Stitch Workshop

Herringbone Stitch

basic techniques, advanced results

KB
KALMBACH BOOKS

From the publisher of
Bead&Button magazine

Kalmbach Books
21027 Crossroads Circle
Waukesha, Wisconsin 53186
www.Kalmbach.com/Books

Published in 2012
16 15 14 13 12   2 3 4 5 6

Manufactured in the United States of America

ISBN: 978-0-87116-454-4

The material in this book has appeared previously in *Bead&Button* magazine. *Bead&Button* is registered as a trademark.

Editors: Elisa Neckar, Erica Swanson
Technical Editor: Jane Danley Cruz
Art Direction: Lisa Bergman
Layout: Rebecca Markstein
Illustration: Kellie Jaeger
Photography: Bill Zuback, Jim Forbes

Library of Congress Cataloging-in-Publication Data

Herringbone stitch : basic techniques, advanced results / from the publisher of Bead&Button magazine.

   p. : ill. (some col.) ; cm. – (Stitch workshop)

"The material in this book has appeared previously in Bead&Button magazine."–T.p. verso.

ISBN: 978-0-87116-454-4

1. Beadwork–Patterns. 2. Beadwork–Handbooks, manuals, etc. 3. Jewelry making--Handbooks, manuals, etc. I. Kalmbach Publishing Company. II. Title: Bead&Button magazine.

TT860 .H47 2012
745.594/2

Contents

Basics

Projects

Introduction
by Diane Fitzgerald

Once again, the richness of African cultures offers us a most versatile beadwork technique: the herringbone stitch, fondly referred to by many as the Ndebele stitch after the African tribe that created and used it widely in ornamentation. The word "Ndebele" seems to roll off our tongues in a fascinating way, creating a link among beaders worldwide and the women of this South African group recognized widely for their geometric style of personal and home adornment. Cousins to the Zulu, who are also noted for their beadwork prowess, we can thank them for a stitch so basic and easy to learn, yet so open to myriad variations.

Ndebele people

Ndebele women shine when it comes to artistic talent. They paint the outside of their houses with bold, colorful and distinctive geometric designs, an eye-catching style that proclaims it is an Ndebele home. These vivid polygonal shapes are reflected as well in their beaded headbands and aprons, bead-embellished fertility dolls, and decorative beaded panels that are hung inside their homes. Besides being known for their beading ability, Ndbele women are often portrayed wearing two types of their traditional personal adornment: rings of brass or copper stacked around the neck, arms, and legs and large donut shapes beaded over coiled grass and worn as collars, bracelets, or anklets.

The projects

The projects in this book, all based on or derived from the original herringbone stitch of the Ndebele, will amaze you. They were developed by creative beaders who saw the potential in this stitch and experimented with it until beautiful new jewelry blossomed in their hands. From Carol Perrenoud's "Lentil Bracelet" to Linda Gettings' "Helix," we see transformations and evolutions from the basic flat stitch to three dimensional contours and textures. Judith Golan's "Flame Tree Flowers" shows us how natural forms can be interpreted with this stitch while Melissa Grakowsky's "Draped Expectations" exhibits curves and movement in a graceful and appealing necklace.

So, get out your beads and join me in learning or revisiting this wonderful gift of the Ndebele—the herringbone stitch.

"Fire Blooms", designed by Debbie Nishihari, p. 61

Herringbone Stitch Basics

Herringbone is a traditional stitch that has been used by beaders of the Ndebele tribe in southern Africa for centuries. Its distinctive weave places pairs of beads side by side so that they stack at a slight angle. This creates a zigzag effect across the horizontal rows and a ribbed effect in the vertical stacks.

The stitch can either start from a row of beads that is gathered into stacks as the second row is sewn, which allows the beads in the base row to angle slightly, following the overall pattern of the weave, or from a row of ladder-stitched beads, in which the first row will be straight. The angled bead pairs begin in the second row.

Herringbone stitch, traditional start

Start with a length of thread with a stop bead (see p. 7) attached to the end, leaving a tail equal to the width of the band plus 6 in. (15cm). Pick up an even number of beads in multiples of four. Allow a small amount of space between the beads and the stop bead. These beads will form the first two rows.

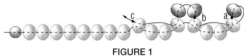

FIGURE 1

Pick up a bead, and sew back through the end bead. Skip two beads, and sew up through the next bead **(figure 1, a–b)**.

Pick up two beads, and sew down through the next bead. Skip two beads, and sew up through the next bead **(b–c)**. Repeat across the row.

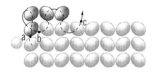

FIGURE 2

To finish the row and begin the next: With the thread exiting the end bead, pick up two beads, and sew down through the first bead just added **(figure 2, a–b)**.

Sew up through the next bead, and pick up two beads. Sew down through the following bead, and continue up through the subsequent bead **(b–c)**. Continue adding pairs of beads across the row. Begin to snug up the stacks.

When you have completed the beadwork, remove the stop bead. Use the tail to sew across the first row to connect the stacks.

a

This method will create a half-stack along the edge with thread showing on every other bead **(photo a)**. To avoid exposed thread, pick up two beads at the first turn and three beads at all other turns. Sew into the first bead just picked up. This will position a bead at the edge of every other row **(photo b, left edge)**. You may choose to fill in the gaps between the edge beads to create the effect of a stack on each edge **(right edge)**.

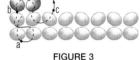

b

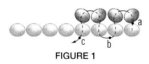

FIGURE 1

FIGURE 2

FIGURE 3

Even-count herringbone, ladder start

Using an even number of beads in the row will stack pairs of beads across the beadwork. Start with an even number of beads stitched into a ladder (see p. 7). Turn the ladder, if necessary, so the thread exits the end bead pointing up.

Pick up two beads, and sew down through the next bead on the ladder **(figure 1, a–b)**. Sew up through the third bead on the ladder, pick up two beads, and sew down through the fourth bead **(b–c)**. Repeat across the ladder.

To make the turn, sew down through the end bead of the previous row and back through the last bead of the pair just added **(figure 2, a–b)**. Pick up two beads, sew

down through the next bead in the previous row, and sew up through the following bead **(b–c)**. Continue adding pairs of beads across the row. You can hide the edge thread by picking up an accent or smaller bead before you sew back through the last bead of the pair just added.

To make a turn without having thread show on an edge or adding an edge bead, sew down through the end bead of the previous row, up through the second-to-last bead in the previous row, and continue through the last bead added **(figure 3, a–b)**. Pick up two beads, sew down through the next bead in the previous row, and up through the following bead **(b–c)**. Continue adding pairs of beads across the row. Using this turn will flatten the angle of the edge bead, making the edge stack look a little different than the others.

Odd-count herringbone, ladder start

Using an odd number of beads in the row will create a half-stack of beads on one edge. Start with an odd number of beads stitched into a ladder (see p. 7). Turn the ladder, if necessary, so your thread exits the end bead pointing up.

Pick up two beads, and sew down through the next bead on the ladder. Sew up through the third bead on the ladder, pick up two beads, and sew down through the fourth bead. Repeat across the ladder.

To make the turn, sew up through the last bead in the row. Pick up two beads, and sew down through the first bead just added (figure, a–b). Sew up through the next bead on the previous row (b–c). Continue adding pairs of beads across the row. Make the turn on the other edge the same way as the turn for the even-count ladder.

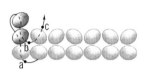

Straight tubular herringbone

Tubular herringbone usually starts from a ladder of beads formed into a ring, though it can also begin with a simple ring of beads. In either case, begin with an even number of beads. Once you get started, you can choose to make the ribs of the stitch straight or twisted (photo).

For a ladder start, stitch a ladder with an even number of beads and form it into a ring. The thread should exit the top of a bead. Pick up two beads, and sew down through the next bead in the previous round (figure 1, a–b). Sew up through the following bead, and repeat around the ring to complete the round (b–c).

You will need to step up to start the next round. Sew up through two beads—the next bead in the previous round and the first bead added in the new round (c–d).

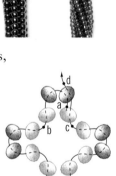

FIGURE 1

Alternatively, begin by picking up four beads, and sew through them again to form a ring. Sew through the first bead again, and snug up the beads (figure 2, a–b). Pick up two beads and sew through the next bead (b–c). Repeat three times, and step up through the first bead added in this round (c–d).

Whether you began with a ladder or a ring, continue adding two beads per stitch. As you work, snug up the beads to form a tube, and step up at the end of each round until your rope is the desired length.

FIGURE 2

Twisted tubular herringbone

Form a base ring with an even number of beads. Pick up two beads, and sew through the next bead in the previous round (figure, a–b). Sew up through the next bead, and repeat around the ring to complete the round (b–c).

You will need to step up to start the next round. Sew up through two beads — the bead from the previous round and the first bead added in the new round (c–d). Work one round of straight herringbone (d–e).

To create a twist in the tube, pick up two beads, sew down through one bead in the next stack and up through two beads in the following stack (e–f). Repeat around the ring, adding two beads per stitch. Step up to the next round through three beads (f–g). Snug up the beads to form a tube. The twist will begin to appear after the sixth round. Continue until your rope is the desired length.

To create a twist in the other direction, work the first two rounds as described. Pick up two beads, sew down through two beads in the next stack and up through one bead in the following stack. Repeat around the ring, adding two beads per stitch. Step up to the next round through two beads.

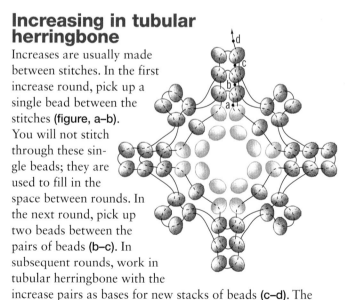

Increasing in tubular herringbone

Increases are usually made between stitches. In the first increase round, pick up a single bead between the stitches (figure, a–b). You will not stitch through these single beads; they are used to fill in the space between rounds. In the next round, pick up two beads between the pairs of beads (b–c). In subsequent rounds, work in tubular herringbone with the increase pairs as bases for new stacks of beads (c–d). The increase stacks may initially seem shorter than the other stacks, but they will catch up as you work additional rounds.

Accelerated herringbone is worked as straight herringbone, but instead of adding two beads, add four beads per stitch and step up through four beads to begin the next round.

Basic Techniques

THREAD AND KNOTS

Adding thread
To add a thread, sew into the beadwork several rows prior to the point where the last bead was added. Sew through the beadwork, following the thread path of the stitch. Tie a few half-hitch knots (see **Half-hitch knot**) between beads, and exit where the last stitch ended.

Conditioning thread
Use either beeswax or microcrystalline wax (not candle wax or paraffin) or Thread Heaven to condition nylon thread. Wax smooths the nylon fibers and adds tackiness that will stiffen your beadwork slightly. Thread Heaven adds a static charge that causes the thread to repel itself, so don't use it with doubled thread. Stretch the thread, then pull it through the conditioner.

Ending thread
To end a thread, sew back into the beadwork, following the existing thread path and tying two or three half-hitch knots (see **Half-hitch knot**) between beads as you go. Change directions as you sew so the thread crosses itself. Sew through a few beads after the last knot, and trim the thread.

Half-hitch knot
Pass the needle under the thread between two beads. A loop will form as you pull the thread through. Cross back over the thread between the beads, sew through the loop, and pull gently to draw the knot into the beadwork.

Overhand knot
Make a loop with the thread. Pull the tail through the loop, and tighten.

Square knot
[1] Cross the left-hand end of the thread over the right, and bring it under and back up.
[2] Cross the end that is now on the right over the left, go through the loop, and pull both ends to tighten.

Stop bead
Use a stop bead to secure beads temporarily when you begin stitching. Choose a bead that is distinctly different from the beads in your project. String the stop bead, and sew through it again in the same direction. If desired, sew through it one more time for added security.

STITCHES

Brick stitch
Traditional
[1] Begin with a ladder of beads (see **Ladder stitch**), and position the thread to exit the top of the last bead. The ends of each new row will be offset slightly from the previous row. To work the typical method, which results in progressively decreasing rows, pick up two beads. Sew under the thread bridge between the second and third beads in the previous row from back to front. Sew up through the second bead added, down through the first bead, and back up through the second bead.
[2] For the row's remaining stitches, pick up one bead per stitch. Sew under the next thread bridge in

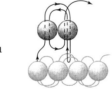

the previous row from back to front, and sew back up through the new bead. The last stitch in the row will be positioned above the last two beads in the row below, and the row will be one bead shorter than the previous row.

Increase
[1] To increase within a row, add a second stitch to the same thread bridge as the previous stitch.
[2] To increase at the end of the row, add a second stitch to the final thread bridge in the row.

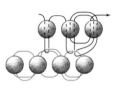

Ladder stitch
Traditional method
[1] Pick up two beads, sew through the first bead again, and then sew through the second bead (**a–b**).
[2] Add subsequent beads by picking up one bead, sewing through the previous bead, and then sewing through the new bead (**b–c**). Continue for the desired length.

This technique produces uneven tension, which you can easily correct by zigzagging back through the beads in the opposite direction.

Alternative method
[1] Pick up all the beads you need to reach the length your pattern requires. Fold the last two beads so they are parallel, and sew through the second-to-last bead again in the same direction (**a–b**).

[2] Fold the next loose bead so it sits parallel to the previous bead in the ladder, and sew through the loose bead in the same direction (a–b). Continue sewing back through each bead until you exit the last bead of the ladder.

Forming a ring
To work in tubular brick or herringbone stitch: Form the ladder into a ring to provide a base for the new technique: With your thread exiting the last bead in the ladder, sew through the first bead and then through the last bead again.

Peyote stitch
Flat even-count

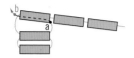

[1] Pick up an even number of beads (a–b). These beads will shift to form the first two rows as you stitch row 3.
[2] To begin row 3, pick up a bead, skip the last bead strung in the previous step, and sew through the next bead in the opposite direction (b–c). For each stitch, pick up a bead, skip a bead in the previous row, and sew through the next bead, exiting the first bead strung (c–d). The beads added in this row are higher than the previous rows and are referred to as "up-beads."
[3] For each stitch in subsequent rows, pick up a bead, and sew through the next up-bead in the previous row (d–e). To count peyote stitch rows, count the total number of beads along both straight edges.

Flat odd-count
Odd-count peyote is the same as even-count peyote, except for the turn on odd-numbered rows, where the last bead of the row can't be attached in the usual way because there is no up-bead to sew through. Work the traditional odd-row turn as follows:
[1] Begin as for flat even-count peyote, but pick up an odd number of beads. Work row 3 as in even-count, stopping before adding the last two beads.
[2] Work a figure-8 turn at the end of row 3: Pick up the next-to-last bead (#7), and sew through #2, and #1 (a–b). Pick

up the last bead of the row (#8), and sew through #2, #3, #7, #2, #1, and #8 (b–c).

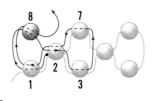

[3] You can work this turn at the end of each odd-numbered row, but this edge will be stiffer than the other.

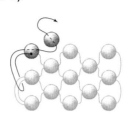

Instead, in subsequent odd-numbered rows, pick up the last bead of the row, and then sew under the thread bridge immediately below. Sew back through the last bead added to begin the next row.

Zipping up or joining
To join two sections of a flat peyote piece invisibly, match up the two pieces so the end rows fit together. If they don't nestle together properly, add or remove a row so that they do. "Zip up" the pieces by zigzagging through the up-beads on both ends.

Tubular
Tubular peyote stitch follows the same stitching pattern as flat peyote, but instead of sewing back and forth, you work in rounds.
[1] Start with an even number of beads in a ring.
[2] Sew through the first bead in the ring. Pick up a bead, skip a bead in the ring, and sew through the next bead. Repeat to complete the round.
[3] You need to step up to be in position for the next round. Sew through the first bead added in round 3 (a–b).

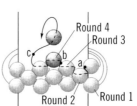

Pick up a bead, and sew through the second bead in round 3 (b–c). Repeat to achieve the desired length.

Circular
Circular peyote is also worked in continuous rounds like tubular peyote, but the rounds stay flat and radiate outward from the center as a result of increases or using larger beads. If the rounds do not increase, the edges will curve upward and become a tube.

Decrease
[1] At the point of decrease, go through two beads in the previous row.

[2] In the next row, when you reach the two-bead space, pick up one bead.

Square stitch

[1] String all the beads needed for the first row, then pick up the first bead of the second row. Sew through the last bead of the first row and the first bead of the second row again. The new bead sits on top of the bead in the previous row, and the holes are parallel.

[2] Pick up the second bead of row 2, and sew through the next bead in row 1 and the new bead in row 2. Repeat this step for the entire row.

Whip stitch
To join two layers of fabric with a finished edge, exit one layer. Cross over the edge diagonally, and stitch through both layers in the same direction about 1/16 in. (2 mm) away from where your thread exited. Repeat.

WIREWORK TECHNIQUES

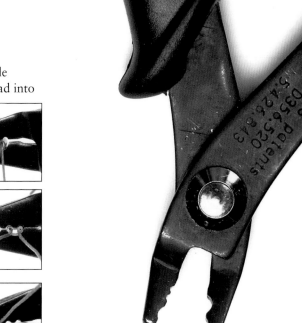

Plain loops

[1] Using chainnose pliers, make a right-angle bend about ⅜ in. (1cm) from the end of the wire.

[2] Grip the tip of the wire with roundnose pliers. Press downward slightly, and rotate the wire into a loop. The closer to the tip of the roundnose pliers that you work, the smaller the loop will be.

[3] Let go, then grip the loop at the same place on the pliers, and keep turning to close the loop.

Wrapped loops

[1] Using chainnose pliers, make a right-angle bend about 1¼ in. (3.2cm) from the end of the wire.

[2] Position the jaws of the roundnose pliers in the bend.

[3] Curve the short end of the wire over the top jaw of the roundnose pliers.

[4] Reposition the pliers so the lower jaw fits snugly in the loop. Curve the wire downward around the bottom jaw of the pliers. This is the first half of a wrapped loop.

[5] To complete the wraps, grasp the top of the loop with chainnose pliers.

[6] Wrap the wire around the stem two or three times. Trim the excess wire, and gently press the cut end close to the wraps with chainnose pliers.

Crimping

Use crimp beads to secure flexible beading wire. Slide the crimp bead into place, and squeeze it firmly with chainnose pliers to flatten it. For a more finished look, use crimping pliers:

[1] Position the crimp bead in the hole that is closest to the handle of the crimping pliers.

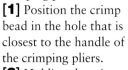

[2] Holding the wires apart, squeeze the pliers to compress the crimp bead, making sure one wire is on each side of the dent.

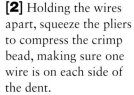

[3] Place the crimp bead in the front hole of the pliers, and position it so the dent is facing the tips of the pliers. Squeeze the pliers to fold the crimp in half.

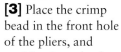

[4] Tug on the wires to ensure that the crimp is secure.

Opening and closing loops and jump rings

[1] Hold a loop or a jump ring with two pairs of pliers.

[2] To open the loop or jump ring, bring the tips of one pair of pliers toward you, and push the tips of the other pair away from you. Reverse the steps to close the open loop or jump ring.

[3] Attach the open jump ring as needed.

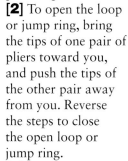

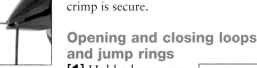

Tools & Materials

Excellent tools and materials for making jewelry are available in bead and craft stores, through catalogs, and on the Internet. Here is a list of the essential supplies you'll need for the projects in this book.

head pin

TOOLS

Chainnose pliers have smooth, flat inner jaws, and the tips taper to a point. Use them for gripping and for opening and closing loops and jump rings.

Roundnose pliers have smooth, tapered, conical jaws used to make loops. The closer to the tip you work, the smaller the loop will be.

Use the front of a **wire cutters'** blades to make a pointed cut and the back of the blades to make a flat cut. Do not use your jewelry-grade wire cutters on memory wire, which is extremely hard; use heavy-duty wire cutters or bend the memory wire back and forth until it breaks.

Crimping pliers have two grooves in their jaws that are used to fold or roll a crimp bead into a compact shape.

Beading needles are coded by size. The higher the number, the finer the beading needle. Unlike sewing needles, the eye of a beading needle is almost as narrow as its shaft. In addition to the size of the bead, the number of times you will pass through the bead also affects the needle size that you will use; if you will pass through a bead multiple times, you need to use a finer needle.

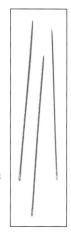

FINDINGS

A **head pin** looks like a long, blunt, thick sewing pin. It has a flat or decorative head on one end to keep beads on. Head pins come in different diameters (or gauges) and lengths.

A **jump ring** is used to connect two loops. It is a small wire circle or oval that is either soldered closed or comes with a split so you can twist the jump ring open and closed.

Crimp beads are small, large-holed, thin-walled metal beads designed to be flattened or crimped into a tight roll. Use them when stringing jewelry on flexible beading wire. **Crimp bead covers** provide a way to hide your crimps by covering them with a finding that mimics the look of a small bead.

Earring findings come in a huge variety of metals and styles, including post, French hook, hoop, and lever-back. You will almost always want a loop (or loops) on earring findings so you can attach beads or beadwork.

Clasps come in many sizes and shapes. Some of the most common are the toggle, consisting of a ring and a bar; lobster claw, which opens when you pull on a tiny lever; S-hook and hook-and-eye, which link two soldered jump rings or split rings; slide, consisting of one tube that slides inside another; snap, consisting of a ball that inserts into a socket; and box, with a tab and a slot.

Bead caps are used to decorate one or both sides of a bead or gemstone.

Spacers are small beads used between larger beads to space the placement of the beads.

jump rings

crimp beads

crimp bead covers

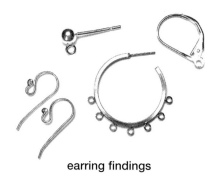

earring findings

clasps

bead caps   spacers

STITCHING & STRINGING MATERIALS

Thread comes in many sizes and strengths. Size (diameter or thickness) is designated by a letter or number. OO, O, and A are the thinnest threads; B, D, E, F, and FF are subsequently thicker.

Plied gel-spun polyethylene (GSP), such as Power Pro or DandyLine, is made from polyethylene fibers that have been spun into two or more threads that are braided together. It is almost unbreakable, doesn't stretch, and resists fraying. The thickness can make it difficult to make multiple passes through a bead. It is ideal for stitching with larger beads, such as pressed glass and crystals. **Parallel filament GSP**, such as Fireline, is a single-ply thread made from spun and bonded polyethylene fibers. Because it's thin and strong, it's best for stitching with small seed beads.

Other threads are available, including **polyester thread**, such as Gutermann (best for bead crochet or bead embroidery when the thread must match the fabric); **parallel filament nylon**, such as Nymo or C-Lon (best used in bead weaving and bead embroidery); and **plied nylon**

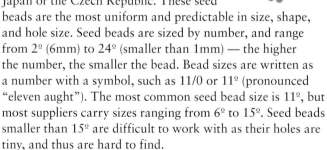

threads

thread, such as Silamide (good for twisted fringe, bead crochet, and beadwork that needs a lot of body).

Flexible beading wire is composed of steel wires twisted together and covered with nylon. This wire is much stronger than thread and does not stretch; the higher the number of inner strands (between three and 49), the more flexible and kink-resistant the wire. It is available in a variety of sizes. Use .014 and .015 for most gemstones, crystals, and glass beads. Use thicker varieties, .018, .019, and .024, for heavy beads or nuggets. Use thinner wire, .010 and .012, for lightweight pieces and beads with very small holes, such as pearls.

flexible beading wire

Memory wire is steel spring wire. It comes in several sizes and can be used without clasps to make coiled bracelets, necklaces, and rings.

memory wire

BEADS

Most projects in this book will call for **seed beads** as the main elements of the design. The most common and highest quality seed beads are manufactured in Japan or the Czech Republic. These seed beads are the most uniform and predictable in size, shape, and hole size. Seed beads are sized by number, and range from 2º (6mm) to 24º (smaller than 1mm) — the higher the number, the smaller the bead. Bead sizes are written as a number with a symbol, such as 11/0 or 11º (pronounced "eleven aught"). The most common seed bead size is 11º, but most suppliers carry sizes ranging from 6º to 15º. Seed beads smaller than 15º are difficult to work with as their holes are tiny, and thus are hard to find.

Cylinder beads, which are sold under the brand names Delicas, Treasures, or Aikos, are very consistent in shape and size. Unlike the standard round seed bead, they're shaped like little tubes and have very large, round holes and straight sides. They create an even surface texture when stitched together in beadwork. These beads are also sold in tubes or packages by weight. In addition to round and cylinder beads, there are several other seed bead shapes: **Hex-cut beads** are similar to cylinder beads, but instead of a smooth, round exterior, they have

six sides. **Triangle beads** have three sides, and **cube beads** have four. **Bugle beads** are long, thin tubes that can range in size from 2 to 30mm long. You might also find tiny teardrop-shaped beads, called **drops** or **fringe drops**, and **magatamas**. Cube, drop, and bugle beads are sold by size and measured in millimeters (mm) rather than aught size.

Some projects may also use a variety of **accent beads** to embellish your stitched pieces, including **crystals**, **gemstones**, **fire-polished beads**, and **pearls** — to name only a few types.

Mata Hari
Bracelet

Turn to history for design inspiration

designed by **Sue Sloan**

Spice up basic herringbone stitch with accent beads.

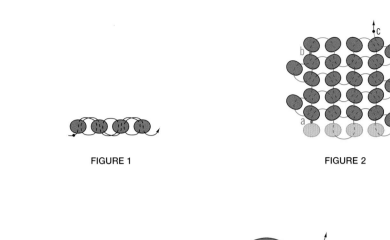

FIGURE 1

FIGURE 2

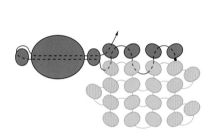

FIGURE 3

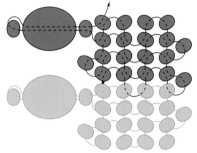

FIGURE 4

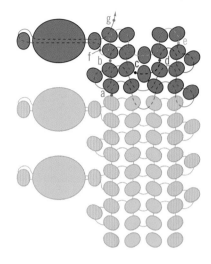

FIGURE 5

The intriguing story of Mata Hari, an exotic dancer who was executed for being a spy for Germany in World War I, inspired this bracelet. An easy-to-stitch herringbone design, it evokes the attire of that famous femme fatale.

MATERIALS
bracelet 6 in. (15cm)
- 3 10mm Czech cathedral beads
- 3g 11º seed beads in each of 2 colors: A, B
- hook-and-eye closure
- Fireline 6-lb. test
- beading needles, #12

stepbystep

[1] On 2 yd. (1.8m) of Fireline, use color A 11º seed beads to make a ladder (Basics, p. 7) four beads long **(figure 1)**, leaving a 10-in. (25cm) tail. Zigzag back through the ladder so the working thread exits the first bead in the opposite direction as the tail.

[2] Work in even-count herringbone stitch (Basics, p. 5) as follows:

Rows 2–5: Work four rows with As, picking up an A for each turn **(figure 2, a–b)**.

Rows 6–34: Continue working in herringbone using an A and a color B 11º seed bead for the first stitch and a B and an A for the second stitch, picking up an A for each turn **(b–c)**, until your beadwork measures about 3 in. (7.6cm).

Row 35: Work a row as in rows 6–34, but alter the turn: Pick up an A, a 10mm Czech cathedral bead, and an A. Sew back through the 10mm and the first A, and then sew up through the last A added in the new row **(figure 3)**.

Rows 36–39: Work three more rows, then work a row with a 10mm in the turn **(figure 4)**.

Rows 40–42: Work two rows **(figure 5, a–b)**. Work the first stitch of an increase row **(b–c)**. Pick up an A, and sew up through the next B **(c–d)**. Work the second stitch, and turn as usual **(d–e)**.

Row 43: Work another increase row with an A inserted between the stitches **(e–f)**, and add a 10mm bead on the turn **(f–g)**.

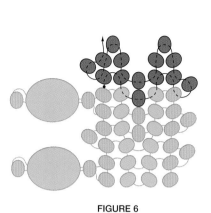

FIGURE 6

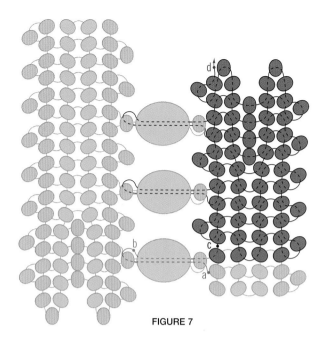

FIGURE 7

Rows 44–45: Work two more increase rows with an A inserted between the stitches, but in the second row, pick up an extra A in each stitch **(figure 6)**. End the working thread (Basics, p. 7) but do not end the tail.
[3] Repeat rows 1–34 to begin the second strap. Work as in row 35, but don't add the turn beads. Instead, sew through the outer A next to the third 10mm bead added on the first strap, the 10mm bead, and the adjacent turn bead **(figure 7, a–b)**. Sew back through the 10mm and A, and step up to the next row **(b–c)**. Continue as in rows 36–45,

connecting the second band to the corresponding 10mms in the first band **(c–d)**. End the thread.
[4] Using the tail at one end of the bracelet, work two stitches with three As each to create two picots at the end. Determine where you want to position the hook-and-eye closure, and sew through the beadwork to exit at that spot. Sew half of the closure to the bracelet, and end the thread. Repeat this step at the other end of the bracelet, and end any remaining threads.

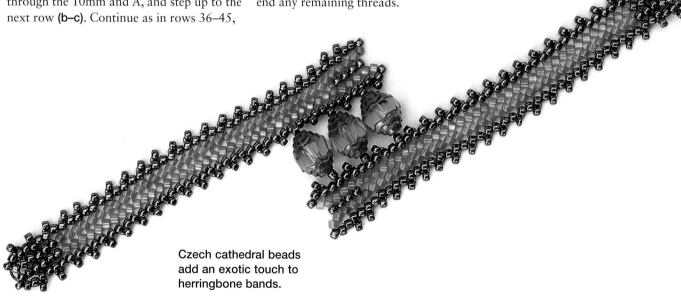

Czech cathedral beads add an exotic touch to herringbone bands.

Spiked
with Pearls

Lustrous pearls reach out
from a herringbone cuff and
grab your attention

designed by **Lisa Olson Tune**

Herringbone stacks are
crowned with pearls in this
graceful cuff.

MATERIALS
bracelet 7½ in. (19.1cm)
- 18g 11º Japanese seed beads, color A
- 8g 11º hex-cut Japanese cylinder beads or 13º seed beads, color B
- 16-in. (41cm) strand 4–5mm rice pearls or stone chips
- 4 4mm jump rings
- 2-strand box clasp
- nylon beading thread, size B
- beading needles, #12

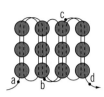

FIGURE 1

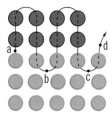

FIGURE 2

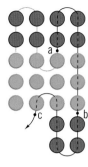

FIGURE 3

The impressive display of richly colored pearls works best when paired with a band of seed beads in a similar hue and accent beads in a bright metallic finish.

stepbystep

[1] Working with a 2-yd. (1.8m) length of conditioned thread (Basics, p. 7) pick up six color A 11º seed beads. Sew through the beads again in the same direction, leaving a 6-in. (15cm) tail. Arrange the beads into two stacks of three (figure 1, a–b).

[2] Pick up three As. Sew through the three beads in the previous stack from top to bottom, and then sew through the new stack from bottom to top (b–c). Continue working in ladder stitch (Basics, p. 7 and c–d) for a total of 82 stacks for a 7½-in. (19.1cm) bracelet. Adjust the length of the bracelet by adding or removing four stacks.

[3] Turn your work so the thread exits the top left bead of the ladder. Work in even-count herringbone (Basics, p. 5) as follows: Pick up four As, and sew down through the second edge bead on the ladder (figure 2, a–b). Sew up through the third edge bead, pick up four As, and then sew down through the fourth edge bead (b–c). Sew up through the next edge bead (c–d) and repeat.

[4] When you add the last stack of beads, sew through all three beads in the ladder's last stack (figure 3, a–b). Pick up four beads, and continue working in herringbone along the bottom edge (b–c).

[5] Once you've added the last stack of beads, sew through all three ladder beads and the two end herringbone beads (figure 4, a–b). Work a second row of herringbone along the top edge (b–c), sew through the beads on the end of the band after adding the last stack, and then stitch a second row of herringbone along the bottom edge.

[6] Work a third row along both edges as follows: Pick up four As and sew down through the next bead on the previous row (figure 5, a–b). Pick up a color B cylinder bead, and sew up through the next bead (b–c). Repeat across the row (c–d). After stitching the third row along the bottom edge, end with the thread exiting the top left bead of the band.

[7] Pick up a B, a pearl, and a B. Sew back through the pearl and the first B (figure 6, a–b). Sew down through the three As in the next stack, the B, and the next three As (b–c).

[8] Pick up two As, a B, a pearl, and a B. Sew back through the pearl and the first B (c–d). Pick up two As and sew down through three As in the next

EDITOR'S NOTE:
You need to sew through most of the beads several times, so when adding a new thread, secure it in the beadwork without tying knots.

stack, the B, and then sew up through three As in the next stack (d–e).

[9] Repeat steps 7–8 along both edges of the band, alternating between short and long pearl fringes (e–f). As you work the second edge, make sure it is the mirror image of the first – a short fringe across from a short fringe, and a long fringe across from a long fringe.

[10] Weave through the beadwork so the thread exits the first B between the herringbone rows (figure 7, point a). Pick up two Bs, positioning them in front of the long herringbone stack, and then sew through the next B (a–b).

[11] Pick up two Bs, position them behind the short herringbone stack, and then sew through the next B (b–c).

[12] Repeat steps 10–11 across the band (c–d), sewing through each B. When you reach the end, weave through the beadwork and exit the first B between the herringbone rows on the other side. Repeat steps 10–11 and end the threads.

[13] Connect the clasp to the end rows of beads with jump rings.

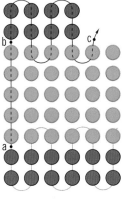

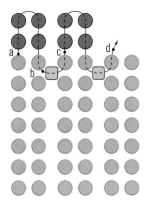

FIGURE 4

FIGURE 5

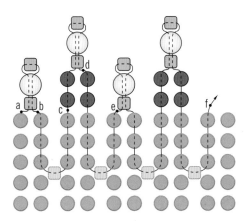

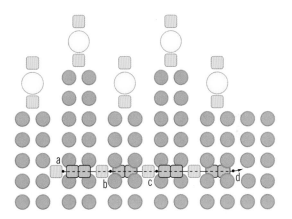

FIGURE 6

FIGURE 7

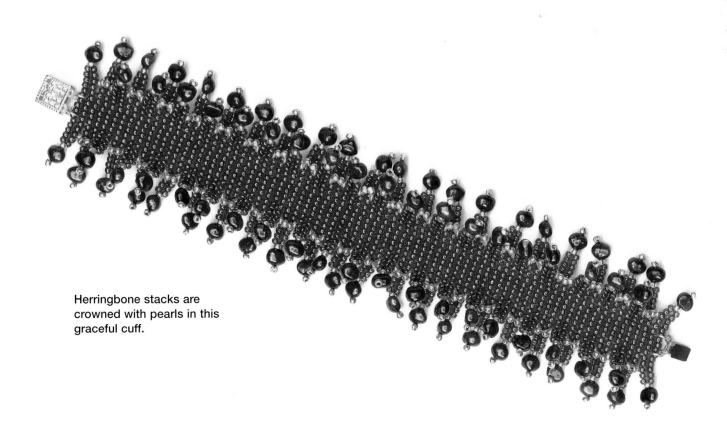

Herringbone stacks are
crowned with pearls in this
graceful cuff.

Pillars of Strength

Twisted bugle beads line up like Ionic columns when they're inserted between herringbone stitches

designed by **Jill Wiseman**

MATERIALS
bracelet 7½ in. (19.1cm)
- 3g 12mm twisted bugle beads
- Japanese seed beads
  5g 8º
  11g 11º
- Fireline 6-lb. test
- beading needles, #10

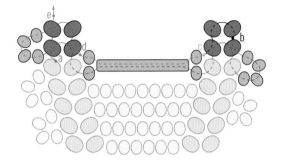

FIGURE 1

FIGURE 2

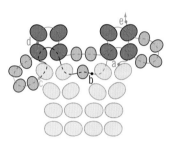

FIGURE 3

FIGURE 4

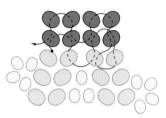

FIGURE 5

The graduated lengths of seed beads used in this band lend a graceful taper to each end. The bugle beads in the brown bracelet are 2.7mm in diameter, while the others are 2mm in diameter. Either size works well in this design.

stepbystep

Bracelet

[1] On a comfortable length of Fireline, leave a 6-in. (15cm) tail, and pick up four 8º seed beads. Sew back through all the beads, and position them so you have two pairs side by side (figure 1, a–b). Work in ladder stitch (Basics, p. 7) until you have a strip that is four beads wide by two beads tall (b–c).

[2] Work two stitches in even-count herringbone (Basics, p. 5 and figure 2, a–b). Step up to complete the row (b–c). Work another row of herringbone.

[3] Work one herringbone stitch (figure 3, a–b). Pick up an 11º, sew through the next 8º, and then work another stitch (b–c). Pick up four 11ºs, and sew up through the last 8º added (c–d).

[4] Repeat step 3, but pick up two 11ºs between stitches instead of one (d–e).

[5] Repeat step 3 seven times, increasing the number of 11ºs picked up between stitches by one in each row until you have completed a row with nine 11ºs between the two herringbone stitches.

[6] Work as in step 3, but replace the group of 11ºs with an 11º, a 12mm bugle bead, and an 11º (figure 4, a–b).

[7] Work one herringbone stitch (b–c). Pick up an 11º, sew through the bugle added in the previous stitch, and then pick up an 11º (c–d). Work the next herringbone stitch, add four 11ºs, and then step up (d–e).

[8] Repeat steps 6 and 7 until the bugle bead section is the desired length. To determine how long the bugle bead section should be, first add the length of the clasp to the length of the two 11º end sections of the bracelet, and then subtract that sum from your wrist circumference. The clasp will require

about 1 in. (2.5cm). The herringbone rows with 11ºs between them are approximately 1¼ in. (3.2cm) per side, or 2½ in. (6.4cm) total. For a 7½-in. (19.1cm) bracelet, the bugle bead section should be 4 in. (10cm) long. Add thread (Basics, p. 7) as needed.

[9] Work a section using 11ºs between the stitches, as in step 3. Begin with nine 11ºs, and decrease the number of 11ºs used between stitches by one bead per row until you have completed a row with one 11º between stitches.

[10] Work two more rows of herringbone, as in step 2 (figure 5). Sew through the last row in ladder stitch to straighten the beads. End the threads.

Clasp

[1] On 2 ft. (61cm) of Fireline, leave a 6-in. (15cm) tail, and pick up a stop bead (Basics, p. 7) and 10 11ºs. Work in flat, even-count peyote stitch (Basics, p. 8) to make a strip 10 beads wide and 10 rows tall (photo a). The completed strip will have five beads on each edge.

[2] Remove the stop bead, and zip up (Basics, p. 8) the jagged edges (photo b) to form a tube. End the threads.

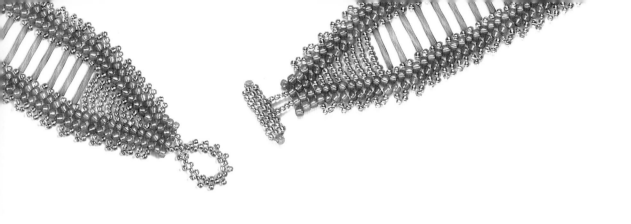

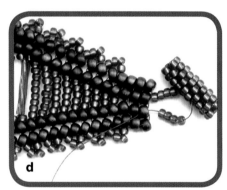

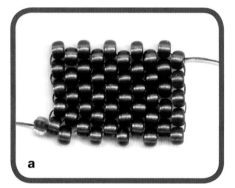
a

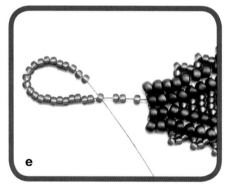
b

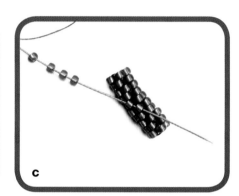
c

d

e

f

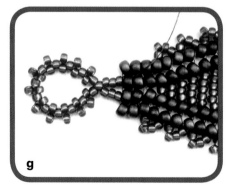
g

[3] Add 18 in. (46cm) of Fireline at one end of the bracelet. With the thread exiting the second 8º in the end row, pick up four 11ºs, and then sew diagonally through two 11ºs at the middle of the peyote toggle bar (photo c). Pick up four 11ºs, and sew through the third 8º in the end row (photo d). Retrace the thread path two or three times, and end the threads.

[4] Add 18 in. (46cm) of Fireline to the other end of the bracelet. With the thread exiting the second 8º in the end row, pick up approximately 27 11ºs, or enough 11ºs to form a ring around the toggle bar. Sew through the fourth 11º added (photo e), pick up three 11ºs, and

then sew through the third 8º in the end row (photo f).

[5] If desired, work a row of peyote stitch around the loop (photo g). Retrace the thread path two or three times, and end the thread.

EDITOR'S NOTE:
While it's not necessary to finish the ends of the toggle bar, it adds a professional touch to the clasp. To do so, exit any 11º seed bead at one end of the bar, and sew an 8º over the open end. Retrace the thread path a few times, and repeat at the other end.

Collier
du
Soleil

Stitch a radiant neckpiece with hex beads and cubic zirconia teardrops

designed by **Anna Elizabeth Draeger**

MATERIALS

15-in. (38cm) choker

both necklaces
- Fireline 6-lb. test
- beading needles, #12

gold/red
- 30g 8º Japanese hex beads
- 5g 11º Japanese cylinder beads
- **35** 6mm faceted, teardrop cubic zirconia
- **36** 4mm Swarovski bicone crystals
- hook clasp
- soldered jump ring

silver/purple
- 30g 10º Japanese twisted hex beads
- 5g 11º Japanese cylinder beads
- **22** 6mm faceted, teardrop cubic zirconia
- **69** 4mm Swarovski bicone crystals
- S-clasp
- **2** soldered jump rings

earrings
- **6** 6mm faceted, teardrop cubic zirconia
- **6** 4mm Swarovski bicone crystals
- 2g 8º or 10º Japanese hex beads
- **2** 6mm flat spacers
- **2** 4–6mm accent beads
- 10 in. (25cm) fine chain
- **12** 1 in. (2.5cm) head pins, 22-gauge
- 6 in. (15cm) 22-gauge wire
- **2** 3mm soldered jump rings
- **2** earring findings
- chainnose pliers
- roundnose pliers
- wire cutters

FIGURE 1

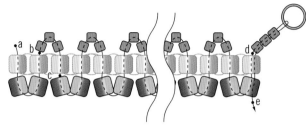

FIGURE 2

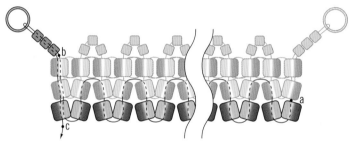

FIGURE 3

Many ancient peoples worshiped the sun. Now, another divine example of solar power takes center stage. This neckpiece features faceted teardrops of cubic zirconia set in a glistening herringbone collar. Wearing this knockout, you'll believe that the sun never sets on a good time.

stepbystep

Choker

[1] Determine the finished length of your necklace (mine is 15 in./38cm), and then subtract the clasp length to find the desired beaded length.

[2] On 3 yd. (2.7m) of Fireline, leave a 6-in. (15cm) tail and work in ladder stitch (Basics, p. 7 and **figure 1**) with hex beads to the desired length. End the tail (Basics, p. 7), but don't end the working thread in case you need to adjust the length.

[3] Add 3 yd. of Fireline (Basics, p. 7), and sew through the first bead in the ladder, leaving a 10-in. (25cm) tail. Work in modified herringbone stitch by picking up two hexes and sewing through the next bead (**figure 2, a–b**). Pick up three cylinder beads, and sew through the next bead (**b–c**). Repeat across the ladder,

using hexes along the bottom edge and cylinders along the top.

[4] Exit the last bead in the ladder with the needle at the top edge (**c–d**). Use the working thread from step 1 to add or remove beads as needed to adjust the length. End the thread.

[5] With the new thread, pick up three cylinders and a soldered jump ring. Sew back through the three cylinders, the last bead in the ladder, and the last bead added (**d–e**).

[6] Work a second row of herringbone in hexes (**figure 3, a–b**).

[7] Finish the other end as in step 3 (**b–c**). End the remaining threads.

Embellishments
gold/red collar

[1] Add 3 yd. of Fireline at either end of the collar. Pick up two hexes, a cylinder, a 4mm crystal, and three

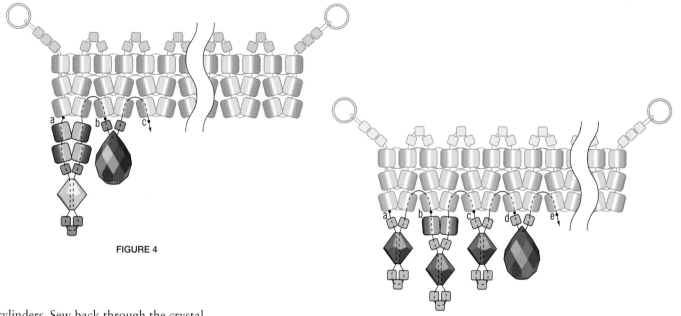

FIGURE 4

FIGURE 5

cylinders. Sew back through the crystal. Pick up a cylinder and two hexes. Sew through the next two beads in the previous row (figure 4, a–b).

[2] Pick up a cylinder, a teardrop, and a cylinder. Sew through the next two beads in the previous row (b–c). Alternate between crystals and teardrops to complete the row.

[3] To finish, reinforce the soldered ring when you reach the end of the row. End the working thread. Repeat with the 10-in. tail on the other end.

[4] Attach the clasp to the soldered jump rings.

silver/purple collar

[1] Add 3 yd. of Fireline.

[2] Pick up a cylinder, a 4mm crystal, and three cylinders. Sew through the 4mm crystal and pick up a cylinder. Sew through the next two hexes on the previous row (figure 5, a–b).

[3] Pick up a hex, a cylinder, a crystal, and three cylinders. Sew through the crystal, pick up a cylinder and a hex, and then sew through the next two hexes in the previous row (b–c).

[4] Repeat step 2 (c–d).

[5] Pick up a cylinder, a teardrop, and a cylinder, and sew through the next two hexes in the previous row (d–e). Repeat steps 2–5 to complete the row.

[6] Repeat steps 3–4 of the gold/red collar to finish the ends.

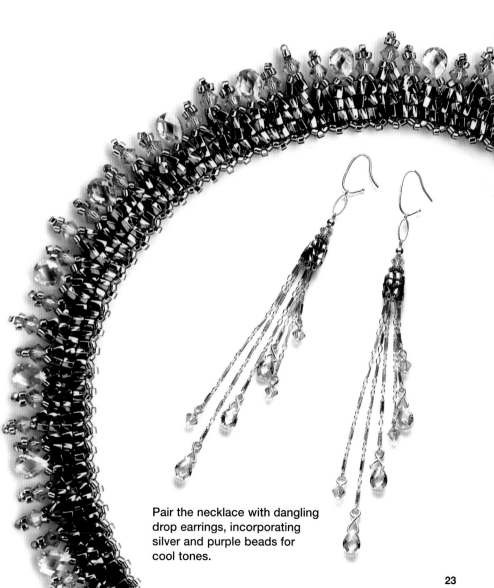

Pair the necklace with dangling drop earrings, incorporating silver and purple beads for cool tones.

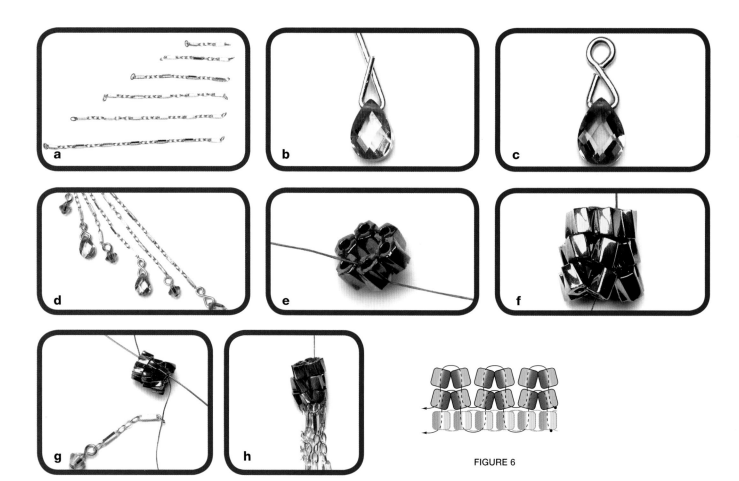

FIGURE 6

Earrings

[1] Cut the chain into six pieces of graduated lengths, starting with ½ in. (1.3cm) and ending with 2½ in. (6.4cm) **(photo a)**.

[2] String a crystal on a head pin and make a plain loop (Basics, p. 9) above the crystal. Make a total of three crystal dangles.

[3] Make a 45-degree bend ¼ in. (6mm) from the end of the wire and slide a teardrop to the bend. Bend the straight wire to a 45-degree angle to form a triangle over a bead **(photo b)**. Cut the wire about ⅛ in. (3mm) above the triangle and make a plain loop (Basics, p. 9 and **photo c)**. Make a total of three teardrop dangles.

[4] Open the plain loops on the dangles and connect one to the end link of each chain cut in step 1 **(photo d)**. Close the loops and set aside.

[5] On 1 yd. (.9m) of Fireline, stitch a six-bead ladder, leaving a 6-in. tail. Connect the first bead to the sixth **(photo e)**.

[6] Work two rows of straight tubular herringbone (Basics, p. 6, and **figure 6**), exiting one of the hexes in the last row **(photo f)**.

[7] Sew through the top link on the shortest dangle and back up through the stack of hexes that the thread is exiting **(photo g)**.

[8] Sew down through the next stack, pick up the second shortest dangle, and then sew back up through the same stack.

[9] Repeat step 8, attaching each remaining chain from shortest to longest. End with the needle exiting one of the hexes on the ladder **(photo h)**.

[10] Pick up a spacer, an accent bead, a cylinder, a crystal, a cylinder, and a soldered jump ring. Go back through all the beads and sew through the ladder opposite where the thread is exiting. Reinforce with a second thread path, and end the threads. Make a second earring to match the first.

Anchor the earring dangles to short rows of straight tubular herringbone.

Layered LOOPS

Repeat a simple technique to produce a wearable bracelet

designed by **Smadar Grossman**

Make the strips of herringbone along the edges of the base a contrasting finish to really highlight the design.

A herringbone band provides the foundation for strips of seed beads that curve delicately as they are stitched in place. The look resembles basket weaving while creating spaces to showcase tiny glass drops.

stepbystep

Base

[1] On a comfortable length of Fireline, use color A 11º seed beads, and work a row of ladder stitch (Basics, p. 7) 76 beads long, leaving a 12-in. (30cm) tail. Add or omit beads to achieve the desired length, making sure you end with an even number of beads.

[2] Working in even-count herringbone stitch (Basics, p. 5) using As, stitch a total of 13 rows, ending and adding thread (Basics, p. 7) as needed. If your working thread is shorter than 30 in. (76cm), end it and add a new thread.

[3] Work a ladder stitch thread path through the last row, and position the working thread and tail at opposite ends.

[4] Exit the fifth bead in the edge stack. Sew through the loop of one half of the clasp and back into the end stack of As, exiting the A that lines up with the next loop of the clasp. Repeat to attach the other clasp loop. Retrace the thread path several times to secure the connection. End the working thread. Repeat on the other end using the tail.

Embellishment

[1] Add a new thread, and exit the first A on one edge of the base.

[2] Pick up two As, and sew through the next A in the edge row, the A your thread exited at the start of this step, and the first new A.

[3] Pick up two As, and sew through the second A in the previous stitch, the first A in the previous stitch, and the first A in the new stitch. Repeat for a total of 12 stitches, and then work one stitch using color B 11º seed beads **(photo a)**.

[4] Bend the strip over so the Bs align with the two As in the fourth row from the opposite edge, and sew through the two As and the two Bs **(photo b)**.

[5] Pick up a 15º seed bead, a drop bead, and a 15º. Sew through the two Bs again and the next four As in the first stack on the base **(figure, a–b)**. Pick up three 15ºs, and sew through the next two As in the row **(b–c)**.

[6] Repeat steps 2–5 until you reach the other end of the bracelet, ending and adding thread as needed.

MATERIALS
bracelet 6½ in. (16.5cm)
- 38 3mm drop beads
- 11º seed beads
  25–30g color A
  2g color B
- 4–5g 15º seed beads
- 2-strand sliding tube clasp
- Fireline 4-lb. test
- beading needles, #12

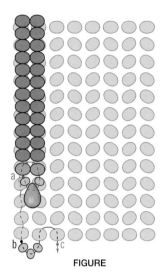

FIGURE

a

b

DESIGNER'S NOTE:

For a chunkier version of this bracelet, use 8º seed beads in place of the 11ºs, 11ºs in place of the 15ºs, 4mm drops in place of the 3mm drops, and a three-strand tube clasp in place of the two-strand clasp. Stitch 10 rows of herringbone for the base, and for steps 2 and 3, work nine stitches with As and one stitch with Bs. In step 4 of "Embellishment," sew through the As in the third row instead of the fourth row.

Add a Splash of Sparkle

Crystal inclusions create nestled treasure for a herringbone cuff

designed by **Elizabeth Nance**

FIGURE 1

FIGURE 2

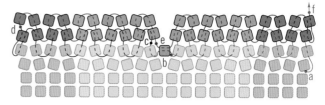

FIGURE 3

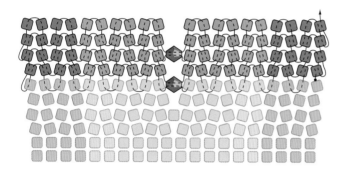

FIGURE 4

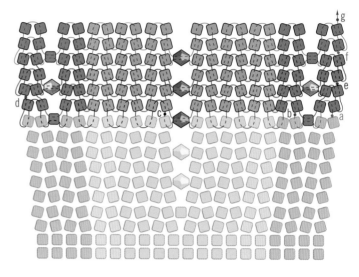

FIGURE 5

Looking for an easy way to do something special with herringbone? Intersperse crystals to create a little drama in a classic band.

stepbystep

Herringbone band

[1] On a comfortable length of Fireline, pick up four color E 11º cylinder beads, leaving a 24-in. (61cm) tail. Sew through all four Es again, and snug them up to form two stacks of two Es each **(figure 1, a–b)**.

[2] Working in ladder stitch (Basics, p. 7), pick up two Es, and sew through the previous pair of Es and the two Es just added **(b–c)**.

[3] Continue working in ladder stitch to add a stack of two Es, two stacks of color F 11º cylinders, eight stacks of color G 11º cylinders, two stacks of Fs, and four stacks of Es.

[4] To step up, with your thread exiting downward, skip the bottom E, and sew through the top E **(figure 2, a–b)**. Work a herringbone stitch (Basics, p. 5) with two Es **(b–c)**. Work in even-count herringbone across the row, following the established color pattern, and then work another row.

[5] Work two rows with an increase stitch in the center column: Work the first four stitches of the row, add the beads for the next stitch, and then sew down through the next G **(figure 3, a–b)**. To work an increase, pick up a G, and sew up through the next G **(b–c)**. Continue working in herringbone across the row, following the established color pattern, and step up **(c–d)**. Work in herringbone until you reach the increase stitch **(d–e)**, sew through the G, and then continue working herringbone stitch across the row, and step up **(e–f)**.

[6] Repeat step 5 twice, and note the following: The increase stitch created a channel; add a color A 3mm bicone crystal as an inclusion in each even row, and sew through the A in each odd row **(figure 4)**.

[7] Add the beads for the first stitch of the next row, and work an increase with an E **(figure 5, a–b)**. Continue working in herringbone with an A inclusion in the channel **(b–c)**. Work herringbone through the second-to-last column of

Es, work an increase with an E, work a herringbone stitch, and step up **(c–d)**. Work another row of herringbone, following the established pattern and sewing through the increase beads **(d–e)**.

[8] Work two rows of herringbone as in step 7, but use a color B 3mm bicone crystal as an inclusion instead of an E for each increase stitch **(e–f)**. Work two more rows using an E for a decrease stitch **(f–g)**.

[9] Work three stitches without an increase, add the beads for the next stitch, and then work an increase with a G **(figure 6, a–b)**. Continue working in herringbone with an A inclusion in the channel **(b–c)**. Add the beads for the

MATERIALS
bracelet 7 in. (18cm)
- 3mm bicone crystals
  47 color A
  8 color B
  12 color C
  6 color D
- 11º cylinder beads
  4–5g in each of **2** colors: E, G
  2–3g color F
- Fireline 6-lb. test
- beading needles, #12

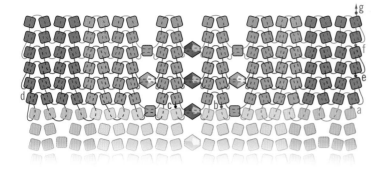

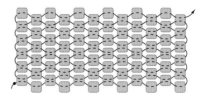

FIGURE 6

FIGURE 7

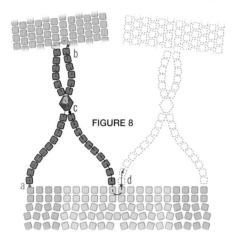

FIGURE 8

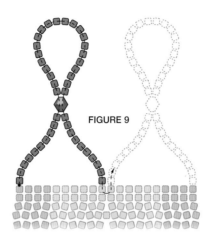

FIGURE 9

next stitch, work an increase with a G, work herringbone through the end of the row following the established pattern, and then step up (c–d). Work another row of herringbone following the established pattern, and sewing through the increase beads and inclusions (d–e).

[10] Work two rows of herringbone as in step 9, but use a color C 3mm bicone crystal instead of a G for each new increase (e–f). Work two more rows using a G for the decrease (f–g).

[11] Repeat steps 7–10 five times, alternating between Bs and color D 3mm bicone crystals in step 8. Repeat steps 7 and 8 again.

[12] Work four rows using As for the channel inclusion and two rows using ag for the decrease. Work two rows without an increase, and work a ladder stitch thread path through the last two rows. Do not end the thread or tail.

Clasp

[1] On 1 yd. (.9m) of Fireline, attach a stop bead (Basics, p. 7), leaving a 6-in. (15cm) tail.

[2] Pick up 12 Es, and work a total of 12 rows of flat even-count peyote stitch

(Basics, p. 8) to make a strip that is 12 beads wide with six beads on each straight edge (figure 7).

[3] Remove the stop bead. Zip up (Basics, p. 8) the strip to form a tube, and end threads (Basics, p. 7).

[4] Repeat steps 1–3 to make a second toggle bar.

[5] With your working thread exiting an end E, pick up 10 Es, an A, and six Es, and then sew through two center Es in a toggle bar (figure 8, a–b). Pick up six Es, and sew through the A (b–c). Pick up 10 Es, and sew down through the fourth G and up through the fifth G in the band (c–d). Repeat to add a second toggle bar. Retrace the thread path a couple of times, and end the thread.

[6] Thread a needle on the tail, and sew through the beadwork to exit an end E on the opposite end of the band. Pick up 10 Es, an A, and 22 Es or enough to form a loop to fit around the toggle bar. Sew back through the A, pick up 10 Es, and sew down through the fourth G and up through the fifth G in the band (figure 9). Repeat to add a second loop. Retrace the thread path a couple of times, and end the tail.

EDITOR'S NOTE:
I used invisible turns for the red and peach bracelet, which changed the alignment of the pairs of edge beads. You can work invisible turns two ways:

• With your thread exiting downward, sew up through the second-to-last bead of the previous row and the last bead of the row just added. Pick up two beads, and sew down through the next bead and up through the following bead (figure a).

FIGURE A

• With your thread exiting downward, sew under the thread bridge between the two beads in the previous row and back up through the two edge beads. Pick up two beads, and sew down through the next bead and up through the following bead (figure b).

FIGURE B

Coin-shaped lentil beads create the texture and pattern that make these designs both elegant and daring.

Lentil Herringbone Weave

Accentuate herringbone stitch with offset-hole lentil beads

designed by **Carol Perrenoud**

FIGURE 1

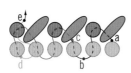

FIGURE 2

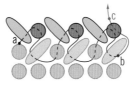

FIGURE 3

MATERIALS
both projects
- Power Pro 20-lb. test
  or Spectra Fiber 15-lb. test
- beading needles, #11

bracelet 8 in. (20cm)
- 6mm offset-hole lentil beads:
  192 for six-bead-wide bracelet (**96** in
  each of **2** colors: A, B) or **256** for
  eight-bead-wide bracelet
- 10g 8º seed beads
- flat bar clasp

pin 2⅛ x 1⅞ in. (5.4 x 4.8cm)
- **112** 6mm offset-hole lentil
  beads (**56** in each of **2** colors: A, B)
- 6g 8º seed beads
- Nylon beading thread to coordinate
  with the Ultrasuede
- pin-back finding
- clean scrap plastic (from a milk jug or
  a deli-container lid)
- Ultrasuede

Coin-shaped lentil beads create the texture and pattern that make these designs both elegant and daring. Carol was experimenting to find a way to highlight the pattern created by herringbone stitch, when she discovered that using one seed bead and one larger bead in each stitch created a dramatic look.

step by step

Bracelet

This bracelet can be made either six beads across, as in the bracelet on p. 32, or eight beads across, as in the bracelet on p. 30.

[1] On a comfortable length of thread, pick up two 8º seed beads, and, leaving a 6-in. (15cm) tail, sew back through both beads (**figure 1, a–b**). Picking up one 8º per stitch, work in ladder stitch (Basics, p. 7) until you have either six or eight beads (**b–c**).

[2] Pick up a color A 6mm lentil bead and an 8º, and sew down through the next bead on the ladder (**figure 2, a–b**). Step up through the following bead (**b–c**) to get into position to work the next stitch. Working in even-count herringbone stitch (Basics, p. 5), continue across the row, picking up a lentil and an 8º with each stitch (**c–d**). Position each lentil at a 45-degree angle (pointing away from the 8º), and tighten your thread before continuing to the next stitch.

[3] To get into position to begin the next row, sew up through the second-to-last bead in the ladder and continue up through the last 8º added in the second row (**d–e**).

[4] Repeat step 2, sewing down through the next lentil and up through the following 8º in the previous row for each stitch (**figure 3, a–b**). If you're using two colors, use color B lentils for this row. To get into position to start the

next row, sew back up through the last 8º added (**b–c**). Some thread will show on the edge of the lentil when you make this turn. The surface with the thread showing will be the back of the bracelet, so in subsequent rows, make sure to orient the lentils toward the front.

[5] Repeat step 4 until your bracelet is the desired length minus the length of the clasp. Switch lentil colors with each row if you're using two colors. End and add thread (Basics, p. 7) as needed.

[6] At the end of the band, stitch a final row of herringbone, using only 8ºs to match the initial ladder row.

[7] Exiting the last 8º added, work six or eight more ladder stitches (the same number as the width of your bracelet) with 8ºs (**photo a**).

[8] Work a row of herringbone off the beads added in step 7, making sure your beadwork is going in the direction of the body of the bracelet (**photo b**).

[9] Fold the two-bead-high flap over the back of the bracelet, lining up half of a clasp between the two layers. Sewing through the holes in the clasp, stitch the flap to the bracelet (**photo c**), sandwiching the clasp between the bracelet and the flap. Stitch through all the holes several times to ensure a secure connection between the bracelet, the clasp, and the flap.

[10] Repeat steps 7–9 to attach the other end of the bracelet to the remaining half of the clasp, and end the threads.

a

b

c

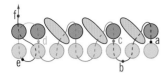

FIGURE 4

FIGURE 5

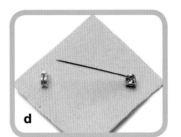

d

e

Pin

[1] On a comfortable length of thread, make a ladder (Basics, p. 7) with an even number of 8° seed beads. This pin started with a 14-bead ladder.

[2] Pick up an 8° and a color A 6mm lentil bead, and sew down through the next 8° on the ladder (figure 4, a–b). Step up through the next 8° to get into position to work the next stitch (b–c). Working in even-count herringbone stitch (Basics, p. 5), repeat for the rest of the row, positioning the lentils at a 45-degree angle to the 8°s, except for the final stitch (c–d). Make the final stitch of the row with two 8°s (d–e). To turn, sew up through the second-to-last 8° in the ladder, and come up through the last 8° just added (e–f).

[3] Repeat step 2, sewing down through the next 8° and up through the following lentil on the previous row for each stitch (figure 5, a–b). If you're using two colors, use color B lentils for this row. Remember that the last stitch is made with two 8°s. To get into position to start the next row, sew under the thread bridge between the two end beads on the previous row, and then sew up through the two edge 8°s above (b–c).

[4] Repeat step 3 for the desired number of rows. This pin has 16 rows of lentils.

[5] Stitch a final row of herringbone, using 8°s only. Zigzag back through the last row of 8°s to close up the spaces between the herringbone stitches and to straighten out the row of beads.

[6] Cut a piece of Ultrasuede the same size as the beadwork, and cut a piece of scrap plastic one bead's width smaller than the beadwork. Mark the spots where the hinge and catch of the pin-back finding will go, and cut tiny holes in each piece.

[7] Push the pin hinge and catch through the holes of the plastic and the Ultrasuede (photo d). Using nylon beading thread, whip stitch (Basics, p. 8) the Ultrasuede to the beadwork all the way around the perimeter of the pin, catching the thread between beads as you stitch (photo e).

EDITOR'S NOTE:
If you make a pin, try to stitch somewhat loosely to lessen the curve caused by the size difference between the seed beads and the lentils. If you stitch too tightly, the beadwork will curl in, making it difficult to attach the backing.

Whether you choose colors that are bright or burnished, the pattern created by the angled lentil beads makes a dramatic statement.

DESIGNER'S NOTE:
The exact colors of lentil beads I used may not be available, but you'll have plenty of pretty options. I like using offset-hole lentils because they create a strong line that looks great with casual attire.

Elegance
Squared

Create a clever collar with two-hole Tila beads

designed by **Diane Fitzgerald**

Is there anything that gets your creative juices flowing more than a new bead? Try two-hole beads!

stepbystep

Herringbone unit

[1] On 2 yd. (1.8m) of Fireline, leaving a 12-in. (30cm) tail, sew through both holes of a 5mm Tila bead. Tie the working thread and tail together with a square knot (Basics, p. 7), and sew back through the second hole.
[2] Working in ladder stitch (Basics, p. 7), pick up two 8° hex-cut beads, and

sew through the second hole of the Tila bead and the 8°s (figure 1, a–b). Pick up two 8°s, and work another stitch (b–c).
[3] Work in modified ladder stitch: Pick up a Tila bead, and sew through the previous pair of 8°s, the first hole of the Tila bead, and the second hole of the Tila bead (c–d).

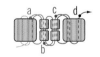

FIGURE 1

MATERIALS
necklace 16 in. (41cm)
- **6** 8mm round faceted fire-polished beads
- 18g 5mm Tila beads
- 17g 8° hex-cut beads
- 3g 11° seed beads
- hook clasp
- 1-in. (2.5cm) head pin
- 5 1-in. (2.5cm) eye pins
- Fireline 6-lb. test
- beading needles, #10 or #12
- chainnose pliers
- roundnose pliers
- wire cutters

33

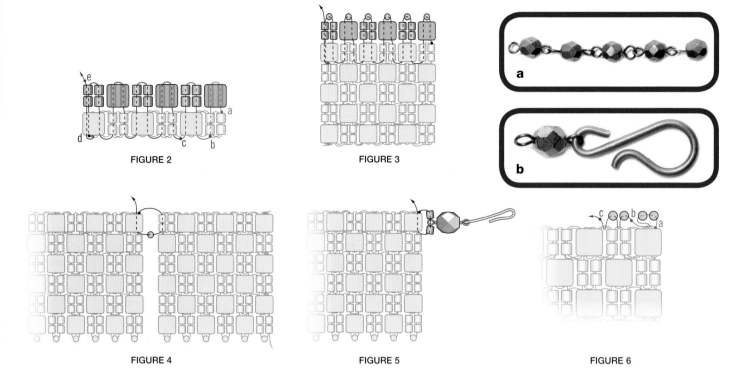

FIGURE 2

FIGURE 3

a

b

FIGURE 4

FIGURE 5

FIGURE 6

[4] Continue working in even-count ladder stitch and modified ladder stitch to add an alternating pattern of a Tila bead and two pairs of 8ºs for a total of three sets.

[5] With your thread exiting the end pair of 8ºs, pick up a Tila bead, and sew down through the second hole and the second pair of 8ºs (figure 2, a–b).

[6] Sew up through the first hole of the next Tila bead, pick up four 8ºs, and then sew down through the second hole of the Tila bead (b–c).

[7] Sew up through the next pair of 8ºs, and repeat steps 5 and 6 across the row (c–d).

[8] At the end of the row, sew under the adjacent thread bridge, and back up through the end hole of the Tila bead and the corresponding pair of 8ºs (d–e).

[9] Work three more rows as in steps 5–8, alternating Tila beads and groups of 8ºs to create a checkerboard pattern.

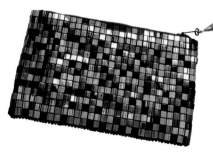

[10] Work the sixth row as in steps 5–8, but pick up an 11º seed bead between the two holes of each Tila bead and between each pair of 8ºs (figure 3). End the thread (Basics, p. 7) but not the tail.

[11] Make 11 to 13 units, as desired.

8mm units

[1] On a head pin, string an 8mm round faceted fire-polished bead, and make a plain loop (Basics, p. 9).

[2] Using eye pins instead of a head pin, repeat step 1 five times.

[3] Open the loop (Basics, p. 9) of the head pin unit, attach a loop of an eye pin unit, and then close the loop. Open the remaining loop of the eye pin unit, attach a loop of another eye pin unit, and then close the loop. Repeat to connect four eye pin units (photo a).

[4] Open a loop of the remaining eye pin unit, attach the hook clasp, and then close the loop (photo b).

Diane made a purse in square stitch and a pair of earrings in ladder stitch.

Assembly

Turn the herringbone units so the edge 11ºs are at the bottom of each unit.

[1] To connect the herringbone units, thread a needle on the tail of one unit, and exit the end edge hole of a Tila bead. Sew through the end pair of 8ºs of the next unit and the hole of the Tila bead your thread just exited (figure 4). Retrace the thread path, and end the thread. Repeat to connect all the units.

[2] Thread a needle on the remaining tail, and sew through the Tila bead to exit the end edge hole. Pick up an 8º, the loop of the 8mm clasp unit, and an 8º, and sew through the hole of the Tila bead your thread just exited (figure 5). Retrace the thread path.

[3] Pick up two 11ºs, and sew under the thread bridge between the two holes of the end Tila bead (figure 6, a–b). Pick up an 11º, and sew under the thread bridge between the first pair of 8ºs. Pick up an 11º, and sew under the thread bridge between the next 8º and Tila bead (b–c). Repeat across all the units, ending and adding thread (Basics, p. 7) as needed.

[4] Sew through the end edge pair of 8ºs, pick up an 8º, the end loop of the connected 8mm units, and an 8º as in step 2, and then sew through the pair of 8ºs your thread just exited. Retrace the thread path, and end all remaining threads.

MATERIALS
necklace 22 in. (56cm)
- Japanese seed beads
  10–20g 11º
  5g 15º
- 5–10g 11º Japanese
  cylinder beads
- shank button, ½–¾ in.
  (1.3–1.9cm)
- Fireline 4-lb. test or nylon
  beading thread
- beading needles, #12

Infinity
Necklace

Multiple beaded links are chained together for a loopy necklace

designed by **Kim Spooner**

The lemniscus (∞) was introduced by John Wallis in 1655 and has since become the symbol for infinity. Proclaim your infinite love of beading with this extended variation.

stepbystep

Infinity links

This necklace can be made with large or small links. The links are made the same way but in different bead combinations. In the larger version, use 11º seed beads on the edges and 11º cylinder beads in the center. Each link measures about 1¾ in. (4.4cm) long. In the smaller version, reverse the bead types, using 11º cylinders on the edges and 11º seed beads in the center.

Each of these links measures about 1½ in. (3.8cm). In both versions, the beads on the edges will be called As and the center beads will be called Bs. The instructions and illustrations show the small-link bead combination. In both versions, the peyote segments between the infinity links are made with 15º seed beads.

[1] On 4 ft. (1.2m) of Fireline or thread, pick up an 11º cylinder (an A), an 11º seed bead (a B), and three As, leaving a 6-in. (15cm) tail. Sew through all five beads again to form a ring. Sew through the first A again **(figure 1)**.
[2] Pick up an A, a B, and two As, skip the B in the previous stitch, and then sew through the next two As **(figure 2, a–b)**. Skip the bead your thread is exiting, and sew back through the previous three As **(b–c)**.

[3] Pick up two As, a B, and an A, skip the B in the previous stitch, and then sew through the next two As on the other edge **(figure 3, a–b)**. Skip the bead your thread is exiting, and sew back through the previous two As **(b–c)**.
[4] Repeat steps 2 **(figure 4, a–b)** and 3 **(b–c)** until you have a total of seven Bs in the center **(c–d)**. The beadwork is now curved with distinct outer and inner edges. Work one more stitch, using four As instead of an A, a B, and two As **(figure 5)**. This leaves an A in the center instead of a B.
[5] To make the second arch going in the opposite direction, repeat steps 2–4 **(figure 6)**.
[6] Repeat step 3 and then steps 2–4 to make a third arch.
[7] For arch 4, which curves back toward the rest of the beadwork, repeat step 3 and then steps 2–4. Cross the end of arch 4 over the intersection of arches 2 and 3, aligning the center As. Using a square stitch (Basics, p. 7) thread path, connect the three end As of arch 4 to the corresponding beads of arch 2 **(figure 7, a–b)**. Retrace the thread path between each pair of beads, exiting at **point c**.
[8] For arch 5, repeat steps 2–4. Cross the end of arch 5 under the intersection of arches 1 and 2 (on the surface opposite the arch 4

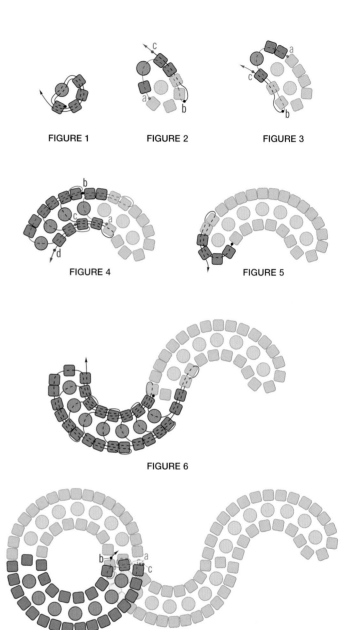

FIGURE 1   FIGURE 2   FIGURE 3

FIGURE 4   FIGURE 5

FIGURE 6

FIGURE 7

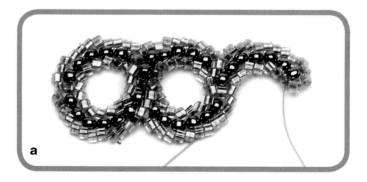

a

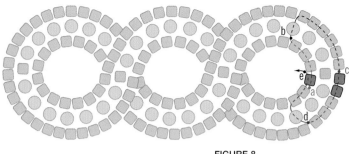

FIGURE 8

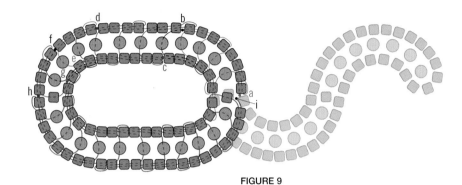

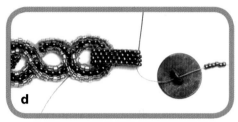

FIGURE 9

connection) **(photo a)**, and join the layers as in step 7.
[9] For the final arch, repeat step 3 and then steps 2–4, without picking up the final four As. Your thread should be exiting the last inner edge A of arch 6. Pick up an A, and sew through the first three inner-edge As of arch 1 **(figure 8, a–b)**. Tie a half-hitch knot (Basics, p. 7), sew through the adjacent B and the corresponding outer-edge As of arch 1 **(b–c)**. Pick up two As, sew through the end three outer-edge As of arch 6 **(c–d)**, and tie a half-hitch knot. Sew through the adjacent B and the corresponding inner-edge As, exiting next to the tail **(d–e)**. Tie the working thread and the tail together with a square knot (Basics, p. 7), and end the thread.
[10] Repeat steps 1–9 10 times if you're making large links or 12 times if you're making small links.
[11] Make a button-hole link as in steps 1–9, but extend the loop made by arches 3 and 4 as follows:

Work the first four stitches of arch 3 as usual **(figure 9, a–b)**. Work the next stitch with an A, a B, and two As **(b–c)**. Work three stitches with two As, a B, and two As **(c–d)**. Resume the pattern for arch 3 by working one stitch with two As, a B, and an A **(d–e)**; one stitch using an A, a B, and two As **(e–f)**; one stitch using two As, a B, and an A **(f–g)**; and one stitch using four As **(g–h)**. Work arch 4 as a mirror image of arch 3 **(h–i)**.

Assembly
[1] On 18 in. (46cm) of Fireline or thread, attach a stop bead (Basics, p. 7), leaving a 4-in. (10cm) tail. Pick up four 15º seed beads.
[2] Working in flat even-count peyote stitch (Basics, p. 8), make a 1¼-in. (3.2cm) strip that is four beads wide.
[3] Slide the strip through the end loops of two infinity links **(photo b)**. Remove the stop bead, and zip up (Basics, p. 8) the ends **(photo c)**. Retrace the thread path through the join, and end the threads.

[4] Repeat steps 1–3 until all the infinity links have been joined, making sure the button-hole link is at one end of the chain, positioned with the large loop at the end.
[5] To attach the button, repeat steps 1 and 2 on 1 yd. (.9m) of thread or Fireline. Slide the strip through the remaining loop of the infinity link at the end opposite the button loop. Remove the stop bead, zip up the ends, and then retrace the thread path through the join. Secure the working thread with half-hitch knots, but don't trim.
[6] Weave through the beadwork, exiting an edge bead that is roughly opposite the knots you just made. Pick up the button and enough 15ºs (approximately six) to make a small loop spanning the peyote strip, and sew through the opposite edge bead **(photo d)**. Retrace the thread path through the loop a few times, and end the threads.

EDITOR'S NOTE:
If the shank of your button is large enough, make a second loop to secure it to the peyote strip.

Hang in There

MATERIALS

bail 1½-in. (3.8cm) span

- art bead, about 1 in. (2.5cm) long
- 2g 11º Japanese seed beads in each of **2** colors: A, B
- 2g 15º Japanese seed beads in each of **3** colors: C, D, and E
- Power Pro 10-lb. test or Fireline 6-lb. test
- beading needles, #12

Cleverly combined herringbone and peyote stitch create a custom bail

designed by **Carol Cypher**

Fine-tune your stitching skills with herringbone increases and decreases as well as a smattering of peyote. Together, the stitches create a framework that fans out to become a sturdy structure from which to hang your treasured art beads.

EDITOR'S NOTE:
Longer art beads can easily be accommodated by using 11º seed beads throughout.

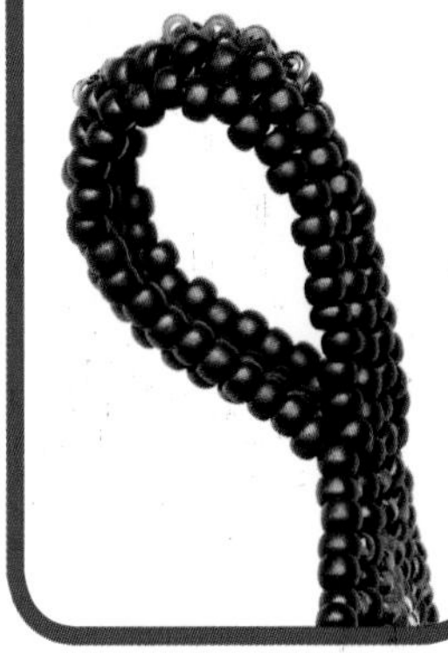

stepbystep

The bail is largely made up of herringbone, with a peyote inclusion at the bottom that helps it fan out to span the length of your art bead. Use tight tension, and refer to **figure 1** as you work.

[1] On a 2-yd. (1.8m) length of thread, stitch a bead ladder (Basics, p. 7) two beads wide and four beads long, using color A 11º seed beads. Leave an 8-in. (20cm) tail. Sew back through the ladder to the first two beads **(figure 1, a–b).**

[2] Work a row of even-count herringbone (Basics, p. 5) in As, turning as shown **(b–c).**

Row 4: Work a row of herringbone in As, with a modified turn **(c–d).**

Rows 5–12: Work the next eight rows as in row 4 **(d–e).**

Rows 13–20: Work increases in herringbone with As, color C 15º seed beads, and color D 15º seed beads **(e–f)**

Rows 21–22: Work decreases in herringbone with As and Cs **(f–g).**

Rows 23–30: Work in herringbone as in row 4 **(g–h).**

Rows 31–32: Work a row of modified herringbone using As and Ds **(h–i).**

Row 33–35: Work in modified herringbone **(i–j).**

Rows 36–43: Work in herringbone and peyote (Basics, p. 8) **(j–k).**

Rows 44–45: Complete two modified herringbone stitches on one side. Sew through the last row of peyote to get to the other side. Complete two rows of modified herringbone **(k–l).**

[3] Sew through the last row added, and turn as before **(figure 2, a–b).** Pick up five As, three color B 11º seed beads, the art bead, three Bs, and five As. Sew through the B on the opposite side of the bail **(b–c).**

[4] Using As, work in flat peyote (Basics, p. 8) for the next three stitches. Pick up three Bs, and sew through the art bead **(c–d).**

[5] Mirror step 4 on the other side of the art bead **(d–e).**

[6] Reinforce these beads with a second and third thread path. Secure the thread in the bail, and end the working thread (Basics, p. 7).

[7] Use the tail to connect row 1 to row 29 by sewing back and forth through the beads in both rows to finish the bail. End the tail.

FIGURE 1

A
B
C
D
E

FIGURE 2

Seed bead bails can easily accommodate different sizes and shapes of art beads.

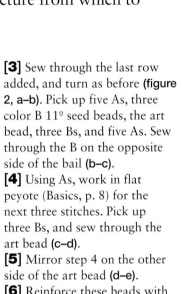

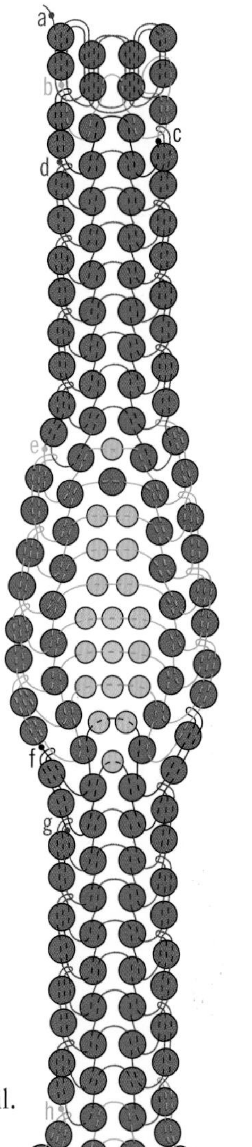

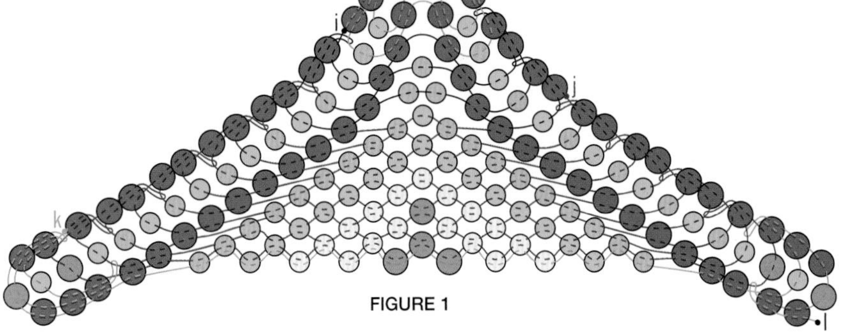

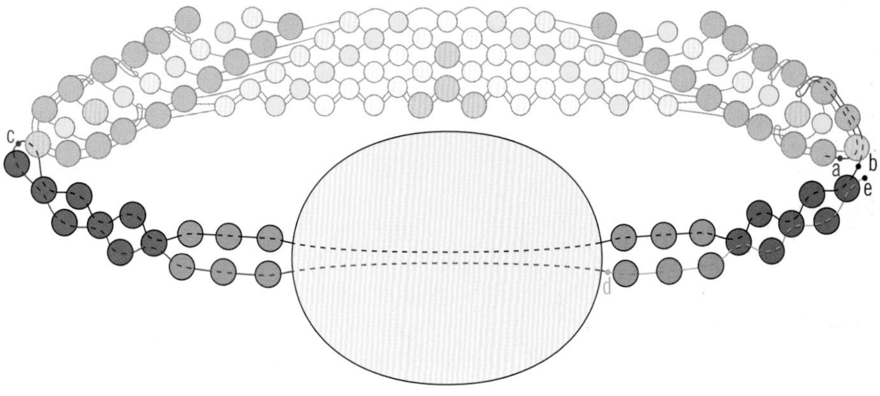

Cabled Bracelet

Adapt herringbone stitch with a classic fiber technique for an undulating bracelet

designed by **Rae Arlene Reller**

A simple twist of one stitch over another adds dimension and shape to this colorful band.

MATERIALS
bracelet 6¼ in. (15.9cm)
- 11º seed beads
  5g color A
  3g color B
  3g color C
- 2g 15º seed beads
- ⅝-in. (1.6cm) shank button
- nylon beading thread, size D
- beading needles, #12

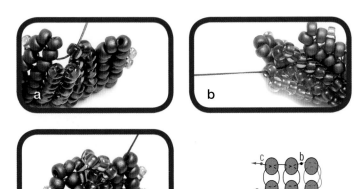

FIGURE 1

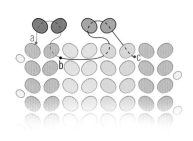

FIGURE 2

FIGURE 3

Twist one stitch over another to create a cabled band that plays with color and shape. Simple repetition creates a bracelet that's perfect for everyday wear.

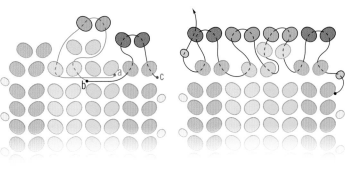

FIGURE 4

FIGURE 5

stepbystep

[1] On a comfortable length of thread, pick up four color A 11º seed beads, leaving a 12-in. (30cm) tail. Sew through the third and fourth As again **(figure 1, a–b)**. Continue across the row in square stitch (Basics, p. 8), adding one A per stitch **(b–c)**.

[2] Continue working in square stitch, adding two rows of color B 11º seed beads, two rows of color C 11º seed beads, and two rows of As **(figure 2)**. Turn the beadwork so the thread is exiting up out of the last A added. You will now work the rows horizontally across the different colors.

[3] Work five rows in even-count herringbone stitch (Basics, p. 5), following the established color pattern, and using a 15º seed bead at each turn.

[4] Work the first stitch of the next row using As **(figure 3, a–b)**. Skip the next two Bs in the previous row, and sew up through the following C, passing behind the skipped beads, and

pulling the thread tight **(photo a)**. Pick up two Cs, and sew down through the next C **(b–c)**.

[5] Sew up through the first B you skipped, passing behind the skipped beads again **(photo b)**. Pick up two Bs, and sew down through the next skipped B **(figure 4, a–b)**, keeping the new pair of Cs in the back. Sew up through the next A **(photo c)**, pick up two As, and then sew down through the last A in the previous row **(b–c)**.

[6] Pick up a 15º to make the turn, and work the next row using the new color pattern. Pick up a 15º to make the turn **(figure 5)**.

[7] Work 11 rows in even-count herringbone, and then flip the bracelet over.

[8] Repeat steps 4–7 until the bracelet reaches the desired length, ending and adding thread (Basics, p. 7) as needed. End with at least three rows of even-count herringbone stitch. Do not end the thread.

[9] Thread a needle on the tail, and weave through the beadwork to exit the second

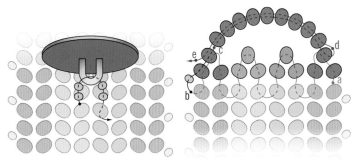

FIGURE 6

FIGURE 7

B in the third row. Pick up two 15ºs, the shank of the button, and two 15ºs, and then sew through the next C in the row **(figure 6)**. Retrace the thread path several times to secure the button, and end the tail.

[10] With the remaining thread, work a row of herringbone stitch, picking up three beads per stitch, instead of two **(figure 7, a–b)**.

Turn, and come out the center A of the last stitch worked **(b–c)**. Pick up enough As to fit around the button, and sew through the center A in the first stitch of the previous row **(c–d)**. Sew back through the loop of beads and the center A of the last stitch **(d–e)**. Retrace the thread path several times, and end the thread.

Turquoise Ropes

Make a herringbone necklace and bracelet using turquoise and onyx

by **Anna Elizabeth Draeger**

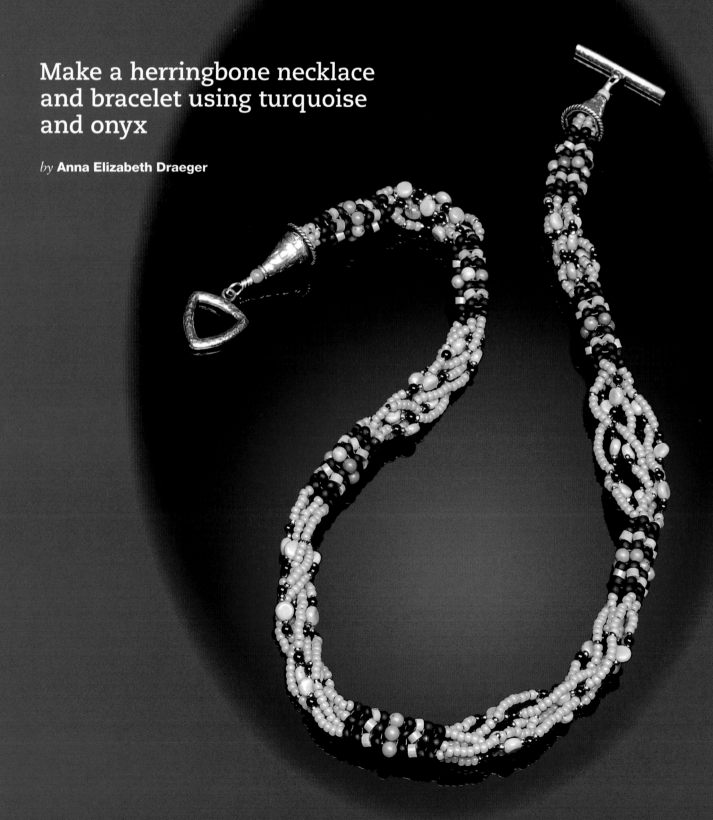

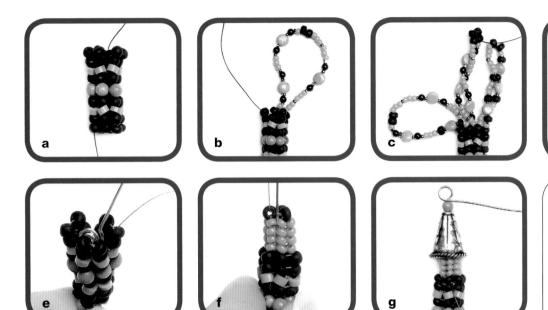

Although turquoise doesn't originate in Turkey, it earned its name because it was traded in Turkish bazaars. Throughout history turquoise has been thought to protect and bring good fortune to those who wear it. With its rich history, people born in December could not ask for a birthstone with greater heritage and meaning. The color is even used in hospitals to evoke a calming effect on patients who suffer from anxiety or depression.

stepbystep

Necklace

[1] On 3 yd. (2.7m) of Fireline, using 8º seed beads, make a bead ladder (Basics, p. 7) six 8ºs long. Leaving a 12-in. (30cm) tail, connect the ladder into a ring by sewing through the first and last bead in the ladder.

[2] Using 8ºs, work a round of straight tubular herringbone (Basics, p. 6).

[3] Work the next seven herringbone rounds using the following beads (photo a):
Round 3: 3mm heishi beads
Round 4: 8ºs
Round 5: 3mm round beads
Round 6: 8ºs
Round 7: 3mm heishis
Rounds 8 and 9: 8ºs

[4] Exiting an 8º in the last round, pick up: three 11º seed beads, a 14º Charlotte, three 11ºs, a Charlotte, a 2mm bead, a Charlotte, a 4mm bead, Charlotte, a 2mm, a Charlotte, three 11ºs, a Charlotte, three 11ºs, two 8ºs, an 11º, a Charlotte, a 2mm, a Charlotte, a 4mm, a Charlotte, a 2mm, a Charlotte, three 11ºs, a Charlotte, a 2mm, a Charlotte, a 4mm, a Charlotte, a 2mm, a Charlotte, and an 11º. Sew through the next 8º in the last round (photo b). Repeat twice to make three loops.

MATERIALS

necklace (18 in./46cm)

- turquoise beads
  54 4mm coin
  84 3mm heishi
  42 3mm round
- **108** 2mm round onyx beads
- 7g 8º seed beads
- 20g 11º seed beads
- 5g 14º Charlottes
- 10 in. (25cm) 20-gauge, half-hard wire
- **2** cones, with a 6mm bottom opening
- toggle clasp
- Fireline 6-lb. test
- beading needles, #12

bracelet (7 in./18cm)

- turquoise beads
  27 4mm coin
  48 3mm heishi
  24 3mm round
- **54** 2mm round onyx beads
- 7g 8º seed beads
- 10g 11º seed beads
- 5g 14º Charlottes
- 2-strand clasp
- Fireline 6-lb. test
- beading needles, #12

EDITOR'S NOTE
Using turquoise-colored glass seed beads throughout the design stretches your dollar.

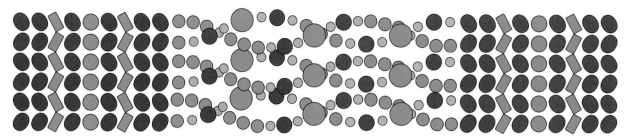

FIGURE

[5] Sew through the first loop, exiting the first 8º. Pick up two 8ºs and sew through the next 8º in the loop. Twist the first two loops two to three times, holding them in place between your index finger and thumb. Sew through the first 8º in the second loop **(photo c)**. Pick up two 8ºs and sew through the next 8º. Twist the third loop, and sew through the first 8º in the third loop. Pick up two 8ºs, and sew through the last 8º in the third loop. Sew through the first two 8ºs from the first loop to connect the first two new rounds **(photo d)**.

[6] Repeat step 3.

[7] Alternate sections of twisted loops and straight tubular herringbone, picking up six 11ºs instead of three throughout the next loop section, and picking up nine 11ºs instead of three throughout the third loop section. Work a tubular herringbone section, then mirror the first side of the necklace. End with a herringbone section.

[8] Cut a 5-in. (13cm) piece of wire. On one end of one wire, make a small coil. Place the coil in the end of the tubular herringbone **(photo e)**. Using 11ºs, work four rounds of herringbone to secure the wire **(photo f)**.

[9] Work the last row of herringbone, decreasing to use only one 8º per stitch. Sew through the last round several times to reinforce it. End the working thread (Basics, p. 7).

[10] On each end, string a cone and a 3mm round on the wire. Make the first half of a wrapped loop (Basics, p. 9 and **photo g**). Slide half of the clasp into the loop and complete the wraps. Trim the excess wire.

Bracelet

[1] Make the bracelet herringbone sections using the same bead counts as the necklace, but work in even-count herringbone (Basics, p. 5, and **figure**).

[2] Keep the loop sections the same length as in step 4 of "Necklace." Alternate between herringbone and loop sections to the desired length. Retrace the last row to mimic a bead ladder.

[3] To add the clasp, exit the end 8º in the last row, pick up two Charlottes, and then sew through the thread bridge between the next two 8ºs. Repeat. Then pick up 10 Charlottes, sew through the first loop of the clasp and back through the same thread bridge your thread is exiting. Work one stitch of two Charlottes, another loop of ten Charlottes, and then two more stitches of two Charlottes. End the working thread and tails.

Flame Tree Flowers

Turn to nature for botanical inspiration

designed by **Judith Golan**

Stitched with 11° cylinder beads (far left), each blossom measures about 1 x ¾ in. (2.5 x 1.9cm). Stitched with 15°s (left), each comes in at ⅞ x ⅝ in. (2.2 x 1.6cm).

Each spring, the Australian flame tree (*Brachychiton acerifolius*) covers itself in brilliant red bell-shaped flowers. Use herringbone stitch to create your own tiny bells. Stitch them in the authentic red, or get creative and experiment with multiple colors.

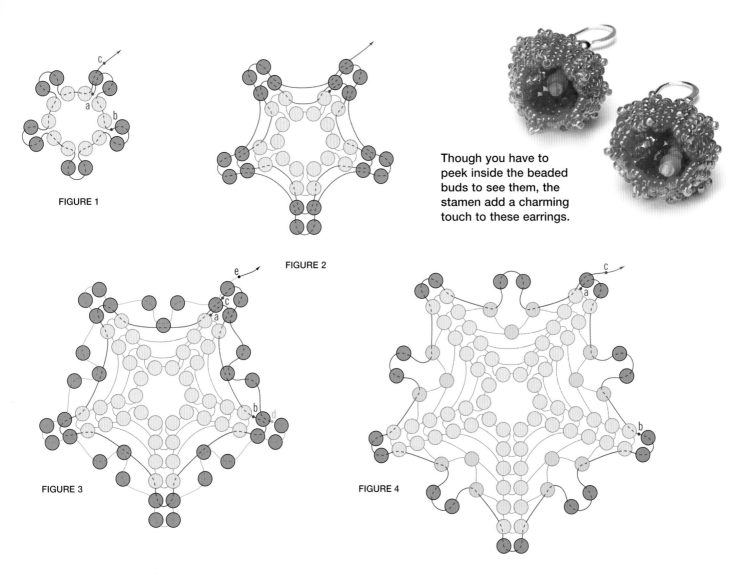

FIGURE 1

FIGURE 2

FIGURE 3

FIGURE 4

Though you have to peek inside the beaded buds to see them, the stamen add a charming touch to these earrings.

stepbystep

The following instructions are for the three-color version of the flower, with fuchsia used for color A, violet for color B, and orchid for color C. The red version used opaque red luster for color A and transparent red AB for colors B and C.

[**1**] On 1½ yd. (1.4m) of Fireline, pick up 10 color A 11º cylinder beads or 15º seed beads, leaving a 10-in. (25cm) tail. Sew through all the beads again to form a ring, and sew through the first bead once more. This is round 1.

[**2**] Work in straight tubular herringbone stitch (Basics, p. 7) as follows:

Round 2: Pick up two As, and sew through the next two As in the ring (figure 1, a–b). Repeat four times, and step up through the first A added in this round (b–c).

Rounds 3–4: Work two rounds of five stitches per round using two As per stitch (figure 2).

Round 5: Pick up two As, and sew down through the next A. Pick up a B, and sew up through the next A (figure 3, a–b). Repeat four times, and step up (b–c).

Round 6: Pick up two As, and sew down through the next A. Pick up a B, and sew through the next B. Pick up a B, and sew through the next A (c–d). Repeat four times, and step up (d–e).

Round 7: Pick up two As, and sew through the next A and B. Pick up two Bs, and sew through the next B and A (figure 4, a–b). Repeat four times, and step up (b–c).

Rounds 8 and 9: Work two rounds with an alternating pattern of a stitch with two As and a stitch with two Bs five times. Pull tight so the beadwork curves.

Rounds 10 and 11: Pick up two As, and sew down through the next A. Pick up a C, and sew up through the next B (photo a). Pick up two Bs, and sew down through the next B. Pick up a C, and sew up through the next A. Repeat four

times, and step up. Work another round.

Round 12: Work as in Rounds 10 and 11, but pick up two Cs between the stitches instead of one **(photo b)**.

Rounds 13 and 14: Work two rounds as in Rounds 10 and 11, positioning the Cs as in Rounds 10 and 11.

Round 15: Work a stitch with two As, skip the C, and sew up through the next B. Work a stitch with two Bs, skip the next C, and then sew up through the next A. Repeat around, and step up. Pull tight after each stitch so the beadwork begins to curve inward.

Round 16: Work 10 stitches with two As per stitch.

Round 17: Pick up one A per stitch to create a picot at the end of each herringbone column. Step up through the first picot A **(photo c)**.

Round 18: Pick up two As, and sew through the next picot A and the following three As to exit the following picot A **(photo d)**. Repeat four times,

and step up through the first A added in this round.

Round 19: Pick up an A, a C, and an A, and sew through the next six As **(photo e)**. Repeat four times, and end the thread (Basics).

[3] With the tail, pick up a 6º seed bead or 4mm bead, six As, and the loop of an earring finding. Sew back through the 6º or 4mm, and sew through a bead opposite where your thread exited at the start of this step **(photo f)**. Retrace the thread path a few times.

[4] If desired, add a stamen: Sew through the 6º or 4mm so your needle exits inside the flower. Pick up five or more color D seed beads. Skip the last one, and sew back through the rest of the Ds and the 6º or 4mm. Sew through the hanging loop again, and end the thread.

[5] Repeat steps 1–4 to make a second earring.

MATERIALS
pair of earrings
- **2** 6º seed beads or 4mm beads
- **11º** cylinder beads or 15º seed beads
  5g color A
  3g color B
  2g color C
- **10** or more color D seed beads in assorted sizes for stamen (optional)
- pair of earring findings
- Fireline 6-lb. test
- beading needles, #12 or #13

Supple
Herringbone Ropes

A pattern of bugle beads and cylinder beads creates interesting surface texture

designed by **Jill Wiseman**

MATERIALS
both projects
- Fireline 6-lb. test
- beading needles, #10 or #12

necklace 16 in. (41cm)
- 8g 3mm bugle beads
- 7g 11º Japanese cylinder beads

bracelet 7 in. (18cm)
- 4g 3mm bugle beads
- 4g 11º Japanese cylinder beads

Enjoy this graceful herringbone rope as a necklace, or make a shorter version to wear as a bracelet. Finish both with a peyote stitch toggle clasp.

step by step

Herringbone rope

[1] On 2 yd. (1.8m) of Fireline, pick up four cylinder beads. Sew through them again in the same direction, leaving a 6-in. (15cm) tail. Align the beads to start a ladder (Basics, p. 7), as in **figure 1, a–b.**

[2] Continue stitching a ladder with two cylinders per stitch until you have a total of eight stitches **(b–c).**

[3] Join the last stitch to the first to form a tube **(figure 2, a–b).**

[4] Work one round of straight tubular herringbone (Basics, p. 5) using cylinders **(figure 3, a–b).**

[5] To start the next round, step up through the top two cylinders in the next stack **(figure 4, a–b).** Continue in herringbone using cylinders **(b–c),** and step up as before.

[6] Work the next round using bugle beads.

[7] Continue stitching two rounds of herringbone using cylinders and one round using bugles until the tube is 1 in. (2.5cm) short of the desired length of your necklace or bracelet. End with three rounds of cylinders.

[8] Pick up two cylinders, and sew down through the top cylinder in the next stack **(figure 5, a–b).** Sew back through the top two cylinders in the previous stack **(b–c),** and continue through the top two in the next stack **(c–d).** This straightens the two sets of cylinders so they look like the

FIGURE 1

FIGURE 2

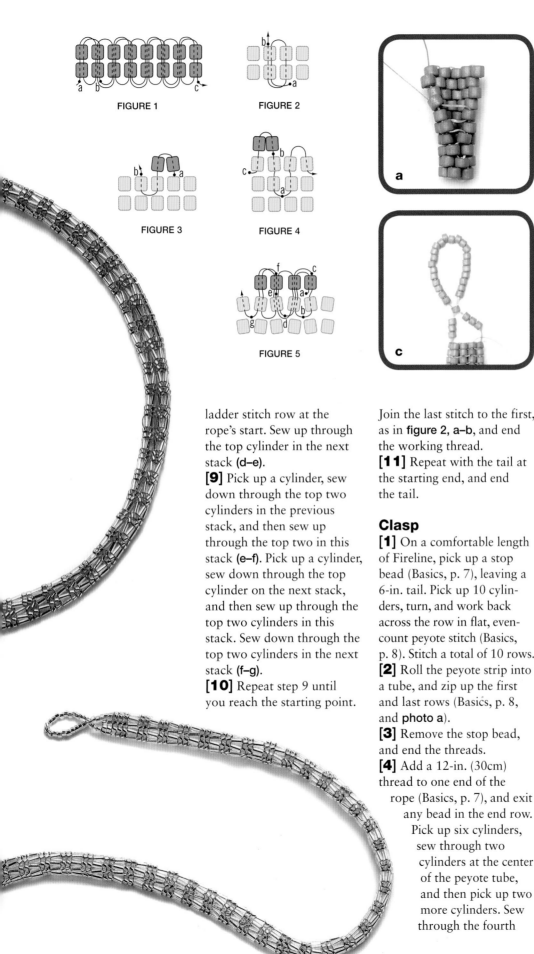

FIGURE 3

FIGURE 4

FIGURE 5

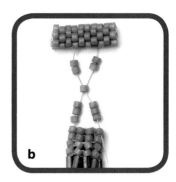

a

b

c

d

ladder stitch row at the rope's start. Sew up through the top cylinder in the next stack (d–e).

[9] Pick up a cylinder, sew down through the top two cylinders in the previous stack, and then sew up through the top two in this stack (e–f). Pick up a cylinder, sew down through the top cylinder on the next stack, and then sew up through the top two cylinders in this stack. Sew down through the top two cylinders in the next stack (f–g).

[10] Repeat step 9 until you reach the starting point.

Join the last stitch to the first, as in **figure 2, a–b**, and end the working thread.

[11] Repeat with the tail at the starting end, and end the tail.

Clasp

[1] On a comfortable length of Fireline, pick up a stop bead (Basics, p. 7), leaving a 6-in. tail. Pick up 10 cylinders, turn, and work back across the row in flat, even-count peyote stitch (Basics, p. 8). Stitch a total of 10 rows.

[2] Roll the peyote strip into a tube, and zip up the first and last rows (Basics, p. 8, and **photo a**).

[3] Remove the stop bead, and end the threads.

[4] Add a 12-in. (30cm) thread to one end of the rope (Basics, p. 7), and exit any bead in the end row. Pick up six cylinders, sew through two cylinders at the center of the peyote tube, and then pick up two more cylinders. Sew through the fourth

cylinder of the first six, pick up three cylinders, and then sew through a bead on the rope's end row opposite the starting point (**photo b**). Retrace the thread path twice, and end the thread.

[5] To make the loop end of the clasp, add a 12-in. thread to the other end of the rope. Exit a bead in the end row in the same column of beads as the toggle connection. Pick up enough cylinders (about 27) to form a loop large enough to go over the toggle. Sew through the fourth cylinder of the 27, pick up three cylinders, and then sew through a bead on the end row opposite the starting point (**photo c**).

[6] Retrace the thread path three times. If desired, work a row of peyote stitch around the loop (**photo d**). End any remaining threads.

Link to Creativity

Clever links connect your favorite colors

designed by **Shirley Lim**

Add texture to each link by using a combination of shiny and matte beads.

Successful execution of design displays the talent of the designer. Here, Shirley Lim has created a necklace that catches the eye from beginning to end. From an intriguing color gradation to seamless joins and a well-planned clasp, this piece of jewelry is bound to attract attention.

stepbystep

Herringbone links

[1] On 2 yd. (1.8m) of thread, attach a stop bead (Basics, p. 7), leaving a 6-in. (15cm) tail. Pick up four color A 11º seed beads, and sew through the first A again to form a ring (figure, a–b).

[2] Pick up two As, and sew through the next two beads in the ring (b–c). Repeat, and step up through the first A in the new round (c–d).

[3] Working in straight tubular herringbone (Basics, p. 6), repeat step 2 until you have 70 rounds.

[4] Remove the stop bead. Using a tubular herringbone thread path, join the last round to the first round, making sure the tube is not twisted. End the threads (Basics, p. 7). Make a second color A ring, and set the two aside.

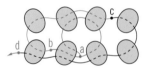

FIGURE

[5] Repeat steps 1–4 with colors B–N. Make three rings for color O, as this will be the center point of the necklace.

Clasp

Herringbone toggle ring

[1] On 1 yd. (.9m) of thread, follow steps 1–3 of "Herringbone links," but in step 3 work only five rounds.

[2] For Round 6, decrease to help the ring maintain a circular shape when the ends are stitched together: Pick up two color As, and work one herringbone stitch. Work the second stitch using a herringbone thread path without adding any beads. Step up through the last two beads in the first column.

[3] Work the next six rounds as in steps 1 and 2 using Bs, adding only two Bs in the first stitch of the sixth round. Repeat, alternating six rounds of As and six rounds of Bs for a total of 36 rounds.

[4] Join the tube into a ring by stitching the last round to the first using a herringbone thread path, making sure the tube is not twisted and the decrease stitches are on the inside of the ring. End the threads (photo a).

Peyote toggle bar

[1] On 1 yd. of thread, pick up 20 As, leaving a 6-in. tail. Work a strip of even-count peyote stitch (Basics, p. 8) that is 10 rows long.

[2] Roll the strip into a tube, and zip up (Basics, p. 8) the ends.

[3] To make a loop on the peyote bar, sew through the beadwork to exit the fourth A from one edge of the bar. Pick up 15 As, skip three As in the same row of the bar, and then sew through the next A in the next row of the bar (photo b). End the threads.

Assembly

[1] On 1 yd. of thread, pick up 22 As, leaving a 6-in. tail. Go through the loop of the toggle bar, and, folding the first color A ring in half, go around the center of it to create the first link. Sew through the first A of the 22 again (photo c).

[2] Work a round of square stitch (Basics, p. 8) on the connecting ring. End the threads (photo d).

[3] Pick up a color B ring, fold it in half, and then slip it through the two loops of link A (photo e).

[4] Working as in step 3, connect one link of each color C–O to the previous link, picking up all three color O rings in succession to make the center point. Work backward, connecting colors N–A to make the colors of the second half of the necklace a mirror image of the first half.

[5] Repeat steps 1 and 2 to connect the last A link to the toggle ring.

MATERIALS
necklace 21 in. (53cm)
- 11º seed beads
  15g in each of **2** colors: A, O
  10g in each of **13** colors: B–N
- nylon beading thread, size A
- beading needles, #12

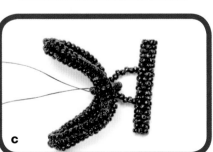

a

b

c

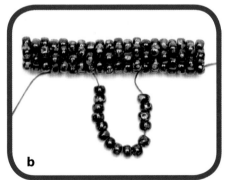

d

e

Fiesta Bangle

Liven up a herringbone tube with hundreds of colorful loops

designed by **Marcia Katz**

Marcia Katz's bangle is made with 14 different colors of Charlottes. Each loop is worked in a separate color.

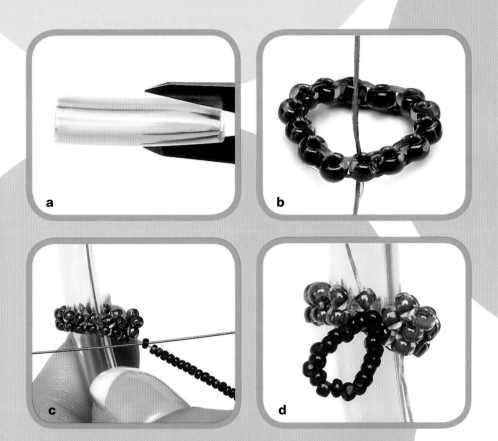

a

b

c

d

This bangle really makes a statement in color and movement. With a few simple stitches and seed beads, you can watch this plain tubular herringbone bracelet evolve into an accessory that will complement your next festive summer outfit.

stepbystep

[1] Cut a piece of tubing large enough to fit loosely over the largest part of your hand. Cut a ¾ in. (1.9cm) piece of tubing, then cut it in half lengthwise (photo a). Discard one half. Dab glue inside one end of the long tubing. Push the ¾ in. tubing halfway into the long piece, smearing the glue around. Set the tubing aside to dry.
[2] Work with comfortable lengths of thread, as you will have to end and add thread many times (Basics, p. 7). Stitch a ladder (Basics, p. 7) 14 beads long, using size 11º seed beads. Connect the ladder into a ring (photo b).

[3] Work a round of straight tubular herringbone (Basics, p. 6). Step up through the first 11º in the new round. (You may want to put your work over the long tubing as you stitch so you know your work will fit over the tubing when you assemble the bangle.)
[4] Modify the remaining rounds as follows to add colorful loops to each round: Work a stitch in herringbone with 11ºs, but do not sew through the first bead in the next stack. Pick up 20 color A Charlottes. Sew back through the first Charlotte, making a loop (photo c). Sew up through the first bead in the next stack (photo d). Complete the round, adding herringbone stitches with 11ºs and loops with Charlottes in

MATERIALS
bangle
- **7 or 14** hanks 13º Charlottes, in each of **7–14** colors: A–G or A–N
- 30g size 11º Japanese seed beads
- 10 in. (25cm) plastic aquarium or surgical tubing, 7mm diameter
- superglue
- nylon beading thread, size B or D
- beading needles, #13

This bangle uses only seven colors, but it delivers the same impact as 14 by having a mix of bead colors within the loops.

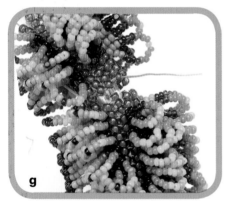

EDITOR'S NOTE:
Charlottes have holes with inconsistent sizes. If a specific bead seems to be a tight fit, discard it since it is unlikely that you'll be able to make a second pass through it.

colors B–H. Work the next round in the same manner, using colors I–N for the loops.

[5] Repeat step 4 until the bangle is 1½ in. (3.8cm) short of the desired length.

[6] Center the herringbone tube on the plastic tubing. Dab glue on the exposed end of the ¾ in. tubing **(photo e)**. Push the open end of the long tubing over the remainder of the ¾ in. piece. Hold the two together until the glue sets **(photo f)**.

[7] Work as many extra rounds of herringbone as needed to cover the tubing, but don't add loops to the last two rounds. Twist the herringbone tube, pick up an 11º, and then sew into the corresponding 11º in the first row **(photo g)**. Pick up another 11º, and

sew into the corresponding bead in the last row **(photo h)**. Repeat to complete the round.

[8] Add colorful loops to the last few rounds of herringbone to cover the join, and end the threads.

Draped Expectations

Connect herringbone scallops and add fringe for an elegant necklace

designed by **Melissa Grakowsky**

MATERIALS

necklace 13 in. (33cm)

- **91** 4mm bicone crystals
- **28** 4mm fire-polished beads
- **140** 3mm magatama or fringe drops
- **91** 15mm bugle beads
- **26** 6mm bugle beads
- **8–10g** 8º seed beads in 2 colors: A, B
- **8–10g** 11º seed beads
- **1–2g** 15º seed beads
- Fireline 6-lb. test
- beading needles, #12

FIGURE 1

FIGURE 2

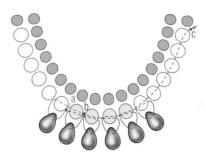

FIGURE 3

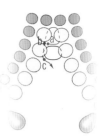

FIGURE 4

This necklace took careful planning to create, but it is deceptively simple to work up. Once you get the hang of your tension — tight scallops and relaxed fringe — the units come together with ease.

stepbystep

Scallops

[1] On 1 yd. (.9m) of Fireline, pick up four 11º seed beads, and tie them into a ring with a square knot (Basics, p. 7), leaving a 10-in. (25cm) tail. Sew through the first two 11ºs again (figure 1, a–b).

[2] Pick up two 11ºs, and sew through the next two 11ºs in the ring (b–c). Pick up two color A 8º seed beads, sew through the next two 11ºs, and then step up through the first 11º in this round (c–d).

[3] Pick up two 11ºs, and sew through the next 11º and up through the next A (figure 2, a–b). Pick up two As, and sew down through the next A and up through the next two 11ºs (b–c). Working in straight tubular herringbone (Basics, p. 6), repeat until you have six rounds of As. Work four rounds with color B 8º seed beads, six rounds with As, and a round with 11ºs only.

[4] Sew through each column, and pull the Fireline snug to reinforce the curvature of the scallop. Sew through the beadwork to exit an A adjacent to a B, pick up a 3mm magatama or fringe drop, and then sew through the A again and the next B (figure 3, a–b). Working in square stitch (Basics, p. 8), add five more 3mms for a total of six 3mms, and sew through the remaining As in the

column to exit the A adjacent to the 11º (b–c). Do not end the working thread or tail.

[5] Repeat steps 1–4 to make 13 scallops.

Assembly

[1] Thread a needle on the tail of a scallop thread, and sew through the beadwork to exit the first A. Using a square stitch thread path, sew through the corresponding A in the next scallop, and continue through the A your thread exited in the previous scallop (figure 4, a–b). Sew through the next A, and use a square stitch thread path to connect the corresponding A in the adjacent scallop (b–c). Sew through the beadwork to exit an A on the back side, and repeat to connect the top two As of each column. End the tail (Basics, p. 7).

[2] With the remaining thread, sew through the beadwork to exit the fourth A on the back (figure 5, point a). Pick up an 11º, a 6mm bugle bead, two 11ºs, an A, a 4mm fire-polished bead, a B, and a 15º seed bead (a–b). Skip the 15º, sew back through all the beads just added, and then continue through the next A (b–c).

[3] To add the next fringe, pick up an 11º, a 15mm bugle bead, a B, a 4mm bicone crystal, a B, and a 15º. Skip the

FIGURE 5

15º, sew back through all the beads just added, and then continue through the next 8º (c–d). Repeat six times with the following changes: Pick up two 11ºs for the second fringe, three 11ºs for the third through fifth fringes, two 11ºs for the sixth fringe, and one 11º for the seventh fringe (d–e).

[4] Pick up an 11º, a 6mm, two 11ºs, an A, a fire-polished, a B, and a 15º. Skip the 15º, and sew through the B, fire-polished, A, and an 11º (e–f). Pick up an 11º, a 6mm, and an 11º, and sew through the fourth A in the next unit (f–g).

[5] Sew through the remaining beads in the column to exit an end 11º (g–h). Pick up a fire-polished and a 15º, skip the 15º, sew back through the fire-polished, and then continue through the 11º in the previous scallop (h–i). Sew up

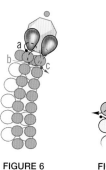

a

b c

FIGURE 6

FIGURE 7

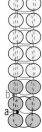

c

b

a

FIGURE 8

EDITOR'S NOTES:
- At 13 in. (33cm), this necklace fits only the smallest necks. To make your choker a little longer, add more scallops. Each scallop will add about ⅞ in. (2.2cm).
- You can substitute 12mm bugles for the 15mm bugles, which are slightly easier to find and won't change the look of the necklace too much.
- The toggle bar fits through the loop snugly. To give it a little more room, stitch two more rounds in the loop and two more rounds on the toggle bar connector.

a

b

c

through the adjacent 11º at the end of the column of 8ºs, and sew through the fire-polished, 15º, fire-polished, and corresponding 11º in the next scallop.

[6] Sew up through an 11º at the end of an inner column of 11ºs, pick up a 3mm, and then sew back down through the 11º **(figure 6, a–b)**. Sew up through the 11º at the end of the next inner column, and repeat **(b–c)**. Sew through the beadwork to exit an 11º at the end of an inner column in the previous unit, and add two more 3mms as before. End the thread.

[7] Repeat step 1 to connect the remaining scallop, and steps 3–6 to add fringe and embellishments.

Clasp
Loop

[1] On 1 yd. of Fireline, pick up two 11ºs and two As, and tie them into a ring with a square knot, leaving a 6-in. (15cm) tail. Sew through the first 11º again. Work six rounds of tubular herringbone as in "Scallops," following the established pattern until you have seven rounds of As.

[2] Work four rounds with Bs, seven rounds with As, and four rounds with Bs.

[3] To form the curved beadwork into a ring, work a herringbone thread path connecting the last beads added to the first beads added in step 1 **(figure 7)**.

[4] Use a square stitch thread path to connect the As of two rounds of the loop to an end scallop, as in step 1 of "Assembly." Sew through the beadwork to exit an edge 11º of an inner column at the end of the scallop. Pick up a 3mm, sew back through the 11º, and exit the adjacent 11º. Repeat to add a second 3mm, and end the thread.

Toggle bar

[1] On 1½ yd. (1.4m) of Fireline, attach a stop bead (Basics, p. 7), leaving a 10-in. (25cm) tail. Pick up 14 11ºs. Work a total of 10 rows of flat even-count peyote stitch (Basics, p. 8) to make a panel that is 14 11ºs wide with five 11ºs on each straight edge. Remove the stop bead, and zip up (Basics, p. 8) the panel to make a tube.

[2] Sew through the beadwork to exit an edge 11º. Pick up a fire-polished and three 15ºs. Sew back through the fire-polished and an 11º opposite the one your thread exited **(photo a)**. Sew up through an adjacent 11º, and through all of the beads just added, and the 11º opposite the one your thread exited.

[3] Sew up through an adjacent 11º, pick up a 3mm, and then sew back through the 11º your thread exited **(photo b)**. Repeat around the edge to add five 3mms.

[4] Thread a needle on the tail, and repeat steps 3 and 4 on the remaining end of the toggle bar. End the tail.

[5] With the working thread, sew through the beadwork to exit a center 11º on the toggle bar. Pick up two As, and sew through an adjacent 11º **(photo c)**. Sew through all the beads again to reinforce the connection, and exit an A.

[6] Pick up two As, and sew down through the adjacent A, up through the A your thread exited, and sew through the first A added **(figure 8, a–b)**. Repeat with another pair of As, five pairs of Bs, and a pair of 11ºs **(b–c)**.

[7] Use a square stitch thread path to connect two rows of the toggle bar's connector to an end scallop, as in step 1 of "Assembly." Sew through the beadwork to exit an edge 11º of an inner column at the end of the scallop. Pick up a 3mm, sew back through the 11º, and then exit the adjacent 11º. Repeat to add a second 3mm, and end the thread.

Queen
of the Sea

Nestle pearls in an
undulating wave of
herringbone rope

designed by **Jenny Van**

MATERIALS

necklace 16 in. (41cm)

- **12mm** rivoli
- **18** 10mm pearls
- **3** 4mm pearls
- **57** 3mm bicone crystals
- **15g** 8º seed beads
- **5g** 11º seed beads
- **1g** 15º seed beads
- Fireline 6-lb. test
- beading needles, #12

Turn the centerpiece into a sparkly stand-alone pendant by adding a soldered jump ring to one of the fringes in step 5 of "Centerpiece."

Simple modifications of stitches can produce the most stunning results. Placing smaller beads opposite larger ones in tubular herringbone produces a gentle curve, and switching the beads sends the curve in the other direction, creating the perfect places to tuck in crystals and pearls.

stepbystep

Centerpiece

[1] On 2 yd. (1.8m) of Fireline, pick up an 11º seed bead and an 8º seed bead, leaving a 12-in. (30cm) tail. Working in ladder stitch (Basics, p. 7), make a four-bead strip with the following bead sequence: 11º, 8º, 8º, 11º. Form the strip into a ring, making sure your working thread is exiting an 11º.

[2] Working in straight tubular herringbone (Basics, p. 6), pick up an 11º and an 8º for the first stitch, and an 8º and an 11º for the second. Step up after each round. Repeat for a total of 24 rounds.

[3] Insert the rivoli into the center of the beadwork (photo a), and work a tubular herringbone thread path through the beads in the first and last rounds to form a ring (photo b). Retrace the thread path of the join.

[4] Sew through the beadwork to exit an 11º on the back of the centerpiece. Pick up three 15º seed beads, skip two 11ºs, and then sew through the next 11º in the round (figure, a–b). Repeat to

complete the round, and step up through the first two 15ºs in the first stitch (b–c). Pick up two 15ºs, and sew through the center 15º of the next stitch in the previous round (c–d). Repeat to complete the round, and step up through the first two 15ºs in the first stitch (d–e). Retrace the thread path of the inner ring, and sew through the beadwork to exit an 8º in the outer ring.

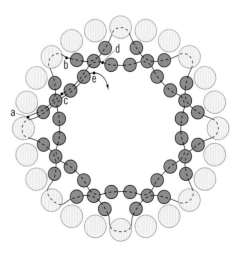

FIGURE

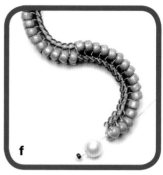

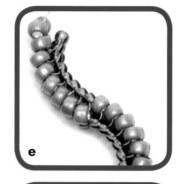

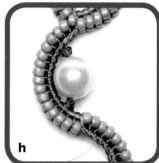

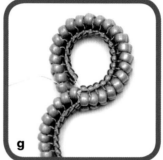

e

f

g

h

i

EDITOR'S NOTE:
If you have trouble with your rivoli slipping out of the herringbone bezel, sew through the front ring of 11ºs to tighten up the bezel.

[5] Sew under the thread bridge between the next two 8ºs, and pick up a 3mm bicone crystal and a 15º. Skip the 15º, and sew back through the 3mm and under the next thread bridge **(photo c)**. Repeat to complete the round, adding a fringe between each pair of thread bridges. End the tail (Basics, p. 7) but not the working thread.

Herringbone rope
[1] On a comfortable length of Fireline, work steps 1 and 2 of "Centerpiece" until you have 16 rounds.
[2] Continue in tubular herringbone, but substitute 8ºs for 11ºs and 11ºs for 8ºs **(photo d)**. As you work, your beadwork will begin to curve in the opposite direction **(photo e)**. Work a total of 16 rows. Continue in this manner until you have nine curved sections, ending and adding thread (Basics, p. 7) as needed. Repeat to make a second rope.
[3] At the end of one half of the necklace, work 16 rounds as in step 2, substituting 15ºs for 11ºs and 11ºs for 8ºs. Exiting an 11º, pick up a 4mm pearl, a 3mm, a 10mm pearl, and a 15º. Skip the 15º, and sew back through the

remaining beads just added and into the adjacent 11º. Sew through the adjacent 15º in the end round, and retrace the thread path of the beads just added. Sew through the remaining 11º and 15º in the end round. Retrace the thread path, and sew through the beadwork to exit the first three 11ºs in the previous curve. Don't end the working thread.
[4] Using the tail at the other end of the rope, exit an 8º. Pick up a 4mm pearl and a 15º, skip the 15º, and then sew back through the pearl and the 8º **(photo f)**. End the tail.
[5] On the other rope, work 22 rounds as in step 2, and then join the end to the end round of the previous curve, creating a ring **(photo g)**. Make sure it accommodates the 10mm pearl at the end of the other rope, adjusting rounds as needed. Don't end the thread.
[6] Repeat step 4.
[7] Using the working thread on the rope from step 5, pick up a 3mm crystal, a 10mm pearl, and a 3mm. Skip 10 11ºs, and sew through the next six 11ºs **(photo h)**. Repeat to add crystals and pearls to each curve except the last. End the thread. Repeat on the other rope.

Assembly
[1] Using the working thread from the centerpiece, exit a 15º at the end of a fringe. Sew through the sixth 8º in the last curve of one rope **(photo i)**. Retrace the thread path, then sew through the beadwork to exit the fifth fringe. Connect the centerpiece to the other rope in the same manner.
[2] Sew through the next three 8ºs on the rope, pick up a 10mm pearl, and sew through the corresponding 8º on the other rope. Retrace the join, and end the thread.

Fire
Blooms

A stunning floral
bead ignites a crystal
herringbone rope

designed by **Debbie Nishihara**

MATERIALS

necklace 18 in. (46cm)
- hibiscus focal bead
- 4mm Swarovski bicone crystals
  - **224** color A
  - **224** color B
- **2** 10mm cones
- **2** 8mm faceted rondelles
- **2** 6mm accent beads
- **4** 5mm daisy-shaped spacers
- **4** 5º triangle beads
- toggle clasp
- **2** crimp beads
- Fireline 6-lb. test
- flexible beading wire, .014–.015
- beading needles, #12
- crimping pliers
- wire cutters

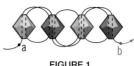

FIGURE 1

FIGURE 2

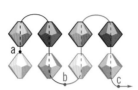

FIGURE 3

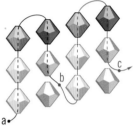

FIGURE 4

Highlight a gorgeous focal bead with a rope of twisted crystals. Choose colors that pop for a truly showstopping necklace.

stepbystep

Herringbone tubes

The number of crystals in the materials list makes two 7-in. (18cm) herringbone tubes for an overall necklace length of 18 in. (46cm). I used approximately 32 crystals per inch (2.5cm), so if you want to lengthen or shorten the tubes, be sure to adjust the number of crystals as well.

[1] Using a comfortable length of Fireline, make a ladder (Basics, p. 7) following the color pattern shown **(figure 1, a–b)**.

[2] Join the beads into a ring by sewing up through the first color A, down through the last B, and back up through the first A **(figure 2, a–b)**. The bicone shape prevents this row from lining up as usual, so be sure to note which are the tops of the beads.

[3] Pick up an A and a B, and sew down through the next B **(figure 3, a–b)**. Sew up through the next A, pick up an

A and a B, and then sew down through the next B **(b–c)**.

[4] To add a gentle spiral to the herringbone tube, modify the stitch slightly, as follows: Sew up through both As in the next stack, pick up an A and a B, and then sew down through the first B in the next stack **(figure 4, a–b)**. Sew up through both As in the next stack, pick up an A and a B, and then sew down through the next B **(b–c)**. Repeat until the tube is 7 in. long. When you finish the tube, leave the needle on the working thread, but end the tail. Make a second herringbone tube.

Assembly

[1] Add 6 in. (15cm) to the combined measurement of both tubes and cut a piece of flexible beading wire to that length. My beading wire is 20 in. (51cm) long.

[2] String a cone, a spacer, a rondelle, a spacer, and an accent bead **(photo a)**.

Then string a triangle, a crimp bead, a triangle, and a clasp half **(photo b)**. Go back through all the beads and the cone, and then crimp the crimp bead (Basics, p. 9). With the clasp faceup, the end components should look like **photo c**.

[3] Hold the tube vertically, trimmed-end first, and drop the beading wire down into it in small increments **(photo d)**. Slide the tube to the cone.

[4] With the working thread, sew through several beads to close the tube around the beading wire. Make half-hitch knots (Basics, p. 7), and end the thread.

[5] String the focal bead and the other herringbone tube **(photo e)**. Close the other end of the tube around the beading wire as in step 4.

[6] Repeat step 2 to finish the other end of the necklace. Do not pull the wire too tightly before you crimp or the tubes will buckle.

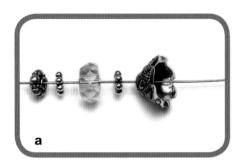

a

b

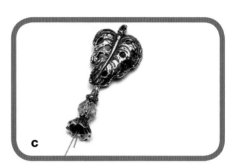

c

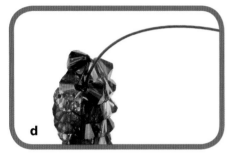

d

e

Fall Leaves

A supple herringbone base supports a graceful embellishment

designed by **Deborah Staehle**

MATERIALS
bracelet 9 in. (23cm)
- 15g 8º Japanese seed beads in each of **4** colors: A, B, C, D
- 15g 11º Japanese seed beads in each of **2** colors: E, F
- 12mm flat flower with a single hole, or a shank button
- Power Pro 10-lb. test
- beading needles, #12

This lavish bracelet, as well as the choker, are much easier to make than they look. Simply stitch a spiral herringbone base of 8º seed beads and embellish it with leaves as you work. This time-saving step will have you wearing a flattering fringe around your neck or wrist in no time at all.

Varying the amount of leafy fringe gives you the option of a delicately or richly embellished version of this bracelet.

stepbystep

[1] On 3 yd. (2.7m) of Power Pro, stitch a three-bead ladder four rows long (Basics, p. 7), leaving a 20-in. (51cm) tail, using 8º seed beads and following the color sequence in **figure 1**.

[2] Sew through the first, last, and first rows again to connect the ladder into a tube. Exit the top of a stack of color A 8º seed beads.

[3] Work in twisted tubular herringbone (Basics, p. 6) as follows: Pick up an A and a color B seed bead. Sew down through the top bead in the B stack and up through the two top beads on the color C seed bead stack **(figure 2, a–b)**.

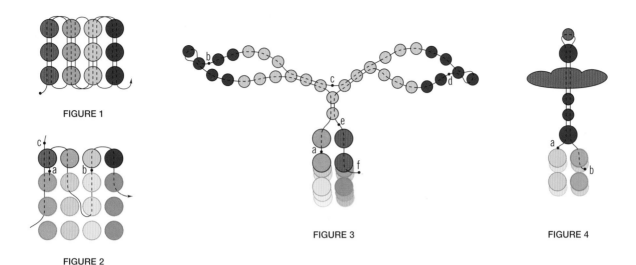

FIGURE 1

FIGURE 2

FIGURE 3

FIGURE 4

[4] Pick up a C and a color D 8º seed bead. Sew down through the top bead in the D stack and up through the three top beads on the A stack (**b–c**).

[5] Pick up an A, eight color E 11º seed beads, and four color F 11º seed beads. Skip an F and sew back through the next F (**figure 3, a–b**). Pick up two Fs and three Es. Skip two Fs and three Es, and sew through the next three Es (**b–c**).

[6] Pick up six Es and four Fs. Skip an F and sew through the next F (**c–d**). Pick up two Fs and three Es. Skip two Fs and three Es, then sew through five Es (**d–e**).

[7] Pick up a B, and sew down through the top B on the B stack (**e–f**), and then sew up through the two top beads on the C stack.

[8] Pick up a C and a D, sew down through the top bead in the D stack, and then sew up through the three top beads in the A stack.

[9] Pick up an A and a B. Sew down through the top bead in the B stack and up through the two top beads in the C stack.

[10] Repeat steps 5 and 6, but pick up a C instead of an A.

[11] Pick up a D, and sew down through the top bead on the D stack and up through the three top beads on the A stack.

[12] Repeat steps 3–11 until you reach the desired length.

[13] Exit the top bead in the A stack, pick up an A, two Fs, a flat flower or button, an A, and an F. Skip the F and sew back through the beads just added to the bracelet (**figure 4**). Retrace the thread path to reinforce the beads, and end the working thread.

[14] On the tail, pick up enough 8ºs to accommodate the clasp. Go into the bead opposite where the thread is exiting. Make a second pass through the beads just added to reinforce them. Make three sets of leaves on the loop, and end the thread.

EDITOR'S NOTE:
Lengthen the bracelet to make a choker. Stitch a few leaf fringes near the back of the necklace and gradually make it fuller near the front. Add crystals to the base, if desired.

Dripping with an abundance of copper-coated leaves, this lovely lariat is the perfect autumn accessory.

Fall Fascination

Copper-dipped leaves contribute an authentic fall motif to this vine-like lariat

designed by **Babette Borsani**

Free-form fringe clusters disguise a herringbone rope — a stylishly practical way to taper the thickness of the lariat.

stepbystep

Lariat

Herringbone rope

[1] On a comfortable length of thread, use 8º seed beads to work a row of ladder stitch (Basics, p. 7) eight beads long, leaving a 6-in. (15cm) tail. Join the ends of the ladder to form a ring, and exit the first bead.

[2] Working in straight tubular herringbone (Basics, p. 6), work five rounds using 8ºs.

[3] Continue, using 6º seed beads, 8ºs, and 11º seed beads to create a bumpy texture in the rope **(photo a)**. End and add thread (Basics, p. 7) as needed.

[4] When the herringbone rope is about 7 in. (18cm) long, reduce the four-stitch rope to a three-stitch rope: Begin by adding two beads for the first stitch. Skip two columns, and sew up through the top 8º in the following stack **(photo b)**. Work two more stitches to complete the round. You will return to the two columns you skipped to stitch a branch after you have completed the herringbone rope.

[5] Continue stitching three-stitch rounds for 3–5 in. (7.6–13cm). Reduce the three-stitch rope to a two-stitch rope as in step 4.

[6] Continue stitching two-stitch rounds for another 9 in. (23cm).

[7] Repeat steps 3–6 to complete the other half of the herringbone rope.

Branches

[1] Add a new thread near a point where you reduced the beadwork from four stitches to three, and exit a bead in the skipped stitch. This stitch will be referred to as the base stitch.

[2] Pick up four 8ºs, and sew through both beads of the base stitch to form a ring **(photo c)**, and then sew through the first bead just added. This ring will be the basis for a new herringbone tube.

[3] Pick up two 8ºs, and sew through the next two beads in the ring **(photo d)**. This is the first herringbone stitch in the

a

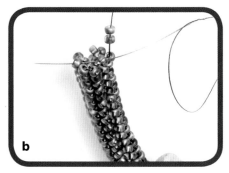

b

c

d

e

f

g

h

i

j

k

branch. Pick up two 8ºs, and sew through the fourth bead in the ring and the first bead in the base stitch (**photo e**). Pick up two 8ºs, and sew through the next bead in the base stitch and the top two beads in the first herringbone stitch (**photo f**).

[4] Working off the beads added in step 3, continue in herringbone for the desired number of rounds. If desired, taper the branch by replacing the 8ºs with 11ºs, and then the 11ºs with 15º seed beads for four or five rounds.

[5] Sew back to the reduction point, and secure the unattached part of the first round of the branch to the rope.

[6] Repeat steps 1–5 at the remaining reduction points.

Embellishments

Enhance the ends of the rope and branches, the column reduction points, and any other desired spots using one or more of the following embellishments.

Surface embellishment

Pick up a combination of five to nine seed beads and crystals, and sew through a bead in the herringbone rope to create a ridge (**photo g**). Repeat as desired, altering bead counts to your liking.

Fringe

Pick up a combination of seed beads, rondelles, pearls, or bicones, ending with one or three B 11ºs. Skip the B 11ºs, and sew back through the rest of the fringe beads and into the rope (**photo h**). Repeat as desired, altering bead counts to your liking.

Leaf-shaped fringe

[1] Pick up four to 15 A 11ºs and 11 B 11ºs, skip the end B 11º, and sew back through the next B 11º (**figure 1, a–b**). Pick up nine B 11ºs, and sew back through the last two A 11ºs added in this stitch (**b–c**).

[2] Pick up two A 11ºs and 11 B 11ºs, skip the end B 11º, and sew back through the next B 11º. Pick up nine B 11ºs, and sew back through the two A 11ºs added in this stitch and the next two A 11ºs in the stem (**c–d**).

[3] Repeat step 2 to fill the stem with leaves (**d–e**), substituting a 3 or 4mm bicone crystal in place of the B 11º, if desired, and altering bead counts to your liking.

Tendril

Pick up a repeating pattern of a 15º and a B 11º until you have the desired length, and end with a 15º. Skip the end 15º, and sew back through only the 11ºs (**figure 2**). Tighten the thread to curl the tendril (**photo i**). Sew into the herringbone rope, and tie a half-hitch knot (Basics, p .7).

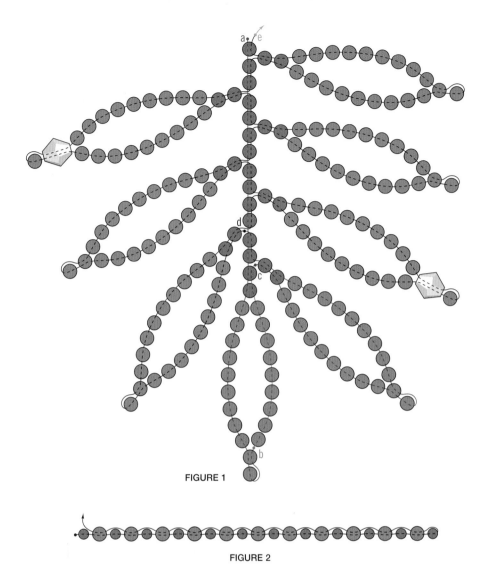

FIGURE 1

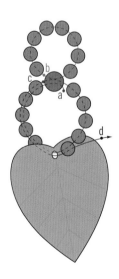

FIGURE 2

MATERIALS

both projects
- nylon beading thread, size D
- beading needles, #12

lariat 46 in. (1.2m)
- **28–35** 25–51mm 1-hole copper-coated leaves
- **2–3** 16-in. (41cm) strands 5–7mm pearls
- **30–35** 6mm crystal rondelles
- **70–85** 3–6mm bicone crystals
- **10–15g** 6º seed beads
- **75–90g** 8º seed beads
- 11º seed beads
  5–10g color A
  5–10g color B
- **3–5g** 15º seed beads

pair of earrings
- **2** 25–30mm 1-hole copper-coated leaves
- **2** 3–4mm crystals
- **2** 8º seed beads
- 1g 11º seed beads, color A or B
- 1g 15º seed beads
- **2** 4mm jump rings
- pair of earring findings
- **2** pairs of pliers

Pearl "berry" cluster

[**1**] Pick up five to 10 8ºs, two or three 15ºs, a pearl, and two or three 15ºs, and then sew back through the last 8º (photo j).

[**2**] Pick up two or three 15ºs, a pearl, and two or three 15ºs, and sew back through the next 8º. Repeat to add one or more loops to each 8º in the stem, altering bead counts to your liking.

Leaf dangle fringe

Pick up two to four 8ºs, five to nine A 11ºs, a leaf, a rondelle, and five to nine A 11ºs, and sew back through the 8ºs (photo k). Sew into the branch, and exit another column. Repeat as desired to add more leaves, altering bead counts to your liking.

Earrings

[**1**] On 1 yd. (.9m) of thread, pick up an 8º seed bead, five 11º seed beads, a leaf, and five 11ºs. Sew through the 8º to form a loop (figure 3, a–b).

[**2**] Pick up eight 11ºs, and sew through the 8º again to form a loop above the first loop (b–c). Sew through the beads of the lower loop to exit an 11º on the front of the leaf (c–d).

[**3**] Working as in "Embellishments: Tendril," pick up a repeating pattern of an 11º and a 15º seed bead 11 times, and sew back through the 11ºs. Pull tight to curl the strand. Sew through the next 11º on the front of the leaf.

[**4**] Repeat step 3 twice, substituting a 3mm or 4mm crystal for the last 11º on one of the tendrils, if desired.

[**5**] Sew through the 8º and the loop of 11ºs above it, and end the threads.

[**6**] Open a 4mm jump ring (Basics, p. 9), attach the top loop of 11ºs and the loop of an earring finding, and close the jump ring.

[**7**] Make a second earring.

FIGURE 3

69

Herringbone *Helix*

Make a twisted bracelet by joining two lengths of tubular herringbone

designed by **Linda Gettings**

I don't have a favorite beading stitch. Instead, I constantly play with all sorts of techniques, and right now, I'm crazy for herringbone. With that on the brain, I envisioned this twisting design and sketched it. Days and many redesigns later, my work revealed this deceptively simple bracelet — one of my favorites. Try mixing up different colors and sizes of beads. After all, that's where the fun is!

step by step

Single twists

[1] On a comfortable length of Fireline, leaving an 8-in. (20cm) tail, stitch a ladder (Basics, p. 7) two beads tall and six beads wide, making the first two bead stacks using 8º seed beads, and the next four bead stacks using color A 11ºs.

[2] Join the ladder into a ring by sewing down through the first pair of beads and then back up the last pair. Sew back through the first stack again to exit an 8º (photo a).

[3] To begin the first round of twisted tubular herringbone, pick up two 8ºs, and sew down into the two 8ºs of the next stack of the base (photo b). Sew up through the top A of the next stack (photo c). Pick up two As, sew down into the two As of the next base stack, and then sew up through the top A of the next stack. Pick up two As and repeat once to complete the round, sewing up through the top two 8ºs of the next stack to step up for the next round (photo d).

[4] Repeat step 3 to make a twisted herringbone rope that is about 7½ in. (19.1cm) long, and end the threads.

[5] Repeat steps 1–4 to make another strand of the same length using 8ºs and color B 11ºs (photo e).

Joining

[1] Twist the two strands together, making sure that the ends line up.

[2] Add 1 yd. (.9m) of Fireline in one of the twists, and exit an end 8º. Sew through two or three 8ºs, cross over to the corresponding 8º on the other twist, and then sew through two or three 8ºs on that side. Continue in this manner, sewing back and forth between the twists to connect them (photo f). End the threads.

[3] Repeat step 2 to connect the aligned inside 11ºs, sewing through three to five beads at a time on each side. Use chainnose pliers to maneuver the needle if needed, and end the threads.

[4] Add 2 ft. (61cm) of Fireline in the beadwork, and exit one joined end. Pick up a bead cap, a B, a 6mm bead, a B, three As, half of a clasp, and three As. Sew through the B and the 6mm, and pick up a B (photo g). Sew through the bead cap and into the beadwork. Pull tight, and retrace the thread path several times for support. To center the bead cap, sew into the beadwork at different points around the end of the twist. End the remaining threads. Repeat on the opposite end with the other half of the clasp.

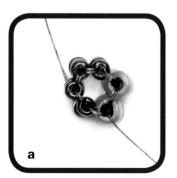

a

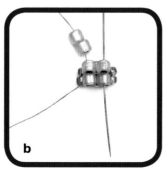

b

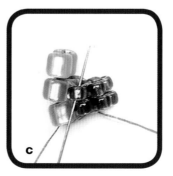

c

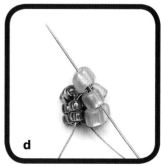

d

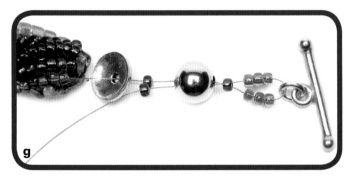

MATERIALS

bracelet 8 in. (20cm)
- 2 6–8mm accent beads
- Japanese seed beads
  16g 8º
  7g 11º, in each of **2** colors: A, B
- 2 10–12mm bead caps
- clasp
- Fireline 6-lb. test
- beading needles, #12
- chainnose pliers (optional)

DESIGNER'S NOTE:

Here's an easy way to add new thread: With at least 4 in. (10cm) of thread remaining, make sure that your thread is exiting an 8º. Remove the needle, and tie a new length of thread to the old tail with a square knot (Basics, p. 7). Attach a needle to the new thread and, without adding any beads, sew down through four to seven beads in the next stack of 8ºs. Sew back up the original stack of 8ºs, hiding the knot within the 8ºs. Proceed to pick up two 8ºs to begin your next stitch, and stitch a few rounds before you trim the tails.

EDITOR'S NOTE:

- Instead of using 11º seed beads in two colors to get a two-tone interior twist (as in these three bracelets), try using both sets of 11ºs in a single color, as in the two bracelets on the right on p. 70.
- Tall, square-holed 8ºs like those used here will create an angular look. If you prefer a more fluid helix, choose shorter, round-holed 8ºs.

Do the Twist

Create a wide cuff of twisted ropes
with crystal connections

designed by **Jimmie Boatright**

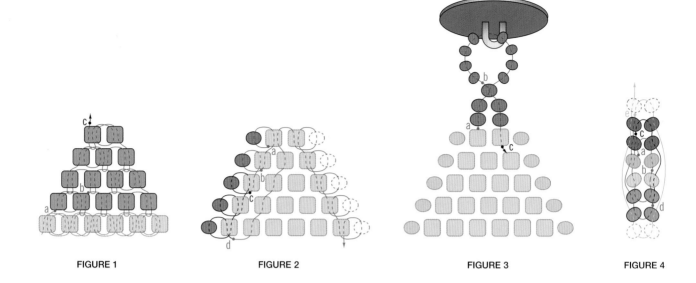

FIGURE 1   FIGURE 2   FIGURE 3   FIGURE 4

This multistrand bracelet offers plenty of opportunities to have fun with color and texture. Three colors play across the twisted ropes while round crystals and a button closure add playful accents.

stepbystep

Triangular ends

[1] On 1 yd. (.9m) of thread or Fireline, pick up two 3mm cube beads, leaving a 6-in. (15cm) tail. Sew through the 3mms again so they sit side by side. Continue working in ladder stitch (Basics, p. 7) until the strip is six 3mms long. Weave through the 3mms to stabilize the ladder, exiting the first 3mm.

[2] Pick up two 3mms, sew through both again, sew under the thread bridge between the second and third 3mm in the previous row, and then sew up through the second 3mm just added **(figure 1, a–b)**. Work in brick stitch (Basics, p. 7), decreasing one 3mm in each row, until the final row has two 3mms **(b–c)**.

[3] Exit the bottom of a 3mm in the top row **(figure 2, point a)**. Pick up an 8º seed bead, sew down through the 3mm again, and then continue through the next edge 3mm **(a–b)**. Pick up an 8º, and sew down through the 3mm your thread just exited and the next edge 3mm **(b–c)**. Repeat to add an 8º to the edge of each row **(c–d)**, sew through the beadwork to exit the other top 3mm, and then repeat along the other edge.

[4] Sew through the beadwork to exit a top 3mm **(figure 3, point a)**. Pick up three 8º's, four 11º seed beads, the shank of the button, and four 11º's **(a–b)**. Sew back through the last 8º added, pick up two 8º's, and then sew through the other top 3mm **(b–c)**. Retrace the thread path, and end the threads (Basics, p. 7).

[5] Repeat steps 1–3 to create and embellish another triangular end. Sew through the beadwork to exit a top 3mm, and pick up enough 8º's to make a loop around the button. Sew through the other top 3mm, retrace the thread path, and then end the working thread and tail.

Ropes

[1] On a comfortable length of thread, leave a 10-in. (25cm) tail, and work in ladder stitch to create a ladder of two color A 11º seed beads and two color B 11º seed beads. Join the ends of the ladder to form a ring, and exit up out of the first A.

[2] Pick up two As, and sew down through the next A in the previous round **(figure 4, a–b)**. Sew up through the next B, pick up two Bs, sew down through the following B, and then sew up through the two As in the next column **(b–c)**.

[3] Pick up two As, and sew down through the next A in the previous round and up through the top two Bs in the following column **(c–d)**. Pick up two Bs, sew down through the next B in the previous round, and then step up through the top three As in the following column **(d–e)**. Continue working in twisted tubular herringbone (Basics, p. 6), following the established pattern, until the rope is 5 in. (13cm) long, ending and adding thread (Basics, p. 7) as needed. Do not end the working thread or tail.

[4] Repeat steps 1–3 to make a second rope with As and Bs.

[5] Work in twisted tubular herringbone as in steps 1–3 to create two ropes using Bs and color C 11º seed beads, one rope using just As, and one rope using just Cs, for a total of six ropes.

Assembly

[1] Using the tail of an A-and-B rope, attach it to the bottom of an edge 3mm in a triangular end: Sew through the 3mm, and continue through the 3mm above it. Sew through the beadwork to exit the bottom of the edge 3mm, and sew back into the rope **(photo a)**. Exit the next 11º in the round, and sew back into the triangular end. Continue sewing between the rope and the triangular end until the join is secure, and end the thread.

MATERIALS

bracelet 7 in. (18cm)

- **11** 8mm round crystals
- 5g 3mm cube beads
- 3g 8º seed beads
- 8g 11º seed beads, in each of **3** colors: A, B, C
- shank button
- nylon beading thread, size D, or Fireline 6-lb. test
- beading needles, #12

[2] Join the remaining ropes to the same triangular end as in step 1, working across the bottom of the end to join an A-and-C rope, the B rope, the C rope, an A-and-C rope, and the remaining A-and-B rope.

[3] Wrap an A-and-B rope over and under the adjacent A-and-C rope, and join the ropes to the other triangular end as in step 1, but do not end the threads. Repeat with the B and C ropes and the other A-and-B and A-and-C ropes **(photo b)**.

[4] Using a thread from an A-and-B or A-and-C rope, sew through the rope to exit the middle of the bracelet. Pick up an 8mm round crystal, and sew through an 11º in the next rope, positioning the 8mm between the ropes. Sew back through the 8mm and the 11º your thread exited on the first rope. Retrace the thread path, and exit an 11º on the other side of the inner rope **(photo c)**.

[5] Use a ladder stitch thread path to join the rope to the next rope, a B or C rope **(photo d)**. Exit the other side of the rope. Add an 8mm between the B and C ropes as you did in step 4, and attach the next two ropes. Add another 8mm

between the other A-and-B and A-and-C ropes, and end the thread. These 8mms form a line across the middle of the bracelet.

[6] Add an 8mm between the A-and-B and A-and-C ropes about one-third of the way between a triangular end and the middle. Repeat to add a second 8mm aligned with the first, and two 8mms at the other end.

[7] Find the point halfway between each row of 8mms where the ropes cross each other. Using one of the remaining tails, sew through the beadwork to exit a rope at this point, and stitch the ropes together. Repeat to join the other ropes where they cross each other.

[8] Exiting between the ropes where they are joined together, pick up an 8mm, and then sew into the next pair of ropes where they are joined. Sew back and forth through the 8mm between the ropes. Repeat to add an 8mm between the center ropes and the pair of ropes on the other side. Repeat at the other end of the bracelet to add two more 8mms, and end all the threads.

That's a wrap

Twisted tubular herringbone winds around itself to hang a pretty pendant

designed by **Melissa Grakowsky**

MATERIALS

necklace 16 in. (41cm)
centerpiece 3 in. (7.6cm)

- 28 x 16mm pendant
- **6** 6mm rondelles
- **36** 4mm fire-polished glass beads
- 2–3g 3mm magatama fringe beads
- 8º seed beads
  8–10g color D
  3–4g color E
- 11º seed beads
  5–6g color A
  1g color B
  3–4g color C
- 4–5g 15º seed beads
- Fireline 6-lb. test
- beading needles, #12

This clever technique could also be used to suspend a stone donut or other pendant with a large hole.

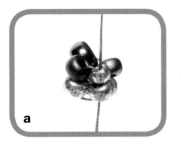 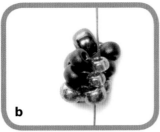 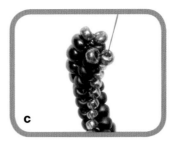 

Using several sizes of beads allows ordinary stitches to be used in extraordinary ways.

stepbystep

Neck strap

[1] On 3 yd. (2.7m) of Fireline, make a four-bead ladder (Basics, p. 7) with color B 11º seed beads, leaving an 18-in. (46cm) tail. Join the beads into a ring.

[2] Work in straight tubular herringbone (Basics, p. 6) for the first round: Pick up a 15º seed bead and a color A 11º seed bead for the first stitch, pick up a color D 8º seed bead and an A for the second stitch, and step up through two beads **(photo a)**.

[3] Continue the bead sequence established in step 2, but switch to modified twisted tubular herringbone stitch by stepping up through only the first bead in the new round instead of two beads (Basics, p. 6, and **photo b**). Work a total of 50 rounds.

[4] Work a round of twisted tubular herringbone using Bs **(photo c)**, a round using 4mm fire-polished beads **(photo d)**, and a round using Bs **(photo e)**.

[5] Working in twisted tubular herringbone,

continue in the bead sequence from step 2 for 20 rounds, stepping up through two beads.

[6] Repeat step 4.

[7] Repeat step 3 for a total of 50 rounds.

[8] Repeat step 4.

[9] Working in twisted tubular herringbone, pick up a color C 11º seed bead and an A for the first stitch, pick up a D and an A for the second stitch, and then step up through two beads. Work a total of 85 rounds to make a neck strap with an overall length of 16 in. (41cm). Note: 11 rounds equal about 1 in. (2.5cm), so to change the length, add or omit rows in this section. End and add thread as needed (Basics, p. 7).

[10] Repeat step 4.

[11] Repeat steps 3–7.

[12] To finish the end, repeat step 4. Exiting an end B, pick up a B, sew through a B in the opposite stitch, the adjacent B, back through the new B, into the remaining B in the first stitch, and then through the next 4mm in the previous round **(photo f)**.

[13] Sew through the beads in the last round to exit an A. Pick up three 3mm fringe beads, skip one A in the same column, and then sew through the next three As **(photo g)**. Repeat until you reach the last cluster of 4mms before the long curve of the back of the neck strap. Exit a 4mm.

[14] Sew through the adjacent 4mm so the thread is facing the nearest end of the neck strap. Pick up enough As to make a loop that will accommodate the end cluster of 4mms, and sew through the adjacent 4mm **(photo h)**. Retrace the thread path of the loop, and end the thread.

[15] Repeat steps 12–14 on the other end of the neck strap using the tail.

Centerpiece

[1] On 3 yd. (2.7m) of Fireline, make a four-bead ladder with two Cs and two Ds, leaving an 18-in. (46cm) tail. Join the beads into a ring. Work in straight tubular herringbone stitch using two As in the first stitch and two

Larger beads at the ends of the rope slip into hidden loops for security.

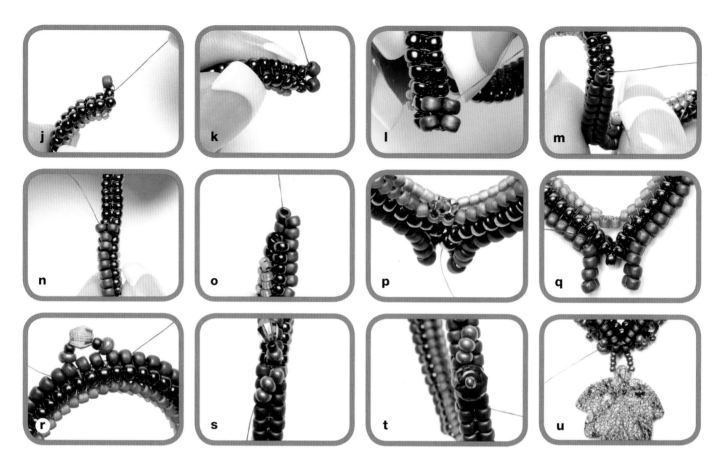

Ds in the second. As you work, the tube will begin to curve (photo i). Work a total of 62 rounds.

[2] Exiting a D in the last round, pick up a color E 8º seed bead, and sew through the D your thread just exited (photo j). Sew through the adjacent D, pick up an E, and then sew through the D your thread just exited. Work a modified ladder stitch by sewing through the two Es just added (photo k).

[3] Pick up two Es, and sew down through the adjacent E in the previous round and up through the next two stacked Es. Work a modified ladder stitch to join the two Ds and two Es in this round, and exit an E (photo l). Work a total of 23 rounds.

[4] Work the next round by picking up only one E, working a ladder stitch thread path to join it to both Ds in the same round (photo m). Work a total of 16 rounds, then switch back to picking up two Es (photo n) for the remaining rounds.

[5] To stagger the length of the rows of each color, work a round of straight tubular herringbone, adding Ds and Es but omitting the Cs. Work two modified ladder rounds, but add only Es (photo o). Repeat using the tail.

[6] Exit a C at one end, and join the two end stitches of Cs using a ladder stitch thread path (photo p).

[7] Sew through the beadwork to exit an end D. Pick up a D, and sew through the D on the other end (photo q). Sew through the adjacent D, and repeat on the other side.

[8] Exit an end E, join the end four Es as in step 6, and end the thread.

[9] Center 1 yd. (.9 m) of Fireline in the two center Es at the top of the pendant.

[10] Pick up a fringe bead, an A, a 4mm, an A, and a fringe bead. Skip two Es, and sew through the next two Es (photo r). Repeat once. Sew through an E in the next round. This will be referred to as the first column.

[11] Pick up three fringe beads, skip an E in the first column, and then sew through the next E in the adjacent column (photo s). Sew through the next E in the first column. Repeat three times.

[12] Pick up a 6mm rondelle and a B. Skip the B, and sew back through the 6mm. Sew through the next E in the adjacent column, then sew through the next E in the first column (photo t). Pick up three fringe beads, skip an E in the first column, and then sew through the next E in the adjacent column. Sew through the next E in the first column. Repeat twice.

[13] Repeat steps 10–12 using the tail.

[14] For a top-drilled pendent with a hole drilled front to back, pick up four Bs, and then sew through the hole in the pendant. Pick up four As, and sew through the E on the opposite surface. Repeat with the adjacent pair of end Es, and end the thread. For a top-drilled pendant with a hole drilled side to side, add both sets of Bs to the front Es first (photo u), then add the As to the back Es.

Assembly

Position the centerpiece in the section of beadwork from step 5 on each end of the neck strap, wrap the twisted sections around each other, and attach each end cluster of 4mms to the appropriate loop of As.

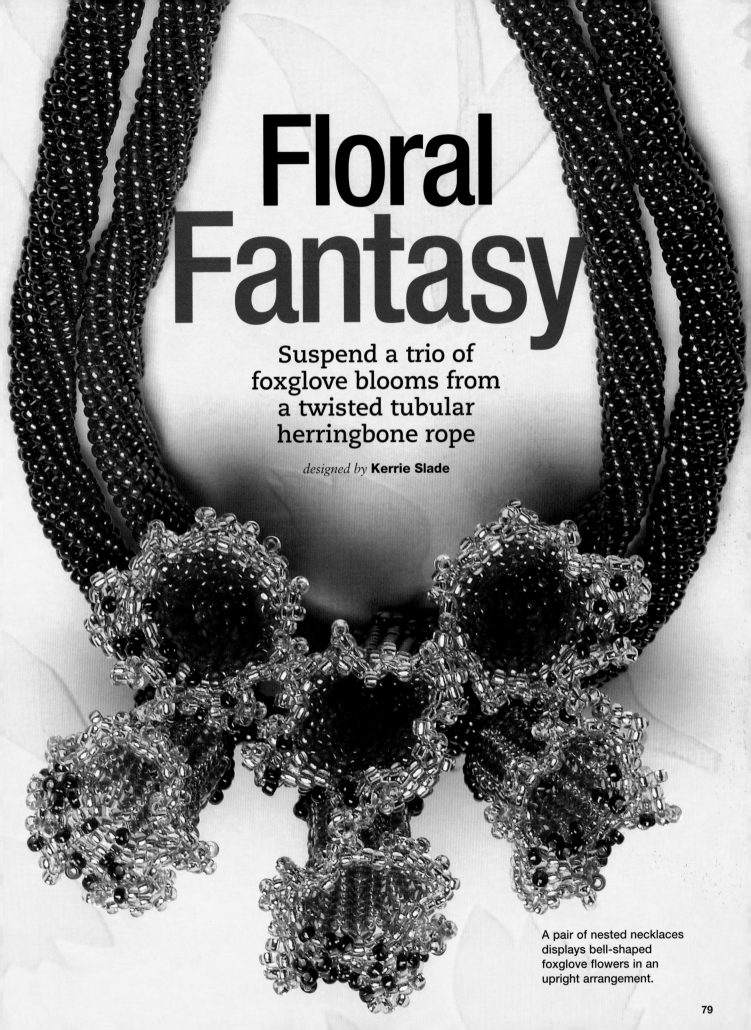

Floral Fantasy

Suspend a trio of foxglove blooms from a twisted tubular herringbone rope

designed by **Kerrie Slade**

A pair of nested necklaces displays bell-shaped foxglove flowers in an upright arrangement.

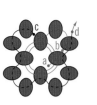

FIGURE 1

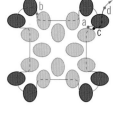

FIGURE 2

I love looking at the foxglove flowers in my garden. I spent a long time working with different stitches until I found the ones that best suited my flower design. The beaded foxgloves can be worn as a single pendant or grouped together to form a floral cluster.

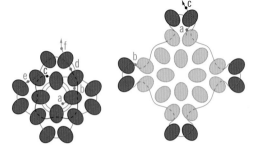

FIGURE 3   FIGURE 4

stepbystep

Tubular rope

[1] On 2 yd. (1.8m) of color A thread, pick up four color A 11º seed beads, leaving a 10-in. (25cm) tail. Sew through the As again to form a ring. Sew through the first A again, and snug up the beads **(figure 1, a–b)**.

[2] Pick up two As, and sew through the next A **(b–c)**. Repeat three times, and step up through the first A added in this round **(c–d)**.

[3] Pick up two As, and sew down through the A in the previous round and up through the next A **(figure 2, a–b)**. Working in straight tubular herringbone (Basics, p. 6), repeat to complete the round **(b–c)**. Step up through one A **(c–d)**.

[4] Work the remaining rounds in twisted tubular herringbone (Basics, p. 6) by picking up two As, sewing down through the A in the next stack, and up through two As in the following stack. Step up through three As. Maintain tight thread tension to form a tube as you add rounds. Make the rope the desired length, adding thread as needed.

[5] To close the end of the tube, pick up one A instead of two in each stitch. Snug up the beads. Retrace the thread path through this round.

[6] Sew through the four single As twice, and snug up the beads.

[7] Pick up a 6º seed bead. Sew through the A opposite the A the thread is exiting. Continue back through the 6º and the As in a figure-8 pattern **(photo a)**. Retrace the thread path three or four times. Secure the thread in the beadwork with a few half-hitch knots (Basics, p. 7), and end the thread. Repeat on the other end of the rope using the tail.

[8] Open a jump ring (Basics, p. 9), and attach a 6º on one end of the rope and

half of the clasp **(photo b)**. Close the jump ring. Repeat on the other end of the rope.

Foxglove flower

The necklace shown has one large and two small foxglove flowers.

[1] On 8 ft. (2.4m) of color B thread, pick up four color B 11º seed beads, leaving a 10-in. (25cm) tail. Sew through the Bs again to form a ring. Sew through the first B again, and snug up the beads **(figure 3, a–b)**.

[2] Pick up a B, and sew through the next B **(b–c)**. Repeat three times, and step up through the first B added in this round **(c–d)**.

[3] Pick up two Bs, and sew through the next B **(d–e)**. Repeat three times, and step up through the first B added in this round **(e–f)**.

[4] Pick up two Bs, and sew down through the B in the previous round and up through the next B **(figure 4, a–b)**. Working in straight tubular herringbone, repeat three times to complete the round. Step up through two Bs **(b–c)**.

Round 2: Begin working an increase (Basics, p. 6) between each pair of stitches. Pick up two Bs, and sew down through the B in the previous round **(figure 5, a–b)**. Pick up a B, and sew up through the next B **(b–c)**. Repeat to complete the round. Step up through the first B added in this round **(c–d)**.

Round 3: Increase to two beads between the stitches. Pick up two Bs, and sew down through the B in the next stack **(d–e)**. Pick up two Bs, and sew up through the B in the following stack **(e–f)**. Snug up the beads. Repeat to complete the round **(photo c)**. Step up through the top two Bs of the first stack **(f–g)**.

Rounds 4–17 or 4–14: Work 14 rounds in straight tubular herringbone for the large flower. Work 11 rounds for the small flower. Maintain a tight tension,

FIGURE 5

a

b

c

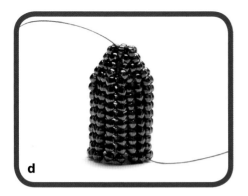

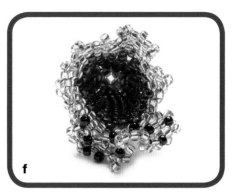

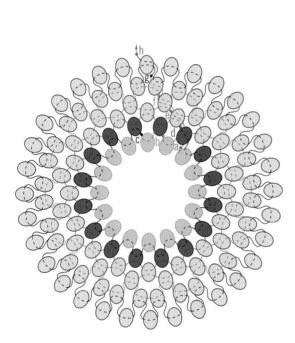

FIGURE 6

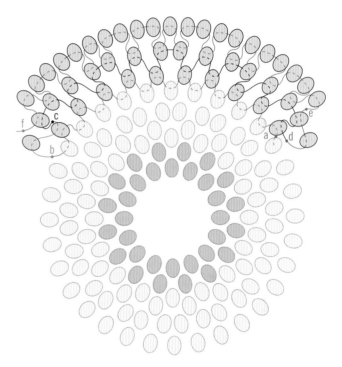

FIGURE 7

pulling the stacks together to form a tube (photo d). Step up as though starting the next round.

[5] Pick up a B, and sew down through one B in the next stack (figure 6, a–b). Pick up a B, and sew up through the first B in the following stack (b–c). Repeat to complete the round. Step up through the first B added in this round (c–d).

[6] Working with color C 11º seed beads, pick up a C, and sew through the next B. Repeat to complete the round. Step up through the first C picked up in this round (d–e).

[7] Working in peyote stitch (Basics, p. 8), add another round of Cs, and then

step up through the first C added in this round (e–f).

[8] Begin a round of peyote increase by picking up two Cs per stitch. Step up through the first C added in this round (f–g).

[9] Complete the increase by adding a C in the middle of the pairs in the previous round, as well as between each pair, and step up through the first bead added in this round (g–h).

[10] To add the lip of the foxglove flower, exit a C in the last row that is aligned with an increase bead from step 4 (photo e). Work 10 peyote stitches using one C per stitch (figure 7, a–b).

[11] Pick up a C, and sew back through the last C added in step 10 (b–c). Work nine peyote stitches in the other direction, alternating between picking up one C or two Cs per stitch (c–d). Begin with two Cs.

[12] Pick up a C, and sew back through the last C added in step 11 (d–e). Pick up one C between the Cs in a pair and two Cs on either side of a single C. Work across the lip (e–f).

[13] Weave through the lip, randomly adding color D 11º seed beads between beads. Secure the thread in the beadwork, and trim (photo f). Secure and trim the tail.

MATERIALS
necklace 17 in. (43cm)
- **2** 6º seed beads, color A
- 11º Japanese seed beads
  25–30g color A
  10–14g color B
  10g color C
  5g color D
- clasp
- **2** 7mm inside diameter (ID)
  19-gauge jump rings
- nylon beading thread, size D, colors
  to match A and B 11ºs, conditioned
- beading needles, #12

DESIGNER'S NOTE:
You can stiffen the flower by running a doubled length of thread through each stack before attaching the calyx.

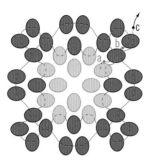

FIGURE 8

FIGURE 9

FIGURE 10

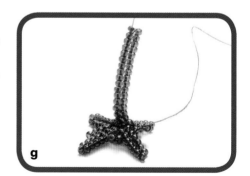

g

h

Flower calyx and bail

[1] On 4 ft. (1.2m) of color A thread, begin a color A herringbone tube as in steps 1 and 2 of "Tubular rope," leaving an 18-in. (46cm) tail.

[2] Begin to increase by adding an A between each pair of stitches, stepping up at the end of the round (figure 8, a–b).

[3] Work another round, increasing to two As between stitches (b–c).

[4] Pick up two As, sew down through two As in the next stack, and up through the A in the following stack (figure 9, a–b). Pick up three As to form a picot, and sew down through the A in the next stack and up through the two As in the following stack (b–c). Repeat to complete the round. Step up through the top three As in the first stack (c–d).

[5] Extend the remaining stacks to form spines. Pick up two As, sew down through three As in the next stack, through the base pair of the picot, and then sew up through three As in the following stack (figure 10, a–b). Repeat to complete the round. Step up through the top four As in the first stack (b–c).

[6] Pick up three As, sew down through four As in the next stack, through the base pair of the picot, and then sew up through four As in the following stack (c–d). Repeat to complete the round. Step up through the top five As in the first stack, exiting the first A added in this round (d–e). Do not end the working thread.

[7] Thread a needle on the 18-in. (46cm) tail, and sew through the base pair of As

of an extended spine. Pick up two As, and sew back through the base pair of As and the first A added in this step. Pick up two As, sew down through one A, and up through two As. Repeat to make a two-bead-wide stack that is 16 beads long (photo g).

[8] Attach the end of the stack to the pair of As at the base of the opposite spine. Check that your clasp fits through the loop. Add pairs of As if needed for the loop to slide over the clasp. Retrace the thread path to secure the base of the loop, and trim.

[9] Repeat steps 1–8 to make two more calyx/bails.

[10] Align the calyx/bail loop front to back with the foxglove lip. Position the calyx at the base of the flower with the spines over the foxglove stacks not created from an increase. With the working thread, sew through a B, the A on the tip of a calyx spine, and a B in the next stack. Sew through the As on the calyx spine in the direction of the loop (photo h).

Sew through the beadwork and down the next calyx spine. Repeat to attach the remaining three calyx spines. Sew through the bail two or three times to stiffen the loop. Secure the thread, and trim.

[11] Repeat step 10 for the two remaining flowers and calyx/bails.

[12] Slide the rope through the three flower bails.

Spiral Transcendence

Make a statement of quiet elegance with cylinder beads, pearls, and fire-polished beads in a monochromatic palette

designed by
Gwen Simmons

Branch fringe combined with stick pearls gives this necklace an opulent look. You can achieve other effects by varying your bead choice and fringe technique.

Fire-polished beads inserted between rows of spiraling cylinder beads take you beyond standard herringbone stitch. A blend of playfulness and precision, this subtly asymmetrical necklace is as beautiful as it is intriguing.

step by step

Necklace
Side one, spiral tube
[1] On 2 yd. (1.8m) of conditioned nylon beading thread (Basics, p. 7), leave a 6-in. (15cm) tail, and pick up two color A and two color B cylinder beads. Sew through all four beads again in the same direction. Alternating pairs of As and Bs, work in ladder stitch (Basics, p. 7) until you have a two-bead ladder that is eight beads long **(figure 1)**. Join the ladder into a ring by sewing through the first two As, the last two Bs, and the first two As again.
[2] Work the next rounds as follows:
Round 3: Work one round of straight tubular herringbone (Basics, p. 6), using an A and a B in each stitch.
Rounds 4–65: Working in twisted tubular herringbone (Basics, p. 6), pick up an A and a B, sew down through the next B, and then sew up through two As in the next stack **(figure 2, a–b)**. Repeat around for four stitches **(b–c)**.

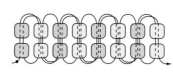

FIGURE 1

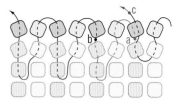

FIGURE 2

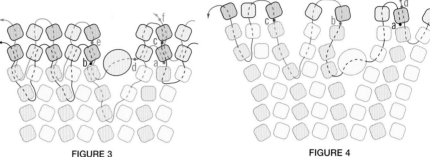

FIGURE 3

FIGURE 4

At the end of 65 rounds, the tube is approximately half the length it will be when finished. Make this section longer or shorter as desired.

Fire-polished embellishment
Continue working in twisted tubular herringbone as follows:

Round 66: Work the first stitch, but sew down through two Bs and come up through three As (**figure 3, a–b**). This creates an opening where you'll insert a 4mm fire-polished bead on the next round. Complete the round (**b–c**).

Round 67: Work the first half of the first stitch (**c–d**), pick up a 4mm, and then sew up through two As in the next stack (**d–e**). Complete the round (**e–f**).

Round 68: Work the first stitch, but sew through the two Bs and the 4mm added in the previous round. Sew up through three As on the next stack (**figure 4, a–b**). Work the second stitch, and, following the method used in round 66, create an opening for a 4mm (**b–c**). Complete the round (**c–d**).

Round 69: Work the first stitch, retracing the thread path through the 4mm as in the previous round (**figure 5, a–b**). Work the second stitch, adding a 4mm (**b–c**). Complete the round (**c–d**).

Round 70: Work the first stitch, sewing down through one B and up through two As on the next stack (**figure 6, a–b**).

Sew back down through the second B from the top on the previous stack, continue through the two As of the next stack (**b–c**), and then tighten to close up the gap above the 4mm. Work the second stitch, retracing the path through the 4mm (**c–d**). Work the third stitch, leaving an opening for the next 4mm (**d–e**). Work the fourth stitch (**e–f**).

Round 71: Work the first stitch, and then work the second stitch, retracing the path through the 4mm. Work the third stitch, adding a 4mm, and then work the fourth stitch.

Round 72: Work the first stitch, and then work the second stitch, closing the gap above the second 4mm. Work the third stitch, retracing the path through the 4mm, and then work the fourth stitch, creating an opening for the fourth 4mm.

Round 73: Work two stitches. Work the third stitch, retracing the path through the 4mm. Work the fourth stitch, adding a 4mm.

Round 74: Work two stitches. Work the third stitch, closing the gap above the third 4mm. Work the fourth stitch, retracing the path through the 4mm.

Round 75: Work the first stitch, creating an opening for a 4mm. Work two stitches. Work the fourth stitch, retracing the path through the 4mm.

Round 76: Work the first stitch, adding a 4mm. Work two stitches. Work the fourth stitch, closing the gap above the 4mm.

Rounds 77–83: Repeat rounds 68–74.

Round 84: Work three stitches, and then work the fourth stitch, retracing the path through the last 4mm.

Round 85: Work three stitches, and then work the fourth stitch, closing the gap above the last 4mm as in Round 76.

Rounds 86–93: Work in straight tubular herringbone.

Four-sided bead cage
Continue working in twisted tubular herringbone as follows:

Round 94: Create an opening after the first stitch. Work three stitches.

Round 95: Add a 4mm after the first stitch. Work three stitches.

Round 96: Retrace the thread path through the 4mm, and then work three stitches.

Round 97: Retrace the thread path through the 4mm, and create an opening for a 4mm after the second stitch, and then work two stitches.

Round 98: Work the first two stitches, adding a 4mm after each, and then work two stitches.

Round 99: Retrace the thread path through the 4mms. Work two stitches.

Round 100: Retrace the thread path through the 4mms, create an opening

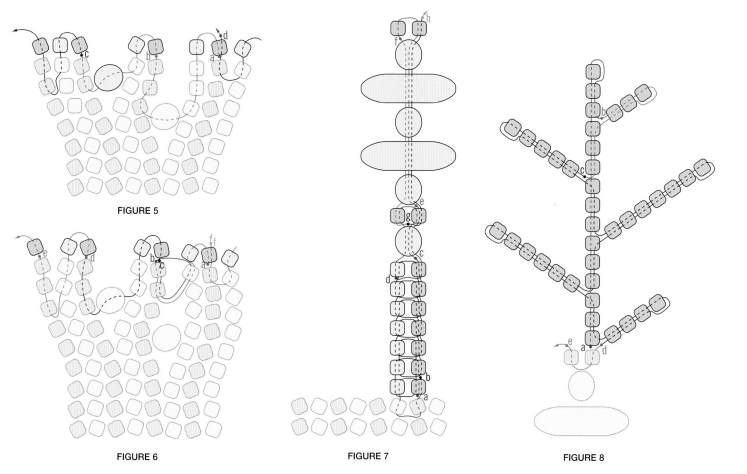

FIGURE 5

FIGURE 6

FIGURE 7

FIGURE 8

for a 4mm after the third stitch, and then work one stitch.

Round 101: Work the first three stitches, adding a 4mm after each, and then work one stitch.

Round 102: Retrace the thread path through the 4mms. Work one stitch.

Round 103: Retrace the thread path through the 4mms. Create an opening for a 4mm after the fourth stitch.

Round 104: Work four stitches, adding a 4mm after each.

Rounds 105–106: Retrace the thread path through the 4mms.

Rounds 107–130: Repeat rounds 104–106 until you have 12 4mms in the first stack.

Rounds 131–142: Continue stitching as in rounds 104–106, closing the gap after the 12th 4mm in each stack. Work in straight tubular herringbone after each stack is closed.

Fringe

[1] After all four stacks are closed, resume twisted tubular herringbone for about 10 more rounds.

[2] Work three more rounds of twisted tubular herringbone, retracing the thread paths between the stacks to separate them.

[3] Choose a stack, and extend it by several rows: Pick up an A and a B, and sew through the previous B and A. Continue through the last A added (figure 7, a–b). Repeat until the stack is about ½ in. (1.3cm) long (b–c).

[4] Pick up a 4mm and two As or Bs, and sew back through the 4mm and the other cylinder previous to the 4mm (c–d).

[5] Sew back through the adjacent cylinder, the 4mm, and the first cylinder added in the previous step (d–e).

[6] Pick up a 4mm, a stick pearl, a 4mm, a stick pearl, a 4mm, and two cylinders (e–f). Sew back through the 4mms, stick pearls, and one cylinder of the pair added in step 4 (f–g). Sew through the adjacent cylinder, sew back through the same five beads, and then continue through the first cylinder added in the previous step (g–h).

[7] Pick up approximately 1 in. (2.5cm) of cylinders, skip the last one, and sew through the next two or three cylinders (figure 8, a–b).

[8] Pick up three to six cylinders, skip

EDITOR'S NOTE:
If you want the spiral on the second side to go in the opposite direction of the first side, work your twisted tubular herringbone by going down two and up one bead on each stitch. You'll need to work the embellishment and cage beads in the opposite order also, adding a 4mm bead after the fourth stitch and working backward.

the last one, and then sew back through the bead just added and the next two or three stem cylinders (b–c).

[9] Repeat step 8 until you've made several branches on the stem (c–d). Sew into one of the cylinders below the last 4mm, and sew through the adjacent cylinder (d–e).

[10] Repeat steps 7–9 twice to make a total of three fringes. Sew back through the fringe beads and the separated stack, and exit the end cylinder of the adjacent separated stack.

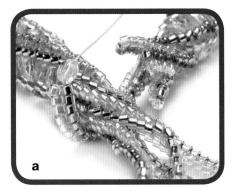

a

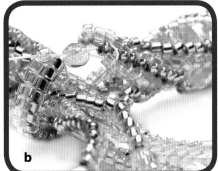

b

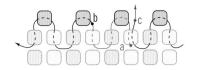

FIGURE 9

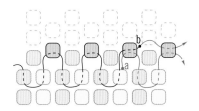

FIGURE 10

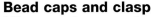

FIGURE 11

[11] Repeat steps 3–10 on each separated stack, varying the length of each fringe. Secure the tails with a few half-hitch knots (Basics, p. 7) between beads, and trim.

Side two, spiral tube
[1] Repeat the instructions for "Side one" up through step 2 of the fringe.
[2] Choose a separated stack, and add 14 pairs of cylinders as in step 3 of "Fringe."
[3] Pick up a 4mm, and wrap the stack around side one, between the fire-polished cage and the fringes (photo a). Sew into an end cylinder of the opposite separated stack of side two, and sew through the adjacent cylinder, the 4mm, and the adjacent cylinder of the extended stack (photo b). Retrace the thread path a few times to reinforce the connection.
[4] Sew back through the beadwork, and exit an end cylinder of one of the remaining stacks.
[5] Repeat steps 2 and 3 to join the two remaining stacks. Secure the tails, and trim.

Bead caps and clasp
[1] Secure 2 ft. (61cm) of conditioned thread at the ladder end of one side, and exit any cylinder. Pick up a cylinder, sew through the next cylinder, and exit the following cylinder (figure 9, a–b). Repeat around to add four cylinders (b–c).
[2] Working in the opposite direction, add a cylinder in the spaces between the beads added in step 1 (figure 10, a–b).
[3] Work two or three rounds of tubular, even-count peyote stitch (Basics, p. 8). Sew through the final round of peyote to taper the end.
[4] Pick up a cylinder, a 4mm, a cylinder, a 4mm, a stick pearl, a 4mm, and three cylinders. Skip the last three cylinders, and sew back through the last six beads. Sew into the cylinder opposite the one your thread is exiting.
[5] Retrace the thread path several times, and then sew through the beadwork to exit a cylinder in the first row of peyote where the herringbone tube and the peyote cap join. To camouflage the join with three-bead picots, pick up three cylinders, and sew through the next cylinder in the

first peyote round. Repeat around, adding picots to the first two peyote rounds. Secure the tails, and trim.
[6] Repeat steps 1–3 on the other end. Pick up a cylinder, a 4mm, and enough cylinders to form a loop around the stick-pearl toggle. Sew back through the 4mm and into the bead cap. Repeat step 5.

Earrings
[1] Thread a needle on 2 ft. (61cm) of conditioned nylon beading thread, and, leaving a 6-in. (15cm) tail, pick up four cylinder beads. Sew back through the first two cylinders (figure 11, a–b).
[2] Stitch two more pairs of cylinders, as shown (b–c).
[3] Pick up a stick pearl, a 4mm fire-polished bead, a stick pearl, and two cylinders. Sew back through the pearls, the 4mm, and a cylinder above the top pearl (c–d). Sew through the adjacent cylinder, the next three beads, and an end cylinder (d–e).
[4] Add fringe as in steps 7–10 of "Fringe."
[5] Sew back up through the pearls, the 4mm, and one stack of cylinders. Pick up five or six cylinders, and sew back through the adjacent cylinder. Retrace the thread path a few times. Secure the tails, and trim.
[6] Open the loop of an earring finding (Basics, p. 9), attach the earring, and close the loop. Make a second earring.

Contributors

Jimmie Boatright is a retired school teacher and lifelong crafter who teaches jewelry making at the Atlanta Bead Market in Buford, Ga. Contact Jimmie by phone at (678) 714-8293, via email at atlantabeadmarket@hotmail.com, or see a list of her classes at atlantabeadmarket.com.

Babette Borsani of Savannah, Ga., has been beading since 2004. Contact Babette at borsani@att.net.

Carol Cypher teaches beadwork and feltmaking workshops worldwide. Contact her at carolcypher@gmail.com or through her website, carolcypher.com.

Anna Elizabeth Draeger is an Associate Editor at *Bead&Button* magazine, and author of *Crystal Brilliance*. Contact her via email at adraeger@kalmbach.com, or visit her website, http://web.mac.com/beadbiz.

Diane Fitzgerald is an internationally recognized teacher, designer, and author. Among her numerous awards, she received the Spun Gold Award from the Textile Center of Minnesota for her lifetime commitment to fiber art. Diane has written 10 beading books, including her latest, *Diane Fitzgerald's Favorite Bead Projects*. Diane teaches classes at many locations. Visit her website, dianefitzgerald.com.

Although **Linda Gettings** played with pop beads as a child, she only started working with more intricate bead designs and wirework about ten years ago. Now she teaches classes of her beaded designs, always encouraging her students to experiment to achieve new looks. Her book, *Great Beaded Gifts*, was re-released in soft cover in March 2007. Contact her via email at ladybeading@aol.com, or visit her website, beadpatterns.com.

Judith Golan of Rehovot, Israel, began beading in 2006 after receiving her master's degree in plant sciences. She enjoys 3-D beadwork and often finds inspiration in the natural world. Email Judith at judith27k@gmail.com, or visit her website, judith27k.blogspot.com.

Beading is a natural fit for **Melissa Grakowsky**, who has bachelor's degrees in physics and painting. The craft combines science and artistry in a creative outlet that fits into her busy life. Melissa started beading in 2007 and now teaches beading classes worldwide. Contact Melissa by email at grakowsky@gmail.com, and visit her website, grakowsky.net.

Smadar Grossman lives in Modi'in, Israel. She fell in love with beadweaving in 2005 and has been exploring its endless possibilities ever since. Contact her via email at smadarstreasure@gmail.com or visit Smadar's website at smadarstreasure.blogspot.com.

Marcia Katz is the author of two books, *Sculptural Flowers I: The Trumpet Flower* and *Adorned Wrists*. Contact her via email at mkatz@gate.net, or visit her website, festoonery.com.

Shirley Lim resides in Singapore and has been beading since 2000. She loves combining peyote with herringbone, her favorite stitch. Contact Shirley at beadingfantasy@me.com, visit her online at web.me.com/beadingfantasy or beading-fantasy.blogspot.com.

Elizabeth Nance started beading in 2004 after going to a bead shop to replace the findings on a pair of earrings. When she's not beading, Elizabeth is a landscape designer, estate gardener, wife to Steven, mother of three, and enjoys mountain biking and running. Visit her website, beaddiddy.com, or email her at enance@gmail.com.

Contact **Debbie Nishihara** in care of Kalmbach Books.

Carol Perrenoud is an internationally recognized bead artist, teacher, and entrepreneur whose work has been widely exhibited and featured in many beadwork books and magazines. Contact Carol via email at carol@beadcats.com, or visit her website, beadcats.com.

Rae Arlene Reller is a self-taught beader who lives in Northfield, Minn. She's been beading since 1999, and works and teaches at the Glass Garden bead store. Contact her via email at rareller@aol.com.

Gwen Simmons sells her beaded jewelry in shops throughout North Carolina and Florida. She also teaches beading classes at The Art Room in Franklin, N.C. Contact Gwen in care of Kalmbach Books.

Kerrie Slade lives in Mansfield, England, carrying on a family tradition of making beaded flowers. Her grandmother made French beaded-flower pins during the 1930s. Contact Kerrie via email at mail@kerrieslade.co.uk, or visit her website at kerrieslade.co.uk or her blog at kerrieslade.blogspot.com.

Sue Sloan is a self-taught beader who has been experimenting with color, texture, and technique for over 20 years. Contact Sue in care of Kalmbach Books.

A designer and instructor based in central Massachusetts, **Kim Spooner** spotted a copy of *Bead&Button* magazine in a doctor's waiting room in 2005 and has been beading ever since. Contact Kim at cisraydesigns@yahoo.com, or visit her website, cisraydesigns.etsy.com.

Deborah Staehle began beading in the mid-1990s as a member of the Bead Society of Hawaii, Oahu chapter. It was meant to be just a hobby. But after moving back to California in 2001, she began working and teaching full time in the bead business. You can find her six days a week at Bead Dreams in Stockton, where she teaches and sells beads. Contact her at (209) 464-2323 or via email at bead_demon@hotmail.com.

Contact **Lisa Olson Tune** via email at tunebdbdbd@aol.com.

A microbiologist and jewelry designer based in Huntington Beach, Calif., **Jenny Van** is a frequent contributor to *Bead&Button* magazine. Contact her via email at jenny@beadsj.com, or visit her website, beadsj.com.

Jill Wiseman is a full-time beadweaving designer and nationally known instructor. Contact her via email at jill@tapestrybeads.com, or visit her website, tapestrybeads.com.

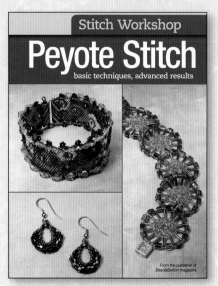
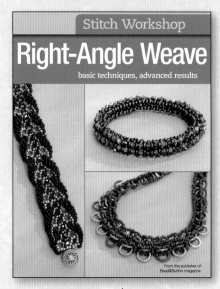

Herringbone Stitch: learn it, love it!

The best of *Bead&Button* magazine

Make 26 fantastic beaded jewelry projects, including:

- broad collars, slinky lariats, and other stunning necklaces
- bracelets using remarkable combinations of flat herringbone, tubular herringbone, and fringing techniques to produce a wide variety of looks
- petite blossom-shaped earrings, and even a brooch

Herringbone stitch stands among the most popular of the off-loom beading stitches — and for good reason! *Stitch Workshop: Herringbone Stitch* highlights the best of those reasons, with 26 projects in a variety of styles and patterns, selected from among the best *Bead&Button* has to offer. Each has been editor-tested and features precise step-by-step directions, clear photos and illustrations, and useful materials lists.

Organized in order of difficulty, the pieces include a range of materials as well: lentil beads, Tila beads, crystals, gemstones, and of course, plenty of gorgeous seed beads! A basic techniques section takes the reader through the steps needed to use traditional, tubular, and twisted tubular herringbone stitches. Beginning beaders and seasoned pros alike will appreciate the gorgeous projects packed into the book that demonstrate plenty of ways to show off the textured patterns of herringbone in jewelry!

www.KalmbachBooks

KALMBACH BOOKS

From the publisher of *Bead&Button*, *Bead Style*, and *Art Jewelry* magazines

Contents

Takedown

Prologue

Art is power.

Since the beginning of time, works of art have had an extraordinary ability to elicit human emotion. From one century to the next, from one medium to the next, art has mesmerized, repelled, titillated, terrified, shocked, and enraged viewers across the Western world. And because of its unique impact on humankind, it has been viewed with suspicion by individuals in positions of political power.

For generations, those individuals were kings and courtiers, popes and cardinals, dictators and their flunkies. They monitored, controlled, censored, and suppressed art and artists to keep themselves in power and prevent social upheaval. Artists were at their beck and call, in their pay, at their mercy; their lives depended on keeping the powerful sweet.

Today, artists in the West have finally thrown off the shackles of crown and court, church and clergy, and one-party tyranny. They are freer than ever to express themselves without fearing retribution from a prince, a pope, or a president. Their works no longer face censorship, or even censure, from people in official positions of authority.

Instead, artists are increasingly being held to account by individual citizens and voters—people like you and me. As liberal democracy becomes ever more entrenched in the Western hemisphere, the voice of the citizen is getting louder and louder. And that voice is demanding equality for all those who were previously overshadowed, overlooked, and overpowered: women, ethnic minorities, colonized peoples. For the first time, younger generations in the West are seeking to atone for a history of exploitation and discrimination, and to wipe out the misogyny, racism, and colonialism that prevailed in the past. A wave of citizen-led, social-media-enabled advocacy and activism is overtaking all aspects of society.

And it's quickly spreading to the art world. Suddenly, thanks to the powerful impetus of two global movements, both in response to serial crimes—#MeToo and Black Lives Matter—groups that were long underrepresented if not erased are being foregrounded in art. Museums and galleries that, for decades, paid lip service to gender and racial equality are now actively rushing to collect, exhibit, and hire women and people of color, and to put on shows that highlight the legacy of colonialism and slavery.

Institutions in major Western capitals, in other words, are waking up, smelling the proverbial coffee, and making sudden and seismic changes. Seemingly overnight, women and artists of color are appearing in museums, galleries, auction houses, and art fairs everywhere, and issue-driven exhibitions are multiplying. The art market, needless to say, is in on the game. Meanwhile, using the bullhorn that is social media, citizen-activists are watching these gatekeepers carefully, and judging their efforts with a raft of new egalitarian and ethical yardsticks.

This digitally enabled revolution is long overdue. For centuries, museum-goers, amateurs, and collectors of art have been exposed to extraordinary talents, but mainly white and male ones—to the exclusion of all others. Half of humanity, meaning the female half, has been ignored. So have artists who are not descendants of white Europeans. How can such a sizeable population be silently disqualified by the world's most important cultural institutions? What good is social progress if it stops at the museum gates? Are museums not mausoleums in that case?

Takedown takes a close look at that revolution, at its durability, and at the impact that citizen-led activism and demands for diversity and inclusivity are having on art, as they transform it into a broader and much richer church. The book shows how women and long underrepresented minorities are now, finally, getting a seat at the table—sometimes the top seat. It examines the implications for art and museums, some good, some less good.

While the effects of misogyny, sexual harassment, cultural appropriation, and racism have been examined in other disciplines—film (Harvey Weinstein, Roman Polanski), music (Michael Jackson, R. Kelly), and publishing (Jeanine Cummins, Woody Allen)—no mainstream book has yet tackled the impact on the visual arts. *Takedown* is my effort to fill that void. It brings all sides together—those pushing for change and those with the power to deliver it. It exposes their views and allows the debate to play out on its pages.

TAKEDOWN IS, IN short, about the overlap between art and politics. As it happens, the twin forces of politics and art have dominated my life both personally and professionally. And I seem to bring that dual vantage point into everything I do—including this, my first book.

I was born in London into a family of Iranian diplomats, and spent my childhood in Iran as well as in countries to which my father was assigned (Morocco, Egypt). The Islamic Revolution of 1978–79 derailed the trajectory that was laid out before me. I was catapulted into a life of exile—and of aesthetic enchantment. We moved to Paris, the city where I had always longed to live. The wondrous art and architecture, the infinite cultural possibilities were enthralling to a young girl who, until then, had never lived in Europe.

I had always had a proclivity for the arts—particularly music, to which I almost dedicated my life. But I had next to no talent in the visual arts. My elementary-school drawings and paintings were lousy, and to this day, my sketches remain ham-fisted and embarrassing. Plenty of talented people have told me that anybody can draw. But I don't believe it. To me, drawing, painting, sculpture, and the plastic arts are innate gifts, and I seem to have had a talent bypass in that department.

So art was not something that I paid much attention to in childhood and early adolescence, let alone understood. All that I remember of a trip to the Louvre at the age of thirteen is locking gazes with the Mona Lisa, and gaping at the headless Venus de Milo as I walked up the stairs. I was like the millions of kids who were dragged to museums every year: not there by choice.

Within a few years, all of that changed. Paris became my first art instructor. Culture was hard to avoid in the French capital: it was what most Parisians partook in. Daily conversations were peppered with talk of the latest book, movie, or *expo*. On weekends, come rain or come shine, dozens of people stood in line outside the Grand Palais, the Centre Pompidou, or the Musée d'Art Moderne, patiently waiting to see this or that blockbuster exhibition. I was one of them.

I vividly remember seeing the Amedeo Modigliani retrospective at the Musée d'Art Moderne in 1981 and being mesmerized by those elongated faces and almond eyes. Pontus Hultén's *Paris-Paris* exhibition at the Centre Pompidou later that year left an even more lasting mark. It was a vast survey of artists living and working in Paris in and around the war years, many of whom I was unfamiliar with. Its catalogue became my first art-history manual.

Paris also led me to a great mentor: Michael Brenson, the art historian, curator, and critic. He taught English literature at the American School of Paris at the time, and I was one of his students. Michael's passion for art was contagious, and by the time I had graduated from high school, I had caught the art bug.

What sealed my conversion to the cause of art was Italy. Somehow, that boot-shaped, midsized country had the highest number of UNESCO world cultural sites of any. Starting in my early twenties, I set out to visit as many of those sites as I could and taught myself Italian along the way. Every chance I got, I escaped to some corner or another of the Italian peninsula, visiting or revisiting the great art cities—Rome, Milan, Venice, Florence, Naples.

Florence was a frequent stop. On my trips there, I would set off every day, fresh-faced and excited, to discover one of the city's mind-blowing art-historical sites: the San Marco monastery, where the monks' cells were frescoed by the divine Fra Angelico; the Duomo, with its gorgeous dome and its sculpted baptistery doors; the Uffizi Galleries, containing Sandro Botticelli's twin miracles, *The Birth of Venus* and *Primavera*. In the evenings, my art education continued. I would take my latest tome to the nearest trattoria and eat a plate of pappardelle with my book open to the page.

I learned the vocabulary of art by looking at it a great deal. I toured the major museums of Europe over and again, studied the lives and creations of great masters, visited every art exhibition on my radar.

In my journalism career, I covered culture only episodically, at first. My main focuses were politics, foreign policy, and economic policy. It wasn't until 2003 that I started covering culture full-time, initially for Bloomberg, then for the *New York Times*.

As a daily occupation, it was a source of unadulterated pleasure. Instead of going to the office on most mornings, I would go to the press preview of this or that museum exhibition. I felt my soul come alive as I lingered in front of this painting or that sculpture. The job's other incredible perk was that it allowed me to have one-on-one conversations with artists.

Not that interviewing artists was easy. Unlike movie stars or pop musicians, they were unaccustomed to the media game and sometimes incredibly timid, unforthcoming, and even awkward. Winning their trust and getting them to open up took time and gentle persuasion. It was like releasing a precious pearl from a sealed oyster. Yet it was never anything less than rewarding.

At their best, artists were oracles of our time, deeply empathetic beings who asked the big metaphysical questions and offered answers through their art. Their works were like visual riddles, or poems: thought-provoking, evocative, atmospheric, mysterious. Art was emotion, just as music was. With a few strokes on a canvas or a few chips in a stone, an artist could lift your spirits, speak to your soul.

OVER THE YEARS, I became a regular interviewer of artists and architects. I was determined to find out what made them tick, discover telling details of their lives. The Chinese artist Ai Weiwei remembered how, as a little boy, he watched his poet father serve out a sentence to hard labor, cleaning messy public toilets that were fly-infested in the summer and frozen in the winter. Richard Serra recalled being taken at the age of three to the launch of a ship that his father had helped build, and spending the rest of his life making towering sculptures of industrial steel.

Zaha Hadid described how she found her calling at home in Baghdad at age eleven when an architect dropped off intriguing maquettes of her aunt's future house. She asked her parents what you called people who made buildings, and went around thereafter declaring, "I want to be an architect." David Hockney explained why he had turned down a commission to paint

Queen Elizabeth II. "She has majesty," he told me. "How do you paint majesty today?"

My focus was not just on living artists and creators. I also delved into the lives of departed masters. On trips to the south of France, I stopped off at the home of one or another of the great artists who had made the Riviera their stomping ground. There was Pierre-Auguste Renoir's grand one-story villa in Cagnes-sur-Mer, surrounded by vines and olive trees, where he and Madame Renoir hosted a steady stream of visitors. Walking through his vast atelier, I saw brushes and dried-up paint tubes last touched by him nine decades earlier, as well as the tall wooden wheelchair that he used late in life, and the rug-draped bed where he had young village girls pose for him.

A half-hour drive away was the smaller but no less spectacular villa in Le Cannet where Pierre Bonnard lived and worked to the end of his life. I had the dizzying experience of standing in the tiny, blue-and-white-tiled bathroom with the clawfoot tub where his wife endlessly bathed, and which is the subject of many of his most celebrated paintings.

Back in Paris, I was taken behind the scenes at the Picasso Museum by one of the world's top Picasso specialists, Anne Baldassari, who ran the museum for years and spearheaded its redevelopment. Meeting Anne there was like being at home with Picasso himself. I remember standing with her in front of Picasso's *Grand Nu au Fauteuil Rouge* (1929), a screaming, contorted nude with dangling limbs, and Baldassari telling me that while some might see this as a depiction of his jilted wife Olga, it was simplistic to view Picasso through a purely biographical prism. Years later, Anne took me on a hard-hat tour of the museum as it underwent redevelopment, and just before it reopened, she let me look on as she and her team positioned a delicate terracotta figurine in a museum vitrine, and hung a giant oil painting on a bare wall.

All of this gave me an incredible taste for art's so-called masters. And I certainly saw many an exhibition of their work inside the great museums of

Paris and London. In the case of Picasso, the shows just kept on coming. They were a surefire hit and they helped museums pay the bills.

In a word, I found myself attending exhibitions of, and writing about, one white male artist after another. It was the way of the world—and certainly the way of the art world. Gender discrimination was endemic and a somehow tolerated aspect of the status quo. What was not apparent to me at the time was how radically these great male masters were snuffing out artists of other genders, origins, and orientations.

Campaigns for gender and racial equality inside museums and art institutions would regularly come up. Yet they would simmer without ever coming to a boil. The institutions in question were like supertankers: hard to turn around. Meanwhile, they regularly put on exhibitions of (white male) art that no one in their right mind could fault them for. These were once-in-a-lifetime shows, breathtaking spectacles. So few paid attention to the underlying disparities.

In a word, we had blind spots—transmitted to us by generations of Western art historians, museum directors, curators, and critics, who identified the greatest masters as being male and of European descent. These were called Leonardo, Michelangelo, Titian, Rembrandt, Caravaggio, Monet, and Picasso. Their talent and genius were beyond dispute, and everyone just assumed that they were the only game in town. Women and nonwhite artists were, in the meantime, invisible.

Artists who were lucky to be part of the canon got away with murder—sometimes literally. Caravaggio was a confirmed murderer and died a fugitive from justice. Yet that did nothing to diminish the admiration so many (including myself) had—and still have—for his art. Would contemporary audiences worship a prodigiously gifted killer? Less unconditionally, I would think.

Paul Gauguin, a married father of five, lived in Tahiti with girls in their early teens. Yet until recently, Western museums programmed one Gauguin blockbuster after another without pointing out what today would be viewed as pathological pedophilia. Egon Schiele drew and painted underage girls who struck graphic poses in his studio; he even spent twenty-four days in prison for seducing one of them. Yet until very recently, he was widely exhibited and admired. Somehow, white male masters, even those who lived well into the twentieth century, were above the law. Their art spoke louder than their misdeeds.

Gradually and incrementally, as the #MeToo and Black Lives Matter movements shook societies on both sides of the Atlantic, museums and cultural institutions started feeling the winds of change. They realized that the decisions they made—who they showed and collected, and who they didn't—merited more careful and evenhanded consideration. There were risks to resisting change: long-silenced minorities suddenly had access to an instant global platform called social media. With a single hashtag, they could summon up an army of loud and angry voices and shame a museum.

The time had come for museums and cultural institutions to give attention to categories they had shunned forever: women, artists of color, and colonized peoples. A revolution got underway.

That revolution is still going on. As a result, *Takedown* is a work in progress. It's a starting point, not a culmination—the beginning of an investigation of art's many blind spots across the ages, the political consequences of those blind spots, and how those blind spots are now being reversed. Through thematic chapters on gender, sex, race, religion, money, public art, and vandalism, I will look at the art world's excesses and how they are finally being called out. I will examine the forces at play, and explore the challenges of this new age of art and activism.

1.

The Clash of Art and Politics

"A robust compendium of adults-only art": that's how one critic described the exhibition that opened in Los Angeles in January 1969. It had a slightly naughty title—"Erotic Art '69"—and the works on display featured men and women engaged in various forms of sexual activity. A watercolor by George Grosz showed a maid and her employer locked in a carnal embrace. A painting by Pablo Picasso depicted a couple having full-blown intercourse.

One Friday afternoon, six weeks after the show opened at the David Stuart Gallery on North La Cienega Boulevard, the Los Angeles Police Department's Hollywood vice squad burst onto the premises. They had received complaints from members of the public about the erotically themed exhibition. Warrants in hand, the LAPD promptly confiscated around twenty artworks (a third of the exhibition's content) and charged the gallerist, David Stuart, with exhibiting indecent materials for sale. Stuart was released after posting $625 in bail. Drawings, paintings, and sculptures with a combined value of $20,000 were hauled off to Parker Center, a police administration building in downtown L.A.

The charges were serious enough for Stuart to have to defend himself in two separate trials that lasted more than nineteen months. In the end, he was acquitted of all charges. An elite lineup of witnesses—cultural personalities, museum curators, critics—testified in his defense. As one witness, the curator Maurice Tuchman, told the *Los Angeles Times*, "The key thing was the feeling of outrage that the city was prosecuting an art dealer when the town is full of sexual permissiveness."

This brazen act of police-led art censorship happened not very long ago, and it happened in Los Angeles, not Leningrad. The episode offers proof that the censorship of art by people in power took place until fairly recently, and in a country that describes itself as the leader of the free world—a country where freedom of expression is a staunchly defended constitutional right. In other words, only months away from the year 1970, law-enforcement officers in the United States of America engaged in what we will refer to henceforth as an act of top-down censorship.

TOP-DOWN ART CENSORSHIP has been around for about as long as art itself. The officers seizing erotic paintings in 1969 in Los Angeles are no different from the disciples of the power-hungry preacher Girolamo Savonarola in Renaissance Florence, who charged into the city's opulent palazzi and sequestered artworks they considered profane. When the L.A. art dealer David Stuart stands trial for an exhibition, he faces the same line of questioning as the Venetian master painter Paolo Veronese, who answered for his art before a sixteenth-century Inquisition tribunal.

History, in other words, repeats itself. Far from being a fusty activity reserved for nerds, it offers plenty of parallels, and mistakes from which we can learn. History is a leading indicator for the present, a flashlight showing us the way. What it reveals is that human life is a never-ending case of *plus ça change*—and that humankind has forever felt the urge to censor art.

The question is, *why?*

Because artists are seldom mere eccentrics operating on the margins of society. They are active participants in society; they hold a mirror up to it. And the art that they create is there to be seen by society. Art is always a dialogue, never a monologue. It lives or dies depending on how much—or how little—it is looked at. The interaction with the viewer is crucial to its existence.

Equally crucial is the length and depth of that interaction. The greatest art pulls the viewer in, captivates and enthralls, provokes feelings. Art is nothing if not a direct appeal to human emotion.

When the Virgin Mary mourns the dead Christ in Michelangelo's *Pietà*, every ripple and fold of that marble miracle is an expression of her grief. Michelangelo's evocation of pathos makes *Pietà* one of the most beautiful sculptures ever made.

Rembrandt's self-portraits are masterpieces because of the inner feelings that they convey. In the early ones, Rembrandt appears fearless and intrepid, a young man on the move. In the final ones, he looks weary of life; his brow is rumpled and lined, and his eyes exude pain.

Even simple works of art can stir the viewer. A line drawn on a sheet is no random doodle: it's a decision made by the artist, a composition that evokes something. It divides the space in two. A simple line drawing—by Henri Matisse, for instance—is an action that invites a reaction.

Art's uncanny ability to press emotional buttons gives it enormous power over the beholder. And that power has forever been feared by people of authority. Generation after generation, rulers and leaders have sought to control and curtail the production and exhibition of art by resorting to top-down censorship. Art is, after all, the perfect scapegoat: a visible, tangible enemy that they can point to as the source of evil and equate with artifice, extravagance, and sin. As ever in politics, it's easier to condemn than to commend.

To be sure, in modern-day Western democracies, top-down censorship has by and large been neutered. Individual freedoms have been conquered to such a degree that art censorship today seems pointless. Besides, policymakers no longer have an arsenal of censorship tools that they can deploy at will.

Nonetheless, the urge to censor lurks beneath the surface. And, as we'll see in the chapters that follow, it still, occasionally, manifests itself.

HUMANKIND HAS BEEN making art for tens of thousands of years. The earliest artworks date back to prehistory: to the Paleolithic period, also known as the Old Stone Age, meaning from about 40,000 B.C. until 8,000 B.C. Those pioneering creations are the famous cave paintings that schoolchildren all over the world learn about: in Altamira, Spain, and in Lascaux, France.

On the rugged surface of the cave wall, prehistoric human hands drew and painted wild animals—bison, mammoths, ibexes, horses. According to experts, the paintings were not there for decoration: they served as a channel for prayers, incantations, and ritual dances aimed at improving the fortunes of animal hunters and their kin.

In other words, for tens of thousands of years, art was vested with invisible, magical, and spiritual powers. The cave paintings of Lascaux and Altamira were pictorial prayers, visual appeals for better days. Their makers appeared to believe that the paintings transcended their physical reality and somehow extended into the realm of the metaphysical.

By the time Christianity emerged as an organized religion, images were everywhere. The dominant cultures in the West were those of Greece and Rome, cultures replete with paintings and sculptures of human and mythological figures. The concern was that the makers of these artworks would take the place of God, the creator, and that their works would become objects of worship, encouraging idolatry and driving the faithful away from the religions of the book. So images were proscribed.

In the second of the Ten Commandments, image making was summarily banned—even before such sins as adultery, thievery, and murder. The second commandment declares: "Thou shalt not make unto thee any graven image, or any likeness of any thing that is in heaven above, or that is in the earth beneath, or that is in the water under the earth: Thou shalt not bow thyself to them, nor serve them." As Julian Bell wrote in his book *What is Painting?*, "The first words in Western culture concerning man-made images categorically warn us against them."

As it turned out, the second commandment inspired the first large-scale and organized campaign of art censorship in the Western world—a campaign that took place in the eighth and ninth centuries in the Byzantine Empire, and is referred to as early Christian Iconoclasm.

Bands of early Christians stormed into Byzantine churches and whitewashed or plastered over the images adorning their interior. Paintings, frescoes, and mosaics of Christ were destroyed, and pictures of other human figures were replaced with plain white crosses. Even Hagia Sophia, the most important of the Eastern Christian churches, was attacked. For roughly a century, figurative art was categorically banned.

From the mid-800s onward, the exact opposite happened: holy figures became the primary focus of paintings, sculptures, drawings, and prints. Christ, the Virgin Mary, disciples, and saints were represented over and over in the art of medieval and early Renaissance Europe. Individual artists were for the first time recognized as creators of works. And eventually, they were given free rein to represent subjects reaching beyond the hierarchy of Christian figures.

In a revival of the arts of ancient Greece and Rome—hence the term "Renaissance," meaning rebirth—artists were suddenly free to depict mythological figures and to portray the living men and women who were their patrons. Because these figures were not sacred, they could be drawn, painted, and sculpted much more liberally. In this revolutionary period, not only were figures no longer proscribed, but they seemed to breed and multiply on canvas and in marble and bronze. In the paintings of the time—just think of Sandro Botticelli's *Birth of Venus*, or Leonardo da Vinci's (now disappeared) *Leda and the Swan*, or Raphael's *Galatea*—Greek gods and goddesses were depicted in their birthday suits, bathing and frolicking. The finest artists of the day also painted real people. Many of Leonardo's masterpieces—including the Mona Lisa—were commissioned portraits. Raphael's *Baldassare Castiglione*, now in the Louvre, was another example of high Renaissance portraiture.

Every revolution, of course, spawns a counterrevolution. The late fifteenth century ushered in a serious backlash against art, which was perceived as a status symbol and a signifier of wealth and profligacy. In Florence, the very cradle of the Italian Renaissance, art began to arouse suspicion. The vilification came from a Dominican friar by the name of Girolamo Savonarola, who, for a brief period, became the city's effective ruler.

At the time, Florence was one of Europe's most prosperous and dynamic centers. Dominant families flaunted their riches by building vast palazzi and hiring the finest painters, sculptors, and artists of the day to decorate their interiors. Walls and ceilings were covered with masterly frescoes. Interiors rippled with tapestries, embroideries, and Oriental rugs. Halls were lined with glistening suits of armor, precious bronze and porcelain vessels, and jewel-encrusted bibelots. Ladies of the household were swathed in silks and fur-lined robes, and their faces were coated with expensive powder and rouge.

These palazzi played host to impossibly lavish banquets at which there was much eating, drinking, and promiscuity. Dinners involved industrial quantities of game, poultry, and fish, with calves and peacocks among the prized delicacies. Courses were washed down with never-ending goblets of fine wine. Meals ended on servings of luscious fruit, and of flavorsome sugar-coated almonds known as confetti.

These feasts were anathema to Savonarola, the ayatollah of his day. Hook-nosed and altogether unattractive, the Dominican friar had fleshy red lips and eyes that smoldered when he preached. He lived like a hermit, ate and drank little, wore plain rough garments, and slept on a straw mat.

In his impassioned sermons, Savonarola bellowed against Florence's wealthy classes—their drinking and reveling, their gambling and excess, their lewdness and greed. He railed at the treasures in their homes: the paintings and tapestries, the marbles and bronzes, the illuminated texts. He urged his contemporaries to emulate the sobriety of the early Christians (meaning the Iconoclasts of the Byzantine Empire), and to destroy the luxuries in their possession. He called for the elimination of paintings and frescoes that, in his view, gave the Virgin Mary the appearance of a low-life, and he condemned the pagan writings of Aristotle and Plato. "Repent, O Florence!" he roared. "Clothe thyself in the white garments of purification!"

Savonarola's sermons, delivered with extraordinary oratorial skill, were a huge hit with the people of Florence. When he was at the pulpit, Florence's Cathedral, the Duomo, overflowed with worshipers. Even the very young Michelangelo was in his thrall; the artist went on to remember Savonarola's thunderous voice well into old age. The volatile and temperamental Botticelli was another disciple.

Among ordinary Florentines, meanwhile, Savonarola developed a cult following. Many emulated him and took up fasting on a daily basis. Young girls and married women checked themselves in droves into the nearest convents.

Savonarola operated his own vice squad: bands of short-haired children who roamed the streets chanting hymns and carrying crosses and olive branches. These underage enforcement officers stormed into the homes of the rich and famous, and rummaged around for evidence of depravity and sin. They promptly confiscated any artworks, books, or luxury objects they found.

One fine day in February 1497, the followers of Savonarola staged an event that would become forever associated with his name: a bonfire of the vanities. As Florentines cheerily marked the carnival season and poured out into the streets, Savonarola's young vice squad embarked on a campaign of mass repossession. They snatched dozens of incriminating objects from the citizens of Florence and heaped them onto a giant pyramid-shaped pyre positioned in the Piazza della Signoria, Florence's main square.

Portraits of women, racy drawings, books, and stories by the likes of Giovanni Boccaccio were piled around the base of the pyre. Unbelievably, paintings were given up for incineration by their artists, who judged them to be immodest and uncouth. Botticelli was thought to be one such artist. Other repentants included Lorenzo di Credi and Fra Bartolommeo.

Wigs and feathers, fans and mirrors, chessboards, and playing cards also found their way onto the towering pyre, which was topped with the effigy of a Venetian merchant who had offered a large sum to buy the treasures earmarked for destruction. As church bells, horns, and choirs rang out across the city, the pyre was lit, and the vanities were set ablaze.

Savonarola's stranglehold on Florence and the Florentines lasted no more than two or three years. The ambitious friar challenged the pope, and was promptly excommunicated. Eventually, he ended up hanged and burned at the stake on the very spot where his bonfire had seared and sizzled. The rule of Savonarola became an important milestone in European history. And the bonfire named after him is remembered to this day as one of the most spectacular acts of art censorship in the Western world.

WITHIN A COUPLE of decades, a new wave of art bashing broke out, this time in Protestant Europe. History, again, repeated itself. Claiming inspiration from the early Christians and from the Second Commandment, groups of Protestant priests pronounced the paintings and sculptures in Roman Catholic churches to be sacrilegious, and likened them to pagan idols.

This outburst of iconoclasm was (as often happens) politically motivated. It was an angry reaction against Catholic Europe—and in particular against Catholic Spain. The Catholic Church was viewed as extravagant and corrupt, and the widespread worship of reliquaries, statues, and effigies of Christian saints was frowned upon.

Once again, works of art—paintings, sculptures, prints, stained glass windows—became proxies in a purge. Churches and monasteries in the present-day Netherlands, Switzerland, Germany, and France were wrecked and looted, and their treasures were destroyed. Ax in hand, the vandals smashed altarpieces, broke windows, tore tapestries. Sometimes they hurled insults at the images, and smeared them with urine and excrement.

Countless paintings and sculptures were snatched and tossed onto bonfires not unlike Savonarola's, when they were not destroyed straight away on church premises. Elsewhere, the figures in images were mutilated. Their heads and hands were chopped off, and their facial features were scratched out.

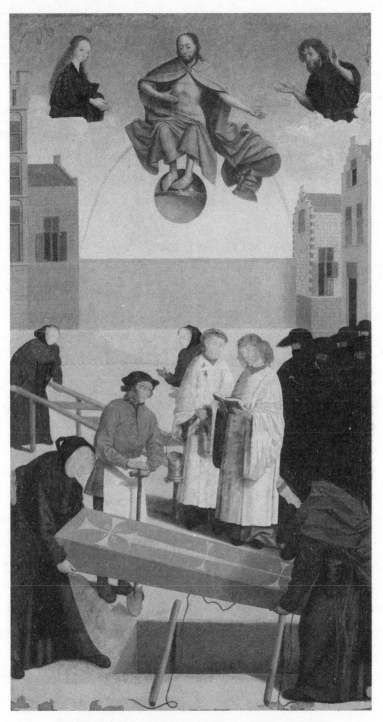

Master of Alkmaar, *The Seven Works of Mercy* (1504).
The faces of several of the figures in this work were
scratched out during the Protestant Iconoclasm.

You can see a telling example of this campaign of religious vandalism at the Rijksmuseum in Amsterdam, where it is on permanent display. *The Seven Works of Mercy*, by the Master of Alkmaar (1504), consists of seven panels illustrating the merits of altruism. Recent restorations of the work revealed that the polyptych had been seriously damaged in the mid-sixteenth century. Vandals armed with knives had sliced out the faces of more than one figure. The restorers left some of that damage visible for museumgoers to see.

Most of the figures on the fourth panel from the left, "Burying the Dead," are faceless: their features have been rubbed out by the Protestant iconoclasts. On the third panel, there are clear scratch marks across the face of a man with a fur collar who is engaging in an act of charity by clothing the poor.

Soon, the puritanical backlash sweeping across Northern Europe spread to Catholic Europe. Beginning in the late sixteenth century, the Roman Catholic Church launched into a Counter-Reformation. Art, once again, became a key tool in this ideological crusade. The Council of Trent—the ecclesiastical conference at which the Counter-Reformation was established—demanded that "all lasciviousness be avoided" and that "figures shall not be painted or adorned with a beauty exciting to lust." Whole swathes of Renaissance art were suddenly called into question, and the practice of representing gods and goddesses in the nude was deemed indecent.

As the Counter-Reformation took hold, three of the greatest artists of all time—Michelangelo, Veronese, and Caravaggio—were accused of irreverence in their portrayal of holy Christian figures. Michelangelo suffered the heaviest damage: several figures in his Sistine Chapel wall frescoes were subsequently clothed, and two saints were actually repainted.

A few decades earlier, Michelangelo's Sistine Chapel ceiling had been unveiled to gasps of wonder and amazement. But times had changed. Now, his *Last Judgment*—the fresco series that covers the altar wall of the cha-pel and was painted between 1536 and 1541—was receiving a more muted welcome, chiefly because many of the figures in it were naked. As prudery took hold in sixteenth-century Rome, Michelangelo faced persistent calls for his nudes to be hidden from view or destroyed. And ultimately, the man whose very name was synonymous with artistic genius was censored.

The censorship didn't happen overnight: it took place more than two decades after *The Last Judgment*'s inauguration, and followed the election of a new pope. Pope Pius IV, the man who concluded the Counter-Reformation, made art—and Michelangelo's frescoes—a topic of discussion by the Coun-cil of Trent. In January 1564, the Council ordered the frescoes to be modified.

By this time, Michelangelo was an ailing man of eighty-eight. To avoid distressing the great master, the decision was made to carry out the altera-tions posthumously. His pupil Daniele da Volterra was quietly charged with the task of figuring out how to do it.

Volterra covered up some of the more overt nudity in the frescoes with clothing and drapery. The figures of Saint Catherine and Saint Blaise posed a particular challenge: in Michelangelo's original, Saint Blaise was seen creeping up on Saint Catherine in what could have been a suggestion of sod-omy. Volterra erased the figures completely and repainted new ones. In the remake, Saint Catherine was clothed, and Saint Blaise, who was positioned immediately behind her in the scene, looked away instead of at her, eliminat-ing any hint of impropriety. (Because of his censorship work, Volterra was forever known as *il braghettone*, or "the maker of breeches." And when *The Last Judgment* underwent restoration in the 1980s and early '90s, the deci-sion was made not to go back to the original Michelangelo, because Volterra might have actually erased certain preexisting body parts and painted them over. A copy of the exact Michelangelo original, by Marcello Venusti, can be seen today in Naples.)

A decade or so later, in Venice, it was Veronese's turn to become a target of the high Catholic censors. Veronese was commissioned to paint a Last Supper for the convent of Santi Giovanni e Paolo in Venice, replacing an earlier one by Titian that had been destroyed in a fire. He produced a sprawling work, atmospheric and richly detailed. Yet because of that very painting, he was hauled before the Tribunal of the Holy Office of the Inquisition in July 1573. Certain details of the work were considered disrespectful—the dog in the foreground, the German (meaning Protestant) soldiers in the far corner, the midget and his parrot, the servant with a nose bleed.

"Does it, then, appear fit to you that at our Lord's Supper, you should paint buffoons, drunkards, Germans, dwarfs, and the like fooleries?" asked the judge. Veronese defended himself by boldly referring to the nudes in Michelangelo's *Last Judgment*. The judge replied that there were no such "drunkards nor dogs nor similar buffooneries" in the Michelangelo work. In a milestone verdict, the Inquisition Tribunal ordered Veronese to change his painting.

Veronese, like most artists, was set in his ways, and wedded to the painting as he originally conceived it. In the end, he made minimal modifications. He basically altered the title, adding an inscription to the painting that read *Feast in the House of Levi*. His painting was no longer called *The Last Supper*. Otherwise, it retained all of its essential characteristics. Today, *Feast in the House of Levi* can be seen in its full glory at the Galleria dell'Accademia in Venice.

The third great Italian artist to fall foul of the Church was Caravaggio. In 1601, the bad boy of Baroque Rome was commissioned by a wealthy lawyer to paint a *Death of the Virgin* for the lawyer's family chapel, located in a new church (Santa Maria della Scala in Trastevere) in a working-class area. The adjoining monastery operated a sort of battered-wives refuge, sheltering women who might otherwise become destitute and fall into prostitution.

Caravaggio, ever the rebel, chose to depict the dead Virgin Mary as an ordinary woman in ordinary surroundings. Mary was represented in a barren room with dirty walls and a red curtain draped across it. She wore a plain red dress and was represented lying down with one hand on her bloated belly, her bare feet sticking out. The saints, including Mary Magdalene, grieved around her in a scene of extraordinary starkness and simplicity.

Caravaggio's painting came as a shock to the monks whose church was set to receive it. As far as they were concerned, the artist had depicted Mary in the guise of a Roman prostitute. (Caravaggio actually used his own lover as a model.) At this time, the Church was still very much bound by the diktats of the Counter-Reformation, and there was no question of mixing the sacred with the profane. Caravaggio's representation of the Virgin as a barefooted commoner was plainly an outrage. The painting was rejected wholesale by the monks. Today, it is one of the proudest displays of the Louvre Museum in Paris.

BY THE EIGHTEENTH century, the progressive ideas of the Enlightenment and its philosophers led human and scientific reason to trump religious faith. There were calls for church and state to be separated, and for the monarchies of Europe to allow greater civil and individual liberties. The power of religious authorities began to wane. In fact, in one of the more unexpected upshots of the Enlightenment (particularly in France), there was a sudden rise of—and appetite for—pornography in literature and in the visual arts. By the late eighteenth century, the French Revolution was overthrowing the monarchy, and imposing a new motto: *Liberté, égalité, fraternité.*

Painters of this period (the so-called Romantic period) openly expressed their thirst for social justice. The Spanish master Francisco Goya produced a trenchant series of 80 prints known as *Los Caprichos* that denounced the power of king and clergy. In the most violent, *The Sleep of Reason Produces Monsters*, reason was threatened by terrifying goggle-eyed owls. The etchings were put on sale via a newspaper announcement. Yet a few days later, the entire series was pulled out of circulation. The 240 remaining sets and their plates entered the collections of the Spanish king. Goya's *Caprichos* were such an irritant to the Inquisition authorities that, much later, Goya briefly stood trial for painting a nude.

In France, Eugène Delacroix produced a triumphant painting for this new freedom-seeking age. His *Liberty Leading the People* (1830) showed a shapely, bare-breasted woman guiding a group of mutineers in a struggle for equality and justice. The same painting that, until recently, appeared on French 100-franc banknotes shocked the public when it went on display at the Paris Salon, the exhibition of officially approved art. The French government bought it to decorate a room of the Tuileries—then promptly took it down for its "glorification of the revolutionary spirit." (This was, in all likelihood, a ruse by the government to keep the painting away from public view without going as far as censoring it outright.)

These episodes were still minor blips compared to the vandalism and Inquisition trials that had come before. Artists of the nineteenth century were undeniably the freest that the world, at that point, had ever seen. Édouard Manet's *Le Déjeuner sur l'Herbe* (1863)—where two men in coattails picnic with a naked woman—was on public display. It scandalized audiences to such a degree that guards were stationed next to it to avoid acts of vandalism.

In 1866, Gustave Courbet painted a brazen close-up of a woman's genitals in *L'Origine du monde* ("The Origin of the World"). (The painting had been commissioned by a Turkish-Egyptian diplomat for his private collection.) Bold and frontal, it left nothing to the imagination. It was, in fact, one of several overt images of the female form that the artist produced at the time. Only a decade or two earlier, pictures of the sort would have been unimaginable.

By the early twentieth century, Western artists pushed the boundaries of art to such extremes that their freedom of expression seemed limitless. Pablo Picasso exploded the norms of two-dimensional representation and pioneered a new movement known as Cubism, where eyes popped out of noses and noses popped out of eyes. Marcel Duchamp, who was invited to participate in a New York exhibition in 1917, submitted a porcelain urinal that he purchased in a store. Salvador Dalí and his fellow Surrealists explored the world of dreams, producing puzzling artworks that were like snapshots of the subconscious.

These hard-won artistic freedoms came under assault in the opening decades of the twentieth century, as totalitarianism swept across the European continent. Art and artists became a prime target for two great European powers of the time: Nazi Germany and the Soviet Union.

Adolf Hitler, an amateur painter, had slicing views on early twentieth-century art, and went to great pains to impose them on everyone else. He abhorred Expressionism, Modernism, abstraction, Cubism, Surrealism, and the other isms of the time. So his rise to power was punctuated by a systematic campaign to exterminate all modern forms of art.

The museums of Germany at the time were chock-full of works by the likes of Picasso, Georges Braque, Henri Matisse, Paul Klee, and Oskar Kokoschka. There were so many modern works in the national collections that they occupied a whole new wing of Berlin's Nationalgalerie. The year 1919 also saw the birth of a new homegrown artistic movement: the Bauhaus, established by Walter Gropius, which drew an elite group of artists, architects, designers, and craftspeople to the movement's hub in the city of Weimar (as well as to other Bauhaus centers in Dessau and Berlin).

The Bauhaus became the Nazis' first artistic target. Within a few years of the movement's creation, its headquarters was emptied of all personnel, and many of the artists who had worked there fled Germany. Site-specific murals in Dessau were painted over, and a German crafts organization moved in.

By 1933, with Hitler now chancellor of Germany and his party commanding its first parliamentary majority, a Reich Chamber of Culture ("Reichskulturkammer") was set up to monitor individuals involved in the arts. Membership became compulsory for artists, architects, writers, and musicians. Museum directors were encouraged to take down modern works, and to show figurative and representational art instead, such as the brooding landscapes of the Romantic painter Caspar David Friedrich.

So-called "degenerate" art was frowned upon, and gallerists dealing in modern art were sanctioned. When the Nierendorf Gallery in Berlin had an opening-night party and exhibition, the Gestapo immediately swooped in and shut it down. Artists such as Paul Klee, Otto Dix, and Max Beckmann were fired from teaching or institutional positions. Other "degenerate" artists saw their work removed, destroyed, or banned from sale, and soon found themselves unable to work at all, as no one would sell them art supplies. Many fled Germany.

Meanwhile, Hitler ordered the construction of the Haus der Deutschen Kunst ("House of German Art") in Munich. As the building neared completion, art was required to fill its galleries. Hitler defined what he considered acceptable art at a rally in Nuremberg in 1934. Cubists, Futurists, Dadaists, and others were "mistaken, if they think that the creators of the new Reich are stupid enough or insecure enough to be confused, let alone intimidated, by their twaddle," he roared. "They will see that the commissioning of what may be the greatest cultural and artistic projects of all time will pass them by as if they never existed."

An open competition was held to assemble the future museum's collections. The only eligibility criterion was German nationality, or "race." More than fifteen thousand works were sent in, and nine hundred were selected. Hitler then fired most of the jury members and appointed his personal photographer and adviser Heinrich Hoffmann as the man in charge of the contest, which was held every year.

In November 1936, the Nazis banned all art criticism, and the following summer, Hitler's Minister of Propaganda, Joseph Goebbels, announced that an exhibition would be organized of "works of degenerate art since 1910" that were in the collections of Germany. Nazi officials fanned out across the museums of Germany and confiscated dozens of such pieces. In Berlin's Nationalgalerie alone, sixty-eight paintings, seven sculptures, and thirty-three graphic works were seized. Museum directors and curators secretly moved to salvage works by the likes of Picasso, Braque, and Edvard Munch, either by giving them back to their owners or by safeguarding them from confiscation and destruction.

On July 18, 1937, in Munich, a solemn procession outside the Haus der Deutschen Kunst aimed at glorifying Germany's past was presided over by Hitler. Thousands of people, animals, and machines participated in the mega-parade, which featured Viking ships, a make-believe Charlemagne, and figures in ancient Germanic garb, as well as more contemporary representatives of the German nation: units of the Wehrmacht and of the SS. From his podium in front of the new museum's marble facade, Hitler thundered at the gathered crowds. He declared that artists were banned from depicting anything but the forms found in nature, and warned that they otherwise risked being banished to a medical institution or put on trial. "We will, from now on, lead an unrelenting war of purification," he bellowed, "an unrelenting war of extermination, against the last elements which have displaced our art."

Inside the Haus der Deutschen Kunst was an exhibition of paintings carefully selected for their traditional and figurative content: majestic war scenes, wholesome nudes, peasant families. Hitler himself was represented as a knight in shining armor, on horseback, brandishing a flag. Yet this heavily edited and rather pompous show drew far fewer spectators than the exhibition of "degenerate" art that opened soon after in a shabby building nearby, a place where plaster casts were previously kept.

There, visitors piled in to gaze at the art that Hitler hated: works of abstraction, Constructivism, and Expressionism, and antiwar paintings by Otto Dix and George Grosz, all described in aggressive wall labels. More than two million people had visited the exhibition by the time of its November 30 closure.

The Nazi crusade against "degenerate art" got nastier still. Within weeks, a ruthless campaign of "total purification" of the German art world began. A dedicated "purification committee" went around the country's museums and confiscated nearly sixteen thousand works from the country's public collections, which were then stored in warehouses, or sold to eager dealers and collectors. (Hermann Goering sold a few seized paintings—works by Munch, Paul Cézanne, and Franz Marc—and used the proceeds to buy Old Masters and tapestries.) An auction was organized in Lucerne for 126 works by the likes of Picasso, Matisse, and van Gogh.

Nazi Germany then organized its own bonfire of the vanities. In March 1939, as many as 1,004 paintings and sculptures and 3,825 drawings, watercolors, and graphics were incinerated in the courtyard of the Berlin Fire Department. The German art world was purified in a chilling foreboding of the racial purification that would soon follow.

Meanwhile, the Soviet Union embarked on its own artistic purge.

Russian artists initially thrived in the run-up to and immediate aftermath of the 1917 Revolution. The founders and proponents of movements such as Futurism, Suprematism, and Constructivism actively participated in the revolutionary wave by directing movies; writing texts; designing sleek and elegant posters, fashion lines, and ceramics; and filling the streets with their art during official holidays.

In the newly established Soviet Union, however, culture came under the control of the government and party. The man put in charge of it was a certain Anatoly Lunacharsky. He believed that art was by no means a politically harmless activity: it had a definite impact on human beings, and that impact, if properly directed, could be useful to those in power.

Lunacharsky laid the groundwork for the propaganda art that dominated the Soviet Union from the 1930s onward. By 1934, a movement known as Socialist Realism became the order of the day. It was championed by the novelist Maxim Gorky. The idea was that art should be accessible by all, including members of the proletariat; that it should represent the lives of ordinary people; that it should be realistic (as opposed to abstract or Futuristic); and that it should promote the aims of the Soviet state and party.

Paintings and sculptures of the period showed youthful and robust Soviet laborers ploughing the land, working factory shifts, and marching with fervor and cheer. Paintings depicted machinery, flowers, and bursts of sunshine. In these works, Soviet-style communism was glorified as a force for good. Artists unwilling to produce works of Socialist Realism were heavily censored, and they disappeared underground. Socialist realism remained the official artistic style of the Soviet Union all the way up to the fall of the Berlin Wall.

IN THE POSTWAR period, the epicenter of art shifted from Europe to the United States. In New York, the Abstract Expressionists, led by Jackson Pollock, produced art that was characterized by a complete and total lack of inhibition. Pollock laid his giant canvases on the floor, and dripped and tossed paint all over them in a form known as a*ction painting*. Pop Art glorified popular, everyday imagery: cartoon strips, billboards, commercials, ads, brands, and labels. Andy Warhol, the Pop Art pioneer, painted series showing nothing but Campbell's soup cans and Coca-Cola bottles, making them subjects as legitimate as human figures and landscapes. Minimalists stripped art down to its barest essentials: Robert Ryman painted canvases that looked like white squares; Donald Judd affixed colored shelves to the wall.

Performance artists took unprecedented liberties in their effort to redefine art. In *Shoot* (1971), the artist Chris Burden had himself shot in the arm by a friend in a California gallery. Vito Acconci's *Seedbed* (1972) involved the artist hiding under a ramp in a gallery and masturbating loudly as his heavy breathing and crude language were beamed through loudspeakers. Art became more extreme than ever, and artists seemed to shatter every remaining taboo. Western visual culture started looking like a level playing field—a place where anybody and everybody was free to express themselves and do whatever they like.

The reality was altogether different. Until the twenty-first century, art remained the tightly guarded preserve of a privileged few. Where once its commissioners were kings, popes, and dictatorships, art was now overseen by a new set of authorities—museums, culture ministries, arts administrators—who kept it white, male, and profoundly unequal.

Until very recently, the world of art and museums left out entire categories of the population: women and artists of color. And it continued to worship and venerate the great male masters of painting and sculpture who, talented though they were, overshadowed, silenced, and sometimes exploited the powerless. Somehow, women—despite representing half of humankind—were callously erased. As the next chapter will show, that erasure still, to some degree, prevails.

2.

Just Not Good Enough

There are an estimated 7.8 billion people inhabiting our planet, and roughly 3.9 billion of them are women. Put another way, half of humanity is female. And yet women are still far from getting equal billing in the world of art and museums. Yes, they get their name on the poster more than they used to, but the underlying picture is still very much skewed against them.

Evidence of this inequality abounds. Only eleven percent of all acquisitions and fourteen percent of exhibitions at twenty-six major American museums between 2009 and 2019 were of work by women, according to the September 2019 Burns Halperin Report, published by Charlotte Burns and Julia Halperin in Artnet News and *In Other Words*. African American women were particularly hard hit: their share was a staggering 3.3 percent.

As a woman, I find gender disparity on this scale—more than two decades into the new millennium—mystifying. Did the women's liberation movement not take on gender bias in the Western world five decades ago?

Did generations of women in between time not fight for, and secure, equal rights?

There's scarcely a profession left in the West today that excludes women. Some are even close to achieving gender parity, or are female-dominated. Yet somehow, women artists have continued to suffer from near-invisibility. Men have consistently dominated the exhibition slate at major Western museums, and held all the sales records at major auction houses. A century after the suffragette movement, and a half-century since women's supposed liberation, art remains a profoundly sexist field.

Somehow, women artists are still being written off as "not good enough." The canon has identified the greatest artists of all time as being men and only men. Women have come into focus as the (mostly naked) figures that those men represented—frolicking in ponds, reclining in plush interiors, picnicking in prairies. Otherwise, they have been relegated to the sidelines as wives, mistresses, sidekicks, assistants, or nameless helpers.

That "not good enough" assessment has somehow stuck for centuries. It's been perpetuated by generation after generation of men, but also women, many of whom adopted the canon hook, line, and sinker, and went along with the prejudices built into it. Even women of my generation, who joined the workforce in the 1990s—a time when women's emancipation was pretty advanced—were somehow inured to the glaring injustices prevailing in the choice of artworks that were studied, exhibited, acquired, and sold.

Why? Because previous waves of feminist rebellion and uproar against the misogyny endemic in the art world led to no noticeable change. The militant feminists who engaged in gender-themed political art and shouted and yelled in protest at the sexism in the art world grew tired and demotivated, and their attention moved elsewhere. By the time my generation came along, feminism was less of a thing; some women even disliked being described as a feminist. We were all fully cognizant of the fact that men outnumbered women in the world of art and museums. But many of us failed to gauge the *magnitude* of the inequity—failed to realize that women had, quite simply, been wiped off the slate.

For research purposes, I went back and leafed through the art-history books that I read and admired as an art-history apprentice and that I still keep in my home library. I was shocked to see how sexist they all were. Take the bestselling *The Story of Art*, by Ernst Gombrich, first published in 1950 and revised in 1989. Rifling through the index, I couldn't find a single woman artist, even though his book starts in prehistoric times and leads all the way up to the 1980s, and is one of the bestselling art books ever.

My French reference books proved no more inclusive. The 1983 edition of the two-volume, pocket-sized *Dictionnaire des Grands Peintres* (first published by Larousse in 1976) was equally devoid of female names. I couldn't find a single standalone entry on a female artist. The few women named were brief mentions in texts on men. Joan Mitchell, universally recognized today as a major Abstract Expressionist artist, appeared in a brief parenthetical under "Willem de Kooning." She was listed with three other names as a member of the younger, second generation of Abstract Expressionists.

And under "Gentileschi," there was a chunky entry on Orazio Gentileschi, but no reference to his daughter, Artemisia, a pioneering painter of the seventeenth century. In short, universally read and constantly reprinted art-history books either omitted women artists completely or mentioned them *en passant* and in connection to men—even though many of these women deserved their own writeups.

Going down the list of artists I myself had interviewed in nearly two decades as a cultural journalist, I noticed there too an overwhelming concentration of white men. Based on a back-of-the-envelope calculation, there were half a dozen women, versus nine times as many men.

Prejudice, in other words, sat at the heart of my own work. That was no fault of my own. As an arts journalist, my job was to cover museums and galleries, and to hold a mirror up to whatever they did. I interviewed those artists who got major museum or gallery solo shows in London and occasionally also Paris. And that landscape was predominantly male.

The women I did encounter in those earlier years in the art world were mostly the wives and partners of the male artists whom I interviewed. These women were key to their husbands' careers. They were highly educated and often artists themselves. They ran their other half's atelier, and made it possible for him to produce work in ideal conditions, as well as to father numerous children. Yet they were systematically eclipsed by their husbands, who introduced them as their long-suffering and "supportive" spouses. I only ever interviewed two male artists who gave their wives equal billing, meaning by cosigning the work: Christo, whose name was forever twinned with his wife Jeanne-Claude's, even after her passing; and Ilya Kabakov, whose wife Emilia is the cocreator of all of his installations.

Toward the end of the last decade, the sands began to shift, slowly but surely. My coverage started foregrounding gender issues more and more. As of 2017, many of the stories and events that I covered and the people whom I interviewed seemed to have tie-ins with the theme of gender inequality. That was not a random date: the year 2017 was when reports of sexual harassment and assault broke out against the Hollywood movie mogul Harvey Weinstein, and when the #MeToo movement was born.

Gender soon became an important focus across all of my coverage areas: classical music, art, film. I wrote about the shockingly small number of female composers whose music was known and performed, and about the longstanding, and frankly staggering, invisibility of female orchestra conductors in classical music. I profiled a string of women who had just been appointed to run major European museums—Tate, the Vatican Museums. They were making history just by virtue of landing the job.

Covering the Cannes Film Festival in 2018—where, some years, there were *zero* female directors competing for the Palme d'Or—I reported on the festival's efforts to be more gender-balanced and less of a stomping ground for the likes of Harvey Weinstein, who had ruled the roost for so many years. The topic of gender was such a big part of the zeitgeist at the time that my main Cannes story landed on the front page of the *New York Times*.

ADMITTEDLY, IN RECENT years, museums, galleries, and auction houses have made noticeable efforts to promote women. There has been some change, at least on the surface. Some of this change has seemed somewhat rushed, as if institutions wanted to play catch-up and look good in a fast-moving world where social-media finger-pointing would be deadly to them. Yet it's still a discernible step forward.

Take Tate Modern, for example. In the last decade and a half—as part of efforts that originated under Nicholas Serota, the longtime director of the four Tate museums—there has been a noticeable escalation in the programming of solo exhibitions by women artists, dead or alive. Louise Bourgeois, Georgia O'Keeffe, Agnes Martin, Anni Albers, and Sonia Delaunay have all had standalone shows at Tate Modern, as have Yayoi Kusama, Marlene Dumas, Joan Jonas, and Mona Hatoum.

For many of these women, success and opportunity came late in life, or posthumously. This was, of course, true in the art world as a whole. In Artprice's 2018 ranking of the top twenty female artists by auction turnover, twelve were dead. They included Bourgeois, O'Keeffe, and Joan Mitchell.

Topping the list was the Japanese artist Kusama, who was born in 1929 and only achieved global stardom in the last decade.

I reached out to Tate Modern's Frances Morris, who runs the London modern-art museum since 2016, to find out more about these programming decisions.

They were all part of "a conscious and deliberate effort," Morris explained. "Things had to change." Tate, like so many other museums around the world, had not done nearly enough until then to acknowledge the work of female artists, she said.

As an example, Morris recalled that on the occasion of Tate's Centenary in 1997, the top 100 works chosen to mark the moment had included only two artworks by women. Her mission was "redressing this balance, which speaks of centuries of patriarchy and female repression, and the erasure of many wonderful careers."

The other very visible sign of gender-related change at Tate was the appointment of Maria Balshaw in 2017 as its overall director. The choice of Balshaw was doubly historic: she also became the first woman ever to run one of Britain's national museums. Men continued to steer the British Museum, the National Gallery, the National Portrait Gallery, and the Victoria and Albert Museum, and still do.

Tate has by no means been the only museum to correct the gender imbalance in its programming. Over at the Serpentine Galleries in London, Artistic Director Hans Ulrich Obrist was also proactive. Obrist told me that when he joined the institution in 2006, he was struck by the "invisibility" of women in the museum world, and saw a "necessity to change that." He and the Serpentine's director Julia Peyton-Jones programmed monographic shows of art by women. It was a good way to get these artists noticed; many had never had an exhibition in a major institution. The shows also served as a very important counterargument: that women artists in fact *were* good enough, and that they deserved to get big solo shows as much as the men did.

Here are two telling examples. In 2019, the Serpentine staged an exhibition of works by Faith Ringgold. Unbelievably, it was Ringgold's very first solo show in Europe. That year, the Serpentine also gave the Venezuelan artist Luchita Hurtado a standalone exhibition. According to Obrist, it was her first solo museum show ever. She was ninety-eight when it opened. And sadly, she passed away the following year.

Also in 2019, the Barbican Centre in London staged a breathtaking retrospective of the work of Lee Krasner—an outstanding artist who had lived and worked at the same time as her painter husband Jackson Pollock. Krasner had been completely overshadowed by Pollock and his outsized reputation, even though she outlived him by nearly three decades, and got a retrospective at MoMA that opened in December 1984, just six months after her death.

The MoMA accolade notwithstanding, Krasner continued to be viewed as playing second fiddle to Pollock. Her name was obscured by his. And yet when I visited the Barbican exhibition in 2019, I found the quality of her work to be staggeringly high. To my mind, it measured up to his. I was not alone.

"Lee Krasner was largely dismissed for the simple reason that she was married to another artist who got all the attention," explained Christopher Riopelle, the curator of post-1800 paintings at the National Gallery in London, as he joined me for a Zoom conversation on gender and art. "Now we're seeing that a wrong was done to her reputation for the simple fact that she was the woman in the partnership."

Artemisia Gentileschi, *Self-Portrait as Saint Catherine of Alexandria* (c. 1615–17)

IF IT TOOK decades for the art world's gatekeepers to recognize Krasner, it took them centuries to recognize the seventeenth-century Italian artist Artemisia Gentileschi. Trained in her artist father Orazio's studio, she was tragically raped at the age of seventeen, then went on to marry and become an artist in her own right. She was celebrated in her lifetime. Yet mysteriously, after her death, she lapsed into art-historical invisibility. Only recently was she retrieved from it.

In the wake of the #MeToo movement in 2018, Gentileschi's *Self-Portrait as Saint Catherine of Alexandria* (about 1615–17) was acquired by the National Gallery in London. It became only the twenty-first work by a woman to enter the permanent collections, versus an estimated 2,300 works by men. As the feminist art historian Griselda Pollock wrote in the preface to *Old Mistresses: Women, Art and Ideology* (the book she coauthored with Rozsika Parker in 1981, which was recently reprinted), it took the National Gallery 196 years from the time of its foundation to present Artemisia to the British public, even though she had once been the guest of Britain's art-loving King Charles I.

The National Gallery staged a massive publicity campaign around the purchase, filming the painting's restoration on YouTube and sending it on a British tour with stopovers in a women's library, a doctor's practice, and a women's prison. By the time the exhibition opened (mid-pandemic) in the fall of 2020, tickets were sold out and Artemisia was the talk of the town.

As someone who had the good fortune of living for a few years (1997 to 2001) in the center of Rome, I had a vague familiarity with Artemisia Genti-leschi. I might even have seen one of her works while I lived there. But I knew her contemporary Caravaggio so much better. His masterpieces hung in the museum I lived above (the Galleria Doria Pamphilj), and graced several of the glorious Baroque churches nearby, which I regularly visited, just to see the Caravaggio's.

As I headed into the Gentileschi exhibition at the National Gallery, I found myself feeling somewhat circumspect, and wondering how good her work would be. I thought the exhibition might ultimately be a case of hype and feminist signposting.

From the very first room, I was proven wrong. There, on the wall directly opposite the entrance, was a painting produced by the seventeen-year-old Artemisia—*Susanna and the Elders* (1610)—showing a young, naked woman desperately fending off a pair of leering older men. This was not just a case of autobiography on canvas; it was an exquisitely composed, powerful painting by a young woman still in her teens.

Making my way through the exhibition, I found a number of other great paintings, as well as a few duds. But what became clear to me was that this artist unquestionably deserved to be in the countless art-history textbooks that had spurned her for so long. In the words of my friend Ali Hossaini—an artist and scientist who co-runs the National Gallery's creative R&D lab, National Gallery X—"you look at her next to a Caravaggio, and neither of them suffers."

To Hossaini, the Artemisia exhibit made one thing clear: the canon needed expanding. It was "exclusive and exclusionary," he said. "A certain amount of rehabilitation" had to be done.

I wondered whether there were other talented women from centuries past who had been shut out by art history and who merited rehabilitation. I put the question to Riopelle (of the National Gallery) in our Zoom call. His answer was yes.

There were several women working in the atelier of the French late-eighteenth-century painter Jacques-Louis David "who have only been rather minor footnotes within the boys' club that was David's studio," Riopelle told me. Their work was being reexamined.

And while abstraction was always believed to have originated with the Russian-born artist Vasily Kandinsky, "now we're seeing that it began much earlier, and almost entirely with women artists," he pointed out. In other words, abstract painting, arguably the most important art movement of the twentieth century, was "the invention of women. That's still a story that has to be told."

An exhibition opening in May 2021 at the Centre Pompidou did just that. *Elles font l'abstraction* examined the history of abstraction from its beginnings until the 1980s, focusing on the contribution of 110 women artists, and highlighting "the process of invisibilization" that they went through. Artists in the show included Georgiana Houghton, a spiritualist medium who painted a number of abstract watercolors in the 1860s and 1870s, but was never recognized as an abstract painter; the Swedish early twentieth-century painter Hilma af Klint; and the Swiss painter Sophie Taeuber-Arp, whose career was long overshadowed by that of her sculptor husband Jean Arp.

PLAINLY, GENERATIONS OF women artists had been unjustly erased from art history. There was growing evidence of that. But why did that erasure happen in the first place? What was behind the perennial sexism in art history? I attempted to piece together an explanation, with a little help from books, essays, films, podcasts, casual chats, and sit-down interviews.

A book I chanced upon in a London bookstore—*The Short Story of Women Artists*, by Susie Hodge—offered preliminary insights. Hodge began by confirming that women had been "excluded, ignored and generally expunged from art history."

According to the author, many prehistoric artists had been women (based on the hand prints they left behind), and in ancient Greece, the first-century writer and philosopher Pliny the Elder had identified six female artists. Yet somehow, from that point on, recognition of female artists was intermittent and rare.

Why? Until the sixteenth century, few women besides nuns received an education. After that, they faced multiple hurdles, marriage and child-rearing being the biggest. For a long time, they were also banned from enrolling at art academies and studying art, and prevented from taking part in art competitions or from showing their work. Even those who were artistically inclined in their youth gave up art after marriage. Those who did not give up art were still stymied by the practice of taking their husband's name; any artworks produced in the household were credited to the husband, particularly if he was an artist.

As a result, women were seldom protagonists. Their contributions to art history were largely anonymous—with a handful of exceptions such as Gentileschi in the seventeenth century, Élisabeth Vigée Le Brun in the eighteenth, and Berthe Morisot in the nineteenth century.

On an extended stay in Paris, I bought another recent illustrated survey of women artists: *Les femmes artistes sont dangereuses* ("Women Artists Are Dangerous"), by Laure Adler and Camille Viéville. The preface gave a vivid description of what it was like to be a woman artist all those centuries ago. It wasn't enough to have a room of one's own; you needed an atelier. And with a pencil, you could draw but not paint; painting required paintbrushes and easels and pigments and models, none of which women had access to.

All in all, it was hard to represent the world when your only missions in life were giving birth and raising children while being confined to the home. Consequently, no matter how talented women were, they could never be on a par with Michelangelo, Rembrandt, Goya, or Picasso. It was "institutionally and politically" impossible.

Admittedly, plenty of women in the medieval and Renaissance periods illuminated manuscripts, sculpted stones, and painted frescoes. Yet they remained completely anonymous. The few who did make a name were the daughters, lovers, or wives of male artists. Women had to go through men to create.

In the eighteenth century, in France at least, women were admitted to certain art academies to work as *petites mains* (which literally means "little hands"), adding flowers or plants to paintings by men. It wasn't until the nineteenth century that they were finally admitted to art academies as full-fledged students. Yet restrictions applied. They were only allowed on the premises at certain hours, when there were no men, and they were barred from certain classes, such as life drawing. It was out of the question for a female art student to be let into a room with a naked man or woman, though there were no such hurdles for male art students. It wasn't until 1897 that women were admitted to the country's finest art school, the École des Beaux-Arts in Paris. And it wasn't until 1900 that they were allowed to have their own ateliers.

Reading Adler and Viéville's book, it became clear that high-profile women artists only emerged in the nineteenth century, and in limited numbers. Two such standouts, who both made a name in Paris, were Berthe Morisot (who was married to Édouard Manet's brother) and Mary Cassatt (who was a close friend of Edgar Degas). Their social status and connections helped get their talents recognized. Then there was the gifted sculptor Camille Claudel, lover of Auguste Rodin, who was long over-shadowed by him until her rehabilitation in a major Musée Rodin show in 1984.

By the turn of the twentieth century, plenty of women artists started to be recognized in the international art world and its undisputed epicenter, Paris. Both books made that clear, as did Catherine Grenier, director of the Fondation Alberto et Annette Giacometti in Paris, and formerly the deputy director of the Centre Pompidou's Musée National d'Art Moderne.

Grenier and I ran into each other at the Institut Giacometti, the intimate research and exhibition center she set up a few years ago. Our lengthy conversation began among Giacometti's emaciated bronze figures and pin-headed busts. What was refreshing about Grenier was that unlike other female art historians, who are prone to trash white male artists and the canon in their drive to denounce gender inequality, she gave credit where credit was due.

What Grenier explained to me that day, and in a follow-up conversation, was that in the Modernist movement that flourished in the early twentieth century, a lot of women were active participants. There were two reasons for that: plenty of women were attending art school, for one thing; and the art world had become less academic in its requirements, acknowledging self-taught women photographers and collage artists. Between 1900 and 1930, a significant number of women made, exhibited, and sold art, said Grenier. When the Mexican artist Frida Kahlo came to France during that period, for example, she immediately got a show.

That may seem paradoxical in a country where women were barred from voting until 1944. Yet paradox lies at the heart of France, Grenier explained. "The French are both the most progressive people you can come across, and the most reactionary," she quipped.

Another manifestation of the progressive France was that in February 1937, Paris hosted one of the first international exhibitions of women's art. The Musée du Jeu de Paume (in the Tuileries Gardens) staged a show titled *Femmes artistes d'Europe* ("Women Artists of Europe") featuring works by artists such as Marie Laurencin and Tamara de Lempicka, who was a star in her day.

Yet strangely enough, after World War II, women artists more or less faded into the woodwork. A group of white male Americans set out to write the history of modern art, and excluded women from that history, said Grenier. Why, I asked? Because those progressive, left-leaning art historians went looking for radical breakthroughs—"the more radical the work, the more it belonged in the history of art." Women, for whom radical artistic innovation was often not a priority, were left out.

Art history was boiled down to a succession of movements, most ending in "ism": Impressionism, Pointillism, Fauvism, Cubism, Futurism, Expressionism, Surrealism, Abstract Expressionism, Minimalism. And the pioneers of these movements were almost invariably white European or American men. This became the canon that prevailed in modern-art museums such as the Museum of Modern Art in New York and the Centre Pompidou in Paris.

There was nothing wrong with this canon, Grenier hastened to add. It was a very useful educational tool, as each movement made small advances and paved the way for the next. But what it ended up doing was sidelining women, despite their breakthroughs in the nineteenth and early twentieth centuries. By the time Grenier started studying art history in the 1980s, the perception was that women were "not good enough."

Was there any truth to that at all, I asked? Certainly not, she said, rolling off a list of women who are art-world superstars today but were forever spurned and scorned before that: Frida Kahlo, Natalia Goncharova, Louise Bourgeois. "Bourgeois waited until she was eighty years old to become famous. Who, today, would say that her art is no good?" The examples are "very clear," Grenier told me. "They're undisputable."

By the early 1970s, the invisibility of women was pretty much absolute. The canon—as embodied by the permanent collections of MoMA—consisted of a suite of movements led by white men, in which women (and artists of color, as we shall later see) played next to no part. That canon was embraced so universally that some began to think that there was some congenital reason why women were absent from the lineup.

When the feminist art historian Linda Nochlin attended a Vassar College graduation ceremony in 1970—where the feminist Gloria Steinem, no less, was the keynote speaker—the gallerist Richard Feigen (whose sister was graduating) came up to her after the ceremony. "Linda, I would love to show women artists, but I can't find any good ones," he said. "Why are there no great women artists?"

That stinging question was the trigger for Nochlin's landmark 1971 essay: "Why Have There Been No Great Women Artists?" Nochlin, of course, intended the question rhetorically, not literally.

In her essay, Nochlin acknowledged that there had been "no supremely great women artists, as far as we know," though there were many interesting and talented ones who had not been studied enough. Nor were there female equivalents of Michelangelo, Rembrandt, Delacroix, Cézanne, Picasso, Matisse, or even Warhol.

But then conditions were "stultifying, oppressive and discouraging to all those, women among them, who did not have the good fortune to be born white, preferably middle class and, above all, male," she wrote. "The fault, dear brothers, lies not in our stars, our hormones, our menstrual cycles or our empty internal spaces, but in our institutions and our education—education understood to include everything that happens to us from the moment we enter this world of meaningful symbols, signs and signals." Given the above, it's a miracle if women or people of color have managed to "achieve so much sheer excellence, in those bailiwicks of white masculine prerogative like science, politics or the arts."

A decade after Nochlin's book came out, the Australian-born art historian Griselda Pollock was so inspired by it and so roiled by the gender inequalities in art history that she cowrote the influential piece of writing mentioned earlier, *Old Mistresses: Women, Art and Ideology.*

In the preface to the 2013 edition, Pollock emphasized how ironic it was that the twentieth century—which had been "named the century of women"—should be the one in which art history should be exclusively male. "Why the contradiction between women's political and educational emancipation," she protested, "and the writing and museum presentation of art history as solely the work of men?"

Her assessment was that art history was *"structurally* sexist." By delivering an image of art and the artist that was exclusively male and "Euro-Americano-centric," meaning white, art history distorted our "views of the world, of history, of ourselves."

I dug out the transcripts of my interviews with female artists to see how much those women were affected by misogyny in the art world.

It was, they said, not easy for them to make their voices heard and their art shown.

The American feminist artist Judy Chicago (born in 1939) found it particularly hard. When I called her at her home in New Mexico in November 2018, she said that most artists needed the support of a major gallerist, collector, or curator to build their careers, but that in her youth, "I had the whole art world arrayed against me." Her only hope was that art history would eventually acknowledge her, "although I knew that for women artists of the past, art history did the opposite: it obscured their achievements rather than recognize them in hindsight."

Part of the reason for her exclusion was that Chicago refused to fit into the minimalist aesthetic of her time. She came up with a highly personal and boldly feminist artistic language to which she dedicated the first fifteen years of her career. The most famous product of that period was *The Dinner Party* (1974–79), a room-sized installation-tribute to the often unsung heroines of history and art history, which is now on permanent display at the Brooklyn Museum in New York. The triangular banquet table has place settings for thirty-nine key women in history: from prehistoric goddesses and the poet Sappho all the way up to the author Virginia Woolf and the painter Georgia O'Keeffe. Each place setting features a plate with a different vulva-shaped design.

"There are all these women at the table who were from different cultures, religions, ethnicities, centuries, professions, and the only thing they all had in common was they all had vaginas, which links to the fact that they were mostly erased from history," Chicago told me. Her aim with that and other works, she said, was to "make images of active female agency"—represent female reproductive organs just as Western art had represented male ones for so long, and show childbirth, another image of female agency, and another taboo subject in art.

The American performance artist Joan Jonas, who belonged to the same generation as Chicago, spoke of the insecurities that she had as a woman artist starting out. Our lengthy conversation took place at Tate Modern in 2018, with her poodle Ozu snoozing on the chair beside her. "Being a woman, I just never thought I could be an artist, frankly," she told me. "I considered myself a student until I was out of school, when I was thirty years old."

"I just thought, 'How can I be an artist?'" said Jonas. "I didn't have confidence until later. But then I got it."

Neither of those women got major museum shows when they were younger. The museum world was stubbornly male—so stubbornly that in the mid-1980s, a group of women artist-activists wearing guerrilla masks and using aliases burst onto the scene to draw attention to its overwhelming maleness.

In a 1985 poster campaign, the Guerrilla Girls asked: "How many women had one-person exhibitions at NYC museums last year?" The answer:

Guggenheim 0
Metropolitan 0
Modern 1
Whitney 0

Subsequent generations of women artists had a slightly easier time, thanks to the trail blazed by the women who came before, and by the feminist movement. Yet they were shocked by the staggering absence of women in the corpus of artists that they studied.

The British painter Jenny Saville was one such artist. I met her in January 2015 at the Royal Academy of Arts in London, as a large-scale exhibition of Peter Paul Rubens was about to open. Saville was busy installing her one-room exhibition of contemporary art inspired by Rubens, an artist she adored.

Saville remembered that when she started studying art in the early 1990s, there were as many male students as female ones. And yet the subject they studied was profoundly sexist. Women were "all over art history visually, in their bodies, but not as the makers of culture," she said. "That was a shock."

Transferring for a semester to the University of Cincinnati, she took classes in women's studies and understood what she described as "the structure of patriarchy." She was so overwhelmed by the power of that patriarchy that she actually gave up painting for a while, unable to "deal with this male-laden historical language." Then, she realized that it was possible to be an artist and to be a woman. She decided to make a body of work that would somehow reconcile the two.

"As an artist, you're all about looking, observing the world," she explained. As a woman, "you are the person that is looked at. My work is about those two worlds coming together."

Saville was both the artist and the model in a series of nude self-portraits where she represented herself in ways that would not be conventionally considered flattering. These were giant close-up paintings of her naked self, exaggeratedly fleshy and flabby, and full of blemishes. In their corpulence, the paintings went further than anything Rubens had ever consigned to the canvas. One of them sold for 9.5 million pounds ($12.4 million) in 2018, making Saville the highest-selling woman artist alive.

To find out how still younger generations of women felt about the gender imbalance in art history, I reached out to the Australian-born art historian Alice Procter (author of *The Whole Picture: The colonial story of the art in our museums and why we need to talk about it*), who leads Uncomfortable Art Tours, a series of guided tours that focus on the imperialist origins of museum collections. Procter recalled that as an eighteen-year-old art-history student in 2013, she went to the National Gallery on a study day hosted by Griselda Pollock to mark the release of the new edition of *Old Mistresses*, a book that Procter found deeply inspiring.

"There was this kind of lopsidedness to the art history I was being taught at school, and the kind of canon that I would be presented with," she said. It was all the more lopsided considering that almost everyone in the course was a woman. There was a strong disconnect between the perception of art history as "a soft female subject," and the mostly male artists who were being taught in art-history books. *Old Mistresses* hit home, because it was the first time that Procter saw art history being challenged from a feminist perspective.

"The most fascinating thing about how the art world excludes is that it makes it look inevitable," she said. Despite the struggles of generations of artists against the overwhelming white maleness of the art world, she observed, women were "either erased or turned into the exception that proves the rule." In the end, the same three, four, or five names popped up over and again, and the going assumption was that they had talents and skills that other women didn't have.

Procter refuted that assessment. "It never occurred to me that women weren't talented," she said. "I would go to galleries and see this history, and think, 'Well, obviously, women are just as capable as men. So what is it that prevented them from making work?'"

Procter said new generations of museum curators and practitioners familiar with feminist theory were now putting on exhibitions that were much more sensitive to the subject of gender—she cited the Gentileschi show as an example. She said social media—the "biggest driver of change" in the museum world—had definitely been an accelerator. Left to its own devices, the museum world took five to ten years to change. So "this incredibly high-speed social media public conversation" was "moving beyond the pace of academic contemplation that institutions usually work at," she said. Institutions were having to speed things up considerably.

When I asked the prominent Cuban-American artist, writer, and curator Coco Fusco to comment on social media's role in bringing about change in the museum world, she replied, "I'm too old to glorify social media," and pointed out that it was "just the latest form of communication." Fusco said she was old enough to remember the days when artists and activists communicated by fax, and used mail art to fight the establishment, including military dictatorships in the 1970s. Fax and mail art were also powerful agents of change, she pointed out.

As for the evolutions afoot in the museum world, Fusco described them as a case of *plus ça change*. "The basic imbalance is still there," she said. "The composition of museum collections is still weighted heavily in favor of dead white men. That has not changed yet, and I don't even know if it will change at all, because the art world is like the advertising world. It's all about show, but that show also acts as a mask for what goes on behind it."

Fusco said there were "cycles in which the wealthy and the powerful basically get a facelift by looking like they're paying attention to everybody else," and we were living through one such cycle. "It is a moment, and we don't know how long it will last," she said. "How long has second-wave feminism been around? When did the Guerrilla Girls start publishing statistics of the institutional sexist practices? When I got out of college in the early 1980s, I saw their paste-up posters. This is an old conversation."

We got talking about the Museum of Modern Art's 2019 rehang of its permanent collections, with MoMA displaying women and artists of color on an unprecedented level, and hanging Ringgold next to Picasso. "I don't see the changes in institutional practice at MoMA being a result of democracy. MoMA is an elite institution," she said.

Her answer boiled down to: follow the money. If MoMA was "vulnerable to change," she explained, it was because "MoMA depends on money, and there isn't enough money coming from longstanding American sources anymore." Female patrons and donors from Latin America and Asia were the real drivers of the change, because they were collecting works by a much more diverse set of artists and donating them to the museum, helping diversify the collections.

The other real driver of change, she said, was that a younger generation of curators trained at much more diverse institutions—such as the Studio Museum in Harlem, led by Thelma Golden—were joining MoMA and bringing in a fresh approach and ethos.

Whatever the reasoning behind it, the MoMA rehang seemed to me to be a very good example of a museum foregrounding gender issues. So I decided to delve into it, and speak to the woman who spearheaded it.

The MoMA Rehang

MoMA is often identified as the first museum dedicated to the art of the modern era. It enjoys quasi-religious status as a pioneering temple of modern art. The artists and works that it showcases in its permanent displays define the canon more than any other modern-art museum on the planet, with the possible exception of Paris's Centre Pompidou.

"MoMA remains enormously important for the role it plays in maintaining in the present a particular version of the art-historical past," Carol Duncan wrote in the summer 1989 issue of *Art Journal*. She could just as easily have written those words today. "For much of the academic world as for the larger art public, the kind of art history it narrates still constitutes the definitive history of modern art."

Founded nearly a century ago—in 1929—with a mission to introduce museumgoers to the art of their time, MoMA today boasts some two hundred thousand works, covering the full sweep of the twentieth century: paintings, sculptures, drawings, prints, photographs, films, and more. It owns a number of gems that are the envy of the world: Picasso's *Les Demoiselles d'Avignon* (one of many top-notch Picasso's), and masterpieces by Paul Cézanne, Henri Matisse, Jackson Pollock, Willem de Kooning, and Andy Warhol, to name but a few. In short, MoMA is a 3D art-history textbook, offering students, museumgoers, and aesthetes the perfect illustrated guide to important artists, movements, and styles.

And yet in the nine decades since the museum's foundation, that history rarely included women, artists of color, or artists living and working outside of North America and Europe. The museum's modern-art timeline remained "a synchronic, linear progression of 'isms' in which one (heterosexual, white) male 'genius' from Europe or the United States influenced another who inevitably trumped or subverted his previous master, thereby producing an avant-garde progression," the feminist art historian Maura Reilly wrote in a 2019 column.

Art by women, artists of color, and international artists—for instance, female Abstract Expressionists such as Lee Krasner, Joan Mitchell, and Helen Frankenthaler—was not often shown. For nearly a century, an institution that was established as the embodiment of the new remained wedded to the old, and blinkered to the seismic societal and cultural shifts taking place in the world around it.

As the twentieth century drew to a close, MoMA's permanent collection started looking seriously staid, and ripe for change. So change came, in a big way. In October 2019, MoMA completed a $450 million expansion that gave it an extra 47,000 square feet (an additional 30 percent) of gallery space. The museum took the opportunity to rehang the permanent collection. As the director Glenn D. Lowry explained, "The real value of this expansion is not just more space, but space that allows us to rethink the experience of art in the museum"—to "reenergize" the place, and make MoMA "a laboratory for the study and presentation of the art of our time, across all visual arts."

Visitors could still find Picasso's *Demoiselles*, Vincent van Gogh's *Starry Night*, and other greatest hits easily and in abundance. But rooms were no longer labeled with "isms," and they were introduced instead by simpler thematic labels. Meanwhile, MoMA's superstar artists, used to being hung in all-male and all-white displays, suddenly found themselves hanging next to artists of a completely different gender, ethnicity and/or historical period.

The most striking juxtaposition was the display of Picasso's *Demoiselles d'Avignon* on a wall adjacent to the African American artist Faith Ringgold's *American People Series #20: Die*—painted sixty years later. Ringgold's mural-like painting from 1967 shows blood-spattered and terrified black and white figures flying all over the canvas. Ringgold was representing the vicious race riots of the 1960s, but she was also paying tribute to Picasso's celebrated war mural *Guernica* (1937), which she had seen in New York before it was returned to Spain. As MoMA explained, this particular display was a way to depart from a purely historical, step-by-step presentation, and start a transgenerational dialogue.

The Picasso–Ringgold juxtaposition was by no means the most radical aspect of the rehang. MoMA pledged to rotating the works in its permanent collection every six to nine months, acknowledging "that there is no single or complete history of modern and contemporary art." While the presentation was still loosely chronological, and major artists of the twentieth century were still well represented, there was now plenty of room to show lesser-known talents who weren't white and male.

To understand the thinking behind the MoMA rehang, I reached out to its principal mastermind: Ann Temkin, MoMA's chief curator of painting and sculpture. She explained that when she arrived at the museum in 2003 (from the Philadelphia Museum of Art), plans for a new building were already underway. It became clear to her that "what we had to do was completely redefine the way that we approached presenting the collection."

The first step was to recognize that "the art history that so many of us are old enough to have learned was written by white men, about white men," explained Temkin. She recalled that as a university student (Temkin attended Harvard and Yale), she did have the option of taking individual courses on woman artists or on African American artists, but "those were not folded into canonical art history. They were byways, and implicitly lesser—or sidebars."

By the time she took the MoMA job, it was "past time" for the museum to set aside its white-male-generated narrative, "especially since a lot of us weren't white men anymore, like me." As a test of this more inclusive curatorial approach, she said, she took over the whole fourth floor of the museum in 2010–11 to show all of the Abstract Expressionist works in the collection: not just the star works by Pollock and Mark Rothko, but also the works of their contemporaries, women artists or artists of color who were recognized in their day. The result was a more representative panorama of the art of 1950s America, and a demonstration that "our history isn't something with a finite set of borders, and it's pretty much an infinite realm. If you just start looking in different places, you make new discoveries."

The notion that you could "sum up the entirety of the truth of the history right now" was clearly "obsolete." And just because Pollock was coupled with these other artists in no way detracted from his greatness. "You're not throwing out the baby with the bath water," she said. "The one doesn't come at the expense of the other."

What took MoMA so long to be more representative of the city, community, and country around it? Art history and the received wisdom are "a slow-moving train," said Temkin. There also had to be a changing of the guard: people who studied in the 1970s or immediately afterward (such as herself) were only just reaching a point where they had "the power to enact the changes" and call the shots, she explained. Had MoMA not moved with the times, the times would have moved without it, and "we would just be the ones that, in retrospect, would have been looking like dinosaurs right now."

Critics greeted the MoMA rehang favorably, on the whole. The *New York Times*'s cochief art critic Holland Cotter wrote that the museum was about to "finally, if still cautiously, reveal itself to be a living, breathing twenty-first-century institution, rather than the monument to an obsolete history—white, male, and nationalist—that it has become over the years since its founding in 1929." Through "the integrated presence of 'difference' itself," MoMA was turning itself into a presentation of "Modernism Plus, with globalism and African-American art added." As for pairing Picasso and Ringgold, Cotter wrote, MoMA traditionalists might find it "sacrilegious," but it was "a stroke of curatorial genius."

Ringgold herself, whom I interviewed via email in the summer of 2019, said she was "ecstatic" about her painting *Die* hanging near Picasso's *Demoiselles*. She was "fully aware of the attention I am now getting in the art world, and grateful," she commented. "But I am also aware that it has taken a very long time, for I had to live to be eighty-nine years old to see it happen."

Other Black female artists continue to be underrepresented, even though "many more women are hanging on the walls of the major museums," she added. "Such women are predominantly white."

Some art historians had a more circumspect, wait-and-see approach to the rehang. The art historian and author Michael Brenson explained in an interview that he "long felt that museums really needed to open up, and I don't have any problem with that." But on MoMA's rotating rehang, "the jury is absolutely out, and it's a new ground," he said. "I hope MoMA really does value the intensity of the art experience more than its brand as an all-consuming institutional behemoth, and is uncompromising in giving its curators free rein to install the collection as they see fit. Good artists are not institutional. I'm interested in curatorial vision and passion."

THOUGH MoMA'S COLLECTIONS start in the 1880s, there are no star paintings by Paul Gauguin within them. Many of the thirty or so works are mostly works on paper. That explains why MoMA's first major monographic exhibition on Gauguin was in 2014, and a focus on his rare and extraordinary prints and transfer drawings.

At the time of writing, none of those Gauguin works were on display at MoMA. No doubt that will change: his works will be brought out of storage and showcased. But Gauguin doesn't score very highly on the gender-balance scale. This was a man who left his Danish wife, Mette, mother of his five children, to set sail for Tahiti. And he entered, on two separate occasions, into "marriages" (according to the local custom) with thirteen- or fourteen-year-old girls, whom he also eventually abandoned. His canvases are full of Tahitian women in varying states of undress whom he coaxed into posing for him, and probably much else besides. As a functionary representing the colonial power that was France, he showed an exaggerated sense of entitlement in his treatment of the women of Tahiti and the Marquesas Islands, where he died. He was, in a word, sexually exploitative.

For a good century after his passing, he got away with it: museums stressed the colonial excesses, but not the sexual ones. That has all changed.

Gauguin Portraits Exhibition (2019)

In May 2019, an exhibition of Gauguin portraits opened at the National Gallery of Art in Ottawa and traveled to the National Gallery in London the following October. The focus was art historical: a studied look at a genre that Gauguin was not known for—portraiture—with the aim of presenting Gauguin's subjects not as generic women, but as individuals he had friendships or relationships with. Yet for the two museums involved, what started out as a classic curatorial exercise turned into a litmus test of their ability to communicate appropriately with audiences in the #MeToo era. After all, here was an already married artist living with underage Tahitian girls on at least two occasions—committing what would legally be defined, today, as pedophilia.

I first heard of the exhibition three years before it opened, in a conversation with its cocurator Christopher Riopelle. He told me that a Gauguin portraits show was in the pipeline. I announced the news to the world in a *New York Times* article, and patiently waited for the exhibition.

As a longtime resident of Paris, I had come across the work of Gauguin early on, both in the permanent collections of the Musée d'Orsay and in multiple exhibitions, such as his landmark Grand Palais show of 1989. He was part of the tapestry of everyday life in Paris. His Tahitian beauties appeared on museum walls, but also on posters, coasters, tea towels, and T-shirts. I was aware that Gauguin had lived with and had sexual relationships with Tahitian girls who were barely past puberty. But this was not a topic of mainstream debate or controversy, nor was it discussed or critiqued by the curators of his many exhibitions.

When Tate Modern staged a retrospective of his work in 2010—*Gauguin: Maker of Myth*, which I visited several times and wrote about—the focus was on how Gauguin was basically something of a mythomaniac who embellished aspects of his life story. A catalogue essay noted that Gauguin had been "judged harshly by feminists" who were reacting to comments by his male supporters. One such supporter was Charles Morice, who, "anticipating future moral indignation about Gauguin's native 'brides,' stressed the equivalence in maturity of a Tahitian thirteen-year-old and a European eigh-teen- to twenty-year-old," said the catalogue. Another was René Huyghe, who expressed similar views in 1951, and blamed Gauguin's Danish wife, Mette, for being cold and for abandoning the artist in a move that spurred his suicide attempt in 1897–98.

The Tate exhibition catalogue, like so many that came before and after, seemed to take no moral issue with Gauguin's private life. After all, the paintings most loved by the public—and likeliest to boost museum ticket sales—were precisely those of the underage Tahitian girls he frequented on the island, who transported Western audiences to an exotic world of luxuri-ant landscapes, crystal-blue seas, and forbidden fruits.

In November 2017, my own perspective started shifting when I inter-viewed African American artist Kehinde Wiley at an exhibition of his work in London and asked him about his upcoming projects. He mentioned Gauguin, who he described as one of his "idols," "even in the age of Wein-stein," yet someone who was "creepy as f—k."

"Let's just face it," Wiley said. "He goes off into the Pacific, and he's looking at these young girls, and the colonial gaze: it's just really problem-atic." Wiley explained that he wanted to go to the Pacific and "use him as a glove or a contact lens or a sleeve through which I see an experience there."

Wiley's words stayed with me. I persuaded my editor to let me cover the *Gauguin Portraits* show through a #MeToo lens when it opened in Novem-ber 2019. The National Gallery, whose collections stop at the year 1900, was the last institution I expected to have its ear to the ground on matters of gender. I was wrong.

Right there on the main entrance wall were references to Gauguin's abuses. The artist "repeatedly entered into sexual relations with young girls, 'marrying' two of them and fathering children," read the text. He "undoubtedly exploited his position as a privileged Westerner to make the most of the sexual freedoms available to him."

When I interviewed him at the exhibition, the show's Canadian cocurator Christopher Riopelle acknowledged that the same show, programmed a couple of decades earlier, "would have been a great deal more about formal innovation, increased use of color, all of those old formalist tropes of modernism." Now, everything had to be seen "in a much more nuanced context."

He described Gauguin as "callous," and explained that while it was customary for Tahitian parents to allow their young daughters to enter into traditional Tahitian marriages with powerful Frenchmen, Gauguin never mentioned to those young girls or their parents that he was already married and a father of five—and on two occasions, he lived with young girls who were barely in their teens. "I don't think any longer it's enough to say, 'Oh well, that's the way they did it back then,' when we have great problems with the way they did it back then," said Riopelle. "We have to contextualize, but at the same time, we can't think that that simply erases the implications."

On my next visit to the exhibition, I found the audioguide to be even more blunt in its condemnation of Gauguin. At one point, a voice asked the rhetorical question: "Is it time to stop looking at Gauguin altogether?" The museum world, it seemed, was finally casting a critical look at Gauguin, the man.

I set off to quiz museum directors, curators, and art historians from Europe, North America, and the Pacific region. I discovered that in the exhibition's first iteration—at the National Gallery of Canada in Ottawa—nine labels had been changed because of culturally insensitive language. Gauguin's "relationship with a young Tahitian woman" was changed to "his relationship with a thirteen- or fourteen-year-old Tahitian girl." The title *Head of a Savage, Mask* given to a work was coupled with an extended label noting that the words "savage" and "barbarian" were "considered offensive today," and were reflective of attitudes at the time.

Among my interviewees, Gauguin's toughest adversary was the feminist art historian Ashley Remer, who described him as "an arrogant, overrated, patronizing pedophile." His biggest defender was Vicente Todolí, who had been director of Tate Modern in 2010 when the Gauguin show was held, and who said, "Once an artist creates something, it doesn't belong to the artist anymore: it belongs to the world." Otherwise, he cautioned, we would have to stop reading the anti-Semitic author Louis-Ferdinand Céline, or shun Cervantes and Shakespeare if we discovered something unsavory about them.

Overall, the consensus was that Gauguin should certainly be shown, but with his private life revealed rather than swept under the carpet. Somehow, Gauguin had enjoyed "the protection of history," concluded the Danish curator Line Clausen Pedersen (who had herself curated several Gauguin shows). It was time to "bring out all the dirty stuff."

When my article was published with the rhetorical headline "Is It Time Gauguin Got Canceled?" the reaction in France was one of outrage. Numerous French publications responded with kneejerk reactions to the headline, in some cases without having read the full piece. "*The New York Times* Suggests Banning a Gauguin Exhibition," wrote the conservative weekly *Valeurs Actuelles*, noting that the newspaper had recommended that the artist's works be taken down (I had done no such thing). Two other French publications recalled that until 1945, the legal age of consent in France was thirteen, so Gauguin was by no means breaking the law. Besides, wrote the art historian Didier Rykner (as quoted in *Le Journal du Dimanche*), if Gauguin were to stand trial with the laws of today, "you would have to eliminate all of art history, and beyond that, all of the history of France."

When it came to Gauguin, there were two clear camps. In English-speaking countries, including Canada and New Zealand, the article sparked debate and led me to be invited on popular radio programs. In France and Italy, where such debates are viewed as manifestations of political correctness gone awry, I was dismissed.

When it came time to write this book, I decided to go back to the two museums that had staged the exhibition and find out how they had put together their preopening communication strategy.

Riopelle acknowledged that for a long time in the museum world, when it came to discussing Gauguin's relationships with young girls, "the head was turned away from it," and "the life did not necessarily inform the art, or you could rather conveniently separate the life from the art." By the time the *Gauguin Portraits* show was in the works, however, the issue "arose early on," and "kept coming up."

"The real change came as we realized that we then had to face the question: how do we present this kind of information to a general public that is also becoming more and more aware with #MeToo?" Riopelle told me. "What happened was a realization that, in the climate then emerging on both sides of the Atlantic, we would need to be more explicit than had been done before in any exhibition."

Over at the National Gallery of Canada, the director and CEO Sasha Suda, who had only just arrived when the show opened there in May 2019, remembered being somewhat surprised when she saw it a few days before opening, particularly by a label that referred to Gauguin's relationships with "young women."

"We were skirting the issue. I expected to arrive in my gallery and have some kind of contextualization happen," she said. In a country such as Canada—where violence against indigenous peoples is "in the news every single day, in the same way that Black Lives Matter is in the headlines in the

States"—an artist such as Gauguin, who was a white settler in a French colony, needed much more careful introduction and contextualization.

"You're essentially talking about a colonial settler arriving in a foreign land, exercising his privilege through his behavior but also identities that he fantasizes about and makes," Suda told me.

Suda recalled that an article by Leah Sandals appeared in *Canadian Art* magazine at the time of the opening of the show in Ottawa. It became all the more clear that the labels had to be changed.

"What's missing from 'Gauguin: Portraits'—at least from my perspective as a white settler Canadian arts writer reporting on our museum sector—are programs and contexts that include perspectives from the Indigenous Pacific peoples Gauguin depicted, or that critically address the problematic issue of Gauguin's relationships with Tahitian girls as young as thirteen years old," Sandals wrote. "All this is especially necessary given that Gauguin's paintings, and his legacy in European art history, have had an outsized impact in defining the Pacific region and its people to outsiders."

Over the duration of the show, the museum received 2,313 feedback cards from visitors, about fifty of which were complaints about Gauguin and the museum programming. One comment card read, "Gauguin, what I learned: he is a narcissist, perhaps a pedophile to a fictional 13/14-year-old girl, crappy parent. A+ guy." Another read, "An 'othering' experience for a person of color." A third said, "As a young Polynesian woman, Gauguin's fixation on young Tahitian girls made me uncomfortable."

Months after the controversy, I visited the Musée d'Orsay in Paris to see whether my feelings about the art of Gauguin had changed after writing the article. I saw paintings in the permanent collection that I'd never seen before, and found them sensational. No part of me was condemning of what I saw on the canvas. I had never asked for Gauguin to be taken down, and I found myself just as eager to see more of his work in the future.

The point is that this was a man who had behaved incredibly callously toward his wife Mette (not to mention his five children) and never divorced her, even though he had gone on to commit serial infidelity in the Pacific islands and "marry" a couple of underage girls, committing an act of polygamy that had been banned in France a century earlier. He behaved as if the women and young girls he came across in Tahiti were exotic fruits, there for the picking.

What the many museum professionals I spoke to recommended—and I agreed—was, simply, far more transparency about his private life in the works' presentation. That's because to twenty-first-century women young and old, and to indigenous populations around the world, Gauguin was no longer blameless, or above the law.

3.

Morally Reprehensible Trash

As the example of Gauguin copiously illustrates, there is one particular area in which male artists have given women *plenty* of
opportunities, and since time immemorial: as subjects of their art. Western
museums swarm with naked muses, voluptuous Venuses, and shapely
pinups who have existed solely for the sake of male aesthetic and erotic
gratification, with no power or agency of their own, and absolutely no
voice. Leaf through any art-history textbook and you'll find untold numbers of depictions of nude women that served, back in the day, as the
pictorial equivalent of *Playboy* centerfolds. The position of these women,
on canvas and in real life, was determined by one set of men—artists—
for the benefit of another set of men—patrons—who, in the great cultural
centers of Europe, happened to be kings, noblemen, and popes. In the
modern feminist parlance, the male gaze was at the center of it all,
determining the direction and tenor of painting and sculpture for
centuries.

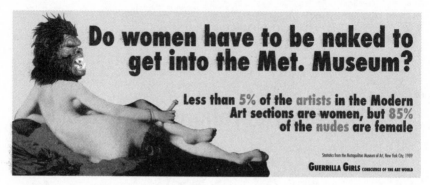

Guerrilla Girls, *Do women have to be naked to get into the Met. Museum?* (1989)

In the 1980s, the feminist campaigners known as the Guerrilla Girls condemned the surplus of nudes in museum collections. In a striking poster plastered all over New York, they howled: "Do women have to be naked to get into the Met. Museum?" Fewer than 5 percent of the artists in the Modern Art sections of the Metropolitan Museum of Art were women, the poster pointed out, "but 85% of the nudes are female."

Four decades later, inside the West's most prominent museums, the status quo ante prevails. The collections of the Met, like those of other museums of its kind in the Western world, remain as dominated by depictions of female flesh as they ever were. How could they not be? Nudes were one of the predominant genres in art, and their representation was a technique that generation after generation of male artists had to master.

In 2018, the prevalence of nudes in art history became the public bugbear of a popular comedian: the Australian-born Hannah Gadsby, who happens also to be an art-history graduate. In her Netflix comedy show *Nanette*, which was watched around the globe, Gadsby humorously explained the conundrum. Gadsby joked that while scientists, philosophers, and thinkers were busy figuring out the world and "naming things," women were doing not very much at all, because they were "too busy napping naked alone in the forest."

Gadsby was exaggerating, of course, but only just. Male artists were nothing but slaves to their own libido, she said. "High art, my arse," she concluded before a cheering audience. "The history of Western art is just the history of men painting women like they're flesh vases for their dick flowers."

As someone who had spent most of her life looking at art through a conventional prism, and not from a feminist perspective, I'll admit that *Nanette* got me thinking. I glanced at a reproduction of Edouard Manet's much-admired *Le Déjeuner sur l'herbe* afterward, and found myself wondering, for the first time, what a naked woman was doing picnicking in a park with a pair of men in coattails. Was she their muse, their mascot, or the post-picnic dessert? Parts of art history did start to look slightly odd.

I set out to explore the high visibility of female nudes in art—having explored the high *in*visibility of female talents in art. Why was it that male artists across the ages were so fixated on representing nude women? How did those women—or young girls, as they often were—end up posing stark naked for the artist in question? Did they have a say in the matter, or were they strong-armed? There was clearly a before and an after to those artworks, which history had totally obscured. Female models had been silenced even more effectively than female artists had been.

TO PROBE ART'S sexual exploitation of women and young girls, I went back to Ashley Remer, a New Zealand–based American curator. Remer was the founder of girlmuseum.org, an online museum focused on the representation of young girls in history and culture. Of all the voices in the Gauguin article I had written for the *Times*, hers had been the most condemning. She had described him as "an arrogant, overrated, patronizing pedophile," and added that if his paintings were photographs, we would find them unacceptable.

When I called her again at her home in New Zealand, I discovered that Remer's remarks about Gauguin had unleashed a torrent of criticism and verbal abuse against her, both on email and on social media. Many of the messages said "you're completely stupid and know nothing about art," she told me, while a few carried unspecified threats. "You're accusing Gauguin of being all of these things, and it would be a shame if that happened to you," Remer remembered them saying. "You're going to get what's coming to you."

That Gauguin lived with thirteen- or fourteen-year-old Tahitian girls is beyond dispute. Yet Remer's description of Gauguin as a "pedophile" subjected her to a stream of criticism and menace. Two decades into the twenty-first century, a female curator who denounced the sexual antics of a dead male artist was being electronically trashed and trolled.

In our second conversation, Remer described Gauguin as "a serial pedophile" who got away with his behavior by projecting an image of the artist as a gifted misfit impossible for society to control. What she found particularly damaging, she said, was that Gauguin's lifestyle continued to spawn copycats—such as the two young Frenchmen she met on separate islands in Tahiti several years ago, who were not painters at all, and told her they were in Tahiti "to live like Gauguin."

Art history was full of examples of men in positions of dominance making women and young girls pose for them. It was a "continuum" of men treating women "as the material of their work," and not as "an equal cultural worker participating in the production." Books had been written about artists' models, yet most of those models remained unidentified. "We don't know if they were slaves or servants, if they were coerced or paid, or if they were just women who liked to get their kit out," she said.

I asked her to name other artists whom she found problematic. She cited a famous painting by François Boucher—*Blond Odalisque* (1752)—showing a pubescent girl lying naked on her stomach, her bare bottom the central focus of the canvas. King Louis XV was so enticed by the girl in the painting that he asked to meet her in person, and the teenager became his mistress, Remer pointed out.

Our discussion reminded me of a more recent example of a naked underage model: Picasso's *Fillette à la corbeille fleurie* ("Young Girl With A Flower Basket," 1905). It shows the skinny young girl from the side, casting a mysterious glance at the viewer, and carrying a basket of blazing red flowers.

The painting—from Picasso's Rose Period, which lasted from 1904 to 1906—sold for $115 million at a Christie's New York auction in May 2018, becoming the sixth most expensive artwork ever sold at auction (at the time). It came from the storied Peggy and David Rockefeller collection, and went on display shortly afterward in a blockbuster Picasso show at the Musée d'Orsay in Paris.

Under what circumstances was it painted, I wondered? Picasso was not one to hold back when he was alone with a young model in a studio. I interviewed one of his former models once, and she told me that while Picasso never touched her or misbehaved in any way, he took her on a tour of the studio, to a little upstairs room with a bed, and started jumping on the bed hoping she would join in (she did not). It was, she recalled, a subtle attempt to seduce her. They became lifelong friends instead.

I asked Remer what she thought of Picasso's *Young Girl With A Flower Basket,* and the enormous price it fetched at auction. "I find it really tragic," she said, describing the girl as a street kid who led a rough life and who, in the painting, looked older than her years. What was most upsetting was "how much it went for, to some private person," she told me. "How could you live in a place with that painting in it?" It amounted, in her view, to the fetishization of a little girl's body.

Our discussion ended with another famous twentieth-century painting of a young girl, this one on permanent display at the Metropolitan Museum in New York: Balthus's *Thérèse Dreaming* (1938). In it, a young girl poses on a bench in an artist's studio, hands clasped over her head, eyes closed. One bent leg rests on the bench, revealing the white underwear she wears beneath her loose, lined skirt.

Remer referred me to an article she had written about the controversial painting on her website. "Most girls Thérèse's age (12 or 13) wouldn't sit like that without being asked or compelled," the article began. "Imagine how it felt to sit with your legs spread and your dress hiked up facing an older man, your next-door neighbor." What did the young girl herself think of the painting? "We don't know. No one asked. No one cared to ask."

Here is how a recent controversy around the Balthus painting unfolded.

Balthus, *Thérèse Dreaming* (1938)

Few painters can have been celebrated more vigorously in their lifetime than Balthus (Balthasar Klossowski, 1908–2001). The Polish-French artist lived long enough to attend career retrospectives of his work at the Metropolitan Museum of Art and the Centre Pompidou in Paris. He was, and is, considered an important twentieth-century artist. Yet he makes the viewer uneasy.

Balthus paintings give you a feeling of not quite knowing where you are, in time and space, or what you're witnessing. They are mysterious, eerie, and somewhat creepy depictions of modern-day scenes. Having come of age in the prewar artistic circles of Paris, Balthus has something of the Surrealist in him. His palette is full of the sickly shades of gray, ochre, and green that the Surrealists also favored.

What Balthus is best known for (hence the unease) are paintings of young girls on the very cusp of adolescence—prepubescent creatures who are about to step across the threshold to womanhood, and don't yet know what that means. Balthus had a lifelong fascination with girls of that particular age group (though he was never accused or suspected of misconduct). His paintings of these children are heavily suggestive and have erotic overtones, which can come across as inappropriate nowadays.

One particular Balthus work is, in fact, so disturbing that it hasn't been exhibited since the late 1970s. *The Guitar Lesson* (1934) shows a music session between a young teacher and her pupil that has descended into what looks like an erotic, sadomasochistic game. Inside the music room, the instructor has laid her half-naked preadolescent pupil across her lap as if she were a guitar; she pulls at the girl's tresses with one hand, and looks set to finger her pudenda with the other. It is a profoundly unnerving work, even when glimpsed online. (Balthus told a reporter that he had done it as an attention-seeking device.)

When the painting wound up in the collections of the New York dealer Pierre Matisse (son of the painter Henri Matisse) in the 1940s, he kept it in storage for three decades, exhibited it in his gallery in 1977, and then offered it as a donation to the Museum of Modern Art. But it was returned by MoMA in 1983 after the museum's president deemed it obscene and unfit for public display. (MoMA owns another Balthus, *The Street* [1933], a street scene suitable for all audiences.)

The Metropolitan Museum's own Balthus, *Thérèse Dreaming* (1938), hangs in Gallery 907 as part of the museum's permanent collection. According to the Met website, the sitter, Thérèse Blanchard, was about twelve or thirteen when she posed for the painting. "Many early twentieth-century avant-garde artists, from Paul Gauguin to Edvard Munch to Pablo Picasso, also viewed adolescent sexuality as a potent site of psychological vulnerability as well as lack of inhibition," reads the text on the Met site, "and they projected these subjective interpretations into their work. While it may be unsettling to our eyes today, *Thérèse Dreaming* draws on this history."

In December 2017—two months after allegations of sexual misconduct were first made about Harvey Weinstein—the daydreaming Thérèse became the stuff of scandal. Mia Merrill, a New York-based entrepreneur, started an online petition urging the Met to "remove Balthus's suggestive painting of a pubescent girl." Merrill said she had been "shocked to see a painting that depicts a young girl in a sexually suggestive pose," especially considering the ongoing debates around sexual assault and suggested that the Met was "perhaps unintentionally, supporting voyeurism and the objectification of children."

Merrill explained that she in no way demanded censorship or destruction of the work, and only wanted contextualizing and explanation to viewers who might otherwise find the painting "offensive or disturbing, given Balthus's artistic infatuation with young girls." It was a "small ask" given the size of the Met's collections, "how overtly sexual the painting is," and in view of the news headlines highlighting "the safety and wellbeing of women of all ages."

Merrill's petition drew 11,600 signatories—just 400 short of her target. Yet the Met refused to take the painting down. "Moments such as this provide an opportunity for conversation," said the museum's chief communications officer, Ken Weine, "and visual art is one of the most significant means we have for reflecting on both the past and the present and encouraging the continuing evolution of existing culture through informed discussion and respect for creative expression."

Supporting the Met in its decision was the National Coalition Against Censorship (NCAC), which said a cultural institution's job was to introduce the public to a wide range of cultures and artworks. It pointed to "a disturbing trend of attempts to stifle art that engages difficult subjects," and concluded, "Art can often offer insights into difficult realities and, as such, merits vigorous defense."

The *New York* magazine critic Jerry Saltz displayed similar reasoning in his column. "Like all good art, *Thérèse Dreaming* presents a paradox; it is about more than one thing at the same time. Even in our rush to protect the innocent, curtail creeps, and assume the moral high ground, art can never abandon paradox," he wrote. "And in the long run, if we remove the Balthus because it offends in the current climate, we pretty much have to remove whole wings of art from the Met."

The *Washington Post* critic Philip Kennicott went still further. Even adjusting the labels at the Met would be "a concession too far," he argued. "By that standard, the museum might have to include hundreds, if not thousands, of warning labels, and not just for works made by heterosexual men with an erotic interest in girls."

The petition was not the first instance of misgivings being publicly expressed about the art of Balthus and its unsettling representation of young girls. As early as 1984, when the Metropolitan Museum of Art gave the artist a full-blown retrospective, the critic Kay Larson expressed discomfort. "And how do I, a woman, feel about Balthus's desire?" she asked in a *New York* magazine column. "That it is a deliberate, calculated affront—an anthropological curiosity to which I claim no connection."

Larson argued that the exhibition presented "a particularly subtle case of the tendency to universalize male experience. Since the artist and almost all his critics and curators are male, his themes are 'universal' to the half of the audience that will do the bulk of the commenting," but not to her. "What if Balthus were a woman, whose paintings were brilliant descriptions of her attraction-repulsion toward men?" she asked. The critical reaction would be completely different.

Larson's argument was rejected wholesale by a male reader named George Harper, who wrote to the magazine the following month. Like many a male museumgoer at the time, Harper seemed oblivious to the possibility that the works of Balthus might seem alien or off-putting to a woman.

Harper recalled that Larson had been embarrassed "when confronted with Balthus's objects of desire (nymphets)," and that she had "made the astonishing suggestion that this obsessive, loving depiction of the female form was nothing but a subtle attempt by the artist and the curators to 'universalize male experience.' My God! So that's what Titian and Rubens and Renoir were up to. If critics like Larson had their way, the ideal nude would be a hermaphrodite."

Today, it is much more widely recognized and accepted that art, art history, and criticism have always been dominated by men, and that in a postfeminist, #MeToo era, when adult men are jailed for their misconduct toward adult women, Balthus's painting of an underage girl with her legs apart can cause profound unease. As the petitioners explained, the point is not to censor Balthus or to take down his work, but rather to explain, contextualize, and, where necessary, provide cautionary wall labels. "If we're unwilling to rethink a bit of wall text because we're scared of the precedent it might set," wrote Jillian Steinhauer in the *Walker Art Center* magazine, "how can we expect to rethink the entire system that brought the painting that wall text elucidates into the museum?"

The Balthus petition was the first major example of visual-arts activism in recent times, and raised questions that are still being asked: Who gets to show art? Where? And why?

The Balthus painting, meanwhile, still hangs on the wall of the Met, with an unaltered label. In its studied ambivalence, it continues to cause occasional discomfort, even among the world's most respected critics. He "puts me in two minds, attracted and repelled, in search of a third," wrote the *New Yorker* critic Peter Schjeldahl as he reviewed a Balthus show at the Met in 2013. "He strains the moral impunity of high art to an elemental limit, assuring himself an august, unquiet immortality."

Personally, I wonder how much impunity and immortality Balthus can enjoy, going forward. The world is heading in the opposite direction. Public opinion nowadays is on high alert when it comes to the interactions of adults and children. Children are increasingly being protected and shielded from prying eyes and from sexual predators. A male artist asking a young girl to pose like Thérèse would immediately be viewed as a child pornographer.

It's been a long time since I saw one or more works by Balthus in a show. I would wager that few, if any, Western museums would be inclined to put on a Balthus retrospective nowadays. And I wonder how long museums such as the Met will keep works such as *Thérèse Dreaming* up as part of their permanent display. Balthus's prolonged interest in underage girls is beginning to look decidedly sinister.

PUBLIC OPINION IN the West has become much more sensitive to the representation of underage girls in art. Artists today no longer have a license to paint, sculpt, photograph, film, or otherwise depict young girls and boys in the nude without risking a backlash from the news media, social media, and public opinion. If they do, they may well find themselves on the wrong side of the law.

One artwork exhibited in London in 2009 led the city's Metropolitan Police to intervene and take it down. *Spiritual America* (1983), by the American artist Richard Prince, was a photograph of a photograph of a ten-year-old Brooke Shields, who was pictured from the side, wearing no clothes and lots of makeup.

Tate Modern included a framed print of the image in its 2009–10 exhibition *Pop Life: Art in a Material World*, a survey of artists' overlaps with money, commerce, and branding. I attended the exhibition's press preview (along with numerous other journalists) and saw the image of the undressed Brooke Shields hanging on the wall—just hours before its sudden removal by the police. I still have, somewhere, a copy of the catalogue, which contains the image in question, and which, under police orders, was also immediately withdrawn from circulation.

What seemed to have alerted the police was the press coverage of the show and, in particular, of the Shields image. Officers from the obscene-publications unit of London's Metropolitan Police swooped in to pull down the picture preemptively, for fear that it breached British obscenity laws. As *The Guardian* reported at the time, the police was "keen to work with gallery management to ensure that they do not inadvertently break the law or cause any offense to their visitors."

That same Brooke Shields image had been publicly exhibited two years earlier—as part of Prince's 2007 retrospective at the Guggenheim Museum in New York. In fact, the show, *Richard Prince: Spiritual America*, was named after the image. And five years after the Tate Modern episode, an editioned print of the image sold for $3.97 million at a Christie's auction in New York. The Tate controversy most probably helped prop up its price.

WHILE SOCIETY HAS grown far less accepting of art involving children and underage models, it has become far more accepting of art that represents sex between consenting heterosexual adults. In the space of a few years, audiences and authorities in the West have gone from censoring graphic, sexually themed art to shrugging it off. This shift reflects the gender revolution that has gone on in the West in the postwar period—women entering the workplace in droves, exercising their right to vote, enjoying newly gained reproductive freedoms, and fighting male domination through the women's liberation movement.

Heterosexual sex, in life as in art, is consequently far less of a taboo. Museumgoers in major Western capitals are now accustomed to seeing explicit heterosexual content in painting, sculpture, installation, film, and performance. When a woman is shown naked in an artwork, the assumption is that it was her choice. Plenty of female artists actually choose to depict themselves in the nude.

From that perspective, art has become freer and more uninhibited than ever. Over the past few decades, ultra-explicit sexual works have been displayed or performed without the slightest intervention or attempt at censorship by the police, the judiciary, or the political authorities—even when they have pushed the boundaries of art to new extremes.

Take *Seedbed*, a previously mentioned 1972 performance by the late artist Vito Acconci. In it, Acconci took over a space inside the Sonnabend Gallery in New York and installed a low wooden ramp from the middle of the space all the way to the back wall. As visitors walked up and down the ramp, he crouched on the floor underneath and masturbated audibly, panting into a microphone, and hurling crude and sexualized words at the audience. His expletive-filled monologue was blasted through loudspeakers, forming the core of the performance, and causing what must have been extreme visitor discomfort.

Yet Acconci's crude spectacle led to no police swoops on the gallery, no naming and shaming of the dealer or artist, and no court injunctions. In fact, the show, which was one in a series of three Acconci performances at the gallery, had an uninterrupted run. (Today, Tate's website defines it as "one of the most important live artworks of the 1970s.")

Imponderabilia is another shock-and-awe art performance from the same period. Staged in 1977 by Marina Abramović and her then partner

Ulay, it involved the couple standing stark naked on either side of a very narrow doorway, which visitors had to squeeze through to enter the gallery. Staged at the Galleria Comunale d'Arte Moderna in Bologna, Italy, the performance went ahead without incidents; there wasn't a carabiniere in sight.

Then, of course, there is Jeff Koons's *Made in Heaven* series from the early 1990s: a set of large, hyperrealistic color paintings of himself and his then wife, the ex-porn star Ilona Staller (Cicciolina), engaging in graphic intercourse, their private parts in close-up view. The series has been exhibited all around the Western world (including in Tate Modern's *Pop Life* show), and never once been censored. Museums merely display it in a separate room with a warning sign (for young or squeamish audiences). *Made in Heaven*, too, is now a classic. The shock factor is pretty much gone.

What did cause scandal and uproar until relatively recently—at least in the United States—was homosexual sex. Until the dawn of the new millennium, it remained something of a taboo in socially conservative circles, and gay men and women remained a marginalized, if not stigmatized, minority.

This latent homophobia was exacerbated by America's spectacular swing to the right during the presidency of Ronald Reagan (January 1981 to January 1989). With the United States still reeling from the trauma of the Watergate scandal, and Americans mistrusting federal government, the religious right made major inroads as a force in conservative opinion—and helped get Reagan elected. Socially and politically speaking, there was a return to family values and to Christian mores. And economically speaking, the push for leaner government and for cuts to nonessential spending ended up targeting contemporary art, particularly when it dealt with topics such as homosexuality and religion. Within two weeks of Reagan's inauguration, his administration suggested that the budget of the National Endowment for the Arts—the federal, tax-funded entity in charge of distributing grants to artists and cultural institutions—be halved.

Historically, this era happened to coincide with the AIDS epidemic. AIDS was first detected in the United States in 1981, when five men were found to have contracted the disease. The following year, it spread to 335 people, 136 of whom died from it. Before long, it became a fully fledged epidemic that afflicted the gay community, mainly. By the end of 1985, some twenty thousand people suffered from it around the world. That same year, AIDS claimed its first celebrity casualty: the Hollywood actor Rock Hudson, who revealed his homosexuality late in life.

The epidemic and the fear associated with AIDS intensified the homophobia prevailing among conservative voters and the Christian right, who portrayed the disease as a punishment for what they viewed as a sinful existence.

In Washington, works of art by and about homosexuality become the target of censorship attempts by people at the highest echelons of power: the Senate, the House of Representatives, the judiciary, and the NEA. Art became the trigger for a series of surreal scenes in the nation's capital. An art catalogue was torn up by a Senator on the floor of the U.S. Senate. A touring exhibition programmed in Washington was canceled before it even opened. A prominent museum director in Cincinnati was hauled into court for daring to host that same exhibition. Senators, prosecutors, and police authorities engaged in conduct that one would expect of a sixteenth-century Inquisition tribunal, or a modern-day Middle Eastern dictatorship—not of policymakers in late-twentieth-century America.

The exhibition at the center of the uproar was the photographer Robert Mapplethorpe's *The Perfect Moment*. That single show led to a historic reshaping of the relationship between the US government, museums, and artists, and to a lasting shift in the dynamics of politics and culture.

Robert Mapplethorpe's
The Perfect Moment Exhibition (1989)

By the time the Corcoran Gallery was preparing to put on *The Perfect Moment* in Washington, D.C., Robert Mapplethorpe had just died of AIDS. The epidemic was decimating the gay community, and Mapplethorpe, who had stayed very much in the public eye throughout his debilitating illness, became one of its most high-profile victims.

At that point, Mapplethorpe was also a darling of the art world—recognized and admired for his sensitive portraits of public figures like Patti Smith, his sensual close-ups of flowers, and his homoerotic imagery. Mapplethorpe's black-and-white photographs were formally flawless: stylized and technically seamless portrayals reminiscent of the work of Edward Weston. Even his most graphic and sexualized pictures were highly sophisticated visual creations, rather than straightforward shots of male arousal such as could be found in gay porn magazines. Some of the compositions even evoked abstraction and geometry.

The Perfect Moment consisted of more than 150 images taken between 1969 and 1988. The exhibition focused on still lifes, nudes, and portraits—of Patti Smith and a host of other celebrities such as David Hockney, Cindy Sherman, and Laurie Anderson. It also included Mapplethorpe's *XYZ* portfolios.

The *Y* portfolio consisted of thirteen suggestive and eroticized photographs of flowers. The *Z* portfolio represented images of Black men. The *X* portfolio—by far the most controversial of the three—featured thirteen explicit black-and-white photographs of men in homoerotic and sometimes sadomasochistic poses. These were hardcore images of faceless, unidentifiable men who introduced dark objects into their own anus, thrust their fist into another man's anus, or urinated into another man's mouth.

Mapplethorpe included himself in that series: he pictured himself from behind, with his head turned toward the viewer, as a whip handle poked out of his naked bottom.

In addition to the *XYZ* portfolio, the retrospective included a pair of images that would almost certainly not be displayed today. They showed prepubescent children—a boy in one image, a girl in the other—whose genitals were clearly visible in the photograph.

BY THE TIME the exhibition was due to open in Washington, it had been seen in Philadelphia and Chicago without the slightest audience objection. After Washington, the show was headed for Hartford, Connecticut; Berkeley, California; and Boston. At every stop on the way, the X-rated images were to be shown in a separate enclosure, with a sign cautioning viewers against the explicit content.

So it was with complete confidence that the Corcoran Gallery announced on May 30, 1989, that the Mapplethorpe exhibition would open there on July 1 and run through September 1. The press release described the show as "an illuminating and complete documentation and examination of the artist's entire career, providing an unedited overview of the maturation of his artistic expression through a diverse range of images."

The release also quoted from a catalogue essay by the exhibition's curator, Janet Kardon, director of the Institute of Contemporary Art at the University of Pennsylvania. The institute had organized the show and received a $30,000 NEA grant for it. "Mapplethorpe captures the peak of bloom," Kardon wrote, "the apogee of power, the most seductive instant, the ultimate present that stops time and delivers the perfect moment into history."

Yet less than two weeks later, the Corcoran canceled the exhibition outright, sending shock waves through the art world and becoming an instant watershed in art history. This was a time when Washington and the Senate were up in arms over *Piss Christ*, a photograph by the artist Andres Serrano—a beneficiary of NEA funding—that pictured a crucifix floating in a container of urine (see Chapter 5). The fear was that the furor over Serrano would spread to the Corcoran and lead to the cancellation of its federal funding, which at the time totaled about $300,000 a year. As a result, the Mapplethorpe show was called off.

Christina Orr-Cahall, the Corcoran's director and chief executive, explained that while the Corcoran was a 120-year-old institution and one of the United States' three oldest art museums and that it didn't shy away from controversy, "our institution has always remained outside of the political arena, maintaining a position of neutrality on all such issues. In a city with such a great federal presence, this has been essential."

"Citizen and Congressional concerns, on both sides of the issue of public funds supporting controversial art, are now pulling the Corcoran into the political domain," Orr-Cahall added, explaining the dropout. She insisted that the move was by no means "a comment on the quality of the artist's work," nor a breach of his freedom of expression, nor was it calling into question the NEA's funding methods.

Evidently, the Corcoran cancellation was a preemptive move. As the Corcoran's board chairman, David Lloyd Kreeger, told the *New York Times* shortly afterward, "You have to consider the larger picture. The endowment has been under attack, its appropriation has been cut by the Executive again and again, only to be restored by Congress. And this is a very critical period in the appropriation process." Going ahead with a Mapplethorpe show, he argued, could result in the NEA scaling back arts funding across the board, and hurting other arts institutions around the country.

The artist community reacted as a bull would to a red rag. How could a museum such as the Corcoran self-censor in this way, calling off a major

Mapplethorpe retrospective which was opening just months after his death? In a furious backlash, a number of artists canceled their donations to the Corcoran and pulled their artworks out of its upcoming exhibitions, forcing the exhibitions to be canceled in turn.

"It is on the basis of quality, not morality, that posterity judges art," the theater critic Robert Brustein, also the artistic director of the American Repertory Theatre, wrote in the *New York Times*. "While awaiting that verdict, arts organizations must not cave in to political intimidation for fear of losing grants . . . Once subsidized artistic activity becomes subject to Government manipulation, we resemble the official culture of Stalinist Russia."

An artist-led organization, the Washington Project for the Arts, stepped in to host the Mapplethorpe exhibition in its entirety and on its own premises. The retrospective opened there on July 20, and fifty thousand people got to see it. The Corcoran cancellation was "an outright cave-in to conservative political forces who are once again trying to muzzle freedom of expression in the arts," said the Project's director, Jock Reynolds.

MEANWHILE, AND DESPITE the Washington exhibition's preemptive shutdown, a group of lawmakers latched onto the most graphic Mapplethorpe photographs and used them as a weapon in their pushback against the NEA. Mapplethorpe became the pet peeve of conservative lawmakers, an excuse for them to bemoan two phenomena that they objected to: immorality and lax government spending.

In June 1989, 105 members of the House of Representatives joined Congressman Dick Armey of Texas in sending a letter to Hugh Southern, the NEA's acting chairman, to denounce what they saw as a misuse of taxpayers' money. "We realize that the interpretation of art is a subjective evaluation," they wrote, "but there is a very clear and unambiguous line that exists between what can be classified as art and what must be called morally reprehensible trash."

Condemning "this horrible abuse of tax dollars," they concluded, "If the NEA has enough money to fund this type of project, then perhaps the NEA has too much money to handle responsibly."

The climax of the anti-Mapplethorpe crusade came the following month. In a late-night Senate session on July 26, the right-wing Senator Jesse Helms introduced an amendment (the Helms Amendment) that sought to limit the kind of art the NEA could fund—or, as Helms declared in his speech to the Senate, "prevent the NEA from funding such immoral trash in the future."

Helms completely dismissed objections by the media and the arts community that restrictions on federal funding amounted to creative censorship. He insisted that there needed to be a third way between "absolutely no Federal presence in the arts" and "granting artists the absolute freedom to use tax dollars as they wish, regardless of how vulgar, blasphemous, or despicable their works may be." That third way meant eliminating grants to "the production or creation of vulgar works."

Senator Helms then turned to the Mapplethorpe exhibition—an admittedly bizarre topic of discussion for a late-night Senate hearing. He condemned the NEA's funding of a "patently offensive collection of homoerotic pornography and sexually explicit nudes of children," and invited fellow senators to look at the catalogue. Senator Helms concluded:

> Federal funding for sadomasochism, homoeroticism, and child
> pornography is an insult to taxpayers. Americans for the most part are
> moral, decent people and they have the right not to be denigrated,
> offended or mocked with their own tax dollars. My amendment
> would protect that right. Mr. President, if Senators want the Federal

Government funding pornography, sadomasochism, or art for pedophiles, they should vote against my amendment.

The amendment he proposed, officially known as Amendment No. 420, recommended that no funds be given toward:

obscene or indecent materials, including but not limited to depictions of sadomasochism, homoeroticism, the exploitation of children, or individuals engaged in sex acts;
material which denigrates the objects or beliefs of the adherents of a particular religion or non-religion; or
material which denigrates, debases, or reviles a person, group or class of citizens on the basis of race, creed, sex, handicap, age, or national origin.

Fortunately, the amendment never became law. It would have been so broad and all-encompassing that it would have made the work of any artist impossible. As Richard Bolton wrote in his introduction to *Culture Wars: Documents from the Recent Controversies in the Arts*, had the Helms Amendment become law, the government would have had the right to "withhold funding from art critical of almost any subject." The art critic Robert Hughes, in his book *Culture of Complaint*, added: "All that a work of art would need to be de-funded, or removed from view, would be to 'offend' anyone for practically any reason at all." The NEA, Hughes warned, would become "hostage to any crank, ideologue and God-botherer in America."

The NEA decided to find a compromise solution and incorporate the spirit of the law in its practices. It asked grant recipients to promise not to make obscene works using government money. Artists preferred to turn down NEA funding than submit to the condition. In the end, that condition was dropped, too.

What the episode illustrated was a desire on the part of some senators to prevent "a progressive agenda"—or, in today's parlance, a gender-balanced and diverse agenda—from taking root. The tactics deployed were reminiscent of the McCarthy era in the late 1950s, when Senator Joseph McCarthy, during the so-called Red Scare, hunted down artists, intellectuals, and personalities suspected of being pro-Communist and enemies of the United States.

The Mapplethorpe controversy raged on into the following year, as the exhibition continued its tour of the United States. In March 1990, a month before *The Perfect Moment* was set to open at the Contemporary Art Center in Cincinnati, an obscenity trial—no less—was brought against its director, Dennis Barrie. While the First Amendment protects freedom of speech and expression, one of the grounds on which an exception can be brought to it is obscenity. The obscenity law precedent was set in a 1973 case, *Miller v. California*, which established three tests:

1. Whether the average person, applying contemporary community standards, would find that the work taken as a whole appeals to the prurient interest
2. Whether the work depicts or describes, in a patently offensive way, sexual conduct specifically defined by state law
3. Whether the work, taken as a whole, lacks serious literary, artistic, political or scientific value

The root cause of the Mapplethorpe court action was a denunciation by Citizens for Community Values, a right-wing religious organization with sixteen thousand members. As the Mapplethorpe show headed for Cincinnati, a letter went out to all of the organization's members and to eighteen thousand other residents of Cincinnati, inviting them to stop the show from opening. The Contemporary Art Center ignored the letter and pressed ahead with its April 7 opening. Only a couple of adjustments were made: people under eighteen would not be admitted, and the price of entry was doubled.

The first day of the exhibition became a moment of high drama. At around 3 p.m., a group of law-enforcement officials moved some 500 visitors off the premises as they proceeded to gather evidence inside the exhibition. Outside, an estimated 1,000 protesters shouted "Fascists!" "Gestapo, go home!"

For ninety whole minutes, the exhibition was shut down while the law-enforcement team shot a video of the photographs on display. The art of Robert Mapplethorpe suddenly turned into evidence to be used against a museum in court. The Center and its director, Barrie, were then indicted by a Hamilton County grand jury of two misdemeanor counts each: pandering, and using minors in pornography.

Barrie—who risked a year's imprisonment and a fine of up to $2,000 for putting on the exhibition—was summoned to court. Cincinnati's Contemporary Art Center became the first American museum or gallery to face prosecution for the art that it chose to display. At stake: the freedom of expression of every artist living and working in the United States of America and beyond.

The jury selected to deliver the verdict in October was, according to the *New York Times*, "mostly working-class." Only three of the eight men and women jurors had ever visited an art museum; one never had. The concern was that such a panel would judge the Mapplethorpe show harshly. The lead prosecutor was certainly severe in his closing statement, as he singled out seven of the 175 photographs in the exhibition—the ones depicting men in sadomasochistic poses, and the ones picturing naked children. "Are these van Goghs, these pictures?" he asked, as he described the images. "Is that art?"

Yet after five days of testimony from a host of American museum directors, and after Barrie's own testimony—that the Mapplethorpe photographs featured "striking . . . light and composition" and were works of art—a not-guilty verdict was pronounced to a chorus of courtroom cheers. The judge had previously explained to the jury that the five disputed photographs had to meet all three conditions laid out in the *Miller* obscenity law test, including that of lacking serious artistic value. The jury ruled that not all conditions had been met. They were citizens with little exposure to art, yet they refused to deny the artistic merit in the work of Mapplethorpe.

Today, the kerfuffle around Mapplethorpe has long died down, and the Senate-floor screams seem a very distant reality. The artist's most explicit series, the X portfolio, is now such an essential part of his oeuvre that his reputation would doubtlessly not be the same without it. Prints from the series appear regularly in exhibitions and art fairs around the world. I've lost count of the number of times I've come across one—and there isn't so much as a warning sign beside it.

There are, however, a couple of Mapplethorpe images that modern audiences would, in all probability, find unacceptable: the ones that picture the little boy and girl not wearing underwear. For reasons mentioned earlier, the world nowadays is profoundly, and understandably, sensitized to the protection of children and to the subject of child pornography. Mapplethorpe intended his photographs as works of art, not as pieces of porn. But they seem so grossly indecent to modern-day eyes that I don't imagine they can be shown any longer, even with explainers and appropriate labeling. Mentalities have shifted too far for child nudity to be tolerated in art.

The NEA Four

A month after the Corcoran cancellation in Washington, the NEA got a new boss: John Frohnmayer. An attorney from Portland, Oregon, he was no Washington insider. Nor was he an arts professional or patron with connections among the men and women steering the country's major cultural institutions. That made the job particularly tough for him to take on at a time like this.

Frohnmayer's first major funding decision, made later that year, proceeded to infuriate the arts community. He suspended a $10,000 NEA grant to an exhibition called *Witnesses: Against Our Vanishing*, which dealt with AIDS and featured images of gay sex. "I think it's essential that we remove politics from grants, and must do so if the endowment is to remain credible to the American people and to the Congress," he said. He admitted that there were works of art—Picasso's *Guernica*, the plays of Bertolt Brecht— that happened to be intensely political. But he wondered whether the Endowment should be "funding art whose primary intent is political," and concluded, "The NEA has always steered clear of that."

Conservative opinion makers were pleased. The columnist William F. Buckley Jr. said: "There remain public representatives who don't believe in the copulative imperative, that art and sex necessarily merit public support." Yet there was widespread revulsion from members of the arts community, who urged the NEA to attribute grants based on quality, not on an individual work's content.

What soon transpired was that the cause of Frohnmayer's concern was not the exhibition itself, but an essay in the catalogue. In that searing essay, the artist David Wojnarowicz (see Chapter 5) had expressed "rage" at being an AIDS sufferer, and dreamed of setting fire to Senator Helms.

Frohnmayer admitted that he was objecting to the catalogue and not to the exhibition. He rushed over to the exhibition's New York venue, Artists

Space, and reassured them that they could keep the NEA grant money—so long as it was not spent on the catalogue (which got funded separately). Yet his explanation did nothing to soothe the art world.

In June 1990, Frohnmayer opened another front in his battle with the art world. He announced that four out of eighteen NEA grants would be discontinued. The four recipients were the performance artists Karen Finley, John Fleck, Holly Hughes, and Tim Miller, three of whom were gay.

To Miller, the NEA's motivations were clear. "My work explores my identity as a gay person and as a person dealing with the AIDS crisis in an active, political way," he said. "So much of this is a homophobic attack on gay people and the visibility of gay people."

In fact, the artist that the NEA considered the most problematic of the four was Finley, a heterosexual woman. Finley had raised NEA eyebrows because of a New York performance—*We Keep Our Victims Ready*—which involved her smearing her bare chest with chocolate cake frosting while shouting out a crude text on the violation of women's bodies.

To Finley, the NEA decision was an act of censorship, plain and simple. As she later explained: "I didn't want to have happen [to me] what happened to [Lenny Bruce.] Which is stopping my ability to create. It's the biggest form of censorship, where you question yourself. When people are attacked it stops the creativity from growing."

THE DECISIONS AROUND the Artists Space catalogue and the NEA Four (as they became known) drew so much attention that some of the United States' most eminent artists cut off all ties with the NEA. In November 1989, composer and conductor Leonard Bernstein refused a National Medal of the Arts (an award that was bestowed by the president but managed by the NEA), invoking the Artists Space grant cancellation. In 1992, Stephen Sondheim, who worked with Bernstein on *West Side Story*, refused the medal too, describing the NEA as "rapidly being transformed into a conduit, and a symbol, of censorship and repression rather than encouragement and support."

Meanwhile, the NEA Four teamed up with the National Campaign for Freedom of Expression, the American Civil Liberties Union (ACLU), and the Center for Constitutional Rights to sue the NEA. The reasoning was that if the NEA could reject grants on the basis of artistic content, and make artists pledge to make "decent" art, then the art produced and shown in the United States was effectively controlled by lawmakers, government officials, and the religious right.

The right fired back with its own arguments. "What does the 'arts community' want?" asked Pat Buchanan in an incendiary *Washington Times* column. "To be honored and subsidized by a society they appear to loathe. Like spoiled children, our artists rant and rail at us; then cry 'repression' and 'censorship' when we threaten their allowance."

In the end, the NEA Four won out. As part of a partial settlement out of court in 1993, the NEA agreed that it would pay the artists sums equivalent to their withheld grants. The artists accepted the sums of money, but pursued their fight against the NEA's "decency clause," which they said was unconstitutional and a breach of First Amendment rights. (In 1998, the Supreme Court pronounced the clause constitutional on the grounds that it contained "advisory" and not "obligatory" language.)

WHAT THE NEA controversies demonstrate is the profound unease that art by and about homosexuals caused until very recently, and at the very highest levels of political power. With the Cold War over and Soviet scapegoating a thing of the past, politicians on the right of the political spectrum, in a classic demonstration of populist tactics, reached for a new enemy that they could blame and point fingers at for their own political gain. Artists living and working outside of the mainstream and receiving government grants provided easy fodder for this late-twentieth-century wave of populism. They became historic test cases in the ongoing tug-of-war between politics and culture—and proof of the enduring complexity of the relations between government and the arts.

The artists in question were all, to use a present-day expression, diverse—"asserting the realities of groups or communities that were still considered less than or un-American," wrote Michael Brenson in his book on the NEA, *Visionaries and Outcasts*. Their art was closely associated with their bodies, and a prime vehicle for the expression of their sexuality. Yet it drew immediate connections with AIDS, a disease so deadly that it had claimed the life of Mapplethorpe himself.

At the same time, the episode demonstrated that censorship of the arts is essentially pointless. Times change, mentalities evolve, and minds open. What shocks and horrifies people today is very likely to be tolerated and accepted tomorrow. The fleshy nudes in the paintings of Peter Paul Rubens surely looked indecent to many when he first showed them, yet they are now in just about every art history textbook, and Rubens is considered not a pornographer but an Old Master. What qualifies as "indecent" and "obscene" is constantly shifting. Images that would have been banned only decades ago are now studied as part of the art-historical canon. The needle is forever moving; the sands are forever shifting.

Consider the kind of pornography that the average person consumes these days on their smartphone or laptop. Until relatively recently, it would have been censored and not authorized for widespread, household consumption. Instead, in the United States today, it is perfectly lawful for a private individual to be in possession of pornographic material—except in the case of child pornography.

Graphic gay images are now considered classics, and sometimes even part of the art-historical canon. They are as widely shown, exhibited, and accepted as the pornographic images of Jeff Koons and Cicciolina. Where twenty-first-century audiences draw the line is in the representation of children in art. So long as it is innocent and decent, it is fine. But any hint of eroticism can lead to the work being taken down and land the artist in hot water.

Mentalities, in short, have evolved. Societies in the West are far less homophobic than they once were. Gay marriage is more and more common-place. Homosexual themes in art are no longer taboo, and are actually pretty widespread. Some of the world's most successful artists are LGBTQ.

These artists, however, tend, for the most part, to be white. That's where the art world still needs work: in its representation of artists of color. They are the focus next.

4.

Still No Seat at the Big Table

An enduring characteristic of Western art history is the invisibility of Black artists—an invisibility even more absolute than that of women. Female artists—or, more specifically, white female artists—started stepping out of the cultural shadows in the immediate postwar period. In the case of Black artists, recognition has taken infinitely longer. And much of it has happened recently and precipitously.

This phenomenon is tellingly illustrated by the trajectory of one particular painting. Faith Ringgold's 1967 *American People Series #20: Die* languished for five decades in the artist's studio without anyone acquiring it. Then, in 2016, it was purchased by MoMA—and ended up as one of the biggest highlights of the museum's collection rehang three years later. In fact, as mentioned in an earlier chapter, it was displayed on the wall adjacent to Picasso's *Les Demoiselles d'Avignon*.

As the Ringgold example demonstrates, American museums have been extremely slow to exhibit and acquire works by nonwhite artists. Only recently have they tried to make up for lost time. Between 2008 and 2018, a meager 2.37 percent of all artworks bought or received as gifts at thirty major American museums were by African Americans (according to a thirty-museum survey conducted in the September 2018 Burns Halperin Report, published by Charlotte Burns and Julia Halperin in Artnet News and *In Other Words*). Only 7.6 percent of exhibitions were of African American art—even though African Americans represent 14 percent of the US population.

In 2016, a student-led survey conducted by CUNY's Guttman Community College of 1,300 artists represented by New York's top forty-five commercial galleries found that 80.5 percent of the artists represented were white, and only 8.8 percent were Black—even though whites represented 64 percent and Blacks 16 percent of the population, according to the poll. (The survey was conducted on the basis of each artist's writings, gallery statements, and media coverage.)

Then came a sudden acceleration. In 2017, there was a 66 percent increase in solo and themed shows of African American artists staged by the thirty institutions polled in the Burns Halperin report. There were sixty-three such shows in total, nearly twice as many as in the previous year. And in the first nine months of 2018, a total of 439 African American artworks were bought by those museums, putting them on track to set a ten-year record.

Admittedly, this sudden attention was not evenly spread: a handful of artists got most of it, as is often the case. Of the 216 solo exhibitions held at thirty museums between 2008 and 2018, nearly a quarter were of the same ten artists. Still, there was progress.

I never entertained any illusions about the world of art and museums being an egalitarian environment granting opportunities to all. The predominance of white male artists was always obvious. Yet I hadn't realized just *how* unequal a space it was. Facts and figures such as the ones laid out above were embarrassing. Artists of color had, since forever, been all but shut out of the Western art-historical canon. Why? How could it be that, six decades after the civil rights movement in America, and after the innumerable inclusivity campaigns across the Western world, racial discrimination should remain so firmly embedded in art?

I reached out to Charlotte Burns, co-author of the report, and discovered that she was just as shocked at the survey's findings. Burns had the idea for the poll in 2018 when she kept seeing media headlines suggesting that it was "a great moment to be an African American artist." At a time of heightened racial tensions, she found it hard to believe that the art world would be a haven for Black artists. So she teamed up with her colleague Halperin to survey thirty major museums and find out more.

When the results appeared on a single spreadsheet, Burns and Halperin were floored. "We were expecting it to be bad, but we weren't expecting it to be *that* bad," said Burns. "This was a great time to be a white male artist, still."

Burns pointed out that the African American community had long been "very vocal about saying 'we are not given the same opportunities,' and people didn't believe them. The numbers showed that it was true."

What the survey also demonstrated, and what I and so many other journalists noticed, was that just as #MeToo had helped jumpstart the foregrounding of women in art, the Black Lives Matter movement was the single biggest catalyst of the sudden representation of nonwhite artists in Western exhibitions and collections. It was right there in the statistics.

Black Lives Matter was established in 2013 after seventeen-year-old Trayvon Martin was shot and killed on his way home from a shop, and his shooter was subsequently acquitted. It began as a Facebook post and a small L.A. gathering of community organizers, mothers, and artists. But in

2014—when police shot the unarmed teenager Michael Brown in Ferguson, Missouri—the movement spread all over the United States. By May 2020, when George Floyd was murdered by a police officer kneeling on his throat, Black Lives Matter had gone global, with massive demonstrations happening (mid-pandemic) all over the planet.

Black Lives Matter led to a surge of interest in Black talent. In 2015—the year after BLM demonstrations spread across the United States—museum acquisitions of African American art shot up by 63 percent (according to data published by the author Jeff Chang).

Even museum directors in Europe were swayed by the activism. "There's no question that the Black Lives Matter movement and #MeToo have given impetus to transforming how museums and galleries operate. There's a huge imperative to do this if we are to remain relevant, let alone increase our audience reach," Tate Modern's Frances Morris told me. She noted that museums were "complex organisations deeply embedded in their institutional conventions," and that while it was "relatively straight-forward to rewrite mission statements and convene racial equality task forces," it took much longer to bring about a "deep, profound, and lasting transformation."

Looking back at my own coverage of the art scene, I realized, once again, that the exclusion of nonwhite artists was implicit within it. In my first decade or so of cultural journalism, I interviewed even fewer artists of color than I did women. This was, again, not intentional. My coverage reflected the exhibitions happening at Europe's big institutions and the artists who were showcased there. Nonwhite artists were simply not getting solo shows, or even group shows, for that matter.

As the Black Lives Matter movement started sending shock waves through the sociopolitical landscape, the cultural scene started shifting, and issues of race, the underrepresentation of Black voices, and the colonial legacy started appearing in my stories. In the fall of 2017, I covered the African American artist Martin Puryear's first-ever show at a British art institution (the Parasol Unit Foundation for Contemporary Art in London). Puryear, a major American sculptor, was little known in London at the time, and my piece was one of the few that were written about the exhibition. Shortly afterward, he was selected to represent the United States at the 2019 Venice Art Biennale. From that point on, coverage on both sides of the Atlantic was never-ending.

Soon afterwards, I interviewed the African American artist Kehinde Wiley when he opened a show of new work at his London gallery (as mentioned in an earlier chapter). At the time, he was working on his painting of President Barack Obama for the National Portrait Gallery in Washington (now one of the Gallery's most popular displays).

We talked about the erasure of nonwhite people from art history, the primary focus of his art. Wiley remembered what it was like going to museums as a boy, gazing at wall after wall of eighteenth- and nineteenth-century portraits, and seeing no one who looked anything like him. When he became an artist, he started reinterpreting Old Master portraits of Napoleon Bonaparte and other kings and noblemen—and replacing those figures with young Black men. As Wiley explained, he was driven by a desire to "talk about us and what we need to see for ourselves as Black Americans," as well as "engage the history of art, and contend with all of those masterpieces."

Wiley had gone through adolescence and early adulthood feeling excluded by the art that he saw hanging in museums. So he had taken it upon himself to remedy that exclusion by replacing the blue-blooded heroes of the past with dark-skinned men of the present. He was reexamining and rewriting art history, critiquing it through a twenty-first-century prism.

In the years that followed, race and racism became a bigger and bigger part of the zeitgeist. As the *New York Times*'s cochief art critic Holland

Cotter wrote in June 2020, the killing of George Floyd spawned a "history-altering human rights movement, potentially the most consequential of the past 50 years," and "left some of our history-writing and history-preserving institutions scrambling to find ways to join."

Big art museums "offered the awkward spectacle of suddenly woke institutions competitively jostling to assert their 'solidarity' with Black Lives Matter," Cotter wrote. "And the gestures have felt both self-aggrandizing and too little too late." He observed that museum websites were suddenly covered with "we-must-do-more statements" and "random postings" of African American artists with no commentary or context.

Other publications highlighted the same trend in different ways. In December 2020, *ArtReview* magazine released its Power 100 list, an annual ranking of the most influential people in the art world. At the top of the list was not a person, but a movement: Black Lives Matter. The movement was, according to *ArtReview*, "a paradigm shift in contemporary culture" whose impact had become increasingly strong in 2020. That impact was evident "in the visibility of Black figurative painting over the past few years; in awards and appointments; in the rush by galleries to diversify their rosters; in the belated attempts to decolonize collections."

Today, nonwhite artists enjoy a higher profile than they ever have. In 2017, Jean-Michel Basquiat (who died in 1988 at the age of twenty-seven) became the most expensive US artist at auction, when his *Untitled* (1982)—a graffiti-style painting of a skull—sold for $110.5 million. That same year, Mark Bradford became the second African American artist to represent the United States at the Venice Art Biennale, the world's largest and foremost international art biennial. (The first African American artist ever to receive the distinction was Robert Colescott, in 1997.) Bradford was followed two years later by Puryear (as mentioned above). And in 2022, Simone Leigh (another prominent Black artist) is representing the United States in Venice.

As of this writing, the hottest names on the art market are African American. And their prices are soaring. One is the painter Kerry James Marshall, who in May 2018 set an auction record for the most expensive work by a living African American artist when one of his works sold for $21 million—more than four times his previous auction record. The buyer was later revealed to be the rapper Sean Combs. Other current art-market darlings include Wiley, Kara Walker, and Amy Sherald, who produced the Michelle Obama presidential portrait hanging beside Wiley's painting of Obama in Washington, D.C.

Such is the buying and selling frenzy that there is a sudden proliferation of forgeries of works by deceased African American artists such as Jacob Lawrence and Romare Bearden. Little research was done into these artists during their lifetime, so their works are harder to authenticate—and easier to fake.

Meanwhile, museums across the United States are busy appointing chief diversity officers. And in the commercial art world, top international dealer David Zwirner announced in September 2020 that he was opening a new Manhattan gallery space with an all-Black management and staff, led by Ebony L. Haynes, a former director at the Martos Gallery in New York. The aim was to give opportunities in the gallery world to people of color.

"While you could argue that strides have been made on the artist side, the art world acts almost shamefully on the employment side," Zwirner told the *New York Times*. The situation would only change "with colleagues of color at the table."

ADMITTEDLY, IN THE last decade or so, a few young African American artists have come to enjoy success and recognition early on in their careers.

I decided to ask two of them how they were being affected by the recent shifts and remedial actions in the art and museum world.

I reached out to Martine Syms (born in 1988), whom I'd met at a London dinner party. Syms—a talented video, installation and performance artist who, at age 29, had a solo show at MoMA and a profile in the *New Yorker*—told me that as of the summer of 2020, she started receiving multiple requests for collaborations from magazines, museums, panel organizers, and brands, "because I'm a visible black woman." They didn't have to do much research to find her, and it helped them "appear as though they're down for the cause." She told me she had turned down most of the offers.

I asked her for examples. She said a fashion magazine invited her to be one of several artists working on an editorial spread about the Tulsa massacre in Oklahoma in 1921, when race riots and violence led to the killing of dozens of people. She told them she didn't want to work on a project about a massacre.

A magazine that still owed her money for a story she'd shot months earlier invited her to work on a Black Lives Matter issue—and said they'd pay her what they owed already to do another shoot. "I'm like: 'If Black lives matter to you, you would already have paid me for a job I did six months ago,'" she deadpanned.

African American artists were admittedly getting more attention and work, she said, but they often still worked with much smaller budgets than their white counterparts. When it came to exhibition funding, white male artists easily got $1 million or $2 million to spend on their first or second big museum shows—far bigger sums than nonwhite artists with comparable careers. That affected the scale and size of the shows.

Another reality that the headlines overlooked was that African Americans getting exhibitions and receiving invitations to join boards and councils still experienced "a lot of microaggressions." She spoke from experience. As a member of an art-institution board and a film council, she was asked "a lot of weird questions," and had to assume that they were well-intentioned to stop herself from getting angry. At a dinner in her honor after one of her exhibitions, she was mistaken for the server. "This is an everyday experience," she said. "It's common, it's endemic. And it's particularly endemic to art, because you're dealing with extreme wealth."

The artist Adam Pendleton (born in 1984) was similarly circumspect about the recent wave of attention paid to nonwhite artists. He said it was not the first time that the spotlight was on them. He told me that he looked at everything from "the funny vantage point of being both a young artist and an old artist at the same time"—he had started exhibiting at age twenty-one, some fifteen years earlier. Every five to ten years, he had seen a group of artists emerge, get picked up by two or three galleries, get attention, "and then everybody moves on," he said.

In short, there was a long history of artists being "in and out of the cultural conversation." The problem was that in the case of Black artists such as Sam Gilliam, for example, "the support was not there to sustain that career, decade after decade, in the same way that it was there for an artist like Gerhard Richter."

What was missing was the follow-up and the attention to detail, because the power structures remained the same. "It's not as though the shape of the table has changed," he said. "It's rather: 'We now have the chief diversity officer, so your voice matters, but you're at that table over there. The big table is still right here.'"

To get a better grasp of race as a marker of identity, I read the American historian Francis Fukuyama's 2018 book *Identity*. It provided a solid historical analysis of how "identity politics" came about.

Back in 1788, at the time of the ratification of the U.S. Constitution, the only people with full political rights in the United States were property-owning white men. Gradually, those rights were granted to non-property-owning white men, African Americans, indigenous people, and women. Yet discrimination remained "shamefully" entrenched: laws banned Black children from being educated alongside white ones and prevented women from voting. So even after desegregation and women's suffrage became law, members of those long-marginalized categories continued to identify themselves by those categories. That's when identity politics was born.

Even when each group was given the choice of being treated in exactly the same way as the dominant groups in society, it remained wedded to the idea of having a separate identity for its members, and define them "as *different* from the mainstream society." Women's movements no longer wished to behave and think like men. Groups such as the Black Panthers or the Nation of Islam took pride in Black people's own traditions, rather than pursuing "what the broader society wanted them to be."

Identity politics was, in other words, "a natural and inevitable response to injustice." But it had been dismissed as "political correctness" after a small number of left-wing thinkers, writers, and students had made "more extreme" identity-related claims—calling for alterations to university curricula, or accusing whites who borrowed from them as committing "cultural appropriation." The words and deeds of this minority were taken to represent the views of the left as a whole. And the result was culture wars.

To Fukuyama, "the reality for many marginalized groups continues as before: African Americans continue to be objects of police violence, and women continue to be assaulted and harassed." To make headway, and be recognized and acknowledged, they have to differentiate themselves from the rest of society. That goes for the art world too. Unless women artists and

Black artists are not singled out and paid attention to, the world will go on as it always has, unjustly and unfairly.

WITH THESE CONVERSATIONS and this research in mind, I looked for further evidence of the marginalization of African Americans in US museums and galleries, and in the art world as a whole. When we spoke, MoMA's Ann Temkin acknowledged the museum's own erratic trajectory, and pointed me in the direction of a 2019 MoMA publication that documented that trajectory. The book was titled *Among Others: Blackness at MoMA*. In the opening essay, authors Charlotte Barat and Darby English referred to MoMA's "paltry track record" in terms of representation of Black artists. But they hastened to add that it wasn't "all bad news."

"The assumption is false that this Museum, a frequent target of criticism because of its authority and capital, has had no meaningful involvement with black artists, or with issues stemming from racial blackness," they wrote. "It has; in truth, MoMA's historical relationship with black artists and black audiences is an uneven one, alternating between moments of pioneering initiative and episodes of neglect and worse."

Temkin validated that assessment. She said the book chronicled "the way in which there was always *almost* change, and then we'd go backwards," she said. That was because "there was just such an incredible amount of current of history against which any innovations had to kind of swim," and so much "built-in conservatism" that came from being a ninety-year-old institution widely regarded as an authority, "even if our roots were completely radical."

The book was organized chronologically, beginning in 1934—five years after the museum was founded. That year also marked the first time that MoMA exhibited a Black American artist: Earle Richardson, who was included in a group show. Two years later, several other Black American artists were shown in an exhibition of "modern primitives" (a term used at the time to describe artists who had not received a formal art education).

Then, in 1937, came MoMA's first solo show by a Black artist: the limestone sculptor William Edmondson, who was an autodidact. The accompanying press release, which appeared to have been copied from a text drafted by the artist's patrons in Nashville, described the artist as "a Negro of Nashville, Tennessee," with "no art training and very little education." Edmondson was, the release added, a "simple, almost illiterate, entirely unspoiled" artist who was likely to have "never seen a piece of sculpture not his own."

The show became a sensation and drew abundant media coverage, focusing predominantly on the fact that the artist was Black. Yet Edmondson himself never got a chance to attend his own exhibition in New York. Nor did he ever meet Alfred Barr, the museum's founding director.

In the years and decades that followed, there were a succession of other firsts. In 1941, Jacob Lawrence became the first African American to be represented by a New York gallery (the Downtown Gallery). In 1970, the Whitney Museum of American Art staged its first solo show by an African American sculptor, Melvin Edwards. In 2014, Carrie Mae Weems became the first African American woman to receive a major retrospective exhibition at the Guggenheim Museum.

Yet many other great African American talents passed away without witnessing the breakthroughs. The painter Norman Lewis, who died in 1979, made a wise prediction, his daughter Tarin Fuller recalled. "He said to us, 'I think it's going to take about thirty years, maybe forty, before people stop caring whether I'm black and just pay attention to the work,'" she told the *New York Times* in 2015. Unfortunately, more than forty years have passed, and people are still not just paying attention to the work: They are still identifying Lewis as Black, and showing, promoting, and collecting his art largely because of it.

Sometime around the early 1990s, a number of smaller and more community-oriented American museums began actively including nonwhite artists. These were often ethnically specific museums, or museums in ethnically diverse neighborhoods, such as the Studio Museum in Harlem—which, under Thelma Golden, would go on to play a pioneering role in this regard—and the Bronx Museum of Art. They nurtured, collected, and exhibited a diverse roster of artists who were largely overlooked by the mainstream art world at the time. These same artists are, today, frenziedly fought over by dealers, auction houses, and collectors.

To find out what it was like working for those institutions back then, I turned to the American curator Lydia Yee, who had been a senior curator at the Bronx Museum of the Arts in New York in the 1990s, and was now the chief curator of the Whitechapel Gallery in London. Yee confirmed that questions of diversity and equality in museum programming and staffing were being raised three decades ago—just not in a far-reaching and enduring way. There were "some changes in mainstream museums," she said. "They would hire one person of color in a curatorial position, but not make any other systemic changes." Had progress been "more sustained from that moment," she noted, "maybe our museums today would look very different."

The early 1990s also saw the staging of one particular exhibition that is now considered a watershed in discussions of art and diversity: the 1993 Whitney Biennial. Artists included in it all tackled questions of gender, race, sexuality, and class—exactly the themes that are now at the top of museum agendas. The Whitney's director, David A. Ross, spelled out the stakes in a catalogue preface that could have been written today.

"Communities are at war, both with and at their borders. Issues of nation and nationality, ethnic essentialism, cultural diversity, dissolution and the politics of identity hang heavy in the air," he wrote. "These issues have impressed themselves upon us with an undeniable urgency. For inherent to a museum of American art is the responsibility to question as we celebrate, to provoke as well as to conciliate."

Highlights of the survey included a real-life video recording by George Holliday of Rodney King being beaten by the Los Angeles police; Pat Ward Williams's photographic mural of five young black men, with the all-caps, graffiti-style inscription "What you lookn at"; and Gary Simmons's row of gold-plated sneakers worn by invisible figures who seemed to be in a police lineup. To top it off, the artist Daniel J. Martinez designed museum admission buttons with the slogan: "I can't imagine ever wanting to be white."

The show was "less about the art of our time than about the times themselves," wrote the *New York Times* critic Roberta Smith in her review, adding that it could easily have been subtitled "The Importance of Being Earnest." Nevertheless, wrote Smith, "this Biennial is a watershed. In some ways it is actually a better show than usual, simply because it sticks its neck out." It was brave enough to take a stance, and was one of the most ethnically diverse Whitney Biennials that the museum had ever put on. Personally, I would have liked to be there to see it.

Other critics found the 1993 Biennial irredeemably bad. "I hate the show," wrote the *New York Times*'s Michael Kimmelman. He said the Biennial displayed "virtually no sensitivity" to "art that aspires to something more than political sloganeering and self-indulgent self-expression." Over at the *Village Voice,* Peter Schjeldahl wrote that it "really may have been the worst ever."

"The show was rough and vulgar," he explained much later, in April 2016, when interviewed for a *New York* magazine article titled "How

Identity Politics Conquered the Art World". "I reacted against that. I resisted the truth that it embodied a necessary force of history, squaring the little art world with big values of democracy. But truth will tell, and I came around. Art survived just fine. The event was good for society and, gradually, by the way, for me."

The exhibition was also a textbook illustration of identity politics being applied to visual art. At the time, it sparked a backlash, and was denounced as the very embodiment of "political correctness." The term, coined by conservatives, soon seeped into general usage and took on derogatory connotations. Artists themselves started feeling uneasy about being defined according to their gender, race, and/or sexuality. As a consequence, diversity was promptly pushed onto the back burner.

Today, critics and curators see that Biennial as a milestone in art history. It "marked the effective end of visual culture's being mainly white, Western, straight, and male," wrote Jerry Saltz and Rachel Corbett in the April 2016 *New York* magazine article. Prefiguring some of the conclusions laid out in this book, they explained, "the transformation unleashed by the culture wars is not just about representation, diversity, numbers, and good little humanists wagging self-righteous fingers. It's about the way culture is formed, how art is made—and what counts as art. For the first time, biography, history, the plight of the marginalized, institutional politics, context, sociologies, anthropologies, and privilege have all been recognized as 'forms,' 'genres,' and 'materials' in art. Possibly the core materials."

By the turn of the millennium, there was a revival of interest in Black artists on the part of galleries and collectors, according to Michael Shnayerson's 2019 book, *Boom: Mad Money, Mega Dealers, and the Rise of Contemporary Art*. That was thanks to a series of exhibitions put on at the Studio Museum in Harlem and its trailblazing director, Golden. The first of those shows, staged in 2001 and titled *Freestyle*, featured the work of twenty-eight artists including Bradford.

"Both mid-level and mega galleries were now vying for black artists," Shnayerson wrote. Why? For one thing, "first-rate black artists had been previously overlooked." Secondly, art by African American artists had started hanging on the walls of white collectors, so mainstream galleries were representing more of these artists. By 2013, Black art was "not just financially appealing to collectors, it was obligatory for dealers."

TODAY, THE QUESTIONS of race and the representation of marginalized minorities have pushed their way to the very forefront of the mainstream cultural conversation in the United States. The debate is no longer taking place in small community centers or among a handful of academics. It tops the agenda at major institutions, dominates the headlines and the hashtags. The question is: Are we witnessing a true revolution this time, an irreversible shift toward the representation of nonwhites in the art world? Are nonwhite artists and art-world professionals finally enjoying equal rights and opportunities? And have we finally put the issue of color behind us, as the African American artist Norman Lewis predicted we would, right around now? When I put the question to American curators and art historians, the answer was—not quite.

One art-world personality I probed was Aaron Cezar, founding director of the Delfina Foundation in London, which runs a high-profile artist residency program in London. Cezar—a Louisiana-born Creole and a Princeton University graduate—moved to London a couple of decades ago and has never left. We met at the Delfina Foundation's elegant headquarters in a townhouse not far from Buckingham Palace.

Cezar remembered touring the Art Basel contemporary-art fair in 2019 and being struck by the sheer number of works by artists who were, as he put it, Black and queer like himself. "There is something unsettling about that," he observed. "It feels like it's completely market driven, not driven by any real intention to diversify the gallery program." Collectors, he said, seemed to be saying: "'It's cool right now to appear more progressive by having a Black queer artist on my wall.'"

He also realized that the shift was driven by the fact that there was money to be made from all this by gallerists and dealers. "You're not going to take that much risk if you don't think that there's a market trend," he pointed out. And there was no telling how long the trend would last: "If the pendulum has gone way over to one side, it's easy to come back from that."

When I subsequently interviewed Cuban American curator Coco Fusco, she also emphasized the importance of money. "This is not the first time in the postwar period that the world has gone through a period of paying attention to people of color," she said.

The difference was the source of the funding. Between the 1990s and the global financial meltdown of 2008, culture was "privatized," she pointed out—meaning there was a boom in contemporary art investing and speculation by private individuals and corporations (accompanied by a reduction in public funding or the arts). Suddenly, collectors from all over the world—with international perspectives and not just Eurocentric ones—became important to auction houses and museums. These collectors came from China, India, Russia, and the Middle East, and showed particular interest in artists hailing from their regions. Cultural funding became much more global.

So museums' collections and programming diversified to reflect those new international benefactors, according to Fusco—not because of sudden pangs of social consciousness on the part of the institutions. "You get a kind of spreading out of where the money comes from," she explained. "That, more than politics or morality, has changed the curatorial policies of major museums that are trying to cater to those of that wealth." In short, the changes we were witnessing were not "some kind of moral awakening on the part of white people with power," but a reflection of what museums could get their boards to approve and acquire.

WHATEVER THE TRUE motivations and the hidden reasons, identity politics now dominates the world of mainstream art and museums. Long-marginalized communities are suddenly being foregrounded, and members of those communities are making their voices instantly heard via the bull-horn that is social media.

In some cases, more activist voices are reacting to centuries of exclusion by being exclusionary themselves—taking offense when their community's history and imagery are represented by white artists. The debate around cultural appropriation has flared up in the art world. And in recent years, it has engulfed two particular artworks, both by white American artists.

The first is Dana Schutz's painting *Open Casket* (2016), which shows the murdered Black teenager Emmett Till. The second is Sam Durant's *Scaffold* (2012), a sculpture that evokes the gallows used in seven historic executions, including one involving Native Americans.

Dana Schutz, *Open Casket* (2016)

On the evening of August 24, 1955, a fourteen-year-old Black boy by the name of Emmett Till walked into a grocery store owned by a white couple in Mississippi to buy some candy. He had an exchange that lasted less than a minute with Carolyn Bryant, the twenty-one-year-old store owner, then walked out. No one knows for sure what he said or did in that time. Before dawn on August 28, he was kidnapped, beaten, and brutally tortured, then shot in the head by a pair of white men (Bryant's husband and brother-in-law). They fastened his disfigured body with barbed wire to a bulky cotton-gin fan and tossed him into the river. After the body was retrieved three days later, a funeral was held for the boy in his hometown of Chicago, drawing tens of thousands of people. His body was placed in an open coffin, at his mother's request, so that everyone could see his mutilated face. Thanks to the photographers present, the face of Emmett Till became etched in the American consciousness.

The tragedy of Till's murder and its place in American history has, unexpectedly, become a focus of the contemporary art world—thanks to *Open Casket*, Schutz's semi-abstract oil painting of that famous posthumous photograph. The painting came to public attention in 2017, when the curators of that year's Whitney Biennial in New York chose to include it, along with two other works by Schutz, in their high-profile exhibition. The canvas tackled the subject of race, which was a primary focus of the exhibition. As its cocurator Mia Locks explained in the exhibition catalogue, while discussions about race and the structural asymmetries in society were taken up in public conservations and by the Black Lives Matter movement, "it's not always been the case in American history, or art history for that matter, that we've talked about these conditions in a direct way. This is happening right now, and it feels necessary to declare this as a moment—to think not just about race but about systemic racism, and how the various power structures that are in place are enmeshed." She dismissed the assumption that "artists of color or women artists or those whose identities are more marked would be the only ones to address these issues. In our show, questions of inequity and asymmetry are driven by artists thinking across lines, developing ideas about allyship and coalition politics that go beyond the limited frameworks of the past." In other words, any artist was free to tackle the subject of race; there were no restrictions or demarcations along identity or racial lines.

What the curators never anticipated was that that very notion would be disputed from the exhibition's opening day, as protests erupted on site and on social media, coupled with demands that the painting be removed and even destroyed. The message was clear: Schutz, a white American artist, had no right to depict—and, by extension, appropriate and profit from—the killing of the Black boy. Evidently, by choosing to paint Emmett in his open coffin, Schutz had stepped on a live wire. For a well-known white artist to represent a Black victim on canvas—and to exhibit that canvas inside a predominantly white New York museum—was, to some, outrageous.

That outrage was transmitted by two people on Facebook. The first was the young African American artist Parker Bright. On March 17, 2017, as the Whitney Biennial opened its doors to the public, Bright staged a peaceful protest in front of *Open Casket*. Holding his cameraphone aloft, he recorded a Facebook live video of himself, rotating the device to give a 360-degree view of the gallery. He then took off his red puffer jacket to reveal a T-shirt with messages scribbled on it with a Sharpie marker. On the front was a circle containing the words "Lynch Mob" (spelled backward). On the back were three words: "BLACK DEATH SPECTACLE." A visitor offered to film Parker with his cameraphone, so he turned to face the painting with his arms spread out, the message on the back of his T-shirt clearly legible.

He then explained on camera that he was demonstrating against the piece because it was an injustice to the Black community, and because Schutz "doesn't have the privilege to speak for Black people as a whole, or for Emmett Till's family." He said African Americans had no access to the museum on account of its $22 admission fee, so the work had no place at the Whitney. "No one should be making money off of a Black dead body. That's what I feel, especially during the Black Lives Matter movement," he said, and especially not Schutz, a white painter, who would "most likely" go on to sell the work for nearly $1 million. His message: "I don't think Black people should be talked for by anyone who is non-Black."

For a few days, Bright continued to demonstrate peacefully in front of the painting. At times he engaged in conversations about it with visitors. At other times, he stood in front of it, alone or with a few other protesters, to try to block it from visitors' view.

Meanwhile, within hours of Bright's Facebook live, Hannah Black (a British-born Black artist and writer) fired the second salvo against the painting. She posted an open letter to the Whitney curators on Facebook. It was signed by thirty other artists whom she identified as nonwhite. The letter went viral. It demanded that the Whitney remove *Open Casket* "with the urgent recommendation that the painting be destroyed and not entered into any market or museum."

Her argument: that "it is not acceptable for a white person to transmute Black suffering into profit and fun, though the practice has been normalized for a long time . . . The subject matter is not Schutz's; white free speech and white creative freedom have been founded on the constraint of others, and are not natural rights. The painting must go."

The Whitney stood firm and kept the painting on display. The Biennial's two curators, Locks and Christopher Y. Lew, were asked to respond to the protests by Artnet News. They explained that the Biennial highlighted different aspects of human experience, including violence, racism, and death. *Open Casket* was "an unsettling image that speaks to the long-standing violence that has been inflicted upon African Americans. For many African Americans in particular, this image has tremendous emotional resonance. By exhibiting the painting, we wanted to acknowledge the importance of this extremely consequential and solemn image in American and African American history and the history of race relations in this country. As curators of this exhibition, we believe in providing a museum platform for artists to explore these critical issues."

Social-media reactions to *Open Casket* ranged from fury at the artist—"Burn This Shit, Bitch"—and questions about why there were no images of Till's murderers, to perplexity that empathy toward Black people should be viewed as racist, and concern that the destruction of art might be followed by the destruction of books and then even people. Clearly the Schutz painting had split opinion right down the middle.

Prominent personalities of color expressed their shock at the condemnations of Schutz. On the daytime television program *The View*, cohost Whoopi Goldberg scolded Black, the anti-Schutz petitioner, without ever naming her. "You may be an artist, but you need to grow up," Goldberg said. "If you are an artist, young lady, you should be ashamed of yourself. Because if somebody decides they don't like your art, then what?"

The artist Kara Walker took to social media to defend Schutz, without naming her. "The history of painting is full of graphic violence and narratives that don't necessarily belong to the artists [*sic*] own life," she wrote. "I am more than a woman, more than the descendant of Africa, more than my fathers [*sic*] daughter. More than black more than the sum of my experiences thus far . . . art often lasts longer than the controversies that greet it. I say this as a shout to every artist and artwork that gives rise to vocal outrage. Perhaps it too gives rise to deeper inquiries and better art."

In a piece in the July 2017 issue of *Harper's* magazine, the British author Zadie Smith recalled going to see *Open Casket* with her two young children after reading the petition against it. Like the petition's initiator, Black, she is biracial and not American, she wrote. "How black is black enough," she wondered, for an artist to be able to engage with a subject? "The solution remains as it has always been. Get out (of the gallery) or go deeper in (to the argument)," she said. "Write a screed against it. Critique the hell out of it.

Tear it to shreds in your review or paint another painting in response. But remove it? Destroy it?"

Within the African American community, sensitivities around the figure of Emmett Till are understandably huge. His murder was one of the principal triggers of the American civil rights movement. Of late, he has become an emblem of black sacrifice in the midst of the Black Lives Matter movement, as white-on-black violence prevails, and unarmed African American youths are routinely killed with impunity.

What makes Till's tragedy resonate with the proponents of the Black Lives Matter movement is that no one was ever punished for his killing, either, even though a trial was held a month later. At the trial, Bryant testified that the boy came in asking for candy, and when she held out her hand for his money, he caught it and said, "How about a date, baby?" According to Bryant, he then grabbed her by the waist, indicated (using an unprintable word) that he had been with white women before, and when she rushed to her car to get the pistol under the seat, he whistled at her. "I was just scared to death," she said.

When all was said and done, Till's two killers were released from custody—although they later confessed to his murder in a magazine interview. Worst of all, when author Timothy B. Tyson interviewed her for his 2017 book *The Blood of Emmett Till*, Bryant admitted that some of the details she gave the court were untrue. "Nothing that boy did could ever justify what happened to him," she said.

For Schutz, *Open Casket* is an unusual work. Unlike her others, it is inspired by real-life events, namely photographs of the teenager as he appeared to mourners in his coffin. A semi-abstract close-up, coarsely painted in parts, it depicts Till from the waist up, dressed in a tuxedo. His features are partially recognizable; you can make out the left eye, and the mouth. The most striking element is a gash across his nasal area. That gash, and the swollen mouth, might suggest aggression; then again, they might not. If it weren't for the title, the average viewer would not associate this canvas with a historic 1950s lynching. There is no sentimentality in the representation, no plea for compassion.

Schutz grew up in suburban Detroit, was raised by Jewish parents who were both teachers, and decided at age fifteen to be an artist. Her mother, an art teacher, taught her how to stretch canvas and let her paint every day in the basement of the family home. After art school in Cleveland and New York, Schutz was spotted for her singular style—a mix of social realism and caricature—and for a set of paintings of figures sneezing. By 2001, the year of her graduation, she was signed on by a gallery, and two years later, showing work at the prestigious Venice Art Biennale.

Schutz became intrigued by the story of Emmett Till when she heard his name repeatedly invoked in the aftermath of the August 2014 police shooting of eighteen-year-old Michael Brown in Ferguson, Missouri. When she met the *New Yorker* writer Calvin Tomkins at her New York studio in 2016 (for a profile piece published after the Whitney Biennial), she told him that she had been wanting to do a painting of Till "for a while now, but I haven't figured out how . . . It's a real event, and it's violence. But it has to be tender, and also about how it's been for his mother. I don't know, I'm trying." When they met again, she appeared still to be haunted by the episode, and riddled with questions about how to depict it. It was hard to avoid making it a painting of the grotesque. Yet it interested her nevertheless, because of its astonishing relevance, she said: "It's something that keeps on happening. I feel somehow that it's an American image."

By October of that year, Schutz had completed the painting, and displayed it without incident in an exhibition at her gallery in Berlin. She told Tomkins that there was "so much uncertainty" around the painting. "You think maybe it's off limits, and then extra off limits," she said. "But I really feel any subject is O.K., it's just how it's done. You never know how something is going to be until it's done."

After the controversy, Schutz commented in a statement issued by the Whitney: "I don't know what it is like to be Black in America but I do know what it is like to be a mother. Emmett was Mamie Till's only son. The thought of anything happening to your child is beyond comprehension. Their pain is your pain," she said. She made the painting to empathize with the boy's mother. "Art can be a space for empathy, a vehicle for connection," she explained. "I don't believe that people can ever really know what it is like to be someone else (I will never know the fear that black parents may have) but neither are we all completely unknowable."

I HAVE SPOKEN about Schutz's work and the accompanying controversy with many of the people I interviewed for this book. They have expressed reservations about it. For example, one curator of color said that by turning the graphic image of Emmett Till's body into a work of abstraction, Schutz had flattened it, diminished its potency, and taken away the very purpose of leaving his coffin open: to convey the extent of the tragedy. Yet no one agreed that Schutz should be banned from making a painting on the subject because she was white. As for the calls for her work to be destroyed, every single one of my interviewees found them inadmissible.

My standpoint is similar. Bright—an artist and arts activist—was completely in his right to stage a demonstration in front of the painting, wear a T-shirt with messages across the front and back, and livestream the demonstration on Facebook. On the livestreamed video (which is available for viewing on his Facebook page), Bright's dialogue with visitors to the

Biennial was peaceful and respectful. Protest is the very stuff of democracy, and museums are places of openness and free expression. Everyone has a right to dislike a painting and voice their displeasure.

I could also understand the perplexity that Bright and other African Americans might feel to discover that what was probably the first mainstream artwork on the subject of Emmett Till should be the work of a successful white artist, and should be displayed at the Whitney Biennial, a ticketed and high-profile exhibition. Emmett Till was a symbol of quasi-prophetic significance to African Americans. Why, they asked, should he not be portrayed by an African American?

Yet I am also of the opinion that Schutz had every right to produce that painting. Her skin color did not disqualify her from doing so. Most of all, I feel, no artist's work—no matter how sensitive or offensive or controversial—should ever be threatened with destruction or destroyed.

Yet not long after *Open Casket,* another artwork exhibited in the United States faced similar calls for destruction, and met a singular fate.

Sam Durant, *Scaffold* (2012)

In 2012, the American artist Sam Durant produced a sculpture titled *Scaffold* that was a monumental wood-and-steel composite of the gallows used in seven US-government-sanctioned executions held between 1859 and 2006. One of those executions was the hanging of thirty-eight Dakota Indian men in Mankato, Minnesota, in 1862, the largest mass execution in the history of the United States—ordered by President Abraham Lincoln during the US–Dakota war, in the week that the Emancipation Proclamation was signed. *Scaffold* also represented the 1996 execution of Billy Bailey, the last execution by hanging in the United States; and the 2006 execution of Iraqi leader Saddam Hussein, three years after his overthrow in a US-led invasion. Durant intended it as a reflection on US history, race, the criminal justice system, and capital punishment.

In May 2017, just months after the Dana Schutz incident at the Whitney Biennial, the sculpture was installed at the Minneapolis Sculpture Garden, an outdoor space curated by, and located next to, the Walker Art Center. Yet a week or so before the sculpture garden was set to reopen after a lengthy closure, angry protesters gathered around the sculpture. Their objections: that a white Los Angeles artist was exhibiting a symbol of Native American tragedy and pain on a site in Minnesota that was once owned by the Dakota people—and that no Native American had been consulted in the installation phases of this project. Placards tacked onto the iron fence around *Scaffold* read: TAKE IT DOWN: GENOCIDE IS NOT ART (with sketches of nooses); BURN IT DOWN; FEELS LIKE 1862: EXECUTION IS NOT ART; NOT YOUR STORY; and NOT IN MY ANCESTORS' NAMES.

"When I first saw it, I had this huge anxious feeling and broke down in tears," said Kate Beane, a Dakota woman working as a community liaison for the Minnesota Historical Society in an interview with *Hyperallergic*. "I don't think the Walker or the artist took into consideration what kind of impact a structure like that would have on a community of people who have been impacted by historical trauma."

Durant immediately responded publicly by saying that his aim had been to denounce "the racial dimension of the criminal justice system in the United States, ranging from lynchings to mass incarceration to capital punishment." His sculpture was "a learning space for people like me, white people who have not suffered the effects of a white supremacist society and who may not consciously know that it exists." And he conceded that the protests had "shown me that I made a grave miscalculation in how my work can be received by those in a particular community."

The Walker's director, Olga Viso, apologized for the "anger and sadness" that the work had produced, and agreed to remove it. After a mediation effort involving Dakota elders, the artist handed over the intellectual property of his work. The work was dismantled, and later destroyed. The Walker, meanwhile, pledged to "make systemic changes" internally to prevent another episode of the kind, admitting that its existing setup had led it "to not sufficiently anticipate community reaction." It was important to "proceed with greater sensitivity around context, intentions, interpretation, and outreach."

I reached out to the artist, who now lives in Berlin, to find out more about the episode. Durant told me that his intention, in making the work, had been to encourage viewers to "think about American history as something that's connected to both imperialism and death and violence and control." He was initially "floored" that the Walker was inviting him to exhibit such an "explicitly political" work in the sculpture garden.

When he heard about the protests, his immediate reaction was to feel "awful that the work was so traumatizing" to Native Americans. He agreed with the Walker that the protests needed to "be deescalated," especially since these were "a group of people that I wanted to accommodate any way I could."

Recalling the mediation meeting, he said there were around thirty people in the room, including Dakota elders and observers from other tribal Native American governments. There were also representatives from the city, the state, and the parks department, a state-run organization. The Dakota elders and representatives said they wanted the sculpture gone— taken down. "Many of them were descendants of the men that were executed. They just talked about all these kinds of traumas that were being triggered," said Durant. "The claims that were made against the work were very serious and valid."

Durant said what he realized in the process was that the Walker was located in a city, Minneapolis, with the largest Native American population in the United States, and that there were "longstanding issues between the Dakota and the city and the state." *Scaffold* seemed to him to be "a kind of lightning rod for all kinds of things that had been happening for a long period of time."

Durant decided right there and then that he no longer needed the work anymore, as it wasn't serving either him or the community, and that he was in no way willing to "traumatize this group of people." Nor would he "insist on my right of freedom of expression and all of this stuff that usually you would do as an artist," because of their history and "the kind of slow-grinding genocide that continues—if you look at one of the definitions of genocide, which is the destruction of language and culture."

The Dakota started talking about whether to bury or burn the work, and how to "subject the physical materials to a transformative process" that would be healing and spiritual. It was, for Durant, a "very moving emotional experience." When they asked him to hand over the copyright to the work, he said, "Yes, why not?"—without, he recalled, measuring what repercussions would have on other artists going forward. "I didn't need to do it. But at the time, in the heat of the moment, it felt okay."

After the meeting, there was a press conference, and it was announced that the sculpture would be taken down, and its components—different kinds of local wood—would be given to the Dakota to dispose of in a ceremonial manner. A few days later, a Native American construction company took the work down. It was stored, then buried by the Dakota in undisclosed locations around Minnesota.

Had the museum consulted the Dakota community, or Native American staff members, the reaction might have been anticipated: "It's very easy to upset people and traumatize people who have a history of oppression," said Durant.

For the artist, the episode was "really traumatic. I'm not going to sugarcoat it. I had a hard couple of years it was and it's still hard." He remembered being portrayed in a very negative way on social media, "being called a racist and a white supremacist and an ignorant white guy who shouldn't be sticking his nose in other people's problems, and just really nasty stuff."

He said that was the nature of social media, and its impact was substantial. "Social media did play a role in kind of blowing us up into a global event," he recalled. "If I had to choose something to be famous for this would not be it." The artist emphasized that while he sometimes felt "terrible" about it, "I didn't do anything wrong. The work was misunderstood because the Walker put the sculpture up without consulting their community. I just have to learn from what happened as I do my work going forward."

Durant said he had been commissioned to produce a new version of the work, referencing European history this time. "They're all representations of executions that took place in European colonies," he said. The sculpture is "highly abstracted, so that nobody would ever be able to recognize a particular structure."

THE EPISODE TAUGHT both the artist and the Walker Art Center a lesson that neither would forget. Yet it also served as a cautionary tale for museums all over the world. The lesson was that they should be in tune with their local communities and recruit staff from those communities to be aware of cultural sensitivities and avoid triggering reactions of the *Scaffold* kind.

This is not a case of excessive political correctness, or of tiptoeing around minorities, or of exaggerated prudence. It's common sense. In contemporary museums, it is advisable to have a staff that reflects the diversity of the population at large. And when exhibitions come up, the institution not only needs to prepare its audiences for them, but it needs to prepare internally for discussions that might come up around those artworks. Decisions about exhibitions need to come to all staff well in advance. That way, if an artwork or theme is likely to cause offense—as was the case with *Scaffold*—an alert system is in place to avoid its display, not to mention its eventual destruction.

The View from Britain

As ever with debates and trends that originate in the United States, there is a spillover effect into the rest of the Western world, starting with English-speaking territories. Britain has recently and very visibly awakened to issues of race and diversity. Exhibitions of works by nonwhite artists are appearing everywhere in the United Kingdom. Much of the attention, there again, has coincided with the Black Lives Matter movement.

As the Tate Modern director Frances Morris told me, artists of color were present and visible in art schools and galleries for many decades. Yet they "remained largely invisible as part of the 'official' narrative," meaning within institutions such as Tate. It was something of a paradox, because London was "one of the most demographically diverse cities in the world," and museumgoers were "increasingly hungry" for art that represented the huge variety of communities and histories.

Tate set out in recent years to correct that imbalance. In 2017, Tate Modern staged *Soul of a Nation: Art in the Age of Black Power*, a survey of African American art between 1963 and 1983. For London museumgoers accustomed to retrospectives of Gauguin and Matisse (gorgeous though such exhibitions were), *Soul of a Nation* was a complete eye-opener, drawing a completely new crowd of visitors. The show became something of a blockbuster in its own right, and traveled to two American institutions including the Brooklyn Museum, making waves there, too. It also received support from three big American foundations, including the Ford Foundation.

Morris wrote in the exhibition's catalogue that while Tate had a long history of collecting and showing American art from the period, "until recently Black American artists' work was under-recognized." The exhibition grew out of "our determination to transform Tate's collection," she noted, "not only by thinking about art made in areas of the world that are new to our research, but by re-examining the art of countries we thought we knew well."

In 2020 came another pioneering exhibition of Black art at Tate Modern: a survey of the work of the South African photographer Zanele Muholi, whose powerful portraits and self-portraits are a combination of art, social history, and queer activism. To a cynic, the exhibition ticked every possible diversity box. In truth, it was a tour de force of an exhibition—spectacular to look at, and a milestone for a London institution.

In the catalogue, Muholi (who uses the pronoun "they") described their work as "visual activism." Being invited to show it allowed members of their community to "see themselves in it. It has taken a long time for us to see ourselves portrayed in a positive way."

On the day I was there, I witnessed a very spontaneous reaction to the show from a young woman named Leanne Haynes, a fashion-brand owner of mixed English and Caribbean heritage. "It doesn't get any Blacker than that," she said, as she gazed in awe at a wall-to-wall display of giant black-and-white Muholi self-portraits.

I tracked Haynes down through a mutual friend to find out more about her. She said she had grown up in Britain in a working-class family, with a sense that art had "nothing to do" with her. Moving to London as an adult, she had started going to galleries off and on, but had been disappointed with representations of Black people in art, because they were often shown in a position of weakness or servility.

Soul of a Nation was an exhibition she saw and liked. But the Muholi show completely blew her away. Why? Because it was unbelievable to see Tate show self-portraits of a woman with very dark skin, and one who was "not apologetic" about it.

"Every famous Black woman in the world has a palatable, Westernized attractiveness, and that's not taking anything away from them," she said, listing Beyoncé and Rihanna as the type of Black women who enjoyed global appeal. In that context, here was Muholi, "saying 'I'm going to show you all of me, and I'm going to emphasize the bits that the Western world isn't comfortable with.' I thought that was extremely empowering."

There were other reasons why the Muholi exhibition stood out. Until very recently, the British art and museum world had lagged behind in terms of exhibiting art by Black people and ethnic minorities, and not because there was any shortage of it. When the Black British artist Sonia Boyce went searching the national collections for works by Black artists, she found some two thousand of them. Shockingly enough, these works had rarely, if ever, been exhibited.

For more on this longstanding neglect, I turned to an artist I knew well: Isaac Julien, the pioneering film artist, whose parents were migrants from the Caribbean island of St. Lucia. "The British art world has been incredibly slow to acknowledge the presence of Black artists," he confirmed. "It's dealt with the idea of exceptionality, instead of looking at true diversity. And it's taken an incredibly long time for it to really come to grips with the diverse pool of artists working in Britain."

Julien's talent was spotted early on. He got his first break in Britain at the age of twenty when he co-founded a film and video collective, Sankofa, to promote independent black film culture. That was in the early 1980s, when there were headline-grabbing race riots in Britain to which the film collective was responding. But the attention soon faded, Julien said.

That didn't stop his career from flourishing. When Julien was twenty-nine, he drew attention with a stylish black-and-white evocation of gay desire—*Looking for Langston* (1989), about the African American poet Langston Hughes. Two years later, his first feature film won a prize at the Cannes Film Festival. In 2001, he was nominated for the Turner Prize, Britain's top art accolade. And in 2013–14, MoMA displayed Julien's multi-screen immersive film installation *Ten Thousand Waves* (2010) in its main atrium for three months, drawing critical acclaim.

Still, Julien has never had a solo exhibition at a major London museum. When I profiled him for the *New York Times* in 2014, MoMA's chief curator of media and performance, Stuart Comer, explained that Julien "falls between the cracks," that people were "still trying to place him," and that he would "get his due, eventually."

As of this writing, Julien may well be getting his due at last. British art institutions are playing catch-up—acquiring, exhibiting, and promoting as much Black talent as they can. And Julien is one of the beneficiaries.

In 2020, Julien was invited by the Royal Academy of Arts—an institution founded in 1768 and run by its elected artists and architects—to curate the first two rooms of its 2020 Summer Exhibition (which was delayed by the COVID-19 pandemic). His sumptuous display included works by Frank Bowling and Sonia Boyce, artists who had spent a long time in the artistic shadows. Bowling had been appointed the first Black British academician in 2005, at the age of seventy-one—nearly two and a half centuries after the academy's foundation. Boyce had been elected to the academy in 2016, becoming the first Black woman academician. (She will represent Britain at the 2022 Venice Biennale.)

As Cezar of the Delfina Foundation told me, there had been previous attempts at diversity in the British cultural establishment. But they were cosmetic and ephemeral. In 2003, a pro-diversity campaign called "Decibel" was launched by Arts Council England, the state-funded body that gives grants to cultural organizations. It was one of multiple approaches that many art professionals and artists deemed "tokenistic" for "ghettoizing" diversity as a separate issue. There did not seem to be a "real commitment" to it, he said.

The situation inside museums with more historic collections was even more problematic. Because of the breadth and depth of the British Empire, and the legacy of British colonialism, exclusion and discrimination were embedded in the very DNA of those collections.

I rang up the young Australian-born art historian Alice Procter (born in 1995), who highlights this loaded legacy in her Uncomfortable Art Tours. Taking visitors around the National Gallery, Tate Britain, and the British Museum, she uncovers the hidden truths behind many pieces of national heritage.

I asked her for an example of an artwork with an uncomfortable back story. She mentioned William Beechey's *Portrait of Sir Francis Ford's Children Giving a Coin to a Beggar Boy* (1793)—which, at first glance, looks like a charming depiction of charity and almsgiving. It shows two rosy-cheeked children dressed in silks and fancy hats giving money to a gaunt boy in rags.

As Procter explained, the two children's father, Francis Ford, was a plantation owner who derived his wealth from exploiting enslaved Africans in the West Indies, and who, as a peer in the House of Lords, was a vocal defender of slavery. Ford argued that the poor in England were worse off than the slaves in the colonies, and that the money made from slavery trickled down to the England's impoverished populations. This painting, according to Procter, was an illustration of that argument.

"When I've spoken to people in the U.K. about the history of colonialism, there's still this overwhelming assumption that imperialism happens somewhere else," she said. Yet so many of the paintings, portraits and objects in museums were instruments in the "writing of colonialism" and in the creation of the British national identity. Just as colonialism "catalogued the world" and set up hierarchies between nations and peoples, museums catalogued objects, created hierarchies, and contributed to the perpetuation of discrimination.

There seemed to be a covert colonialism at the heart of Britain's historic collections, I realized. There was also a much more overt colonialism: in the vast holdings of treasures looted from the colonies.

That was a story I was well aware of, having reported extensively on the growing calls for restitution of objects forcibly removed in imperial and colonial times. The British Museum holds 73,000 objects from sub-Saharan Africa alone, including the so-called Benin Bronzes—extraordinary sculptures and relief plaques that were plundered from royal palaces in what is now Nigeria by British colonial forces in 1897, then brought back to Britain or sold on the open market. Many Africans want these extraordinary masterpieces to be given back. The British Museum—which is prevented by an act of parliament from returning any objects in its collections—is in talks on collaborative projects with Nigeria and on loaning some of the Bronzes to a new museum being built there.

The View from France

Across the Channel in France, the underrepresentation of nonwhites in cultural institutions is endemic. When it comes to general issues of diversity—showing and collecting works, hiring staff—France has an even poorer track record than Britain. Positive discrimination is difficult to implement, because people cannot be categorized according to their ethnicity. So the museum world, in its exhibitions, collections, and management, remains overwhelmingly white and male.

The other issue is that debates around racial equality and identity politics are generally viewed with suspicion by the French, and dismissed as outbursts of American-style political correctness.

In a book published in 2001—a conversation between the French philosopher Jacques Derrida and the author Elisabeth Roudinesco titled *De quoi demain* (and translated and published in 2004 as *For What Tomorrow*)—Derrida took issue with the expression "politically correct" and its overuse in the French discourse. He said it was a way of dismissing genuine and lasting injustices.

Calling someone politically correct "can become an easy technique to silence all those who speak in the name of a just cause," Derrida observed. "Just imagine the scene: someone protests against this or that perversion—let's say racism, antisemitism, political corruption, marital violence, I don't know, delinquency or crime—and they are pointed at with the words: 'Enough of that political correctness!' We all know this is happening everywhere."

Two decades after Derrida's remarks, the expression is still as fashionable as ever, and not just among the French intelligentsia. Politicians (generally, but not exclusively, of the right and far right) use it to denounce a brand of oversensitivity that has been imported directly from North America and that is out of place in France. They use expressions such as "la cancel culture" and "le woke" to describe it.

In her 2020 book *Generation offensée*, the journalist and author Caroline Fourest denounces the excesses of identity politics and cultural appropriation, and the rise of a "culture police" created by a "woke" society and youth ultra-sensitized to injustice.

"The new generation only thinks about censoring what vexes or 'offends' them," she protests. "We live in a furiously paradoxical world where the freedom to hate has never been so out of control on social media, and where the freedom to speak and think has never been so surveilled in real life."

In another book published the same year, *Un coupable presque parfait* ("An Almost Perfect Culprit"), the French philosopher Pascal Bruckner denounces a phenomenon that originated in the United States—"the tribal-ization of the world, the racial obsession, the identity nightmare." He argues that the fall of the Berlin Wall in 1989 has given rise to another ideology based on "race, gender, identity."

In the "neo-feminist, anti-racist and decolonial" discourse, "the guilty party is the white male, reduced to the color of his skin," he writes. In this new hierarchy, and based on this new set of prejudices, you're better-off "dark instead of light-skinned, homosexual or transgender instead of het-erosexual, woman instead of man."

I turned to a French historian with expertise in African American stud-ies to get a better understanding of why the so-called culture wars raged so fiercely in France. Pap Ndiaye had just started his job as the director general of the Palais de la Porte Dorée in Paris—a massive colonial-era edifice that contains the National Museum of Immigration History. He had also just completed a report recommending measures to promote diversity at the Paris Opera.

Ndiaye said France was wedded to the republican principle of univer-sality: that a citizen was an abstract figure with no skin color, gender, or particularity, and that all citizens were equal in terms of their political rights. It was a principle that children were taught from the day they were born, he said, and it explained why the French were more resistant to identity-related debates originating in the United States.

There was another reason. "In the French intellectual world, there is a very deep-rooted anti-Americanism," he pointed out. Initially, that anti-Americanism had been the by-product of communist and socialist ideas, which had been deeply rooted in France for a long time. Today, it manifests itself as "the denunciation of multiculturalism and the excesses of political correctness and wokeness," and of "the U.S. as a country that now finds itself living under a new dictatorship: that of minorities."

France could come across as closed-minded in that respect. At the same time, as a country, it is seldom blinkered or shut off from the rest of the world—on the contrary. As someone who lived there for two decades (and carries a French passport), I found the French to be among the most intellectually curious nations I ever came across—open to learning about the culture and heritage of others in a way that many other Westerners were not. I was reminded of what Grenier had mentioned to me earlier on: that the French were both the most progressive people you could ever come across, and the most reactionary.

A good example was the groundbreaking international exhibition that the Centre Pompidou put on in 1989. *Magiciens de la terre* ("Magicians of the Earth") was an exhibition of contemporary artists from all over the world, including sub-Saharan Africa. The show was curated with equity in mind: there were as many Western artists on display as there were non-Western artists. It was so unprecedented that it is still talked about today, more than three decades later. Wasn't that the most perfect expression of diversity?

And while France today may still look fiercely resistant to the concept of diversity, it's changed a lot in the past twenty years, Ndiaye observed. "There is an awareness that to have exclusively white environments in art, politics, and so on is an anomaly. It's a problem. It's not normal." Such considerations were "nonexistent" before.

Ndiaye speaks from experience. He was one of the advisers to a major exhibition held in the spring of 2019 at the Musée d'Orsay: *Black Models: From Géricault to Matisse*, an exhibition that, for the first time in France, focused on the Black figures represented in nineteenth- and early-twentieth-century paintings, including some of the highlights of Orsay's own collections.

The exhibition was the brainchild of Denise Murrell, a Columbia University postdoctoral research scholar, who staged a smaller version of it at the university's Wallach Gallery. When she approached Orsay for loans, the museum's president, Laurence des Cars, decided to host a bigger show on the subject. (Des Cars was subsequently named the president of the Louvre Museum.)

In the catalogue, des Cars described the exhibition as an unprecedented initiative, and said it was a "true challenge" to "share the heritage and history more widely with new audiences that constitute the multifaceted France of today, as a result, among other things, of its colonial history."

The most prominent display in the show was Edouard Manet's *Olympia* (1863), in which a Black maid brings a large bouquet of flowers to the painting's central subject, a reclining and naked courtesan staring boldly at the viewer with one hand on her groin. The bandana-wearing maid occupies nearly half of the surface of the canvas. Yet generations of art historians have come and gone without paying attention to her. She is a *faire valoir*, there to accentuate the beauty and desirability of the main subject.

In the 2019 exhibition, the maid was the center of attention, and of the conversation. The curators had managed to identify her as "Laure," based on an entry in Manet's notebook describing her as a "very beautiful negress" ("*Laure, très belle négresse*") next to her address. They had tracked down the building where she had lived and determined that it was located in a working-class area inhabited at the time by washerwomen and seamstresses.

Another striking feature of the exhibition was that the museum had renamed paintings with a racial epithet in their original title. *Portrait d'une négresse* (1800), by Marie-Guillemine Benoist, had been redubbed *Portrait de Madeleine*, as research revealed that to be the model's name.

The exhibition had a massive impact on visitors whose families hailed from France's former colonies. One of them was an artist from Benin by the name of Roméo Mivekannin. He was so bowled over by the show that he started a series of monumental works inspired by some of those nineteenth-century masterpieces. The paintings were done not on canvas but on strips of old bedsheets dipped in voodoo potions and patched together. Instead of replicating the paintings exactly, Mivekannin replaced the faces of the Black figures with his own. In Manet's "Olympia," for instance, he was the Black maid.

I saw one of those works—a monumental version of Théodore Géricault's *Raft of the Medusa* in which the artist had drawn his own face in place of that of three Black figures—in the lobby of Christie's Paris in January 2021. It was one of the highlights of the 1:54 Contemporary African Art Fair.

Mivekannin told me that when he saw the Orsay exhibition and discovered the true story of the Black figures in those paintings, he experienced "indescribable emotion." He had often wondered who the Black figures in those nineteenth-century paintings really were: whether they had a say in being portrayed, whether they were fairly remunerated.

"I had an instant desire to relive the past, to put myself in those people's place, to cross over to the other side of the canvas," he explained. "I wanted to make the viewer confront history." He described the resulting works as "decolonial" and "an act of deconstruction."

Roméo Mivekannin, *Olympia d'après Manet* (2020)

Mivekannin spoke of his own connection to France's colonial past. His great-great-grandfather, King Béhanzin of Dahomey, was overthrown by French colonial forces in the late nineteenth century when they conquered the kingdom and ruled over it for more than six decades. I knew exactly which king he was referring to, because France was preparing to give back twenty-six priceless objects that had been looted from that very king's palace at the time of his overthrow. They were due to be restituted to the African state of Benin, the territory where the Kingdom of Dahomey was situated.

The restitution of Africa's cultural heritage was a topic I had been covering for a few years, and France was at the forefront of it. In November 2017, French President Emmanuel Macron stood before hundreds of students at a university in Ouagadougou, the capital of Burkina Faso (a former French colony), and made the following declaration. "I cannot accept that a large part of the cultural heritage of several African countries should be in France," he said. "Africa's heritage must be showcased in Paris, but also in Dakar, in Lagos, in Cotonou. This will be one of my priorities. Starting today, and in the next five years, I want to see the conditions put in place so as to allow for the temporary or definitive restitution of African cultural heritage to Africa."

The repercussions of the presidential statement were huge. Macron then asked two academics to devise a roadmap for the restitution process. The report by Bénédicte Savoy of France and Felwine Sarr of Senegal went very far: it urged France to give back all objects that had been removed without consent, provided the country of origin asked for them. And it labeled everything taken out of Africa before 1960 as being eligible for return, including objects brought back by scientific explorers, missionaries, administrators, or the military.

The report sent shock waves through the French museum world. France held ninety thousand objects from sub-Saharan Africa in its collections, of which seventy thousand were in the Quai Branly Museum in Paris—including the treasures of King Béhanzin. By the academics' definition, practically all of those collections belonged back in Africa. How could that be?

The French cultural establishment subsequently appeared to slam the brakes on the process. Only one other object (a Senegalese sword) was given back. What started out as a lofty presidential promise was shelved in the face of bigger challenges, such as the waves of "yellow vest" protests against President Macron and his government, and the COVID-19 pandemic.

Macron's half-fulfilled promise led one Congolese activist to take the matter in his own hands. In June 2020, Mwazulu Diyabanza bought a ticket to the Quai Branly Museum and visited the collection with four associates. He then staged a dramatic protest action. Shouting anti-colonial slogans, he started tugging at a nineteenth-century wooden funerary post from present-day Chad or Sudan and released it from its iron grip. Holding the object, he then marched toward the museum exit, still shouting slogans, before being stopped by security. Diyabanza subsequently staged two similar actions in museums in Marseille and Berg en Dal, in the Netherlands.

Weeks before his Paris trial (in which he was sentenced to a small fine), I met Diyabanza at an outdoor cafe on the outskirts of Paris. He wore a long ivory necklace over his black tunic and a black beret with an Africa badge, symbol of his organization. He described the Quai Branly as "a museum that contains stolen objects," and added, "There is no ban on an owner taking back his property the moment he comes across it."

The View from the Netherlands

The Netherlands is another European power with a heavy colonial footprint, and one that I was somewhat familiar with. My sister Nazanine lived and worked in Amsterdam for many years, and I spent many a morning at the Rijksmuseum, marveling at the Rembrandts and the Vermeers. So when, in the spring of 2021, I saw that a grand old museum such as the Rijksmuseum was putting on an exhibition titled *Slavery*, I hopped on a Zoom call with the main curator of the exhibition, Valika Smeulders. A Dutch colonial heritage specialist and curator of Surinamese origin, Smeulders said she had been hired by the Rijksmuseum in 2017, four years after the museum's reopening following a lengthy redevelopment. "The focus was very much on the glory of the nation of the Netherlands," she said. At the same time, the museum's management realized that "the historical narrative of the museum could use some renewal." Curators set out to identify "what stories we have not told yet."

When, in 2017, plans were unveiled to put on a slavery exhibition, the museum decided that it would not be an exhibition on "the grand narrative of slavery," but one that would focus on ten different people who were either enslaved themselves, or slave holders, or people who had spoken out against slavery. By the time the exhibition came together, their stories were being told using 140 objects, a third of them from the Rijksmuseum itself.

How could those ten people be identified, I asked, when there were few, if any, written records or archives on the lives of slaves? Smeulders admitted that this was a "huge hurdle," because Dutch historians had, for so long, held on to written sources as the major sources to build history on. This time, a third source had to be brought in, she said: oral history. The curators had access to a precious resource: early-twentieth-century recorded interviews with people who had been born during the time of slavery or right after, and who spoke about themselves, their parents, and their grandparents, meaning people as far back as in the eighteenth century.

The exhibition would focus on the reality of people who were brought as slaves to the Netherlands, where slavery was illegal—through the display of a metal collar that was probably worn by a servant. The Rijksmuseum had several portraits of servants of color who wore a collar around their neck, she said. These servants were long described as being symbols and not real people. Yet subsequent archival research revealed that they were the first Afro-Dutch people, meaning that metal collars such as the ones on display were meant, not for dogs, but for these young men and children.

Smeulders noted that she and the museum had received lots of different reactions to the exhibition when it was first announced. Some were from people who wished to contribute and help out. Others expressed doubts, were critical, and asked: Why are you doing this? Is this really necessary? Is this something I need to feel bad about? Should I be ashamed about my ancestors? Can we still be proud of our history?

After centuries of being told by one set of people—the colonizers—history was being told by another set of people—the colonized. And ideological divisions were rising out of it.

THE EPISODES AND anecdotes contained in this chapter all point to one thing: that it is time to give voice to the previously voiceless—not out of pity or compassion or charity, and not in an effort to tick boxes and satisfy quotas, but because those previously voiceless communities are there as a result of generations of colonization and enslavement by Western powers, and because their stories are, therefore, the West's own. Britain, France, and the Netherlands are former colonial powers with a culpability that they now have to face. Engaging with that culpability will finally make it possible to hear the voices of the colonized and of their descendants, who now compose a not-insignificant percentage of their population. In other words, the story now has to be told from the vantage point of the vanquished and of their descendants, not just from the vantage point of the victors.

The same goes for America. The descendants of the vanquished—African Americans, Native Americans, and Hispanic Americans—can no longer be silenced and rendered invisible in the world of art and museums. Their stories, triumphs, and tragedies must be shown, seen, and heard. And they need to be involved in the running of museums and in the making of exhibitions so that artworks on public display do not end up threatened with destruction, or destroyed.

Race is certainly not the only divisive issue in the world of art and museums. Religion was for a long time an even bigger cause of conflict and controversy in art history. And as we are about to see, it continued to tear people apart until fairly recently.

5.

A Despicable Display of Vulgarity

In the Western world, it's been a very long time since religion determined the direction of politics, society, individual behavior—and, by extension, art. Nowhere do religious authorities have the direct power to censor creativity. The days when popes and cardinals could order the repainting of a racy fresco, or that an Inquisition tribunal could put a celebrated painter on trial, or that Protestant Iconoclasts could scratch out the faces of figures in a painted polyptych, are well and truly over.

The secularization of state and society is not a recent phenomenon. In France, it dates back to the late eighteenth century, when the French Revolution stripped the Catholic Church of its powers and properties and laid the groundwork for the separation of church and state. That separation, and the notion of a completely secular state, are today deeply entrenched in France and elsewhere in Europe. Religious authorities cannot meddle in the affairs of government, society, or culture. Even in a Catholic country such as Italy, church and state have been separate for a century, and the Vatican has no say whatsoever in what kind of art is shown (or not shown) in the museums of the Italian peninsula.

The sharp separation between church and state, and the deep-rooted secularization of Western societies, mean that art, too, has become arch-secular. It was not always thus. There was a time when most of the art commissioned in Europe and in the Western world illustrated Christian themes. Just wander around the painting collections of the Louvre in Paris or the National Gallery in London, and you'll be struck by the frequency of sacred subjects.

That's because for a long time religious authorities were major commissioners of art. For centuries, they were the ones providing work and a career to the finest artists of Europe. Today the commissioners of art are governments—chosen by voters in secular and liberal democracies—and private individuals or corporations. Artists can survive and even thrive without having anything to do with the church. Those who do accept commissions from a church—such as to produce stained-glass windows—do so out of choice, not out of obligation.

Most artists, in fact, go out of their way not to represent religion, as the art historian Ronald Bernier told me. Bernier is a professor of humanities at the Wentworth Institute of Technology in Boston, and he was brought up in the Catholic tradition. He had written a book about the American video artist Bill Viola in 2014, so I interviewed him on the occasion of an exhibition of Viola and Michelangelo at the Royal Academy of Arts in London in 2019. The exhibition featured some striking juxtapositions. In the first room, for example, a set of Michelangelo drawings of the Virgin Mary—carrying the baby Jesus, or holding the dead Christ in her arms—were displayed across from Viola's *Nantes Triptych* (1992), a three-screen video installation that showed one woman giving birth and another (the artist's mother) on her deathbed.

Bernier noted how unusual it was to see such an exhibition be programmed in a mainstream cultural institution. "Art seen as engaging with religion is seen as retrograde and reactionary," he explained. There were reasons for that, including the fact that "there's a lot of bad religious art out there." But as a rule, contemporary artists were "desperately trying not to fall into the trap of being labeled a Christian or a religious artist," because art history "still looks so skeptically at it."

As a result, Bernier explained, Viola—who is of Italian origin, was brought up Episcopalian, and spent time in Florence as a young man, making work inside churches—preferred to connect his art to mysticism, Sufism, or Zen Buddhism, rather than link it to a religion such as Christianity. That ambiguity allowed him to tackle the subject of religion without appearing to do so, "almost as if he's sneaking it in through the back door," Bernier explained.

He had a point. I remember interviewing Viola's wife and closest collaborator, Kira Perov, for the exhibition. When I asked her about the place of God in the exhibition, she replied: "Let's keep God out of it, because who knows what that is?" It was better to describe the show as "addressing the really large questions that we all have in our lives."

Five years earlier, in 2014, Viola—notwithstanding his reluctance to connect his work to Christianity or religion—became the first artist ever to have a multiscreen moving-image work (*Martyrs*) permanently installed in one of the great cathedrals of Christendom: St. Paul's Cathedral in London. I was one of the journalists previewing the work when it was first unveiled. In this ecclesiastical setting, I met the mild-mannered artist in a small press huddle, accompanied by the man who had commissioned him, the Reverend Canon Mark Oakley. Viola spoke about his contribution: a silent four-screen video installation showing four figures being martyred by the four elements—earth, air, fire, and water. The work, I must admit, looked completely unexpected inside a major London cathedral. And yet as always with Viola, the iconography looked very Christian.

Other churches in Europe have commissioned contemporary artists to produce art for them. After World War II, thousands had to be built or rebuilt. Rather than call in traditional artists who would replicate the art of the past, churches started to move with the times and reach out to contemporary artists. Artists who accepted the commissions were by no means religious or even Christian. Marc Chagall, who was Jewish, designed stained-glass windows for churches in England, France, and Germany.

The practice continues to this day. David Hockney, one of the world's best-known living artists, was commissioned to produce a window for Westminster Abbey in London: *The Queen's Window*, marking the sixty-fifth anniversary of Queen Elizabeth II's reign, and inaugurated in October 2018.

Days before the window was installed, I interviewed Hockney at his London home-and-studio. We sat in his cozy, skylit living room, filled with self-portraits and endearing prints of his pooches, and got on to the topic of faith. Hockney told me that despite the fact that his mother was a "keen Christian," he himself, at age sixteen, had stopped going to the Methodist chapel that the family went to, because "I realized all the people who went to church weren't really that good: they were hypocrites. That put me off."

Now in his eighties, he still believed that he was "heading for oblivion," yet had developed his own kind of faith, "a personal God," as he called it, as a way of seeking answers to the big existential questions.

Neither Hockney nor Viola were devout Christians or even religious in the conventional sense of the word. They were two secular artists very much in tune with the beliefs and technologies of their time. Yet the Church of England was reaching out to both of them to produce works that would help engage with people in an overwhelmingly secular society. After a century or more of confrontation, religion and art were, it appeared, reconciled.

THERE WAS A time not long ago, however, when religion and art had a nasty and thunderous clash: in the United States of America in the late 1980s and 1990s. It was a time when religion played an abnormally important role in politics, government, and lawmaking. During this period, artists in the United States were condemned by Christian groups, and that condemnation was sanctioned and seconded by lawmakers and federal and local government officials. Museums exhibiting their artworks either censored the works by not showing them at all or faced lawsuits and threats to their public funding when they did. Somehow, at the dawn of the twenty-first century, religion continued to indirectly influence political, social, and cultural affairs in the United States—and intermittently affect the art that was funded and shown in the country's taxpayer-funded museums.

As Derek Thompson wrote in *The Atlantic* in September 2019, "When it comes to religion, Americans really are exceptional. No rich country prays nearly as much as the U.S., and no country that prays as much as the U.S. is nearly as rich . . . Deep into the 20th century, more than nine in 10 Americans said they believed in God and belonged to an organized religion, with the great majority of them calling themselves Christian."

The mingling of religion and politics became particularly pronounced in the 1980s and early '90s, when the Christian right exercised astonishing influence on the policies and behavior of men and women at the highest echelons of power in Washington, D.C. That's because starting in the 1970s, the country's most powerful Christian groups involved themselves more closely in American politics to prevent society from becoming too secular and straying from conservative Christian teachings. This period coincided with the women's liberation movement, when abortion and divorce became more and more widespread and traditional family values took a back seat.

In its campaign to re-Christianize America, the religious right found a ready political ally: the Republican Party. Christian groups started fundraising for the party and spreading the Republican message among white suburban communities across America. To reflect the views and values of this devout new voter base, the Republican platform turned considerably more conservative on matters of sexuality, morality, and faith. What nobody expected was for this conservatism to spill over into the art world—with lasting and potentially serious consequences. Three famous cases, from the 1980s and '90s, illustrate this censorious atmosphere.

Andres Serrano, *Piss Christ* (1987)

The first artwork to unleash the rage of the religious right in the United States was a 60-by-40-inch color photograph by the New York artist Andres Serrano. The altarpiece-sized image was essentially a misty depiction of a crucifix, with the head of Christ stooped in agony. Tiny bubbles ran across the side of the image, suggesting that the crucifix was submerged in a body of liquid. Jesus had a yellowish glow, as if a burst of sunlight were shining onto him through the surface of the water. The rest of the image was a deep red. There was nothing in the picture itself to suggest profanity or provocation—until you read the title, *Piss Christ*, and realized that the crucifix was, in fact, immersed in the artist's urine.

"I always felt that as an artist and as a former Catholic, I had every right to use the symbols of the Church in my work," Serrano explained in a 1989 documentary (available on YouTube). "As far as I'm concerned, my use of bodily fluids in connection with religion is not that different from the

Andres Serrano, *Piss Christ* **(1987)**

Catholic obsession with the body and blood of Christ. I'm also obsessed with blood."

The HispanicAmerican artist was inspired early on to represent blood and death. From the mid-1980s, he started using bodily fluids in his work. His motivations were also formal and artistic: he wanted to abandon three-dimensionality and perspective in photography and strive for a flat plane. *Milk, Blood* (1986)—a photograph of a half-white, half-red surface intended as a tribute to the Dutch modern-art master Piet Mondrian—was produced with exactly those components: milk and blood.

"I realized I needed a third color added to my palette," the artist explained in the documentary. "So I started using piss." At the same time, he abandoned abstraction and returned to figuration, choosing the cruci-fix—an image omnipresent in his Catholic childhood—as one of his subjects.

"My use of bodily fluids in connection with religion is just my way of personalizing religion for myself and exploring my relationship with God and my Catholic upbringing and the ambivalent feelings I have about that," he explained. "You can't have the sacred without the other side of the coin, the profane, and sometimes it's hard for me to tell the difference."

In December 1989, *Piss Christ* was shown along with thirteen other pieces by Serrano in an exhibition at the Stux Gallery in New York. Review-ing it for the *New York Times*, Michael Brenson described Serrano as a "good artist," and said the work "suggests the arty images and the mass pro-duction of religious souvenirs that have been partly responsible for the trivialization and exploitation of both religion and art." He noted that, like Mapplethorpe, Serrano "struggles against inhibitions about the human body. His use of bodily fluids is not intended to arouse disgust but to chal-lenge the notion of disgust where the human body is concerned."

Nearly three decades later, in a 2014 interview with *Huffpost*, Serrano offered further clues to the thinking behind his work:

> The only message is that I'm a Christian artist making a religious
> work of art based on my relationship with Christ and The Church.
> The crucifix is a symbol that has lost its true meaning; the horror of
> what occurred. It represents the crucifixion of a man who was
> tortured, humiliated and left to die on a cross for several hours. In
> that time, Christ not only bled to dead, he probably saw all his
> bodily functions and fluids come out of him. So if "Piss Christ"
> upsets people, maybe this is so because it is bringing the symbol
> closer to its original meaning.

The work became the focus of public debate in the United States start-ing in 1987, when Serrano was one of ten artists to receive a visual-arts grant from the Southeastern Center for Contemporary Art (SECCA) in Winston-Salem, North Carolina. Each artist was awarded the sum of $75,000, and their work was featured in a touring exhibition in Los Angeles, Pittsburgh, and Richmond (VA). The grants were funded by the Rockefeller Founda-tion (a nonprofit), Equitable Life (a corporation), and the National Endowment for the Arts (a government agency).

The exhibition—which included Serrano's *Piss Christ*—traveled to L.A. and Pittsburgh without the slightest incident. In the early months of 1989, however, opened in Richmond, Virginia, where it was viewed one Saturday by a computer designer named Philip L. Smith. His reaction was one of fury.

He wrote a letter of protest to the *Richmond Times-Dispatch*, his local newspaper, saying that he was "appalled" to see the image of a crucifix dipped in urine prominently displayed in an art exhibition. "The Virginia

Museum should not be in the business of promoting and subsidizing hatred and intolerance," he wrote. "Would they pay the KKK to do a work defaming blacks? Would they display a Jewish symbol under urine? Has Christianity become fair game in our society for any kind of blasphemy and slander?" He objected vehemently to "the tax-supported arbiters of our culture justifying the desecration of a symbol so precious to so many of our citizens."

Smith's missive was a standard letter to the editor addressed by a citizen to his local paper. Yet the letter and its contents quickly turned Serrano's *Piss Christ* into a cause célèbre—with seismic repercussions on contemporary art, censorship, and the relations between government and culture.

One of Reverend Donald Wildmon's followers told him about the letter. Wildmon was a Christian fundamentalist preacher who headed the powerful American Family Association (AFA) in Tupelo, Mississippi. The association had some five hundred local chapters and a $5 million annual budget, and was famous for its tub-thumping protests against film and popular culture. A year earlier, in 1988, the AFA had spearheaded a massive boycott of Martin Scorsese's movie *The Last Temptation of Christ*. And it had just scored a major public-relations triumph: having condemned Madonna's music video "Like a Prayer" as "blatantly offensive," it had compelled Pepsi-Cola to cancel a whopping $5 million advertising deal with the singer.

Serrano, it seemed, was the next artist on the list.

In April 1989 (the very month that Madonna's commercial was canceled by Pepsi), Reverend Wildmon sent a furious letter to his hundreds of thousands of followers. He mentioned that Serrano planned to also use semen in his work. "And, of course, defecation will follow that. The bias and bigotry against Christians, which has dominated television and the movies for the past decade or more, has now moved over to the art museums," Wildmon wrote.

The Reverend said Christians were partly to blame for not reacting to this bigotry, and that as a child, he would "never, ever have dreamed that I would live to see such demeaning disrespect and desecration of Christ in our country that is present today. Maybe, before the physical persecution of Christians begins, we will gain the courage to stand against such bigotry. I hope so."

Later that month, Wildmon wrote to every member of the U.S. Congress, and enclosed a copy of Serrano's *Piss Christ* image. The image—and its maker—soon became headline news.

On May 18, 1989, Senator Alfonse D'Amato, a Republican from New York, took the floor at the U.S. Senate, tore up a catalogue of Serrano's work, and trampled it under his feet. He then declared that he had received letters, phone calls, and postcards weeks earlier from constituents in the state of New York expressing "a feeling of shock, of outrage, and anger" and asking "'How dare you spend our taxpayers' money on this trash?'"

"This so-called piece of art is a deplorable, despicable display of vulgarity," said the senator, noting that the artist had received a $15,000 NEA grant. "Well, if this is what contemporary art has sunk to, this level, this outrage, this indignity—some may want to sanction that, and that is fine. But not with the use of taxpayers' money." He declared that he and more than twenty other senators were writing a letter of protest to the NEA.

Senator D'Amato's address contained an inaccuracy: Serrano's $15,000 grant was only partially funded by the NEA. Still, his message was widely endorsed, including by Jesse Helms, the Republican senator from North Carolina, who took the floor:

> *What this Serrano fellow did, he filled a bottle with his own urine*
> *and then stuck a crucifix down there—Jesus Christ on a cross. He set*
> *it up on a table and took a picture of it.*

For that, the National Endowment for the Arts gave him $15,000, to honor him as an artist . . . That is all right for him to be a jerk but let him be a jerk on his own time and with his own resources. Do not dishonor our Lord . . .

I have sent word to the Endowment that I want them to review their funding criteria to ensure abuses such as this never happen again . . . They are insulting the very fundamental basis of this country.

The pair and other senators wrote to the NEA's acting chairman, Hugh Southern, urging the agency to change its funding procedures. Denouncing the agency's support for "a so-called 'work of art'" that is "shocking" and "abhorrent," the senators noted that millions of taxpayers were "rightfully incensed that their hard-earned dollars were used to honor and support Serrano's work." This objection "does not involve freedom of artistic expression," the senators added. "It does involve the question whether American taxpayers should be forced to support such trash."

Serrano and his photograph became the single most important trigger for the so-called culture wars that erupted around the NEA's funding of the arts—the very conflict that, later that year, engulfed Mapplethorpe and the NEA Four. From then on, the name of Andres Serrano became associated with scandal, controversy, and censorship. Though his grant was not rescinded and his work was never taken down, the episode became a milestone in the history of Western art censorship, and a lightning rod in the debate around what kind of art the taxpayer can and should fund.

To conservative American politicians—then very much under the influence of the religious right—Serrano was doubly to blame: He was a beneficiary of taxpayer largesse, and he had produced a piece of art that was offensive to Christians. Twelve years later, another artist would be disparaged for those same two reasons.

Chris Ofili, *The Holy Virgin Mary* (1996)

Another episode of religion-related art controversy took place exactly a decade later, at the Brooklyn Museum of Art in New York. The work in question was Chris Ofili's *The Holy Virgin Mary* (1996). A tall painting—96 inches by 72 inches—it was, on the face of it, neither crude nor profane. It pictured a sketchily drawn Black Virgin Mary, draped in an ample, shapeless robe, and baring one of her breasts.

There was nothing unusual about that: plenty of paintings in the world's finest museums show a bare-chested Virgin Mary feeding the infant Jesus. Ofili's Mary was set against a background of glitter and orange resin that gave the painting a spectacular glow, and might even recall the illuminated icons of Byzantine and medieval art. Affixed onto the shimmering canvas surface were what appeared from afar to be little butterflies, or cherub-like winged figures.

What did stand out was that the figure's bare breast was, in fact, made of a gob of elephant dung. So were the two dark clumps that the canvas rested on, one marked "Virgin" and the other "Mary." The little butterflies, or winged cherubs, were actually cutouts of women's buttocks from pornographic magazines.

Born in Manchester, England, to Nigerian parents, Ofili grew up and went to school in Manchester; his mother worked in a biscuit factory. He was raised Catholic, was an altar boy in his local church, and believed in God without being "dominated by it," he later recalled. As a young man, he initially dabbled in furniture design, but soon switched to art—specifically, painting—and moved to London, where he got a postgraduate degree from the prestigious Royal College of Art.

In 1992, while in his early twenties, Ofili received funding for a trip to Zimbabwe. That trip turned out to be life-changing, transforming his artistic style and aesthetic. He spent two weeks working alongside Zimbabwean artists in a studio, then traveled for a month: he went on a horseback safari and spent days gazing in awe at animals, in particular giraffes. He was staggered to see the landscape and the animals in their natural habitat.

"When a giraffe taller than the average house in Britain would walk by," he told the *New York Times* in September 1999 (amidst the controversy around his painting), "it gave me that particular feeling of being shocked and simultaneously finding something beautiful. It gave me an excitement and a fear of the new."

The game tracker accompanying Ofili on the safari could tell which animals were in the vicinity by examining the fresh excrement on the trajectory. Ofili hoped to come across elephants on his trip, but because of a drought, the mammoths were not showing up in their habitual drinking locations. What Ofili encountered instead was their excrement: dry elephant dung. He took a clump of it with him and stuck it on a canvas. "It was a crass way of bringing the landscape onto the painting," he later recalled.

On the same trip, he visited the prehistoric cave paintings in the Matobo Hills of Zimbabwe, and was mesmerized by the paintings of animals and beasts but also by a wall covered with dots, which, he was told, may have been the work of someone who did not accompany the hunters and stayed behind in the cave, possibly meditating.

Ofili took clumps of dung back to Britain in his suitcase. In Berlin and London, he staged a performance with the elephant excrement titled *Shit Sale* in street markets, arranging rows of dung on a strip of fabric laid on the pavement. The excrement clumps were not for sale; they were there to solicit responses from visitors. Later, in May 1993, Ofili, still an art student, took a quarter-page ad out in one of the first issues of Frieze magazine that read: ELEPHANT SHIT. The same message appeared on stickers that he put up on the London Underground, on street walls, on cars, and in clubs and art galleries.

Among the earliest artworks he created with dung were three sculptures called *Shithead*, which consisted of a ball of dung adorned with his own dreadlocks and, in one particular case, a set of milk teeth. He also made an abstract work called *Painting with Shit on It* (in many ways a preamble to *The Holy Virgin Mary*) which had, at its core, a blotch of elephant dung from which thick black resin dripped. Two other clumps of elephant dung stood on the floor, supporting the canvas. So central was the animal excrement to the art of Ofili that an article in the March 1994 issue of *Frieze* magazine was headlined "The Elephant Man." The nickname stuck.

Four years later, in 1998, Ofili became the first Black winner of the Turner Prize, Britain's most important contemporary-art accolade. By then, Ofili's art was a fusion of all of the influences important to him at the time: hip-hop and gangsta rap, Blaxploitation movies, Africa, and religion.

The clumps of dung were not randomly positioned: They formed a central part of the composition, and also served as supports for the canvas. "There's something incredibly simple but incredibly basic about it," he explained in the *Times* interview. "It attracts a multiple of meanings and interpretations."

THE HOLY VIRGIN *Mary* was one of five Ofili paintings included in an eye-catching 1997 exhibition of some ninety works of contemporary British art—painting, sculpture, photography, installation art—belonging to the advertising executive and art collector Charles Saatchi. Titled *Sensation*, it opened at the Royal Academy of Arts in London, and would later travel to the Brooklyn Museum in New York.

In London, huge crowds shuffled in to view the provocative artworks, which included Damien Hirst's shark suspended in formaldehyde (*The Physical Impossibility of Death in the Mind of Someone Living*) and Marcus Harvey's portrait of the serial child killer Myra Hindley, made up of small hand prints of real-life children. Ofili's *Virgin Mary* attracted no controversy whatsoever; the scandal was over the serial-killer work. Why? Because in arch-secular Britain—where so many churches had by then been converted into gyms, creches, and community centers—an artist taking liberties with an image of the Virgin Mary was not going to cause as much of a stir as one who represented the murder of multiple children. (The display of the latter work caused four academicians to resign in protest, and *The Sun* to write, "Myra Hindley is to be hung in the Royal Academy. Sadly it is only a painting of her.")

Sensation came to New York at the end of 1999 thanks to Arnold Lehman, the director of the Brooklyn Museum, who was keen to diversify the museum's audience and show more boundary-pushing contemporary art. In 1990 and 1991, the museum had hosted two exhibitions—*The Play of the Unmentionable: BM Collection* and *Too Shocking to Show*—demonstrating how art that was once considered politically, socially or religiously scandalous had become perfectly acceptable. *Sensation* seemed a natural follow-up.

Lehman negotiated for months to persuade Saatchi to show the works in New York, and raised money to make the show happen. The board was kept abreast of the negotiations, as was the City of New York, which funded and oversaw the museum. Mayor Rudolph Giuliani and his staff were given an advance presentation of the Brooklyn Museum's plans, including the *Sensation* exhibition, and were shown a slide of Hirst's shark work. No objections were raised. Meanwhile, the museum rolled out an advertising campaign that played up the more hair-raising aspects of the exhibition.

"HEALTH WARNING," the ad campaign read, in capital letters. "The contents of this exhibition cause shock, vomiting, confusion, panic, euphoria and anxiety."

Two weeks before the exhibition was to open, the *New York Daily News* published an incendiary four-column story with the headline: "BROOKLYN GALLERY OF HORROR: GRUESOME MUSEUM SHOW STIRS CONTROVERSY." The article described a "shocking contemporary art exhibit that features real animals sliced in half, and graphic paintings and sculptures of corpses and sexually mutilated bodies." It noted the "outrage" around "such works as a painting of the Virgin Mary splattered with elephant dung." Mayor Giuliani's press secretary, Sunny Mindel, was reached for comment. She replied that "assuming the description of the exhibit is accurate, no money should be spent on it."

Six days later, with the doors of the exhibition still not open to the public, a member of the City Hall staff suggested to a journalist that they ask the mayor about the show and specifically about *The Holy Virgin Mary* during the morning press briefing. The question was being planted, in other words. The journalist proceeded to probe the mayor, who replied that he had not seen the exhibition itself. (At that point, he had only had a personal briefing with Lehman from the Brooklyn Museum outlining the contents of the show.) Here was the mayor's reply:

> *It offends me. The idea of, in the name of art, having a city subsidize art, so-called works of art, in which people are throwing elephant dung at a picture of the Virgin Mary, is sick. If somebody wants to do that privately and pay for that privately, well, that's what the First Amendment is all about. You can be offended by it and upset by it. You don't have to go to see it if somebody else is paying for it. But to have the government pay for it is outrageous.*

You don't have a right to a government subsidy to desecrate someone else's religion. And therefore we will do everything that we can to remove funding from the Brooklyn Museum until the director comes to his senses. And realizes that if you are a government-subsidized enterprise then you can't do things that desecrate the most personal and deeply held views of the people in society. (. . .) The city should not have to pay for sick stuff.

Within hours, City officials notified the museum's board and director that if the Ofili work was not pulled out of the exhibition, the museum would get no more funding from the City of New York. There were a few other artworks in the exhibition that the mayor had lampooned, but the main target of his opprobrium was Ofili's work, because it was an attack on the Virgin Mary and an insult to Christianity. (This was a time when the religious right still controlled votes and voters.)

Later that month, Giuliani railed that since the Brooklyn Museum's board had no qualms about using taxpayers' money on pickled pigs and dissected cows and on the practice of "throwing dung on important religious symbols," then "I'm not going to have any compunction about having to put them out of business, meaning the board." He vowed to evict the museum from the building it had occupied for a century and to withhold their funding until another board took over.

The museum nevertheless decided to open as planned on October 2. It was a bold move, considering that the City of New York provided 27 percent of its annual operational funding—some $7 million a year—and had pledged an extra $28 million in capital funding.

Three minutes after the board voted to let the show open, the Brooklyn Museum's representatives filed a complaint in court against the City of New York. That evening, the City pulled the plug on all Brooklyn Museum funding, including the $7 million allocated for that year, and the additional $28 million in capital funding.

The court hearing for the museum's complaint against the City of New York was set for very soon afterward, on October 8. In the meantime, Deputy Mayor Joseph Lhota filed an affidavit singling out the artworks in the *Sensation* exhibition that were unsuitable for display. Two pictures that included the Holy Virgin Mary, he wrote, were offensive to Catholics; others were inappropriate for children; another (*Myra*) "inappropriately glorifies a heinous criminal."

During the hearing, Judge Nina S. Gershon asked Lhota how he had determined which works were unsuitable for exhibition. Lhota replied, "I asked myself the following question: One, do they desecrate anyone's religion? . . . The second question is: Would I like my eight-year-old daughter to see this work of art? . . . And the third question that I asked was: Would anyone who believes in animal rights be offended?"

The judge then came back with examples from art history. She asked if Lhota would show Michelangelo's *David* to his eight-year-old daughter, or exhibit it at the Brooklyn Museum. Lhota answered no to the first question and yes to the second. He gave similar responses concerning another artwork he was shown: Jean Broc's *The Death of Hyacinthos*, which represents Apollo and his male lover, both naked, locked in a tender embrace.

On that basis, asked the judge, how can the museum determine ahead of time what and what not to show? This was not, Lhota replied, something that the City of New York "would ever put in some kind of protocol, some kind of procedure."

The court then turned to the primary charge brought by the mayor against the exhibition and the Ofili work: that it was sacrilegious and an affront to religion. The museum's attorney, Floyd Abrams, took the stand, and explained that while the notion of blasphemy may have been recognized by the country two hundred years ago, it was "now not a word heard in American courts," and one that the City of New York could not invoke. "It is the ideas of this art, it is what they offer by way of disagreeable, painful, sometimes offensive ideas, that the mayor and the city are so upset about, and that is precisely what they may not use the funding process to deal with," he said, noting that when the city funded a museum or library or any other institution, the First Amendment protected those institutions, and the City could neither be "the proprietors" nor "the moral censors" of those institutions.

In the end, the museum won on all counts. The judge ruled that there was "no federal constitutional issue more grave" than efforts by government officials "to censor works of expression and to threaten the vitality of a major cultural institution, as punishment for failing to abide by governmental demands for orthodoxy. . . . If there is any fixed star in our constitutional constellation, it is that no official, high or petty, can prescribe what shall be orthodox in politics, nationalism, religion, or other matters of opinion."

The court then barred City Hall and the mayor from taking any action or inflicting any punishment or sanction against the museum for its display of the *Sensation* exhibition.

The mayor was livid, and City Hall appealed. He described the judge as "biased," "totally out of control," someone who has "lost all reason," and "part of the politically correct, left-wing ideology of NYC."

Nonetheless, the City was legally forced to keep funding the museum. On appeal, the City was banned in a permanent order from taking any retaliatory measures against the museum, cutting its funding, or evicting or punishing it.

Mayor Giuliani's vocal objections to the exhibit and the media coverage actually increased public and market appetite for it. An estimated 180,000 people attended the *Sensation* exhibition. It was then acquired by the Australian collector David Walsh (who has a subterranean Museum of Old and New Art in Tasmania), and sold at auction for $4.5 million in 2015.

Subsequently bought by the hedge-fund billionaire Steven A. Cohen, it is now in the collections of the Museum of Modern Art in New York.

Within a couple years of the *Sensation* exhibition in Brooklyn, the attention of politicians and the public had been drawn to far more serious events: the September 11 terrorist attacks. America went to war in Afghanistan and Iraq, and Muslims became the new scapegoats. The battles over religion in art were shelved. Yet fears that they might be reignited lingered on—and led another artwork to get caught in the crossfire a decade later.

David Wojnarowicz,
A Fire in My Belly (1986–87)

In 2010, exactly eighteen years after his death from AIDS, the artist David Wojnarowicz was condemned for one of his works. His name was by no means unfamiliar to the Christian right by that point. Nor was he a stranger to the NEA.

Born in 1954, Wojnarowicz was a photographer, writer, filmmaker, painter, and activist whose work explored the notion of the outsider in society and who, from the late 1980s, became increasingly focused on the gay community and on AIDS sufferers such as himself. His name first came up on the NEA radar in November 1989 when John Frohnmayer, the agency's new director, suspended a $10,000 NEA grant to the avant-garde New York-based Artists Space for an exhibition titled *Witnesses*. What had irked Frohnmayer especially was a catalogue essay by Wojnarowicz in which the artist had expressed his "rage" at the ravages of AIDS, and his dream of setting fire to Senator Jesse Helms (who, earlier that year, had attacked Serrano and Mapplethorpe). Wojnarowicz also assailed other political and religious officials. In the end, Artists Space retained its grant, but the catalogue was funded by other means.

The following spring, works by Wojnarowicz—one of them representing Jesus with a hypodermic needle plunged into his arm—were reproduced in mailings by Reverend Wildmon (founder of the American Family Association) to all members of Congress, as examples of the kind of art that the taxpayer should stop funding. Wojnarowicz furiously fought back, suing the American Family Association on the grounds that they had reproduced his art without permission and violated copyright. In August 1990, AFA was instructed by the U.S. District Court to alter one of the pamphlets. Wojnarowicz walked away with $1 in damages. (From the court's point of view, there was no evidence that he had suffered financial damage because of the reproductions.)

Two decades later, Wojnarowicz was singled out again, this time post-humously, for a video that was actually an edit of a two-part film work that he had shot partly in Mexico titled *A Fire in My Belly*. One segment was a long, thirteen-minute rumination on violence and street life featuring a cockfight, a bullfight, wrestlers, industrial wheels, circus acts, marionettes, and picture cards. The second segment was a more coherent, tightly focused seven-minute work (posthumously discovered on a separate film reel) that represented pain, death, and sorrow.

Shot immediately after the death of the artist's partner, it was a visually disturbing reflection on the AIDS epidemic. It showed ants crawling over coins, coins dropping into a bandaged hand, two halves of a bread loaf being sewn together, a man's lips being sewn together, a petri dish filled with blood, skulls, a gravestone, and an effigy of Christ with a large bleeding scar covered with large ants.

Ants appeared often in Wojnarowicz's work. They could be seen elsewhere in his films—crawling over coins, toy soldiers, a clock, or other items. In a 1989 interview, he explained that animals "allow us to view certain things that we wouldn't allow ourselves to see in regard to human activity," and that in his Mexican images incorporating the figure of Christ, "I used the ants as a metaphor for society because the social structure of the ant world is parallel to ours."

The *Hide/Seek* exhibition that opened at the National Portrait Gallery in Washington, D.C., on October 30, 2010, featured a four-minute mashup, or edit, of the two videos, with the same title that Wojnarowicz had given the originals—*A Fire in My Belly*—even though the artist had never produced a finished version in his lifetime. The Smithsonian showed the edit (created by the exhibition's curator and by the artist Bart Everly) with the permission of the Wojnarowicz estate.

A month after the exhibition opened, CNSNews (part of the Media Research Center, a conservative organization whose mission is to demonstrate the media's liberal bias) published an article titled: "Smithsonian Christmas-Season Exhibit Features Ant-Covered Jesus . . ." The article was illustrated with a still from the Wojnarowicz video, and captioned: "The image shows Christ on the cross with ants crawling over his body and face."

The article pointed out that the Smithsonian Institution had an annual budget of $761 million, and that two-thirds of it came from federal government. The National Portrait Gallery—which was part of the Smithsonian—received $5.8 million in federal funding in the 2010 fiscal year, and the same amount the year before. The article then described the video, quoted from the wall labels and catalogue, and asked cocurator David C. Ward whether the exhibit "might be offensive to people who disagree with the homosexual lifestyle."

"This exhibition identifies specific artists who were gay and discusses how that identity affected their art," Ward replied. "Insofar as Hide/Seek has an over-arching message it is that democratic culture consists of many strands and influences."

The day after the article's publication, the Catholic League (a conservative and Catholic organization) issued a press release about an exhibition at the Smithsonian's National Portrait Gallery "that features a video that shows large ants eating away at Jesus on a crucifix. The exhibit is replete with homo-erotic images."

The Catholic League's president, Bill Donohue, then commented in the release: "We call it hate speech." He said that despite a plaque at the entrance to the exhibit pledging to uphold justice and the right of all people and groups to inclusion and equality, "somehow Christians didn't make the cut," and announced that he was writing to congressional appropriation committees to "reconsider future funding."

In a subsequent interview, Donohue told the *New York Times*: "It would jump out at people if they had ants crawling all over the body of Muhammad." He added: "I'm not going to buy the argument that this is some statement about some poor guy dying of AIDS. Was this supposed to be a Christmas present to Catholics?"

It all looked, sounded, and felt like an exact rerun of the art scandals of 1989—a case of déjà vu all over again. History, or rather art history, was repeating itself. It was as if no progress had been made in the area of art censorship. Once again, a leader of the Christian right was condemning a publicly funded institution for showing a work of art that he found offensive. Once again, a museum that received taxpayers' money was being faulted for showing a piece that the writer of the letter had found shocking, and promoting a way of life that he found reprehensible. Once again political leaders had jumped on the art bandwagon.

Representative Eric Cantor of Virginia, a Republican, described the Wojnarowicz video as an "outrageous use of taxpayer money and an obvious attempt to offend Christians during the Christmas season." Jack Kingston of Georgia, another Republican, labeled it "in-your-face perversion paid for by tax dollars."

So in something of a replay of events two decades earlier—when the Corcoran pulled the plug on the Mapplethorpe exhibition in 1989—the

National Portrait Gallery engaged in an act of self-censorship. It withdrew the video from the exhibition. The museum's director, Martin E. Sullivan, explained that the takedown was because of "a misperception that that video was about that artist intentionally wanting to do a sacrilegious piece on Christ or the crucifix or whatever."

He said he understood if the act was seen as one of self-censoring, but that it was a "very tough call" because of the ongoing debate about federal culture spending. "We don't think it's in the interest, not only of the Smithsonian but of other federally supported cultural organizations, to pick fights," he said.

No sooner did the National Gallery remove the work than a wave of furious counterprotests broke out. The first was by the Transformer gallery in D.C., which played *A Fire in My Belly* on a monitor in a gallery window perfectly visible from the street. The PPOW Gallery, representing the Wojnarowicz estate, put two versions of *A Fire in My Belly* on its website for all to see.

The next day, more than one hundred people marched—with their mouths taped over to suggest censorship—to the Portrait Gallery. The day after that, the Association of Art Museum Directors published an objection to the decision. It describes it as "unwarranted and uninformed censorship from politicians and other public figures," many of whom hadn't even seen the show or the work, and stressed that freedom of expression meant "the rights and opportunities of art museums to present works of art that express different points of view."

Meanwhile, the video became a work that everybody wanted a piece of. What became clear once again was that nothing served an artist more than censorship—or the threat or whiff of it. Wojnarowicz became an overnight star. Several dozen galleries and museums around the world put his video on display.

At the National Gallery, however, the work stayed down. The Smithsonian Board of Regents later gathered a panel of experts who recommended that "in the absence of actual error, changes to exhibitions should not be made once an exhibition opens without meaningful consultation with the curator, director, secretary and the leadership of the Board of Regents."

Today, these controversies have turned into art-school case studies, and the three artists condemned by the Christian Right are now, to all intents and purposes, part of the art-historical canon. The scandals have served to boost their critical recognition, public notoriety, and art-market standing.

A decade after he was slammed by Mayor Giuliani, Chris Ofili went on to get a mid-career retrospective at Tate Britain in London. Serrano had a show at the New Museum less than a decade after his Senate skewering. The works of the late Wojnarowicz are regularly exhibited, and he is considered one of the most prominent artists of the AIDS era.

In the rare instances when there are protests against these artists' religiously themed works, they are so small as to go virtually unnoticed. When *Piss Christ* was shown in an exhibition at the Edward Tyler Nahem gallery in New York in 2012, a small group of Catholics—representing Donohue's group, the Catholic League for Religious and Civil Rights in the United States—demonstrated against it outside the gallery. Donohue was with them.

"I would argue that ethics should dictate that you don't go around gratuitously and intentionally insulting people of faith," Donohue was quoted by a reporter as saying. "I don't care whether you're Muslim or Jewish or Catholic or whatever you might be."

When Donohue and his cohorts got into an argument with the exhibition's security officers, they promptly departed. And they were replaced soon afterward by three counterprotesters, two of them dressed as nuns, who were there to defend the Serrano photograph.

Today, American politicians are no longer scapegoating artists and making political slogans out of controversial artworks. That's because the American taxpayer is no longer the principal funder of artists and their careers. Money now comes predominantly from private sources—corporations, wealthy individuals, trusts, foundations—rather than from a federal government agency or from the mayor of a big city. So politicians feel less entitled to poke their noses into the contents of an exhibition and to quibble with this or that work of art.

The art world is now flush with private-sector money: donations from billionaires and their museums and foundations, sponsorships from big corporations, gifts from rich wives. These new sources of revenue come with a raft of new problems—having to do with ethics, conflicts of interest, and propriety—which I will discuss in the next chapter.

6.

All Money Is Dirty

M odern-day Western museums are incredibly expensive to run. Caring for their permanent collections is already a labor-intensive and complicated task. Then there are all of the other strands to a museum's operations: exhibition making, curating, education and outreach, management and administration, front-of-house and security staffing, marketing and publicity, retailing and events, and development—meaning fundraising from donors and sponsors of all kinds. The annual budgets of top Western modern-art museums range between $100 million and $200 million. In the case of European museums, a sizeable chunk comes from their governments, meaning from the taxpayer. US museums are mostly privately financed and live on their endowments. So philanthropy is the linchpin of their business model.

For all museums, regardless of their location, money from private individuals, trusts and foundations, corporations, and sponsors is vital. Fundraising is absolutely crucial to their survival—so much so that it is now a big part of a museum director's job. Institutions are more and more reliant on philanthropy and donations from people with very deep pockets: the billionaires, the one percent, however you want to describe the mega-rich. Why them? Because as someone with decades of high-level museum fundraising explained in an interview for this book, "You have to have a lot of money to give it away."

For the givers themselves, cultural philanthropy is highly prestigious. Museums are universally perceived as temples of high art, connoisseurship and integrity; they are the major landmarks of the cities they find themselves in; and they are public and high-visibility sites that draw millions of visitors each year. Any person or entity with their name on a museum building, wing, or blockbuster show is sure to be noticed and talked about.

And being talked about as a cultural patron is what many of those high-net-worth individuals look for, especially when their fortunes are newly minted. Arts philanthropy is one of the quicker ways of climbing the social ladder. Since the Renaissance, the patronage and ownership of art has been an important status symbol—and its importance has only increased with the exponential growth in the world's billionaires.

A Forbes ranking showed that there were a total of 2,775 billionaires in the world in 2021—three and a half times as many as there were in 2009. Between 2009 and 2019, the number of billionaires around the world nearly tripled to 2,095. Most billionaires are in the United States and Europe, but China and India boast a few hundred billionaires each. These are the very individuals who engage in heated auction-house bidding wars over star artworks.

Here's a recent example. In November 2015, Liu Yiqian—a former taxi driver turned billionaire who owns two private museums in Shanghai—paid $170.4 million for a nude by Amedeo Modigliani. "Modigliani's works already have a pretty established value on the market," he told the *New York*

Times. "And his nude paintings have been collected by some of the world's top museums."

Of late, billionaires from around the globe have shown incredible largesse toward the world's major museums, helping them fund building expansions and blockbuster exhibitions, and sitting on their boards. Board seats are not just fancy perks: they come with invisible strings attached. In the nonprofit world, to which museums belong, trustees are expected to "give, get, or get off"—meaning either reach into their own pockets or coax others to reach into theirs.

For high-net-worth individuals, being on museum boards is a big responsibility. As trustees, they are the overseers of those high temples of culture. They have a say in who runs them and for how long, which exhibitions are programmed or not, and what the long-term strategy is. They also enjoy the glamour that comes with the territory. Not only can they hobnob with the greatest living artists and collect blue-chip art that is only sold to a select few, but until the global COVID-19 outbreak, they also led a jet-setting lifestyle that involved shuttling from one art fair to another, and from one exclusive art shindig to another.

The preview days of the Venice Art Biennale were a perfect illustration. During those seventy-two exhilarating hours, the Grand Canal was swarmed with the superyachts of billionaires. Members of the one percent were water-taxied from one sumptuous Venetian palazzo to another, from this exclusive vernissage to that Very VIP party. During the day, the Biennale's main exhibition venues—the Giardini and the Arsenale—teemed with wealthy wives wearing high-end sneakers and luxury handbags, who perused the contemporary-art installations as if they were vitrines at Hermès.

Since the turn of the millennium, millions—if not billions—of dollars, euros, and pounds from these high-net-worth individuals have poured into the coffers of the West's top museums. The funds are needed more than ever in Europe, because governments, facing ballooning budget deficits and public debts, have been slashing their spending on culture.

To complete the construction of its new wing, which was inaugurated in 2016, Tate Modern received one of the largest donations in its history: a gift of fifty million pounds from the billionaire Russian émigré Len Blavatnik. His contribution roughly matched that of British national and local government. The new building has now been renamed the Blavatnik Building. The Tate Modern extension, designed by the architects Herzog & de Meuron, has doubled the spaces available to visitors, and allowed the opening of exhibition galleries for film and performance art.

There are plenty of other examples in Europe of donations from deep-pocketed philanthropists that have enabled institutions, their communities, and the art world as a whole to benefit from a richer array of cultural programming. So far, museums have been all too happy to receive such funding.

Yet in an age of scrutiny and accountability, questions are now being asked, if not shouted out, via social media. Where is the money coming from? How was it made? Many museumgoers—who, in Europe, happen also to be the taxpayers funding those institutions—are increasingly demanding that the money given to museums be clean and ethically sound. The definition of "ethically sound" is becoming more and more restrictive. As a seasoned British fundraiser told me, there is a lot of digging and investigating going on nowadays. Had that kind of digging gone on before, many a museum board would have been vulnerable.

"Pretty much all money is dirty somewhere down the line," noted Aaron Cezar of the Delfina Foundation. "If it hasn't been made through a dirty process, it might have been invested in a dirty process. Or you might find that the source of the money from a donor might be all quite legitimate, but then they're supporting other things that you don't agree with. It's very, very difficult."

Cezar, who runs an international artist residency program at the London headquarters of the foundation, said he had introduced ethics into Delfina's funding model. As a smaller institution, Delfina was able to offer its artists a choice in who funded their residencies. If the artist had ethical qualms about a corporation backing their London stay, Delfina would look for another funder.

While large-scale arts philanthropy is a fairly recent phenomenon in Europe, it started more than a century ago in the United States—chiefly because the government was by and large unwilling to dig into its pockets (meaning those of the American taxpayer) to pay for culture. So museums and cultural institutions were largely left to their own devices, and relied heavily on private money to operate.

At the turn of the twentieth century, obscenely wealthy titans of industry—the big steel, oil, and railroad tycoons—became the target of public finger-pointing, in much the same way that the one percent are today. Cultural institutions took the opportunity to appeal to their generosity.

In 1880, when the Metropolitan Museum of Art was inaugurated, one of its trustees—a lawyer named Joseph Choate—made an elaborate fundraising pitch at the dedication ceremony. "Think of it, ye millionaires of many markets," he said, "what glory may yet be yours, if you only listen to our advice, to convert pork into porcelain, grain and produce into priceless pottery, the rude ores of commerce into sculptured marble."

As public rage over extreme wealth and inequality started to boil over, industrialists such as Andrew Carnegie and John D. Rockefeller decided to "give back." They set up private foundations to make it happen. At first, the criticism continued. After all, these foundations were funded by money earned in inappropriate ways by a caste of people widely known as robber barons. As President Theodore Roosevelt pointed out, "No amount of charities in spending such fortunes can compensate in any way for the misconduct of acquiring them."

Yet in the decades that followed, such objections died down. Donations by the super-wealthy and their foundations and charitable arms were universally welcomed and embraced. As the donations paid for impressive buildings and as time passed, the magnates were no longer viewed as robber barons. Far fewer questions were asked about where the money came from. Soon, they would be remembered for funding outstanding cultural and educational institutions.

In the 1970s, one artist started denouncing corporate philanthropy in his work. The German-born, New York-based artist Hans Haacke voiced concerns about what he saw as the insidious role that corporations and executives were starting to play in museums. By sponsoring exhibitions and programs, and by sitting on boards, they were using museums as an instrument of corporate brand building, he objected, and were having potentially undue influence on their decision-making process.

Haacke decried corporate philanthropy in a number of works, including *On Social Grease* (1975), a set of six photo-engraved magnesium plates mounted on aluminum with quotes from a different corporate titan on each. David Rockefeller—then the chairman of MoMA and of the Chase Manhattan Bank—was quoted on one of the Haacke plaques as saying: "From an economic standpoint, such involvement in the arts can mean direct and tangible benefits. It can provide a company with extensive publicity and advertising, a brighter public reputation, and an improved corporate image. It can build better customer relations, a readier acceptance of company products, and a superior appraisal of their quality. Promotion of the arts can improve the morale of employees and help attract qualified personnel."

Haacke's beef with corporate philanthropy drew attention, and became one of his defining characteristics as a contemporary artist. Yet in the decades that followed—which coincided with the explosion of Wall Street and the exponential growth of the financial industry in the world's major capitals—objections such as those raised by Haacke were snuffed out.

Governments in the West embarked on austerity programs and slashed their culture spending because it seemed less essential. Museums and cultural institutions on both sides of the Atlantic started expanding their development departments and sending their directors on fundraising missions seven days a week at the headquarters of corporations and at the mansions of the very rich. They received billions in the process, and for a long time, virtually no questions were asked. Recipient institutions were grateful. To show their gratitude, they readily integrated donors onto their boards and acquisition committees, and put their name on buildings, wings, galleries, and posters.

Today, the tide is turning again, and in unprecedented ways. It is not enough for a billionaire or a top executive to sit on boards and give a lot. The money that gets handed over has to be ethically clean.

Take the example of Warren B. Kanders. In 2015, while he was a board vice chairman of the Whitney Museum of American Art, an article appeared on the *Hyperallergic* art site headlined "The Unlikely Connection Between the Whitney Museum and Riot Gear." It opened as follows. "We all know it costs a lot of money to sit on the board of a major art museum, so naturally the question becomes: where does that money come from? In the case of one trustee of the Whitney Museum of American Art, the answer is selling high-grade weapons to police departments and militaries."

Hyperallergic reported that a brand of the Safariland group, owned by Kanders, was supplying militarized gear (including rubber pellets and tear gas) to US police departments.

In November 2018, another *Hyperallergic* story reported that US guards on the Mexican border were firing tear gas canisters at hundreds of Central American asylum seekers (including children); the canisters had labels that corresponded to brands owned by Kanders. Kanders had been a "significant contributor" to the Whitney's recent Warhol exhibition.

The article sparked outrage. The following month, an angry open letter was sent from the Whitney's staff to its director, Adam Weinberg. Another open letter signed by artists, curators, and critics demanded Kanders's resignation.

Meanwhile, an activist group called Decolonize This Place (DTP) staged weekly protests outside the Whitney in the run-up to the Biennial. Marz Saffore, one of the group's core members, identified herself as "a queer Black woman who also is an artist," and noted: "We're in a moment in the art world right now where the landscape is changing in terms of accountability." Artists wanted "to be a part of that."

Eight artists selected for the Whitney Biennial then vowed to pull out unless Kanders quit. On July 25, 2019, Kanders handed in his resignation letter. "The targeted campaign of attacks against me and my company that has been waged these past several months has threatened to undermine the important work of the Whitney," he wrote. "I joined this board to help the museum prosper. I do not wish to play a role, however inadvertent, in its demise." In June 2020, Kanders announced that he was selling those divisions of his company that sold tear gas and riot gear.

The future of the Whitney Museum does not hang on the vacating of a single board seat, regardless of how wealthy or generous its occupant. One potential side effect of Kanders-style episodes, however, is that in a country where the government does little arts funding and where cultural institutions depend on private donors, other potential givers could be deterred. As the Whitney director Adam Weinberg noted in a statement a month after Kanders's resignation, museums were "fragile institutions" that needed private-sector support to exercise a mission in society that was now more important than ever. "We would hate to see those who wish to support our efforts in bringing the work of American artists to a broad public become discouraged from doing so," he said.

Private-sector support is indeed a crucial component of museum funding nowadays, even in Europe. Capital projects and building expansions are impossible without contributions from corporate sponsors or from the superrich (whose fortunes, as mentioned before, are seldom squeaky clean). Even exhibitions need outside sponsors. They often also need the support of commercial galleries to cover catalogue, insurance, and shipping costs.

And as we all know, gifts seldom come without strings attached. A benefactor can then lean on the museum to program an exhibition of works he collects. A gallery can then coax the museum into exhibiting an artist it represents. That's why it's all the more important for social media to scrutinize the back-scratching and cozy relationships that go into the funding of modern-day museums.

The Sackler family are a very good example of a benefactor with long-standing links to cultural institutions on both sides of the pond. They have

Elizabeth Bick, "Nan Goldin protesting against the Sacklers" (2019)

also been identified as makers of the painkiller OxyContin, a principal cause of US opioid deaths.

The Sacklers

If you go on a museum crawl in New York or London nowadays, it will be hard to find an institution that doesn't have a wing or at least one or more rooms named after the Sackler family. In New York, the Metropolitan Museum of Art has a Sackler wing housing the majestic Temple of Dendur, a sandstone monument from ancient Egypt. The Guggenheim Museum has a Sackler Center for Arts Education—an 8,200-square-foot space with an auditorium and an exhibition space. The American Museum of Natural History has two Sackler-named sections, a genomics institute and an educational laboratory.

Over in London, the field is also crowded. One of the Serpentine Galleries' two buildings still has the name "Serpentine Sackler Gallery" on its facade (though the Serpentine announced in March 2021 that it had renamed the space the Serpentine North Gallery everywhere else, including on its website and in its communications). The Royal Academy of Arts has a Sackler exhibition wing. The British Museum and the National Gallery each have Sackler rooms. And when the Victoria and Albert expanded in 2017, the vast courtyard leading to the new wing was named the Sackler courtyard.

Until a few years ago, there was no public outrage at seeing the Sackler name here, there, and everywhere in major Western museums. It was synonymous with cultural excellence, patronage, and generosity. But today, it has become a label associated with one of the biggest human tragedies in present-day America: the opioid crisis.

OxyContin is a painkiller so powerful that it can be twice as strong as morphine. It was marketed from 1996 by a company named Purdue Pharma, owned and run by members of the Sackler family. It can provide as much as twelve hours of relief from extreme pain. That's because it is an opioid, a devastatingly addictive narcotic. And yet it was promoted by the company to general practitioners all over the United States who were encouraged to prescribe it. In the process, Purdue went from being a small pharmaceutical company to generating sales of nearly $3 billion in 2001, according to *Winners Take All*, Anand Giridharadas's 2019 investigation into US corporate philanthropy. OxyContin was responsible for 80 percent of those sales.

Today, the Sackler family fortune is estimated at around $13 billion. Much of that wealth owes to sales of OxyContin. And yet for a long time, few were aware of the connection. To most people—including top museum directors and artists—the Sackler name was synonymous with high-level cultural patronage.

The veil was lifted by journalists from the *New Yorker* and *Esquire* magazines in 2017. In "The Family That Built an Empire of Pain"—a *New Yorker* article published that October—Patrick Radden Keefe (author of a recent book on the Sacklers called *Empire of Pain*) pointed out that the Sacklers were now among America's richest families, richer even than the Rockefellers or the Mellons, and that most of their money had been made in recent decades. "Yet the source of their wealth is to most people as obscure as that of the robber barons," he wrote. "While the Sacklers are interviewed regularly on the subject of their generosity, they almost never speak publicly about the family business, Purdue Pharma—a privately held company, based in Stamford, Connecticut, that developed the prescription painkiller OxyContin."

The article went on to show how Purdue had generated some $35 billion in revenues from the drug by marketing it across the medical community, and how, since 1999, hundreds of thousands of Americans had died of overdoses linked to OxyContin and other prescription opioids.

"I don't know how many rooms in different parts of the world I've given talks in that were named after the Sacklers," said Allen Frances, a former chair of psychiatry at Duke University School of Medicine, in the *New Yorker* article. "Their name has been pushed forward as the epitome of good works and of the fruits of the capitalist system. But, when it comes down to it, they've earned this fortune at the expense of millions of people who are addicted. It's shocking how they have gotten away with it."

In his subsequent book *Empire of Pain*, published in 2021, Keefe investigated the family and its links to the opioid tragedy. He noted that although the Sacklers, in their heyday, were occasionally likened to the Medicis, the source of their wealth—unlike that of the Medicis'—was long a mystery. "Members of the family bestowed their name on arts and education institutions with a sort of mania," wrote Keefe. "It was etched into marble, emblazoned on brass plaques, even spelled out in stained glass. There were Sackler professorships and Sackler scholarships and Sackler lecture series and Sackler prizes. Yet, to the casual observer, it could be difficult to connect the family name with any sort of business that might have generated all this wealth."

The shock was felt most acutely by the artist and photographer Nan Goldin, who had firsthand experience of the drug. Goldin had been prescribed it for surgery in Berlin a few years earlier, and she initially stuck to the recommended dose, but then developed a dangerous and long-lasting addiction that nearly ended her life. Goldin was prescribed OxyContin by doctors for more than a year. It was not until the fall of 2017, via a *New Yorker* article by Keefe, that she discovered the connection between OxyContin and the Sacklers.

In *Empire of Pain*, Keefe wrote a chapter about Goldin. "As soon as she took the pills, she could see what the fuss was about," he wrote. "OxyContin didn't just ameliorate the pain in her wrist; it felt like a chemical insulation not just from pain but from anxiety and upset. The drug felt, she would say, like 'a padding between you and the world.'" In January 2018, just months after recovering from her addiction, Goldin published a powerful first-person account in *Artforum* magazine (accompanied by self-portraits of herself as addict). The piece doubled as a manifesto, and announced the birth of a movement.

"I survived the opioid crisis. I narrowly escaped. I went from the darkness and ran full speed into the World," it began. "When I got out of treatment, I became absorbed in reports of addicts dropping dead from my drug, OxyContin. I learned that the Sackler family, whose name I knew from museums and galleries, were responsible for the epidemic."

Goldin then recounted her own addiction to the painkiller. She recalled that 40 milligrams were too much, initially, "but as my habit grew there was never enough. At first, I could maintain. Then it got messier and messier."

She moved to New York, where her dealer kept her well supplied. She went from the prescribed dosage of three pills a day to eighteen pills a day, and spent all of her money on the drug. "My life revolved entirely around getting and using Oxy," she wrote. "Counting and recounting, crushing and snorting was my full-time job." The addiction ended only after a two-and-a-half-month period of rehabilitation.

Goldin announced at the end of the piece that she was setting up a group called Prescription Addiction Intervention Now (P.A.I.N.) to go after the Sacklers. "To get their ear, we will target their philanthropy," she wrote. "They have washed their blood money through the halls of museums and universities around the world. We demand that the Sacklers and Purdue Pharma use their fortune to fund addiction treatment and education. There is no time to waste."

The artist started planning performative actions at top Sackler-backed museums. "I felt that the Sacklers lived in their museums, that that's where their reputation was," she told me in a December 2020 interview. "I wanted them to be shamed by their own people. So I started to look into how I could go into the museums and try to affect them."

Until then, the world had seen many an artist or public personality front a campaign for this or that cause. But seldom had a visual artist and recovered addict put themselves and their own life and reputation on the line as boldly as Goldin did. Her very visible participation in P.A.I.N. performance-protests around the world made international media headlines, which in turn embarrassed the institutions in question.

In March 2018, Goldin and a group of fellow activists entered the Met gallery containing the Temple of Dendur and started shouting slogans ("Temple of greed! Temple of Oxy!") "We are artists, activists, addicts," Goldin proclaimed, standing before two big stone statues. "We are fed up." Then her fellow protesters moved up to the reflecting pool around the temple, where so many glamorous fundraising parties had been held, and started tossing orange pill bottles into the pool. "Look at the facts!" they hollered. "Read the stats!"

Appearing on my podcast *CultureBlast* in June 2021, Goldin explained: "With my loud voice, I managed to engage the public into understanding that the Sackler name is not the name of philanthropists, but it's synonymous with the opioid crisis."

In July 2019, at the entrance to the Louvre Museum in Paris, Goldin and her fellow activists staged a similar action demanding that the Sackler name be taken off one of the galleries; they unfurled a banner in front of the glass pyramid, and one activist lay in the surrounding pool of water. And in December 2019, Goldin and a few dozen others staged a "die-in" at the Guggenheim Museum in New York, lying on their backs in the museum's giant foyer as prescription-like pieces of paper rained on them like confetti.

The activism paid off. In March 2019, the National Portrait Gallery in London turned down a promised $1.3 million Sackler grant toward its redevelopment—after Goldin threatened to cancel her upcoming retrospective at the museum. In July of that year, the Louvre announced that it was taking the Sackler name off the gallery that bore it. (The naming agreement, made in 1997, had expired.) The Met, the Guggenheim, the American Museum of Natural History, and Tate Modern all announced that they would no longer take any Sackler donations. And the Met also said that the name of its Sackler Wing was officially being placed "under review."

I asked Goldin on my podcast if she was happy with the way things were going. She described the settlement with the Sacklers as "outrageous" and said she hoped an act would pass in Congress making it "illegal for billionaires to hide behind their corporations in bankruptcy court."

Goldin's other big goal now is to see the Sackler name removed from all institutions. This is already happening on university campuses. In December 2019, Tufts University became the first university to announce that it was taking the Sackler name down from its buildings and programs. That same month, the Smithsonian announced that its two Asian art museums—the Sackler Gallery and the Freer Gallery of Art—were being rebranded as the National Museum of Asian Art. The Sackler name was not coming down, however, because according to the donation agreement, it had to stay on the gallery in perpetuity.

Nevertheless, museum professionals I spoke to—including ones who had received Sackler funding for capital projects and building extensions before the OxyContin scandal broke out—predicted that over time, more and more institutions would take down the Sackler name, irrespective of clauses and contracts. It was becoming too much of a liability, they said. There was a wave of rejections of any future Sackler funding, despite the dearth of other corporate donors and despite the severe cuts to government funding of culture across Europe.

Tufts had been the first to do that, despite its contractual obligations. A spokesman said the association with the Sacklers was "untenable" and contrary to the "values and mission" of its medical school and university.

To Goldin, all Sackler money was bad. "I think you have to look at the degree," she said. "There are degrees of evil, like there are degrees of good, and some are more ambiguous than others. Having the bodies of 450,000 people right in front of you in America alone is pretty much evidence of the degree."

Meanwhile in London, similar ethical questions are being raised—sometimes very vocally—about where museum money is coming from. The corporate sponsor that gets named and shamed with the greatest regularity nowadays is BP, the international oil company.

Demonstrators from the BP or Not BP group stage a protest at the British Museum to denounce its sponsorship by the oil company.

BP

BP has for decades been incredibly active on the British cultural scene. According to a 2019 brochure published on its website, BP has been supporting U.K.-wide arts programs for more than fifty years, and reached more than fifty million people.

In London, it has been the long-term patron of many major arts institutions. For three decades, BP has sponsored the Royal Opera House and the National Portrait Gallery (for its annual BP Portrait Award). The British Museum has had BP as its corporate partner for more than two decades. Other longstanding relationships—now dissolved—were with Tate and with the Royal Shakespeare Company.

These associations presumably grew out of BP's wish to raise its profile, engage in corporate social responsibility, and be less associated with pollution and greenhouse gases. Yet they were also the result of the personal passion that the company's longtime chairman John Browne (now Lord Browne) had for the arts. When Browne resigned as chairman of BP in 2007, he joined the board of Tate that same year, and in 2009 became its chair, a position he held until 2017.

Over time, however, the BP name has become one that institutions are finding more and more difficult to be connected with. Citizens of all ages in the twenty-first century are increasingly concerned about the climate emergency, and increasingly unforgiving of major world oil companies. To make matters worse, in 2010, BP was responsible for a very public, deadly disaster.

That April, a BP offshore rig known as Deepwater Horizon—described by the company as "the deepest well ever drilled by the oil and gas industry," attaining depths in the ocean floor that were the equivalent of the heights reached by jet airplanes—blew up in the Gulf of Mexico during a drilling operation. The explosion left eleven crew members dead, and led oil to burst out of the ocean floor in continuous and devastating convulsions. It took three months for the United States' largest-ever oil spill to be brought under control. By then, four million barrels of crude had polluted the environment.

Two months after the explosion, at Tate Britain in London, a spectacular protest was staged by a group of environmental activists known as Liberate Tate. It took place at the museum's annual summer party, to which various participants in the art world—artists, curators, museum professionals, journalists—were invited. As one of the guests, I arrived just before the protesters began their demonstration at the museum, the original headquarters of Tate. As dozens of guests in tailored suits and cocktail dresses arrived for the summer party, black-clad activists with veils over their heads suddenly appeared, carrying cans of treacle bearing the BP logo. They splashed the entrance to the museum with the thick, dark goo, then sprinkled bird feathers over it. "What do we want? Liberate Tate!" they cried. "When do we want it? Now!"

Inside, as guests bit into their cheese puffs and sipped glasses of Pimm's, another set of activists staged a separate and equally eye-catching action. Having snuck into the party with cans of treacle hidden under their skirts, they suddenly emptied the cans in Tate Britain's vast, columned hall, before the very eyes of the Tate director, Nicholas Serota, who stood by in silence.

I went up to him to ask for his reaction. He pointed out the challenges involved in accepting sponsorship. "It's a very difficult decision for an institution to make," he said. "There's no money that is completely pure."

Meanwhile, the tarred floor of the museum's grand hall, the Duveen Gallery, was quickly and successfully mopped up. But getting the treacle off the entrance ramp outside seemed a much bigger challenge. As I left the party hours later, I saw Tate personnel stubbornly scrub away at the darkened pavement, and use industrial vacuum cleaners to remove the bird feathers stuck to the treacle.

Six years later, after many more such actions and denunciations, and with Tate itself increasingly concerned about the environment, the twenty-six-year-old relationship between Tate and BP was broken off, and Tate said it would turn down all future sponsorship.

"The climate and ecological emergency is one of the greatest challenges of our time," Tate Modern's director, Morris, told me in an interview. She said Tate had committed to cutting its carbon emissions by fifty percent by 2023 and was striving for net zero emissions by 2030. A complete audit of operations had also been carried out, and strategies were being introduced "for doing things differently."

Two art institutions that are still receiving BP funding are the National Portrait Gallery—for its BP Portrait Awards—and the British Museum. These two institutions are the target of continuous protests.

BP has been the British Museum's corporate partner for nearly a quarter of a century. But this relationship is causing increasing unease, including within the institution itself. Many staff members are said to be unhappy about the sponsorship. And in July 2019, a high-profile trustee—the Egyptian author Ahdaf Soueif—resigned from the board, invoking the BP sponsorship as a principal reason. "The world is caught up in battles over climate change, vicious and widening inequality, the residual heritage of colonialism, questions of democracy, citizenship and human rights," she wrote in her resignation statement. "On all these issues, the museum needs to take a clear ethical position."

Soueif said she had raised the issue of BP's "very high profile sponsorship of public exhibitions" with the board and director in early 2016. "The public relations value that the museum gives to BP is unique," she noted, "but the sum of money BP gives the museum is not unattainable elsewhere."

That was true before the 2008 global financial crisis, when multinationals were scrambling to get their logos on the poster at one or another of the big museums of London. Yet the pool of corporate donors has severely shrunk over the last decade, and companies with spare cash prefer to give it to causes that score higher with public opinion—such as climate change, for example. A museum such as the National Gallery in London is lucky to have a lasting relationship with Credit Suisse, the bank. Institutions that had longstanding relationships with BP and that have severed those relationships appear not to have found a substitute partner. That might explain the British Museum's reluctance to part ways with the oil giant.

In February 2020—just before the U.K. and much of the rest of the world went into lockdown on account of the COVID-19 pandemic—a group of demonstrators disguised as ancient Greek warriors dragged a thirteen-foot-tall wooden horse into the main courtyard of the British Museum to protest the *Troy* exhibition, sponsored by BP. They managed to take over the museum premises for much of the weekend with workshops, talks, and creative activities. Many dozens of others joined in.

I reached out to Jess Worth, one of the founders of BP or not BP? (the organizers of the Trojan horse action) to get a better understanding of their goals. Worth said she and others had set up the group in 2012 because she was a climate-change campaigner with heightened sensitivity to the oil industry, and had discovered that BP was sponsoring the World Shakespeare Festival that year, coinciding with the 2012 London Olympic Games. Worth had studied Shakespeare all of her life, and the thought of the BP logo appearing next to the Royal Shakespeare Company stirred her into action. "I just felt: I have to do something about this, because this is really upsetting me," she recalled.

She and a group of friends got together and carried out a series of stage invasions during the Shakespeare festival. Right before the performance of a Shakespeare play was due to start, BP or not BP? activists would hop onstage and, in costume, recite a three-minute anti-BP message in the form of a Shakespearean soliloquy. That's how the group started, and that's why the group gave itself a Shakespearean-sounding name. The British Museum, another beneficiary of BP largesse, was the natural next target.

Why BP in particular? "As a company it has made a bigger contribution to climate change than almost any other entity on the planet," said Worth. They have lobbied to create a society and economy "that are completely hooked on fossil fuels," and "are some of the absolute biggest stumbling blocks in the world to actually solving the climate crisis."

The BP or not BP? protests were "part of a global push to negate the power of the fossil-fuel industry, so that the world has a hope of actually preventing the worst runaway climate change," she maintained.

To the British Museum's director, Hartwig Fischer, BP's sponsorship was part of a very complicated issue. "We've always said publicly that we have a complex funding model for the museum," he told me. "In order to deliver our public mission, we need support from different sources: from the private sector, from private individuals, and also from the corporate world. We do not endorse or promote any product in any way."

Fischer explained that outside funding had become all the more necessary because of cuts in government funding after the 2008 global financial crisis. Without sponsors, the museum could simply not put on major exhibitions. Meanwhile, the museum was "an open forum for these important questions to be debated," and activists and protesters were free to stage demonstrations on the premises.

That openness was something of a double-edged sword, he said. Because the museum was, by definition, an open and public place, it was also "a very easy target" for protesters—just "not the right target," because it had no power to solve the climate emergency.

Fischer brought up a 2020 exhibition at the museum that directly addressed ecological issues: *Arctic: Culture and Climate*, sponsored by Citi. The exhibition focused on the serious impact of climate change on the Arctic—substantial loss of ice; erratic weather patterns—which were challenging the way of life of the populations living there.

I mentioned Fischer's comments to Worth. She brought the Arctic exhibition as proof that the museum was "absolutely recognizing" the climate crisis. And she completely understood the museum's need to have corporate sponsors. She just objected strongly to this particular sponsor.

BP was a profit-making company that could not be persuaded to stop extracting fossil fuels, she said. But it had to be prevented from extracting fossil fuels at the rate it planned to. And sponsoring the British Museum gave BP the "social license to operate" without being called on the carpet for it.

"We're not saying you shouldn't take any corporate sponsorship," she concluded. "We're saying: Taking money from BP at the moment is a political act," and "perpetuating the climate crisis by giving BP the legitimacy that it desperately needs at the moment."

Public scrutiny of the funding that goes to institutions dedicated to the common good—museums, cultural institutions, and other centers of learning— is unquestionably a welcome development. For decades, big corporations, billionaires and the superrich have been able to buff up their reputations by writing big checks. The practice is so widespread that there are now expressions for it: "art washing," or "reputation laundering." It is so effective a strategy that it has allowed former robber barons to be remembered, generations later, as generous arts patrons.

The same glory might have come to the Sackler family had it not been for the investigations led by journalists, and for the high-visibility campaign spearheaded by the artist Nan Goldin. In the meantime, some members of the Sackler family have distanced themselves from OxyContin, arguing that they were descendants of a man (Arthur C. Sackler) who died before the drug was developed. Yet they and other family members nonetheless derived a vast proportion of their wealth from a drug that has contributed to nearly half a million deaths.

There are those who predict that the Sackler name will gradually be taken down from every building it is currently on. They are probably right. Keeping the name up may soon become unsustainable.

In the meantime, museums and cultural institutions that are recipients of funds from big corporations and billionaire donors can no longer hold their noses and take whatever money comes their way. They are having to get serious about due diligence and to commission (admittedly expensive) private security reports on those who sit on their boards and/or give them funding to avoid embarrassment, social-media finger pointing, and PR disasters down the line.

The probable result of this increased monitoring is that private-sector funding, already hit by the 2008 financial crisis and by the global COVID-19 pandemic, will slow further. New, more transparent and less capitalistic funding models will have to be found. It will be much more difficult for museums to be overly reliant on private corporations whose primary mission is to maximize profits. And with government culture funding being cut and cut again, that leaves little to no other option.

As the former Whitney Museum director Maxwell Anderson said in August 2019, "Unless you are prepared to face real setbacks as an institution, it will be hard to find support derived entirely from sources beyond reproach." He recalled how, on his watch, the Whitney received funds from the tobacco company Altria, and even had an off-site exhibition space in Altria's corporate headquarters. "Although it pained me to be complicit," he recalled, "I also knew that the money they provided was supporting our mission."

In short, while the public needs to be made aware of corporate sponsors that are behaving unethically or are major polluters, sponsorship as a source of art funding is a necessity. Museums "have to raise money in terms of what they're doing, and I don't think fundraising will go away," the Serpentine's artistic director Hans Ulrich Obrist told me when I asked him about money. He said the Serpentine, like other museums, had an ethical committee that looked carefully at incoming funds. Beyond that, the post-pandemic era was an opportunity for art institutions to build alliances and partnerships with mission-driven businesses—whose missions overlapped with theirs.

When it comes to matters of money, responding to public outrage is a relatively easy thing to do. One sponsor can potentially be replaced with another, and one board member or administrator can resign to make way for another. But what about when the controversy focuses on a public artwork—installed permanently and outdoors for the benefit of the public? What happens when a monument edified for all time angers the community it is destined for? How should city authorities respond when a work is petitioned against, or knocked down? Public art and its particular challenges will be explored in detail in the following chapter.

7.

Take Them All Down

P ublic art is a genre all onto itself. City squares, esplanades, and piazzas all over the Western world are chockablock with statues, monuments, and murals put up to glorify, celebrate, and aggrandize people who were either in power themselves or who provided help to those in power. These are monuments to great leaders and heroes, tributes to outstanding thinkers and scientists, and memorials to those who lost their lives in battle. They are designed to extol the great and the good, as defined by the powerful and the victorious. This traditional kind of public art is, by definition, undemo-cratic: Citizens have had no say in who or what gets parked on the plinths that are scattered around their cities.

And with the exception of cities such as Rome—where the public mon-uments are so attractive that you never tire of looking at them—most public artworks are ordinary and bland-looking. To the people who interact with them on a daily basis, they become invisible.

Think about it for a moment. You probably walk past a public sculpture every day and never really pay any attention to it. I personally confess that despite the fact that I regularly find myself in London's Trafalgar Square, I have never once made time to look at the statues that are permanently perched there. They are bronze effigies of people I am not curious about, and I don't really rate them as works of art.

Even when an outdoor sculpture is the work of a modern-art master—Henry Moore, for instance, or Alexander Calder—we can be oblivious to it. There are so many sculptures by Moore and Calder scattered around public spaces in the West that they have lost their luster and started to fade into the surroundings. Even works by prominent living artists can go unnoticed when they are not the centerpiece of a major city square.

For years, on my way to work in London, I ambled past a towering steel sculpture of vertical panels leaning against each other. I only realized much later, after interviewing the prominent American sculptor Richard Serra, that it was one of his sculptures. And it was a striking, powerful work. Yet placed at the entrance to a very busy train station, and near a forest of corporate high-rises, it was somehow not getting my attention.

The reality is that until the postwar period, public art was public in name alone: It was chosen for the people, but never by the people, and little attention was paid to their needs and wants. The artists who made those works were selected by rulers and governments, and the works themselves were glorified propaganda. They were designed to boost patriotism and national pride, vaunt the courage and might of the leadership, and justify the sacrifice of soldiers on the battlefield.

In the postwar years, as Western societies became more and more democratic and suffrage became truly universal, governments started to be more mindful of the audience for public art, meaning ordinary citizens. Rather than continue to commission three-dimensional propaganda, they started to commission outdoor sculptures by contemporary artists that had aesthetic and cultural value. From the 1960s onward, works by the likes of Moore, Calder, and Picasso started proliferating in city centers and business districts to add a touch of color and freshness to urban landscapes and introduce citizens to contemporary forms of sculpture.

With time, younger and less established contemporary artists were commissioned to produce public monuments. In 1980, a nonprofit known as the Vietnam Veterans' Memorial Fund received the congressional go-ahead to finance and build a memorial in Washington, D.C., to commemorate the nearly sixty thousand US soldiers who had lost their lives in that theater of conflict between 1954 and 1975. A competition was set up with a highbrow jury of architects, landscape architects and artists, and more than 1,400 submissions were sent in. The surprise winner was a twenty-one-year-old Asian American Yale University graduate named Maya Ying Lin. She moved the jurors with the simplicity, sobriety, and directness of her submission. Rather than produce heroic effigies of soldiers on the battlefield, as past war sculptors might have done, Lin decided to etch the name of every single fallen soldier into two massive walls of lustrous black granite that came together in a V-shaped configuration.

Personally, when I first saw the monument, I found it very moving. Somehow, the black stone monument managed to pay tribute to each and every American victim of that recent war. Lin's work spoke to me, and stayed with me. But not everyone liked it. Some considered those two slabs of stone to be an unsuitable memorial to the tens of thousands of war dead—a monument that many might not understand. So two years later, a more conventional bronze statue was unveiled, showing three soldiers— one white, one African American, and one Hispanic—by the sculptor Frederick Hart. Lin's memorial has definitely grown on people, however. Today, it is a hugely popular feature of Washington, D.C., and an obligatory stop on any tourist's itinerary.

A year before Lin's monument was installed, another public sculpture commissioned by a federal agency in Washington was unveiled. Only this one had a much more troublesome fate.

Richard Serra, *Tilted Arc* (1981)

In 1979, the sculptor Richard Serra was invited to come up with a work to be installed outside a set of government buildings (including the Jacob K. Javits Federal Building) in New York's Federal Plaza. Commissioning him was the General Services Administration (GSA)—the federal agency that oversees the construction of government buildings across the United States. The funding would come from the GSA's Art in Architecture program, a program originated in 1962 by which up to half of 1 percent of the cost of a building's construction would be spent on commissioning art. To date, some two hundred artists had been commissioned under the program, to the tune of $7 million.

Serra created *Tilted Arc*, a curved 73-ton wall of Cor-Ten steel (a self-oxidizing, rust-colored type of steel that is Serra's medium of choice). The work measured twelve feet high and one hundred and twenty feet long, and it effectively sliced the plaza in two. It cost the government $181,000 and was hoisted in the square in the spring of 1981.

Tilted Arc, unlike most public art, was impossible to overlook. Like it or not, it was a somewhat forbidding partition running down the middle of the square. There was no way not to see it, or to go about your business as if it wasn't there. It was, especially to adversaries of modern art, in-your-face.

The other issue was that the people in the community had not been consulted about it at all and had had no say in its commissioning. The GSA had chosen the work and let Serra create it, never once stopping to sound out the public.

And the public was not won over. Office workers found it ugly and unnecessary, and pushed for its removal. Eventually, two petitions against it garnered a total of 1,300 signatures.

The GSA stood firm, noting that the petitioners represented just over one-tenth of the ten thousand workers in the surrounding buildings. The sculpture stayed in place, and the office workers continued to grouch and grumble against it—until the year 1984, when the GSA got a new regional administrator, a Republican appointee by the name of William Diamond.

Diamond scheduled three days of public hearings to determine whether the sculpture should stay or go. Everyone from neighborhood residents to the crème de la crème of New York culture testified, including Louise Bourgeois, Frank Gehry, Philip Glass, Keith Haring, Joan Jonas, Donald Judd, and Frank Stella. Supporters of Serra outnumbered opponents by a ratio of 2 to 1. There were 56 voices against *Tilted Arc* and 118 in favor.

Arguments against the sculpture were that it was ugly to look at, that it blocked the view across the square, that it was a graffiti magnet, and that it prevented performances or social gatherings to be held in the square. Norman Steinlauf, an employee of the Federal Emergency Management Agency working in an adjacent building, said, "The wall of steel in the front yard of this building does nothing for me, and from what I hear from people in this building and the community, nothing for them, except represent an irritant and impediment."

Counterarguments were brought by William Rubin, who headed the department of painting and sculpture at the Museum of Modern Art. Rubin noted that Serra, one of the world's top sculptors, was about to get a MoMA retrospective. He recalled how the Eiffel Tower had been mocked in its day as a "visual obscenity," and how it was due to be dismantled fifty years later, but grew too popular in the interim. "Truly challenging works of art require a period of time before their artistic language can be understood by a broader public," Rubin argued. The "removal-cum-destruction" of the work should be ruled out until the public can have a "more informed opinion," he said, proposing that everyone regroup at least a decade later.

Serra himself then stood up to defend his work. He noted that it was created specifically for the plaza in question and nowhere else, and so it couldn't be displaced and parked elsewhere. "I don't make portable objects; I don't make works that can be relocated or site adjusted," he said. "My works become part of and are built into the structure of a site, and often restructure, both conceptually and perceptually, the organization of the site."

He explained that his sculptures were "not objects meant for a viewer to stop, look and stare at. The historical concept of placing sculpture on a pedestal was to establish a separation between the sculpture and the viewer. I am interested in a behavioral space in which the viewer interacts with the sculpture in its context." Serra reminded everyone that he had been commissioned by the GSA to make a permanent work, meaning one that would be on that spot forever.

"To enable artists to function and work freely, and to avoid governmental or institutional or donor-sponsored dictates of art, artists ought first to be selected objectively and impartially; and then their artistic expression ought to be insulated from censorship, suppression, and destruction," he concluded.

But as the *New Yorker*'s Tomkins wrote, while the tradition of commissioning public art (church monuments, statues, frescoes, altarpieces) was widely accepted in Renaissance times, there was no such tradition when it came to modern art, which was predominantly created for private spaces. Here was a giant artwork created for a very public place, which directly affected the everyday lives of thousands of people. Serra and his supporters could not "dismiss" the objections against the artwork "as a philistine attitude," Tomkins argued. The "social implications of public art" also had to be taken into consideration.

In the end, the five-member panel—including Diamond, an adversary of the *Arc*—ruled that the sculpture had to be moved to a different location. (By then, more than seven thousand people working in the area had petitioned to take it down.)

"The people have spoken, and they have been listened to by their government," Diamond said as he made the announcement. "This is a victory for thousands of New Yorkers who live and work in lower Manhattan." The GSA's acting administrator in Washington, Dwight Ink, said he would ask the NEA to put together a panel of people who would find another place for the work. More importantly, he asked that in the future, when artists were commissioned to make art for government buildings, local communities and people working in those buildings be consulted.

Serra was furious. "To relocate the work is to destroy it," he told the *New York Times*. "It was built specifically for that place." He sued, seeking $30 million in damages, and invoking a verbal understanding with the government that the sculpture would remain on site. He insisted that it was "constitutionally protected expression," and that its removal would be a violation of the contract between him and the GSA.

The lawsuit argued that the decision to move *Tilted Arc* was "based upon reactions to its artistic expression, in part because these meanings, for some, caused anxiety or discomfort," that the GSA had offered no academic or factual substantiation of the work not being "site specific," and that "removing or relocating *Tilted Arc* negates, and therefore destroys, its artistic expression."

Yet the court disagreed with Serra. Even if *Tilted Arc* was speech, it said, the GSA had authority under the Constitution and owned the sculpture. "With that ownership comes a significant degree of control over the structure when exercised in the public interest," the court ruled.

So late one night in March 1989, when nobody was looking, the massive wall of steel was taken down and moved to a warehouse in Brooklyn. There, its three component parts were wrapped up and kept behind barbed wire, never to be seen in public again.

In a *New York Times* commentary, the critic Michael Brenson described *Tilted Arc* as "one of the most bitterly contested of all 20th-century sculptures and a watershed work of public art," and added that there were "wounds here that will not easily heal." He questioned whether it would ever be possible to have truly compelling, independent and diverse public art if that art had to be accepted by the community. "'Tilted Arc' was insistent and imperious; so was Serra," Brenson wrote. "Both public art and the artists who make it are now expected to be more digestible."

At the same time, Serra's own personality and behavior hadn't done him any favors, Brenson pointed out, as he had not shown any empathy toward the office workers who were living every day with his sculpture. "If he had acted differently, the saga might have been different," Brenson concluded. "He might have created a different climate for his work. People might not have liked 'Tilted Arc,' but they probably would have made more of an effort, and the resistance might not have been so extreme."

I would be the last person to condone the dismantling of a work of art as important as *Tilted Arc*, and its disappearance from public view—particularly as it had been commissioned by an arm of the government to be permanently in situ. But a sculpture that is around forever, one that completely reconfigures a widely used community space, and one that divides as much as *Tilted Arc* did—both physically and notionally—cannot be exempted from a dialogue with the people who are to live with it day in and day out. Conversation is so often the answer to so many seemingly intractable problems. Had there been a dialogue between the artist and the office workers, perhaps the work might have survived—and, like the Eiffel Tower and so many other public artworks and monuments that were first perceived as scandalous eyesores, it might have been adopted by the community. Instead, *Tilted Arc* languishes in a warehouse somewhere, and the artist refuses to allow its reinstallation anywhere else but on the square for which he created it.

Tilted Arc became something of a cautionary tale for Western governments commissioning outdoor art. There was an increasing realization that the art had to speak to the community, not alienate it, and be relevant to ordinary people. That was a radical departure from the traditional mission of public statuary in centuries past.

Some artists went out of their way to be relevant to the communities they were asked to intervene in. An example was the British sculptor Antony Gormley and his 1998 *Angel of the North*—a sixty-five-foot steel figure with long, wing-like arms stretching out over the horizon. It was made for Gateshead, a historic mining and shipping town in northeast England ravaged by deindustrialization.

When I asked Gormley about it in September 2019 (as he was opening a show at the Royal Academy of Arts), he explained that the sculpture was born at a moment in British history when Prime Minister Margaret Thatcher was "telling everyone that everything that had come out of the industrial revolution" was "over."

This was, to Gormley, "an absolute betrayal." He set out to make an object that paid tribute to Gateshead's mining and shipbuilding history: *Angel of the North* was made with industrial steel, and stood on the site of historic mines. His aim was to produce a landmark "for a community that's been told it's got no future because its past is meaningless." Its subsequent popularity as one of Britain's most widely recognized monuments was proof that art "can be out there for everybody, and that it can be a focus for life."

Angel of the North is a permanent sculpture, installed for all time, and popular with the British. But producing a permanent monument that everyone will like—in liberal democracies with a free press and a vocal citizenry—has become a major challenge. As a result, cities and governments have sometimes resorted to temporary commissions to get around the problem.

The Fourth Plinth is the best example. Established by the Mayor of London in 1998, it's a program that involves commissioning an artist to produce a work for Trafalgar Square's empty plinth. The artist is chosen by a jury, but the public is also involved. The short-listed artists' maquettes are put on free public display before the winner is picked, and visitors are welcome to comment and opine as they please. Over the years, a multitude of artists have appeared on the plinth, including Michael Rakowitz, Yinka Shonibare, Marc Quinn, Katharina Fritsch, and David Shrigley.

The most attention-grabbing project of all was Gormley's *One & Other* in 2009. For one hundred days, twenty-four hours a day, anybody who was interested could occupy the empty plinth for an hour.

I was there on the day of the unveiling, a sunny July morning. London Mayor Boris Johnson cycled up to the square and scribbled his inaugural speech on a sheet, using the base of the plinth as a writing surface. As he started delivering it from a nearby platform, an agile anti-smoking campaigner managed to scale up the plinth in a split second and unfurl a banner that read: "Save the children. Ban tobacco and actors smoking." Johnson, amused and unfazed, continued his speech, paying homage to the protester, Stuart Holmes, who continued to occupy the plinth with his banner unfurled. Moments later, he was invited to vacate the plinth—making way for its first pre-programmed occupant—and was instantly mobbed by reporters. Holmes told them that he had campaigned against tobacco for more than twenty-five years, and was taking this opportunity to advance the cause.

In those one hundred days, all manner of eccentrics had their hour on the plinth, which was streamed live for anyone who cared to watch. People came dressed as Godzilla, a cow, or a beehive; pitched tents and brought live chickens; campaigned for an infinite range of causes; and, in a few cases, stripped naked.

One & Other (the work's title) was as inclusive an artwork as one might ever see. And it likely emboldened the citizens of Britain into believing that a public sculpture was their business, especially if it was going to be on permanent display.

When a silvered bronze statue of the eighteenth-century British women's rights activist Mary Wollstonecraft (who died after giving birth at age thirty-eight) went up in a leafy square in North London in November 2020, the press and social media reacted with outrage. The problem that people had with the statue by Maggi Hambling was that Wollstonecraft appeared as a naked, doll-like figure atop a cascade of silvery bronze. It was disrespectful to focus on the naked body of the "mother of feminism," instead of celebrating her legacy, the sculpture's adversaries objected. As the historian Simon Schama put it, "I always wanted a fine monument to Wollstonecraft. This isn't it."

Over in Paris, some four years earlier, a far bigger brouhaha erupted over a public sculpture. In November 2016, the superstar American artist Jeff Koons—who had been asked by the US ambassador to Paris to produce a homage to the victims of the terrorist attacks of 2015 and 2016 in France—announced at a press conference in Paris that he was donating a sculpture inspired by the Statue of Liberty to the city of Paris: a tall fist clutching a bunch of colorful tulips. The statue was to be installed in 2017 on an esplanade directly across the river from the Eiffel Tower. "I hope that the *Bouquet of Tulips* can communicate a sense of future, of optimism, the joy of offering, to find something greater outside the self," said Koons.

As it transpired, there was one caveat: Koons was donating the concept, not the physical sculpture. The €3.5 million cost of the sculpture had to be raised from French and American donors. Koons later told the *New York Times* that he had added $1 million of his own money after costs soared and there were delivery delays. In the end, the sculpture was installed, not across from the Eiffel Tower, but outside the Grand Palais, just off the Avenue des Champs-Elysees.

Koons is an important contemporary artist and someone I would describe as a Pop sculptor. He has produced some highly attractive pieces of public art in recent years—monumental sculptures called *Puppy* or *Split Rocker* that are made up of thousands of flowering plants. The former is permanently installed outside the Guggenheim in Bilbao, Spain; the latter was temporarily displayed on the lawn at Versailles in 2008–09.

His thirty-four-ton *Bouquet of Tulips* is not, if you ask me, one of his finest works. To start with, the tulips are balloon flowers, oblong shapes that are pinched at the top. And the hand holding them looks unrefined. It certainly has had its fair share of adversaries. When the French found out that Koons was gifting the concept and not the actual sculpture, there was a mutiny in the French intelligentsia. In January 2018, a group of French artists, politicians, and cultural personalities published an enraged letter in the newspaper *Libération* demanding that the whole project be scrapped. They said the sculpture had been intended as a commemoration of a terrorist tragedy, and yet it had been proposed in an "opportunistic if not cynical" way, and had been selected in an undemocratic process from which French artists had been excluded. "We appreciate gifts, but free ones that come without conditions and ulterior motives," the signatories wrote.

The uproars outlined above show how hard it has become, in the modern age, to put up a public artwork that has everyone's approval. What is the solution? Surely not art that is selected by committee or by referendum. How creative and cutting-edge would that end up being?

The protests against the Koons and the Wollstonecraft sculptures were nothing in comparison to the violence visited on another sculpture in

Demonstrators protesting the killing of George Floyd pull down a statue of the slave trader and benefactor Edward Colston in Bristol.

Britain in the summer of 2020: the statue of the seventeenth-century slave trader Edward Colston.

Edward Colston statue, Bristol (June 2020)

Colston was a hugely wealthy merchant who profited handsomely from the slave trade in the 1670s and 1680s. He transported at least eighty thousand enslaved people from West Africa to the Caribbean. Their chests were branded with his corporation's acronym, RAC (Royal African Company). Roughly twenty thousand of them died of disease and dehydration on board the slave ships.

Yet in 1895—nearly two centuries after Colston's death—a bronze statue was put up in Bristol to honor his many financial and philanthropic contributions to the city. The inscription on the statue identified him as "one of the most virtuous and wise sons" of Bristol.

Colston had endowed the city and helped it build squares and preserve church buildings. Schools, streets, a major concert hall, a parade, and even a sweet local bun were named after him.

Yet when the brutal June 2020 murder of George Floyd took place across the ocean, tempers flared in the multicultural city that is Bristol, and that anger was directed at the bronze statue of Colston. A furious mob tied rope around the hollow bronze statue, tugged and tugged at it until it tumbled over, dragged it over to the edge of the harbor—exactly where slave ships would have docked in Colston's day—and tossed it in. TV footage of the toppling was beamed all over the world as one of the most spectacular acts of Floyd-related protest anywhere.

Soon afterward, on orders from Bristol's mayor Marvin Rees—who describes himself as the first mayor of African descent to run a major European city—the statue was fished out of the harbor.

About a month later, the British contemporary artist Marc Quinn decided to replace the statue. Intervening at dawn on a Wednesday in July, he put up a black resin-and-steel sculpture of a Bristol demonstrator: the activist Jen Reid, who had climbed atop the vacated plinth and raised her fist during the protest. For one day, Quinn's effigy of the young Black activist towered over the square, defiantly replacing Colston.

Quinn recalled in a joint statement with Reid on his own website that after seeing her image on Instagram, "my first, instant thought was how incredible it would be to make a sculpture of her, in that instant." He said the sculpture was not intended as "a permanent solution to what should be there," but as "a spark" to highlight the issue of racism.

Quinn's work was taken down less than 24 hours after it went up on Mayor Rees's orders. In between time, there was a chorus of reactions to it.

The Booker Prize–winning author Bernardine Evaristo said the fact that Quinn had teamed up with Bristol protester Reid, paid for the sculpture himself, and installed it by night showed "a demonstrable commitment to the cause of Black Lives Matter in that it shows active allyship. Isn't this what we need? Allies?"

But the artist Thomas J. Price, whose grandmother was from Jamaica, said Quinn's initiative "feels like an opportunistic stunt." He said it would be "far more useful if white artists confronted 'whiteness' as opposed to using the lack of black representation in art to find relevance for themselves."

I reached out to Mayor Rees months later to find out more about the episode and about Bristol. We began by discussing his childhood and formative years in the city.

Rees told me that he was of mixed heritage—his father was Jamaican-born, and his mother was of English, Welsh, and Irish heritage—and that he faced regular harassment growing up in racially fractured Bristol. He was chased down the street and called names, and people tried to hurt him physically, even though his primary caring family were white. So he was "living across these divides."

For a long time in Bristol, he explained, the city's slaving history was not talked about. It started emerging as a topic of debate in the 1990s. By 2007—the two hundredth anniversary of the Slave Trade Act, which banned the trading of slaves throughout the British Empire—there was "an acceleration" and a desire on the part of many people "to talk about the fullness of Bristol's history."

That was when calls for the removal of the Colston statue picked up. There were concurrent campaigns for the renaming of Colston Hall, of Colston Street, and of other places that bore the slaver's name. Gradually, these cries became part of the mainstream conversation. And, the mayor pointed out, Colston's name recently came off the city's main concert hall: Just before Christmas 2020, mid-lockdown, Colston Hall was renamed the Bristol Beacon.

What did Rees himself think of Colston? "I find him objectionable," and his statue is "an affront to me as someone who is descended from enslaved Africans," he replied.

"Slavery isn't just about picking cotton," the mayor explained. "This is about systems of rape and exploitation and breaking up families and gratuitous violence and torture." Regardless of where people stood on the matter of Colston—and there were plenty who didn't want his name to come down—the reality of slavery had to be openly acknowledged, the mayor said.

Rees found out about the statue's toppling on the afternoon it happened, while he was out with his children. "I was taken aback," he recalled. As a mayor, he could not "condone criminal damage." Yet he was "not going to pretend that the statue was anything other than an affront to me, and I wouldn't pretend that I miss it, or that I'm not glad it's gone."

What will take its place? Rees said he had set up a commission of experts on the history of Bristol, "a city looking for answers," which would help determine what stories needed to be told. Only then would it be possible to determine Colston's replacement.

Rees said that Quinn had contacted him before installing the Jen Reid sculpture, and the mayor had told him that he liked the idea but that it was not the right time for it. Rees told me that just as the Colston statue "went up because a rich white man decided to put it up," the Quinn statue "went up because a rich white man decided to put it up." It did not engage with real issues such as the underrepresentation of Black artists, which Quinn could have helped address. At first glance, the Quinn statue was "great. But the way it was done just spoke to privilege."

I wanted to find out how Bristol residents experienced the Colston episode. I connected via Zoom with Euella Jackson, one of the co-directors of the Rising Arts Agency—a nonprofit that helps Bristol creatives aged eighteen to thirty produce work and lead to social change. In the months that followed the Colston episode, Rising had covered nine billboards and 370 sites across the city with posters bearing slogans such as "We mattered then, we matter now, we matter always."

Jackson, whose parents are of Jamaican origin and grew up in Bristol, moved to Bristol in 2013 to study at the university. She was at home when news of the Colston statue broke out, and was overtaken by a feeling of "absolute panic" at the thought of the possible repercussions. Quite a few of her friends were in the protest, sending texts and pictures and social-media posts. But she stayed away, though she could hear the cheers and jeers, to avoid crowds in the pandemic. Not until much later did she feel that it was safe to celebrate.

And celebrate she did, teaming up with a few of her friends and posing in front of the Quinn statue of Jen Reid. She said she had never heard of Quinn, "but I was thinking, 'Wow, a Black woman up on the plinth, that's beautiful. I've never seen that before.'" Since then, she had had second thoughts about "a white man from London" taking such action. But to her, seeing Jen Reid up there was "still a significant moment."

What should go up on the plinth now? "I really like it bare," she said. "The absence speaks so much about where we are now, and where we could be." The empty plinth could be used as a space for installation, or as a platform for poets and speakers, she said. Why fill it up with something else?

Meanwhile in London, politicians have taken the opportunity to react to the statue's toppling in a myriad of ways. Two days after it happened, London's mayor, Sadiq Khan, put out a statement announcing that he was setting up a Commission for Diversity in the Public Realm that would look at the statues, plaques, and street names across the capital to make sure they represented London's incredibly diverse residents. For the time being, he said, they were largely reflective of Victorian Britain. Landmarks would be reviewed, and a decision would be made as to "what legacies should be celebrated," he said.

"It is an uncomfortable truth that our nation and city owes a large part of its wealth to its role in the slave trade and while this is reflected in our public realm, the contribution of many of our communities to life in our capital has been willfully ignored," he was quoted as saying in the press release. "This cannot continue."

But members of Prime Minister Boris Johnson's conservative government voiced a completely different position. In September 2020, Culture Secretary Oliver Dowden sent a letter to a number of publicly funded institutions emphasizing that the government "does not support the removal of statues or other similar objects." He said even though some of the figures represented could be viewed as "deeply offensive," they were lessons about "our past, with all its faults," and were not to be taken down. He warned the letter's recipients against "taking actions motivated by activism or politics."

The Black Lives Matter movement has certainly been a major trigger for attacks on public art on both sides of the Atlantic. Old-fashioned statues and effigies have been toppled, defaced, and targeted everywhere since the death of George Floyd. Even a statue of Winston Churchill in Parliament Square in London was spray-painted with the words: "was a racist." In the United States, states themselves are taking down Confederate monuments on their own initiative. In 2020, as many as 168 public symbols representing the Confederacy were removed across the United States, more than half of them monuments. All but one of these came down after the killing of Floyd.

To art historians and specialists living and working nowadays, many of the old-fashioned monuments and statues that dot the squares, streets, and sites of major Western cities are, from a purely aesthetic standpoint, dispensable. Few bona fide artists would agree to produce a commemorative work, so "commemorative statues are produced by sub-artists: traditional, academic, ungifted," said Catherine Grenier, the former Centre Pompidou administrator who now runs the Fondation Giacometti.

Grenier said she was "in favor of taking all of those statues down." Looking around Paris, she said, "there's frankly not a lot that's worth keeping," besides the Rodin statue of Honoré de Balzac. It was time for a debate about where these commemorative statues belonged, and what should take their place.

As a matter of principle, I would never endorse acts of violence or vandalism against works of art or outdoor monuments. But when it comes to much of the staid public statuary dotting big cities in the West, I can't say I disagree with Grenier. When I saw the statue of Colston being toppled and tossed into the river in Bristol, part of me felt that that act of vandalism set a dangerous precedent. But another part felt no sorrow at the removal of an effigy of Colston.

Why? Because I find it odd, in the twenty-first century, to have statues in cities glorifying individuals who profited from a practice, slavery, that is a crime against humanity. When I think of the horrific conditions aboard Colston's ships, and of the twenty thousand enslaved people who died crossing the Atlantic, I am shocked and revulsed. When the African American artist Martine Syms tells me that she found the spectacle of the statue topplings "cathartic," I understand. Some of these heroes of yesterday would be condemned as war criminals today. Their effigies deserve, at the very least, to be reexamined.

In the meantime, the pandemic, which shuttered museums and galleries and made it impossible for artists to show their work, has significantly boosted artists' appetite for public art.

When I spoke to Syms, she spoke with affection about a public artwork of hers on display in Florida. It's a text work installed in the design district in Miami, and references a live album recorded by the late singer Sam Cooke at the Harlem Square Club in Miami, a club that was later torn down. Syms recalled feeling "really responsible" when putting up the work, and hoping that people would like it.

Public art "can be a really fun and dynamic way of responding to a community," she said. "I like art that's a part of your life, not just rarefied."

The Serpentine's Obrist confirmed that public art was the medium du jour. "Right now, a lot of artists have a desire to speak directly to the public, and that is definitely something which museums must take into account," he said. Museums had doors, a threshold, and in many cases, admission fees which could be obstacles to the visiting public. So artists living through the global pandemic were increasingly keen to show their work outdoors, in different areas of London, for example, in search of close contact with the public. "This," he observed, "is where art is going."

Exhibiting art in public definitely allows artists to have much more direct and immediate contact with their audience than they would if the art was in a museum, gallery, or private home. Art is visual, after all, and to exist, it needs to be shown. The more people see it, the merrier.

Yet placing art outdoors and within easy reach of the general public also has its hazards. Sometimes members of the public express their distaste for the art, use it as a vehicle for protest, mount a social-media smear campaign against it, vandalize it, and even try to destroy it. The following chapter looks at all of the ways in which art and artists are being taken down by ordinary citizens—and the drawbacks of this new activist age.

8.

A Load of Rubbish

The democratization of art and the proliferation of museums have placed the work of artists within easy reach of the general public. No need to be a person of high birth or high rank to see an artwork from close-up. Anybody with a ticket—or even without one, in the case of free-admission museums—can walk straight up to a masterpiece and stand within a few inches of it. Experiencing art has become as accessible as reading a book or watching a movie. Public appetite for art has soared to unprecedented levels.

That's great news for museums and cultural institutions, which are getting more attention than ever. Museums are receiving millions of visitors a year (when it's not a pandemic year); the Louvre alone attracts roughly ten million under normal circumstances. Millions more are being reached online. Where museums once relied on journalists and broadcasters to get their message out, they now can also communicate directly and digitally with their audiences. This has been a major asset in times of COVID-19, when locked-down parents have been able to take their children on virtual tours of the world's greatest art institutions. Thanks to museums' strong social-media presence, audiences can start instant conversations with and about them using popular and widely followed hashtags. When the reaction is positive, it's a win-win for the institution.

What this also means, however, is that museums are being held to account as never before. There are more eyeballs on them, and more questions asked of them, than at any time in history. As Tate Modern's director, Frances Morris, observed in our exchange: "The massive growth in social media has helped create the sense of a community of practice which feels incredibly exciting and purposeful. It has also seriously enhanced the level of scrutiny and commentary around everything we do."

The very masses that democracy and the Internet have empowered can sometimes engage in a new, bottom-up form of censorship. Young citizen-activists use the yardsticks of gender, race, and sexuality to judge artists and cultural institutions. When the latter are found wanting, they are put on trial in the open courtrooms that are Facebook, Twitter, and Instagram. Artworks that some consider offensive—such as Dana Schutz's *Open Casket*—are called out, often by people who have only ever seen it on screen rather than in person. There are even demands that it be destroyed.

Public opinion has become such an important metric in the digital age that museums do everything they can to stay on the right side of it. A critical social-media campaign can seriously hamper an institution's operations, unseat board members, and directors. One top European curator and former museum director, Daniel Birnbaum, summed up the quandary well when we spoke. Social media is "an accelerator and an amplifier of immense power," he said. "There's also a kind of nervousness surrounding the whole thing. This new populist culture of social media is often very black and white, very plus or minus. You're on the right side or the wrong side. If you say one thing wrong or one thing right, you're either with the bad guys, or you're a hero."

The explosion of smartphones has given rise to another channel of communications on the subject of culture: dedicated Instagram accounts on which art-world employees, former employees, or interns anonymously air their complaints. These accounts give victims of professional abuse a channel to speak out, and they serve as catalysts of change. Potentially, they can also cause undue reputational harm.

I went scrolling down the @cancelartgalleries Instagram feed to read recent posts. The format is basic: white text on a square black background—with no name and no photograph. The posts usually name the offending gallery and its managers and list all kinds of mistreatment. Present and former interns and junior recruits say they were grossly underpaid, if paid at all; never referred to by their name; screamed at and verbally abused; made to clean windows, floors, and bathrooms; and yelled at for not getting the right variety of coffee or noodle or juice. The posts describe terrorizing working conditions imposed by nasty and tyrannical bosses who seem to bully away with impunity. The same gallery names (and gallery bosses) seem to come up with conspicuous regularity.

I have no way of confirming any of these posts. Yet their message is not unfamiliar. I am independently aware of certain gallery bosses' terrifying treatment of underlings, and the abuse that interns undergo just to be able to put a prestigious gallery name on their CV. It is great to see that these underlings now have a channel on which they can lift the lid on these abuses, and that gallery bosses can no longer brutalize their staff blamelessly. Social media is introducing a level of accountability to the commercial art world, which has otherwise been completely unaccountable—and that's a good thing overall. There's just one caveat: these posts do tend to alter one's perception of the galleries in question. What if the charges are unfair, or fabricated? As Coco Fusco cautions later on in this chapter, the culture of naming and shaming can sometimes target people who do not deserve it.

I looked up another well-known Instagram feed, @changethemuseum. The complaints on there were mostly about the lack of diversity at the top of US institutions and managers' insensitivity toward BIPOC (Black, indigenous, people of color). The museums in question were sometimes named, sometimes not.

One post about an unnamed institution described hasty efforts by art-world actors to be seen as promoting diversity. "The only thing I am seeing more of than rushed tokenized efforts to overcompensate for a previous lack of acknowledgement of people of color in institutions is the number of white colleagues who think it is okay for them to determine this programming," it read. "You are not changing things by being another room full of white people deciding what people of color want or get to experience. Get out of the way."

Yet there were also much more mundane and random posts about what seemed like fairly routine actions. One employee of a named institution was called in by the director after describing the workplace as toxic. Another reported that a curator objected to taking down a particular painting just because the artist had misbehaved in the past. Neither of those episodes seemed to be excesses on the scale of the ones reported on @cancelartgalleries.

There were clear benefits to this culture of complaint. But there were also drawbacks. The people who had started those Instagram feeds were determined to correct serious forms of injustice. Yet in the process, they could potentially be enabling other forms of it.

I discussed this dilemma with Coco Fusco. We talked about why Fusco had chosen to come to the defense of the artist Dana Schutz when her painting *Open Casket* had been called out.

Fusco explained that Schutz had been unfairly targeted, that calls for the destruction of an artwork were never justified—and that no individual or individual artist was "the problem, or the carrier of the entire racist tradition."

The Schutz episode, she said, reminded her of when her students went after white professors because they were white, instead of taking aim at the power structure and its perpetuation of racism through education and hiring. "If you really want to address the problems of racism in the arts," she said, "you have to stop screaming at individual people."

She bemoaned the culture of denunciation, which she said was widespread on university campuses. "A lot of kids confuse that naming and shaming with change, and they do it at their peril," she said. "I have colleagues who have been named and shamed erroneously, and had their lives turned upside down. And I'm not in favor of it, because I know how harmful it can be. It is antidemocratic in spirit, and a complete disregard for the rule of law."

As of this writing, fear of being named and shamed hangs over everybody who's anybody in the art world. To preempt such opprobrium, some museums are losing senior staffers and postponing or canceling exhibitions, as in the examples that follow.

SFMOMA and Gary Garrels

In July 2020, the San Francisco Museum of Modern Art (SFMOMA) had a Zoom call for all staff. The call's primary focus was how to keep safe in the midst of a global pandemic, and ensure that the staff had access to hand sanitizer and masks as well as Plexiglas dividers to be protected from the disease. The call proceeded according to plan until the question-and-answer part. The museum's longest-tenured curator, Gary Garrels, was then asked about comments attributed to "the white senior curator" on the Instagram account @changethemuseum. According to the post, the curator "was giving a presentation about a group of new acquisitions by [*sic*] POC artists" (meaning acquisitions of POC artists). "He ended the presentation by saying, 'Don't worry, we will definitely still continue to collect white artists.'"

On the Zoom call, Garrels replied that his remarks had been "a little bit skewed," and emphasized that the museum had concentrated a lot "on collecting women, Black artists, first nation, Native, LGBTQ, Latino and so on."

"I'm certainly not a believer in any kind of discrimination," he added. "And there are many white artists, many men who are making wonderful, wonderful work."

When a staffer asked if that was equivalent to saying "All lives matter," Garrels replied, "I'm sorry, I don't agree. I think reverse discrimination . . ." Gasps were heard on the call, and someone expressed disbelief at what Garrels had just said.

After the Zoom call, an anonymous group of ex-employees called xSFMOMA gathered several hundred signatures to petition for Garrels's resignation, saying he had used "white supremacist and racist language." Employees of the museum store separately emailed management describing Garrels's remarks as racist, and demanding accountability.

The next day, an unsigned email sent to the museum's staff from "Members of the Curatorial Division" expressed collective disapproval of the comments. "We will no longer accept such racism denial; unilateral power over systems, money and colleagues; and comments, made publicly and internally, that are offensive and reckless," they said, demanding "actions and accountability for Gary's conduct."

Five days after the Zoom call, Garrels, who was sixty-three, resigned, expressing his "personal and sincere apology" to all staff in an email.

"I realized almost as soon as I used the term 'reverse discrimination' that this is an offensive term and was an extremely poor choice of words on my part," he said. "I do not believe I have ever said that it is important to collect the art of white men. I have said that it is important that we do not exclude consideration of the art of white men."

Garrels's resignation shocked his supporters in the art world—who recalled that he had vigorously supported artists of color and used the proceeds from the sale of a $50 million painting by Mark Rothko to buy works by Black artists for the collections.

Unfortunately, the expression Garrels had used—"reverse discrimination"—was one with a very ugly history. It had emerged in the 1970s among adversaries of the civil rights movement as a way of undermining the movement and preventing greater racial equality. It was an unfortunate choice of words, as Garrels himself acknowledged, and appeared to be the principal cause of his departure.

The timing of the episode was also complicated. Garrels' remarks came a month after the museum made a second round of layoffs following a COVID-induced plunge in revenues—despite extensive online petitioning for jobs to be preserved through salary cuts. Also in June, the museum faced criticism for responding to the killing of George Floyd with an Instagram image of an artwork by African American artist Glenn Ligon, then deleting a critical comment about it from an ex-employee. The museum subsequently issued apologies.

Philip Guston Retrospective

Another controversy broke out in 2020 over a major retrospective of the work of the painter Philip Guston, who died in 1980. Guston was known for figurative paintings involving cartoonish pink-and-gray figures, which he

produced late in life. These included hooded characters that were deliber-
ately made to resemble Ku Klux Klan members. The figures were depicted
in scenes from everyday life. Guston's message was that he, and we, could
easily be one of them.

This message was conveyed loud and clear in his lifetime, and any curator planning an exhibition of Guston would be conscious of it. As his
daughter Musa Mayer writes in a 2020 biography, Guston witnessed social
injustice as an adolescent growing up in Los Angeles, and the racially motivated violence of the Ku Klux Klan, which he found especially upsetting.
"He experienced this directly when a mural he had painted depicting a
black man, tied up and tortured by the Klan, was defaced," writes Mayer.

The images of hooded Klansmen, who were never prosecuted for their
crimes, stayed with him, and Guston later incorporated them in his art.
They represented "America's racist past—and present, as the tragedies of
the civil rights movement unfolded," and they "became more than embodi-
ments of evil and terror," writes Mayer. Guston started to introduce humor
and complexity in his portrayals of them. "They are self-portraits," he later
explained. "I perceive myself as being behind the hood. In the new series of
'hoods' my attempt was really not to illustrate, to do pictures of the Ku Klux
Klan, as I had done earlier. The idea of evil fascinated me . . . I almost tried
to imagine that I was living with the Klan. What would it be like to be evil?
To plan, to plot."

Before the COVID-19 outbreak derailed museum timetables, the exhi-
bition was due to open in June 2020 at the National Gallery of Art in
Washington, D.C. It was then set to travel to the Museum of Fine Arts,
Houston; Tate Modern in London; and the Museum of Fine Arts, Boston.

Curators from all four museums worked on the exhibition catalogue,
and in their preface, demonstrated full awareness of the sensitivity of the
material. They recalled how Guston shocked New York when he first

showed the KKK paintings fifty years earlier, and how he "threw them in the face of the public, changing the course of contemporary art." They noted that Guston was highly relevant to the "culture wars" going on in the United States and Europe nowadays, and to "levels of racism, violence and polarization" unseen in fifty years. In this "dark time," they concluded, "we see Guston anew." In a separate catalogue essay, the African American artist Glenn Ligon wrote: "Guston's 'hood' paintings, with their ambiguous narratives and incendiary subject matter, are not asleep—they're woke."

The catalogue was proof that the exhibition teams were fully cognizant of the sensitivity of the works they were showing. There was no shortage of explanation and interpretation of the KKK images, including by well-known African American artists.

Yet in September 2020, the four museums jointly announced that the show was being postponed until 2024, "a time at which we think that the powerful message of social and racial justice that is at the center of Philip Guston's work can be more clearly interpreted." The world had changed a lot since the project's launch five years earlier, they argued, and the "racial justice movement" and pandemic had "led us to pause." It was important to "meet the very real urgencies of the moment," and "bring in additional perspectives and voices to shape how we present Guston's work to our public."

The uproar among artists, critics, and curators was instant. The art historian Robert Storr, a biographer of Guston, said, "If the National Gallery of Art, which has conspicuously failed to feature many artists of color, cannot explain to those who protect the work on view that the artist who made it was on the side of racial equality, no wonder they caved to misunderstanding in Trump times."

The exhibition's cocurator Mark Godfrey, of Tate, wrote a riposte on Instagram. "Canceling or delaying the exhibition is probably motivated by the wish to be sensitive to the imagined reactions of particular viewers, and

Still image of a video by Adel Abdessemed, *Don't Trust Me* (2008), in which animals are bludgeoned to death on a real-life Mexican farm

the fear of protest. However, it is actually extremely patronizing to viewers, who are assumed not to be able to appreciate the nuance and politics of Guston's works," he wrote. (Godfrey was briefly suspended from his job by Tate, then reinstated, because of this Instagram post. He resigned from the museum in March 2021.)

Weeks after the postponement was announced, the National Gallery's director Kaywin Feldman explained that after the murder of George Floyd, museum staff members had expressed concerns about the show going ahead. The National Gallery of Art, like other US museums, had also received an anonymous petition pushing for inclusivity and fairness. "Guston has modern relevance, he had anti-racist views, and he used his Klan imagery subversively to examine racism and evil," said Feldman. But "those are triggering images. Regardless of the artist's intentions, the symbol of the Klansman is a symbol of racial terrorism that has been enacted on the bodies and minds of Black and brown people from our country's founding." It was not enough, she argued, to "tell them what to think." (The exhibition was subsequently reprogrammed for 2022.)

There was never any question of canceling the Guston exhibition. Its date was pushed back, then brought forward in the face of art-world protest. Other exhibitions, however, were canceled outright because of protests. One such exhibition was a show by the French-Algerian artist Adel Abdessemed at the San Francisco Institute of Art in 2008.

Adel Abdessemed's
Don't Trust Me Exhibition (2008)

Abdessemed, one of France's most prominent contemporary artists—he had a solo exhibition at the Centre Pompidou in 2012–13—exhibits all over the world. He frequently uses animals in his art. One of his best-known works, *Who's Afraid of the Big Bad Wolf* (2011–12), is a giant bas-relief of taxidermied and charred animals—wolves, rabbits, squirrel, boar, deer, fox—which he bought from specialized shops.

In a series of six videos produced in 2007 called *Don't Trust Me*, Abdessemed showed a single animal (a goat, a lamb, a pig, a horse, a cow, and a fawn) tethered to a brick wall, then killed by a sledgehammer rammed into its skull. The series was shot in an abattoir in Mexico where animals are slaughtered every day for human meat consumption.

But when the video was screened at the San Francisco Art Institute (an art school with an exhibition program) in 2008, there was such an uproar from animal-rights campaigners and the media that the show shut down after just over a week. In the Institute's 137 years of existence, this had never happened before. When the show later traveled to the Fondazione Sandretto Re Rebaudengo in Turin, Italy, its opening was delayed by a lawsuit from animal-rights campaigners.

Chris Bratton, the Art Institute's president, justified the decision to shut down the show. "We've gotten dozens of threatening phone calls that targeted specific staff people with death threats, threats of violence and threats of sexual assaults," he said. "We remain committed to freedom of speech as fundamental to this institution, but we have to take people's safety very seriously."

The Institute said it had also received more than eight thousand irate emails, and some were particularly vicious in their threats to staff members, including one that read: "We're going to gather up your children and bludgeon their heads." As a result, not only was the show canceled, but so too was the accompanying forum, which might have been overtaken by some of the more menacing protesters, Bratton explained.

Animal rights advocates applauded the decision. "There is no artistic merit in cruelty to, or suffering of, living creatures," Jan McHugh-Smith, the director of the San Francisco Society for the Prevention of Cruelty to Animals, said in a written statement. "To take this type of brutality against animals, call it art and use tax money to support it is deplorable."

"This is a snuff film about animals," was the reaction from Elliot Katz, a veterinarian and founder of In Defense of Animals, a national animal-rights group headquartered in San Rafael, California. He said the killings were "done gratuitously, not like someone documenting a slaughterhouse." The article in which Katz was quoted added, importantly, that there was no explanation or context provided in the exhibition, nor any mention that the footage was taken at a real-life animal farm in Mexico.

To understand the artist's intentions better, I paid a visit to his Paris studio in August 2020, a treasure trove of semifinished artworks, sketches, and sculpture models scattered among shelves stocked with Bach recordings, bottles of fine wine, and books on art, philosophy, and poetry.

The artist said he had been deeply upset by reports of rats and dogs in research laboratories on which drugs and cosmetics were tested and experiments were done. It had stirred in him a "feeling of horror."

"Man is the most ferocious animal," he told me. "I started expressing that as an artist who produces images." He pointed out that his videos had no subtitles, no narration, and no story. They were edited films that played over and over in a never-ending loop.

Abdessemed said he got help from his dealer to produce a video showing what went on in the world's abattoirs. A gallery team located the farm in Mexico where the slaughter took place. "I had to show what people refused to see," he said. "A visual artist like myself doesn't speak or write: He screams. I decided to expose the hidden violence."

What neither the exhibition labels nor the curators explained was that the animals filmed by Abdessemed were destined for slaughter and would have died regardless: Not only was he not the cause of their death, but he was defending their dignity. "I just positioned my camera outside, in broad daylight," he said, emphasizing that his mission as an artist was to bear witness to "blind cruelty."

When the show traveled to the Turin foundation, local animal-rights groups tried to shut it down. But Abdessemed's show went ahead—with the Mexican animal slaughter video.

Abdessemed described social media as "a tribunal where the sentence, the fatwa strikes all of a sudden." He spoke of its inhibiting effect on creativity. "Paralysis threatens art," he said. "If we don't resist, art will soon be unable to show anything."

The other side effect of this culture of complaint is that members of the public occasionally take their rage out on works of art. They engage in acts of vandalism, sometimes causing temporary or even lasting damage to the artwork.

Vandalism has been going on since the beginning of time. Just flick back to the first chapter of this book and you'll find plenty of examples of icons, images, and artworks being scratched, torn, bashed, and smashed. With the birth of museums, artworks were exhibited for the first time before the general public. From the middle of the eighteenth century, major museums in Europe flung open their doors to the general public—the British Museum, the Louvre Museum in Paris, and the Uffizi Galleries in Florence—and exposed works of art to the risk of vandalism.

So art collections became intermittent targets of public bile. Some of the greatest masterpieces of all time were attacked, sometimes repeatedly, by attention-seeking visitors. Leonardo da Vinci's *Mona Lisa* suffered four different acts of vandalism (not to mention its theft a century ago). In 1956, a vandal splashed acid on it. Later that year, a Bolivian painter by the name of Ugo Ungaza Villegas hurled a rock at it, causing slight damage to a piece of pigment next to the Mona Lisa's left elbow (which was painted over).

From then on, the *Mona Lisa* was always displayed behind bulletproof glass. But that didn't deter the vandals. In 1974, while it was on loan to the Tokyo National Museum, a disabled woman protesting the museum's poor accessibility sprayed red paint at the shielded masterpiece. And in 2009, a Russian woman threw a cup bought in the museum boutique at the Gioconda to protest her rejected application for French citizenship; the cup hit the bulletproof glass and fell to the floor.

Far more serious damage was incurred by another Italian Renaissance masterpiece: Michelangelo's *Pietà* (1499), the magnificent marble sculpture on display in St. Peter's Basilica in Rome. In May 1972, Laszlo Toth, an Australian geologist of Hungarian origin, walked up to the marble marvel and dealt more than a dozen hammer blows to it, bellowing that he was the resurrected Christ. The Virgin Mary's forearm fell off, as did sections of her nose and eyelid. Toth was wrestled to the ground and neutralized by bystanders. The sculpture was, mercifully, restored.

Rembrandt's *Night Watch*—pride of the Rijksmuseum in Amsterdam— was also mysteriously attacked on three different occasions. In 1911, an unemployed navy cook started slicing into it with a knife, though the coat of varnish prevented damage to the canvas. In 1975, an unemployed school-teacher managed to make dozens of slashes to the canvas before security intervened to stop him. Restoration took months, and by some accounts, traces of the cuts are still visible. And in 1990, a man tossed acid at the paint-ing, which museum guards quickly poured water over, preventing damage.

The culprits in these episodes were either psychiatric cases or disgruntled individuals seeking to draw attention to their plight. Yet the twentieth century also saw the emergence of a new breed of vandal: the vandal with a cause.

In March 1914, the militant suffragette Mary Richardson staged a protest at London's National Gallery in Trafalgar Square—using a work by the Span-ish master Diego Velázquez as her billboard. To protest the arrest of a fellow suffragette, she showed up at the museum with a meat cleaver and hacked away at the *Rokeby Venus* (1647–51), which pictures the naked and reclining Venus contemplating herself in a mirror. Richardson left a half dozen gashes on the surface of the painting (which were subsequently repaired).

Much more recently, another vandal claimed to be acting for a cause. In 2012, the artist Wlodzimierz Umaniec—founder of a movement called Yel-lowism, which defines itself as "not art" or "anti-art"—walked into Tate Modern and, using black ink, scrawled graffiti and his signature on a major Mark Rothko painting, *Black on Maroon* (1958). When he was detained and questioned, he denied being a vandal, and said that it was possible, in art, to take an existing work and "put a new message it."

Restoration took eighteen months, roughly the same amount of time that the vandal spent in jail. He subsequently apologized to the British people. "I suppose I wanted to change the art world, but of course I did it in a very, very wrong way," he said. The Tate director, Nicholas Serota, commented: "I'm really sorry that he felt the necessity to do what he did and from time to time people make mad gestures of this kind. But art endures."

As art has strayed further and further from convention, and new and much more intangible genres of it have come about (conceptual art, performance art), the public's perplexity has grown.

The British artist Martin Creed has firsthand experience of that perplexity. His work is a combination of minimalism and the absurd. Over the years, Creed has exhibited a crumpled piece of paper, a piece of Blu Tack stuck to a wall, and a video of someone defecating. In 2001, he famously won the Turner Prize (the top British art prize) for *Work No. 227: The Lights Going On and Off.*

The work was exactly that: the lights coming on and off, periodically, in an empty museum room. And it was vandalized—pelted with eggs by a fellow artist, Jacqueline Crofton, who said she had nothing against Creed, "although I do not think his work can be considered as art." She added, "What I object to fiercely is that we've got this cartel who control the top echelons of the art world in this country and leave no access for painters and sculptors with real creative talent."

A few decades earlier, Tate was the scene of a much more impactful act of vandalism, which is still talked about, written about, and reported on.

Carl Andre, *Equivalent VIII* (1966)

Carl Andre is one of the best-known proponents of Minimalist art—art that is stripped of all artifice, color, ornamentation, and representation, and whose message to the viewer is: what you see is what you get.

If you look Andre up on the Tate website, you will find an artwork that was purchased by Tate for the British national collections in 1972. It's called *Equivalent VIII*, and it was made in 1966. "Not on display," the entry reads in capital letters. The work consists of "a rectangular arrangement of 120 firebricks. Although the shape of each sculpture is different, they all have the same height, mass and volume, and are therefore 'equivalent' to each other."

Equivalent VIII is one of eight sculptural pieces by Andre composed of 120 bricks each. The pieces each have their own geometric pattern. Andre originally aimed for them to be shown together on the floor of an art gallery. But they were then sold separately (with his consent) by his dealer. They are a textbook example of Minimalist art, and fetch millions on the art market today.

But in the mid-1970s, minimalist art was uncharted territory for the general public. Initial displays in 1974 and 1975 of *Equivalent VIII* (one of three Andre works bought by the Tate at the time) drew no particular press or publicity. The scandal was ignited by a newspaper article.

"The Tate Drops a Costly Brick" was the headline of the business piece published in the *Sunday Times* in February 1976. The journalist Colin Simpson had perused Tate's latest acquisitions report and singled out some of the more eccentric shopping that the museum had done with taxpayers' money, mainly *Equivalent VIII*.

The journalist never referred to the work by its title, but he gave a sarcastic description of its creation. The artist, wrote Simpson, had made a "sudden" decision to lay 120 bricks "in a low pile on the floor of an art gallery, put a price tag of $12,000 dollars on them, and wait for customers."

To the tabloids, Tate had blown a large chunk of taxpayers' money on a pile of bricks that could have been bought for a few pounds. "What a load of rubbish," screamed the *Daily Mirror* on its front page.

There's no such thing, they say, as bad publicity. So rather than shy away from the controversy, Tate decided to face it head on: put the bricks back on immediate display and let the public decide.

Most visitors were unimpressed, and walked away saying that the Andre work was nothing more than "a pile of bricks." And on the face of it, they were not wrong. So as a joke, members of the public started making their own art submissions to the collections of the Tate: a piece of string, one hundred paper clips, a picture of a filing cabinet with paper cups on top, and a vacuum cleaner.

Objections to the bricks "were very very simple: people didn't understand them," said Simon Wilson, of Tate's education department, in a BBC documentary. And Tate failed to give proper explanations. Nor did it disclose the amount paid, which was £2,297, the equivalent of £25,000 today—a very small sum.

More than one thousand articles were published about the bricks, most of them in mockery. Millions of people read them, including the chef Peter Stowell-Phillips. After seeing the bricks on display, he told a friend that he wanted to color them blue in protest. So one day, he put on a new three-piece pinstripe suit and headed over to the Tate Gallery with his bottle of ink.

Stowell-Phillips headed straight for the *Bricks* display, asked people to stand back, undid his bottle, and made "pretty designs and swirl patterns all over the bricks," he later said. He was questioned by security, photographed, and told that he was banned for life from going to Tate.

Any regrets? None at all. "It's like the Emperor's new clothes," he explained. "There are a lot of people in the art world who are scared to be seen as not being with it. Instead of saying, 'Well, that's a right pile of [expletive deleted],' they say, 'Oh, isn't it wonderful, how marvellous, what a wonderful pile of bricks.'"

Equivalent VIII was restored and put back on display the following year. And thanks to the scandal, it is one of the best-known works in the collection. Yet the controversy did have a traumatizing impact on the museum's administration. "That piece was like a lightning conductor for a whole set of attitudes in Britain," Nicholas Serota, the director of Tate, told the *New Yorker* in 2011, "and for a long period afterward, the Tate was rather less ambitious in its acquisitions."

Much more serious acts of vandalism were carried out more recently against two works of contemporary art. Both were outdoor sculptures, and both were displayed in prestigious locations in France.

Contemporary Art
at Versailles (2008–present)

The Château de Versailles is one of the most grandiose heritage sites in all of France—for its scale, its beauty, and its connection to extraordinary episodes in French history. It was built by Louis XIV, the Sun King, and its last royal inhabitants were Louis XVI and his Austrian-born queen, Marie Antoinette, who were overthrown and beheaded in the French Revolution. Few historic sites in France have such a layered and emotionally charged past.

Versailles is where millions of tourists head to every year for reminders of its royal occupants: frescoed salons, heaving chandeliers, a shimmering Hall of Mirrors, and an impeccably landscaped garden that stretches as far as the eye can see. This is not a place where you would expect to see contemporary art. And yet starting in 2008, the Château decided to dust off its image, rejuvenate its audience, and invite a different contemporary artist each year to show work in its halls and gardens.

The first artist to be invited was Jeff Koons, who festooned the ornate royal headquarters with his signature inflatable-toy sculptures made of shiny steel: a rabbit, an elongated balloon dog, a hanging red lobster. At the press unveiling, which I attended, Koons sounded overjoyed to be exhibiting his work in such surroundings. Yet there were rumblings of discontent outside the palace gates.

There, I met a raucous group of mostly elderly French protestors who howled their disapproval of Koons and his creations. Their dark-suited ring leader—Arnaud-Aaron Upinsky, representing the *Union Nationale des Écrivains de France* (National Union of Writers of France)—could not conceal his rage. "This is like a burglary," he cried. "They want to replace Louis XIV with Jeff Koons. They want to replace France with the United States."

I then spoke to a retired upholsterer named Nicole Rigault. She expressed her utter fury at "the horrors being put in a château that represents France." Speaking for all of her fellow demonstrators, she added: "He can have an exhibition anywhere he wants, but not at Versailles."

Since that spectacular Koons show, eight other contemporary artists have exhibited at Versailles, including Takashi Murakami in 2010 and Joana Vasconcelos in 2012. These exhibitions proceeded without hiccups or local mutinies. But in 2015, when it was the turn of the British sculptor Anish Kapoor, he was met not only with anger and fury, but with messages of hatred and anti-Semitism—and acts of vandalism.

Kapoor is one of the world's leading sculptors. He is known for his mirrored sculptures—famously, the giant *Cloud Gate* (2004) in Chicago, which has been nicknamed The Bean. He also makes works that are reminiscent of the human body: sculptures with dark, gaping cavities; a canon firing clumps of blood-red goo; installations made of intestine-like components.

In Versailles in 2015, Kapoor exhibited a giant wide-mouthed horn made of rusted steel, weighing thousands of tons and resting among huge boulders on the lawn. It was placed on the garden's vast central axis, inter-rupting the exquisite vista conceived by the seventeenth-century architect André Le Nôtre.

In a video interview produced by his Paris gallerist, Kamel Mennour, Kapoor said *Dirty Corner* was "a situation with the big stones and this big vulva. It's like the queen, like an Egyptian queen, sitting here, exactly in opposition to the King, who is Louis XIV. She's displaying herself, very sexually, open, dark." In a subsequent interview, he described the sculpture as one with "sexual connotations: the queen's vagina taking power."

The queen in that reference was taken by many in France to mean Queen Marie Antoinette. And the reaction was violent. Between June and late September, the sculpture was vandalized three times: first, splashed over with yellow paint; then, covered with hateful and anti-Semitic slogans applied with white paint; then spray-painted.

The artist decided to leave the inscriptions on, and to make them an integral part of the work. But a French court banned the Château de Ver-sailles from leaving a work covered with invective on public display. So the graffiti was covered with gold leaf.

Soon, another work of art by a foreign artist, installed in another sto-ried French site—the Place Vendôme, established in the late seventeenth century in tribute to King Louis XIV—became a target of vandalism. Here, too, the objection seemed to be that a contemporary artwork with crude connotations was being positioned on a site of French heritage and cultural pride.

Paul McCarthy, *Tree* (2014)

L.A.-based Paul McCarthy is an artist whose works almost inevitably provoke shock, disgust, and revulsion. That's often their aim. They are scatological, crudely sexual, and plainly obscene. McCarthy uses everyday objects and food products such as ketchup, mayonnaise, and chocolate sauce to represent bodily acts and secretions that are usually kept private.

"It's almost impossible not to pay attention to what he does. It's almost impossible to pay attention to it for a sustained period of time without it making me nauseous," explained the American art historian and critic Robert Storr in a video on McCarthy. As Storr explained, McCarthy made art that, like the crude caricatures of eighteenth-century England, "bravely and insouciantly abolishes good taste."

In October 2014, McCarthy was invited to install a work on Paris's majestic Place Vendôme, as part of the outdoor art program of the Foire Internationale d'Art Contemporain, or FIAC, the Paris contemporary-art fair. The work would also signpost his exhibition at *La Monnaie de Paris*—the former headquarters of the Paris Mint.

So McCarthy produced *Tree*, a towering (seventy-nine-foot) green inflatable sculpture which, despite its title and Christmas-tree color, looked like an anal plug. On installation day, McCarthy explained in a video interview that someone had given him a miniature Santa Claus holding a Christmas tree. The object reminded him of an anal plug he had made years ago as part of a "joke sculpture," and he saw the resemblance between the plug and the tree. But his *Tree* for Paris was not to be seen as either.

Right after the video interview, a man walked up to McCarthy and hit him in the face three times, shouted that he wasn't French and that his work did not belong on Place Vendôme, and ran off. The artist was shocked and stupefied, though not hurt.

Tree immediately became the bete noire of the French social-media networks. A group called *Printemps Francais* (composed of Catholic traditionalists and rightwing militants) posted a tweet announcing the installation of "a giant 24-meter anal plug" on Place Vendôme. "Place #Vendome disfigured! Paris humiliated!" read the tweet, as if in a call to arms.

The violence did not end there. Late the following night, vandals went up to the sculpture and cut off the long cords that were holding it up. *Tree* fell on its side, like a bulging, shapeless sack.

Rather than reinflate it, the artist decided to take it down altogether. Video images showed the work being deflated and turned into a vast green pancake before being hauled away.

"Instead of the piece being about a discussion about how objects exist as language with layers of meaning, a violent reaction occurred," McCarthy said in a statement. "I am not interested in the possibility of such confrontation and physical violence, or continuing to put those around the object at risk."

WE LIVE IN an age that is both intensely democratic and intensely digital. Those twin forces have combined to give citizens more of a voice than ever to denounce the longstanding injustices, inequalities, and discriminations that still prevail in society as a whole. And that outspokenness and activism has now reached the world of art.

But as this chapter demonstrates, there comes a point when individual empowerment can go too far. When the climate of activism and finger pointing leads to the resignation of a senior curator, to the postponement or cancellation of an exhibition, and to the vandalizing of works of art by major artists, it is worth asking: Should there be limits to the power of individuals over art? What should those limits be, and who should have the right to set them?

Those are questions that, for the time being, no one has answers to. Art-world clashes and controversies are still frantically playing themselves out. We don't yet know where the cards will fall. And as ever with pendulum swings, we have gone from one extreme to the other and not yet found our point of equilibrium.

When we do, the kinds of excesses listed in this chapter are likely to diminish. Citizens will be less inclined to use art and the institutions connected to it as target practice. But that point of equilibrium will be a long time coming—for art is most definitely, still, not a level playing field.

Epilogue

The Genie Is Out of the Bottle

The social upheavals of the last decade—as epitomized by the #MeToo and Black Lives Matter movements—have been unquestionable catalysts of change in the art world. They have accelerated a process that was otherwise proceeding at a sluggish and erratic pace: inclusivity.

Today, museums, galleries, curators, and patrons all want to be seen as agents of that inclusivity. Their efforts may look, in some cases, like window dressing, hasty and superficial. Yet there's no going back to the way it was before. As MoMA's Chief Curator of Painting and Sculpture Ann Temkin points out, "the genie is out of the bottle."

It would be reductive to attribute these shifts solely to the mutinies triggered by the crimes of Harvey Weinstein and the murder of George Floyd. The art world has unquestionably been undergoing a dramatic and radical transformation for a few decades now. International biennials have multiplied, and new art centers have flourished on all continents. There's a sense that interesting art is being made all over the world. New fields of academic research—feminist studies, African American studies, colonial critique—have opened the minds and broadened the horizons of younger curators. Social media has been a major enabler of this cultural mini-revolution. As the curator Daniel Birnbaum pointed out in a previous chapter, it is "an accelerator and an amplifier of immense power."

Consequently, the art world today, while still a work in progress, is a better, richer and more interesting place than it was before. True, some of the changes are motivated by cynicism, damage control, and fear of bad publicity. Nonetheless, arts programming has become less staid, repetitive, and blockbuster-led. Audiences are faced with a wider and more relevant range of options, and are visiting museums and arts institutions in ever greater numbers. Not only have museums not lost audiences in the process: they have gained new ones.

There are those who are suspicious of this new age of inclusivity, who write it off as a burst of political correctness, and view the beneficiaries as second-rate talents brought in to fill diversity quotas. Yet in the vast majority of cases, the artists emerging from oblivion and getting solo museum shows should have done so a long time ago. They have been unfairly underestimated for far too long.

Take women artists, for example. Forever brushed off as not good enough, they're finally stepping into the global spotlight and being recognized, not for their gender, but for their talent. After generations of being labeled only as wives, lovers, muses, mothers, sisters, daughters, and objects of desire, they are finally getting credit where it is due. Thanks to solo exhibitions, they are marching, one by one, through the guarded gates of major museums—even as they remain absent from the art-history textbooks.

The same goes for nonwhite artists. More and more of them are getting solo shows and exhibiting works so powerful, you wonder why they weren't shown before. As Holland Cotter wrote in the *New York Times* in

February 2021, Black art is "some of the most conceptually exciting and urgent-minded American art, period—a reality only quite recently acknowledged by the art world at large."

Admittedly, there have been other moments in recent history when Black artists received particular attention. And those moments came and went without causing lasting change. What makes *this* particular moment different is that the artists in question are entering museum collections, getting important solo shows, and being reviewed by prominent critics. That, notes the artist Adam Pendleton, makes them "harder to ignore" down the line: "They become a part of the conversation that is concerned with history and not with the market."

What digital communications have done in the meantime is hold museums, arts institutions, and the people running them to account. These institutions exist for the good of society. They are the custodians of priceless collections, and (in Europe at least) recipients of tax money. It stands to reason that they should face greater scrutiny. And they do.

Thanks to heightened media and activist attention, the public today is much more mindful of who the sponsors and managers of major museums are, where the money comes from, and what else it is invested in. And there are increasing demands on the part of that public for that money to be ethically and morally clean.

This is an altogether recent phenomenon. Until the global financial crisis of 2008, museum managers accepted fat checks from billionaires and other members of the global one percent without asking questions about the source of the wealth, even when there was more than a whiff of scandal around it (arms deals, opioids . . .) In those heady days of lavish museum expansions led by star architects, all help was gratefully received. Sometimes, the name of the biggest benefactor ended up emblazoned on the building.

As we now emerge from a deadly and protracted pandemic and look ahead to years of austerity, the era of no-questions-asked extravagance is gone. What we can expect is concern for three things: equality, ethics, and ecology. Museums are going to have a much tougher time taking donations from billionaires whose fortunes were made improperly. If they accept patronage from a louche benefactor, they will risk being named and shamed in the court of digital opinion.

We are, in short, witnessing "the beginning of a process of realignment into a more just and equal world," says Jess Worth, co-founder of the BP or not BP? environmental protest group, which regularly stages protests against BP's sponsorship of U.K. cultural institutions. There are "imbalances of power and privilege" running all the way through the arts, and they need to be addressed.

"What that process looks like in practice," she concludes, "is obviously really messy and complicated."

Sometimes too messy. The art world has swung from one extreme to another, and is still far from reaching equilibrium. And new imbalances are being created in the process.

To start with, as Wesley Morris wrote in the *New York Times* in 2018, "We're talking less about whether a work is good art, but simply whether it's *good*—good for us, good for the culture, good for the world." In this do-gooding art world, where morality determines "which artists can make what art" and "who can speak," we may sometimes end up headlining artists who don't merit the attention. A certain tokenism may enter into play as dealers, auctioneers, and collectors strive to be demonstrably more diverse and grab whoever they can get from the newly favored category.

The artist Adam Pendleton says that happens a lot in the commercial art world. "Not very good artists" with works that "don't have a deeper meaning" can, after just two shows in a big city, become market sensations and end up "where all the dollar bills are flying," Pendleton explains. Those figures are unlikely to be remembered down the line: they "will fade away."

Who's to say that the same thing is not happening in museums, and that the artists being shown are not flashes in the pan? After all, MoMA is being more inclusive than ever, and presenting a fluid and ever-shifting definition of the canon. In its collection rehang, MoMA is keeping the Picassos, Matisses and Cézannes that are its mainstay. But it is also incorporating works by women and artists of color who were long excluded, and indicating that it will be constantly rehanging its permanent collection in a challenge to the very notion of permanence. As Temkin puts it, "We're saying there is no fixity, there is no limit, we don't want just one canon. The canon shifts every six months."

What if the artists who get written into this new and rotating canon are no good? "I don't worry about that at all," replies Temkin. She notes that MoMA has always operated on two tracks: choosing works of the past that seem important "with historical 20/20 hindsight," and works that are brand new and completely untested. She recalls that the museum's second-ever exhibition was dedicated to nineteen living American artists, many of whom are unknown names today. It's impossible to know in advance who will be great, she says. "You just have to forget about that barometer. Otherwise you'd be paralyzed."

The Whitechapel's chief curator, Lydia Yee, agrees. "Museums and galleries have to take risks, and not all of the art will stand the test of time," she says. "Look back at issues of *Artforum* from past decades, and you'll ask, 'Who is this on the cover?'" Some artists will have a lasting career, and others won't. That's not necessarily a gauge of their talent, and can't be "boiled down to that elusive factor of quality."

That's because canons are always being revisited, and artists' importance is constantly being reassessed, notes Birnbaum. Cézanne "was different" after Picasso—he took on much greater significance—as was Marcel Duchamp after Warhol. "The only good definition of a meaningful canon is that the works are still of relevance to people in their lives," Birnbaum explains. Art history is "rewritten and reinterpreted," and it is "through these rereadings that the real canon will emerge."

Fair enough. But on occasion, the baby can get thrown out with the bath water. As Brenson points out, there is now "a real aversion to a lot of the art that we grew up caring about: pretty much the whole history of Modernism." He cites the example of the American sculptor David Smith, whose biography he has just completed; people today have preconceptions about him, judge him as "a canonical male who made welded steel sculpture."

The same goes for Jackson Pollock, I might add. It is fashionable in the art world nowadays to describe him as an artist whose vast canvases were extensions of his masculinity and ego, and who completely crushed the career of his equally gifted wife, Lee Krasner. It's true that Krasner was unquestionably overshadowed as a result of her marriage to Pollock. Yet Pollock's paintings are no less epic.

These new stereotypes will "have to be undone, and will be undone," Brenson predicts, "because the artists are simply too good."

A third consequence of this distorting age is that people, artworks, and exhibitions are being taken down on social media, for better or worse. White artists are being slated for portraying Black subjects, or for representing episodes of Native American pain. Their works are being threatened with destruction, or destroyed. Exhibitions containing one single controversial artwork are being shut down as soon as they open. Outdoor sculptures are being vandalized.

Inside museums and galleries, the daily behavior of those at the top is being denounced (albeit anonymously) on dedicated Instagram accounts citing offensive statements and behavior. People in senior positions are losing their jobs because of verbal slipups that then reverberate online. Such is the impact of these callout accounts that one recent post read: "My museum's director has said one of their biggest fears right now is being featured on this page." Many of the managers targeted by these feeds probably deserve to be called out. But what about those who don't?

It can feel like a witch hunt sometimes. I find it paradoxical that, a couple of decades into the twenty-first century, when people are able to express themselves freely every minute of the day, the world should still also be closed-minded and exclusionary. Round-the-clock digital democracy is empowering, but it can also be paralyzing.

In her book *Dare to Speak*, Suzanne Nossel—chief executive of PEN America—describes the quandary well. "Our callout culture, wherein offensive remarks, infelicitous phrasings, and misstatements can get someone lambasted online and even make their way into news coverage, is remaking the landscape for speech in ways both good and bad," she writes.

On the plus side, we are held to account "by anyone who hears or reads our words." On the minus side, there is a "toxic and censorious" consequence to this, because callouts can "metastasize, delivering a punishment vastly disproportionate to the underlying offense," a punishment that gets further amplified by the fact that it is public and online.

In any event, the art world is indisputably in the throes of a radical and far-reaching transformation. The sands are still shifting, especially with the COVID-19 pandemic, and there is no telling what the landscape will look like in five or ten years.

What remains beyond doubt is that the levers of power and influence are still firmly and predominantly in white and male hands. Take a look at the management of the West's top museums. How many women or nonwhite directors do you see? Ditto when it comes to boards of trustees. A changing of the guard seems in order.

How soon will it happen? "Whenever people ask me about what I think it would take to change the museum, my flippant but absolutely serious answer is, 'I think some people have to die,'" quips the young art historian Alice Procter. "We won't really see change until we have a new generation coming up."

In the meantime, it's all well and good to program exhibitions of artworks by women and artists of color, but those artworks must then be acquired by the exhibiting institutions for change to become entrenched. "Everybody jumps because museums are doing a lot of shows, but how much of that goes into the collections?" asks Coco Fusco. To Fusco, it's the equivalent, in the academic world, of asking: "Should I be happy that a lot of Black people are invited to give lectures, or should I look at how many get tenure?"

"When Black artists start selling for the same as those dead white men, and Black people start managing the institutions, and more Black people are on the boards of those museums, and more Black dealers are able to maintain their galleries open," says Fusco, "then I may start believing this."

Brenson agrees that this revolution will truly be complete only when museums become "a level playing field," where "everything will be able to be considered," irrespective of gender, nationality, race, age, sexual orientation, or political persuasion.

As the British artist Isaac Julien observes, "I think it would be great to come to a position when we don't have to underline things."

For now, we're still in a position of having to underline things—to emphasize and to accentuate them—lest we should revert to our bad old ways. The pendulum still has a way to go before reaching equilibrium point.

Image Credits

Bibliography

CHAPTER 1

Bell, Julian. *What is Painting? Representation and Modern Art*. London: Thames and Hudson, 1999.

Berger, John. *Ways of Seeing*. Penguin, 1977.

Bigham, Steven. *Early Christian Attitudes Toward Images*. Rollinsford, NH: Orthodox Research Institute, 2004.

Cameron, Averil. *Byzantine Christianity: A Very Brief History*. London: Society for Promoting Christian Knowledge, 2017.

Clapp, Jane. *Art Censorship*. Metuchen, NJ: Scarecrow Press, 1972.

Cunningham, Mary B. "The Iconoclast Controversy." In *A World History of Christianity*, edited by Adrian Hastings, 726-843. Grand Rapids, MI: William B. Eerdmans Publishing Company, 2000.

Drummond, William J. "Vice Officers Seize 20 Works but Erotic Art Show Goes On." *Los Angeles Times*, March 9, 1969.

Freedberg, David, "Art and iconoclasm, 1525–1580: The case of the North Netherlands." In *Kunst voor de Beeldenstorm: Noordnederlandse Kunst 1525–1580*. Amsterdam: Rijksmuseum, 1986.

Gombrich, E.H. *The Story of Art*. London: Phaidon Press Limited, 1993.

Hibbert, Christopher. *Florence: The Biography of a City*. London: Viking, 1993.

Iconoclasm—Deutsches Historisches Museum: Blog, dhm.de. http://www.dhm.de /blog/tag/Iconoclasm/.

Kleiner, Fred S. *Gardner's Art through the Ages: A Global History*. Boston: Cengage Learning, 2020.

Langdon, Helen. *Caravaggio: A Life*. London: Chatto & Windus, 1998.

Louvre website. "Caravaggio: La Mort de la Vierge." Entry on Caravaggio painting. https://collections.louvre.fr/en/ark:/53355/cl010062304.

Nicholas, Lynn H. *The Rape of Europa: The Fate of Europe's Treasures in the Third Reich and the Second World War*. New York: Knopf, 1994.

Nickerson, Angela K. *A Journey into Michelangelo's Rome*. Berkeley, CA: Roaring Forties Press, 2008.

Prose, Francine. *Caravaggio: Painter of Miracles*. London: Harper Press, 2007.

Robertson, Clare. *Veronese*. London: Scala Publications with RMN, 1992.

Schlesser, Thomas. *L'art face a la censure*. Paris: Beaux Arts Editions, 2019.

"The Seven Works of Mercy, Master of Alkmaar, 1504." Rijksmuseum website. www.rijksmuseum.nl/en/collection/SK-A-2815-7.

Strathern, Paul. *The Medici: Godfathers of the Renaissance*. London: Vintage, 2007.

University of Nottingham. "Why Study Iconoclasm." Video, YouTube, June 13, 2012. www.youtube.com/watch?v=FGheDcU0cFg.

Vasari, Giorgio. *The Lives of the Artists*. Oxford: Oxford University Press, 2008.

von Geldern, James. "Culture and Revolution." *Seventeen Moments in Soviet History: An online archive of primary sources*. soviethistory.msu.edu/1917-2/culture-and-revolution/.

Wilson, William. "Obscenity Charge Dropped." *Los Angeles Times*, Oct. 25, 1970.

CHAPTER 2

Adler, Laure, and Camille Viéville. *Les femmes artistes sont dangereuses*. Paris: Flammarion, 2018.

Cotter, Holland. "MoMA Reboots With 'Modernism Plus'". *The New York Times*, Oct. 10, 2019. www.nytimes.com/2019/10/10/arts/design/moma-rehang-review-art.html.

Cropper, Elizabeth. "Artemisia Gentileschi: La Pittora." In *Artemisia*, Catalogue of Artemisia Gentileschi Exhibition at The National Gallery, London, 2020. London: National Gallery Company Limited, 2020.

Duncan, Carol. "The MoMA's Hot Mamas." *Art Journal*, Vol. 48, No. 2, Summer 1989.

Farago, Jason. "The New MoMA Is Here. Get Ready for Change." *The New York Times*, Oct. 3, 2019. www.nytimes.com/2019/10/03/arts/design/moma-renovation.html.

Gombrich, Ernst. *The Story of Art*. London: Phaidon Press Limited, 1993.

"The Guerrilla Girls' Complete Chronology." www.guerrillagirls.com/chronology.

Halperin, Julie, and Charlotte Burns. "Women's Place in the Art World." Artnet, Sept. 19, 2019.

Hodge, Susie. *The Short Story of Women Artists*. London: Laurence King, 2020.

Laclotte, Michel, ed. *Dictionnaire des grands peintres*. Paris: Librairie Larousse, 1983.

Nayeri, Farah. "A Contemporary Twist on Rubens's Legacy." *The New York Times*, Jan. 28, 2015. www.nytimes.com/2015/01/29/arts/international/a-contemporary-twist-on-rubenss-legacy.html.

Nayeri, Farah. "Is It Time Gauguin Got Canceled?" *The New York Times*, Nov. 18, 2019. www.nytimes.com/2019/11/18/arts/design/gauguin-national-gallery-london.html.

Nayeri, Farah. "Joan Jonas Endures with Her Strange and Entrancing Rituals." *The New York Times*, March 21, 2018. www.nytimes.com/2018/03/21/arts/joan-jonas-tate-modern.html.

Nayeri, Farah. "Kehinde Wiley on Painting the Powerless. And a President." *The New York Times*, Nov. 27, 2017. www.nytimes.com/2017/11/27/arts/design/kehinde-wiley-obama-portrait-london-exhibition.html.

Nayeri, Farah. "Miami Show Explores the Evolution of Judy Chicago." *The New York Times*, Nov. 30, 2018. www.nytimes.com/2018/11/30/arts/judy-chicago-miami.html.

Olivennes, Benjamin. *L'Autre art contemporain*. Paris: Grasset, 2021.

Parker, Rozsika, and Griselda Pollock. *Old Mistresses: Women, Art and Ideology*. London: Bloomsbury Academic, 2020.

Reilly, Maura. "MoMA's Revisionism Is Piecemeal and Problem-Filled: Feminist Art Historian Maura Reilly on the Museum's Rehang." *ARTnews*, Oct. 31, 2019. www.artnews.com/art-news/reviews/moma-rehang-art-historian-maura-reilly-13484/.

Reilly, Maura, ed. *Women Artists: The Linda Nochlin Reader*. London: Thames & Hudson, 2020.

Sandals, Leah. "What's Missing from the World's First Gauguin Portraits Exhibition?" *Canadian Art*, June 20, 2019. canadianart.ca/features/whats-missing-from-the-worlds-first-gauguin-portraits-exhibition/.

Schjeldahl, Peter. "The Exuberance of MOMA's Expansion." *The New Yorker*, Oct. 14, 2019.

Thomson, Belinda, ed. *Gauguin: Maker of Myth*. Princeton: Princeton University Press, 2010.

Wyma, Chloe. "Loose Canon." *Artforum*, Oct. 21, 2019. www.artforum.com/slant/chloe-wyma-on-the-reopened-moma-81076.

CHAPTER 3

Brenson, Michael. *Visionaries and Outcasts: The NEA, Congress, and the Place of the Visual Artist in America*. New York: New Press, 2001.

Bolton, Richard, ed. *Culture Wars: Documents from the Recent Controversies in the Arts*. New York: New Press, 1992.

Clements, Marcelle. "Karen Finley's Rage, Pain, Hate and Hope." *The New York Times*, July 22, 1990. www.nytimes.com/1990/07/22/theater/theater-karen-finley-s-rage-pain-hate-and-hope.html.

Gamarekian, Barbara. "Corcoran Gallery's Director Resigns Under Fire." *The New York Times,* Dec. 19, 1989. www.nytimes.com/1989/12/19/arts/corcoran-gallery-s -director-resigns-under-fire.html.

Gamarekian, Barbara. "The Corcoran to Apologize for Canceling Show." *The New York Times*, Sept. 19, 1989. www.nytimes.com/1989/09/19/arts/the-corcoran-to -apologize-for-canceling-show.html.

Gamarekian, Barbara. "Corcoran, to Foil Dispute, Drops Mapplethorpe Show." *The New York Times*, June 14, 1989. www.nytimes.com/1989/06/14/arts/corcoran -to-foil-dispute-drops-mapplethorpe-show.html.

Harris, William. "The N.E.A. Four: Life After Symbolhood." *The New York Times*, June 5, 1994. www.nytimes.com/1994/06/05/archives/the-nea-four-life -after-symbolhood.html.

Higgins, Charlotte, and Vikram Dodd. "Tate Modern removes naked Brooke Shields picture after police visit." *The Guardian*, Sept. 30, 2009. www .theguardian.com/artanddesign/2009/sep/30/brooke-shields-naked-tate-modern.

Hughes, Robert. *The Culture of Complaint: The Fraying of America.* New York: Oxford University Press, 1993.

Kidd, Dustin. *Legislating Creativity: The Intersections of Art and Politics.* New York: Routledge, 2014.

Kinsella, Eileen. "The Rockefeller Name Proves Mighty Indeed at Christie's Record $646 Million Sale of Storied Masterpieces." Artnet, May 9, 2018. news.artnet .com/market/christies-rockefeller-sale-648m-1281551.

Larson, Kay. "Balthus the Baffler." *New York Magazine,* March 12, 1984.

Libbey, Peter. "Met Defends Suggestive Painting of Girl after Petition Calls for Its Removal." *The New York Times*, Dec. 4, 2017. www.nytimes.com/2017/12/04/arts /met-museum-balthus-painting-girl.html.

Merrill, Mia. "Metropolitan Museum of Art: Remove Balthus' Suggestive Paint- ing of a Pubescent Girl, Thérèse Dreaming." The Petition Site. www.the petitionsite.com/157/407/182/.

New Museum website. "NEA 4 in Context." www.newmuseum.org/pages/view /residence-1.

Nossell, Suzanne. *Dare to Speak: Defending Free Speech for All.* New York: Dey Street, 2020.

Rasky, Susan F. "Corcoran Head Talks About Her Quitting." *The New York Times*, Dec. 20, 1989. www.nytimes.com/1989/12/20/arts/corcoran-head-talks-about-her -quitting.html.

Remer, Ashley. "#MeToo and Girlhood in Art." Girlmuseum.org, Jan. 5, 2018. www .girlmuseum.org/metoo-girlhood-art/.

Schjeldahl, Peter. "In the Head: Balthus and Magritte Reconsidered." *The New Yorker,* Oct. 7, 2013. www.newyorker.com/magazine/2013/10/07/in-the-head.

Wilkerson, Isabel. "Cincinnati Gallery Indicted in Mapplethorpe Furor." *The New York Times*, April 8, 1990. www.nytimes.com/1990/04/08/us/cincinnati-gallery -indicted-in-mapplethorpe-furor.html.

Wilkerson, Isabel. "Cincinnati Jury Acquits Museum in Mapplethorpe Obscenity Case." *The New York Times*, Oct. 6, 1990. www.nytimes.com/1990/10/06/us /cincinnati-jury-acquits-museum-in-mapplethorpe-obscenity-case.html.

Zeigler, Joseph Wesley. *Arts in Crisis: The National Endowment for the Arts Versus America*. Chicago: A Cappella Books, 1994.

CHAPTER 4

Andres Serrano Documentary 1989. Video, YouTube, Oct. 31, 2012. www.youtube .com/watch?v=LNJIloJiBKE.

Bright, Parker. Video, Facebook, March 17, 2017. www.facebook.com/parker.bright .9/videos/10209898925964379.

Bright, Parker. Video, Facebook, March 21, 2017. www.facebook.com/parker.bright .9/videos/10209933615111586.

Bruckner, Pascal. *Un coupable presque parfait:La construction du bouc-émissaire blanc*. Paris: Grasset, 2020.

Carrigan, Margaret. "African American artists sweep Sotheby's contemporary eve- ning sale in New York." *The Art Newspaper*, Nov. 15, 2018. www.theartnewspaper .com/news/african-american-artists-sweep-sotheby-s-contemporary-evening-sale -in-new-york.

Carrigan, Margaret. "African-American fakes are on the rise." *The Art Newspaper*, Jan. 4, 2019. www.theartnewspaper.com/news/african-american-fakes-are-on-the-rise.

Cotter, Holland. "'Black Art: In the Absence of Light' Reveals a History of Neglect and Triumph." *The New York Times*, Feb. 8, 2021. www.nytimes.com/2021/02 /08/arts/design/black-art-hbo-review.html.

Cotter, Holland. "Museums Are Finally Taking a Stand. But Can They Find Their Footing?" *The New York Times*, June 11, 2020. www.nytimes.com/2020/06/11 /arts/design/museums-protests-race-smithsonian.html.

Derrida, Jacques, and Elisabeth Roudinesco. *De quoi demain . . . Dialogue*. Paris: Fayard, 2001.

Dwyer, Colin. "At $110.5 Million, Basquiat Painting Becomes Priciest Work Ever Sold by a U.S. Artist." NPR.org, May 19, 2017. www.npr.org/sections/thetwo -way/2017/05/19/529096175/at-110-5-million-basquiat-painting-becomes -priciest-work-ever-sold-by-a-u-s-arti.

Earth Guardians New York. "From Sasha Brown: Please share the following letter from Graci Horne . . ." Facebook, May 28, 2017.

English, Darby, and Charlotte Barat. *Among Others: Blackness at MoMA*. New York: The Museum of Modern Art, 2019.

Fourest, Caroline. *Génération offensée: De la police de la culture à la police de la pensée*. Paris: Grasset, 2020.

Fukuyama, Francis. *Identity: Contemporary Identity Politics and the Struggle for Recognition*. London: Profile Books, 2019.

Fusco, Coco. "Censorship, Not the Painting, Must Go: On Dana Schutz's Image of Emmett Till." *Hyperallergic*, March 27, 2017. hyperallergic.com/368290 /censorship-not-the-painting-must-go-on-dana-schutzs-image-of-emmett-till/.

Godfrey, Mark, and Zoe Whitley. *Soul of a Nation: Art in the Age of Black Power*. London: Tate Publishing, 2017.

Greenberger, Alex. "'The Painting Must Go': Hannah Black Pens Open Letter to the Whitney About Controversial Biennial Work." *ARTnews*, March 21, 2017. www.artnews.com/artnews/news/the-painting-must-go-hannah-black-pens -open-letter-to-the-whitney-about-controversial-biennial-work-7992/.

Halperin, Julia, and Charlotte Burns. "The Long Road for African American Artists." Artnet, Sept. 20, 2018. news.artnet.com/the-long-road-for-african-american-artists.

Hamilton, Clive. "Political Correctness: Its Origins and the Backlash against It." *The Conversation*, Aug. 30, 2015. theconversation.com/political-correctness-its -origins-and-the-backlash-against-it-46862.

Hanson, Sarah P. "Kerry James Marshall sets $21m record for a living African American artist at Sotheby's sale." *The Art Newspaper*, May 17, 2018. www.theart-newspaper.com/news/tastes-shift-in-sotheby-s-usd392-3m-contemporary-sale.

Kennedy, Randy. "Black Artists and the March into the Museum." *The New York Times*, Nov. 28, 2015. www.nytimes.com/2015/11/29/arts/design/black-artists -and-the-march-into-the-museum.html.

Kennedy, Randy. "White Artist's Painting of Emmett Till at Whitney Biennial Draws Protests." *The New York Times*, March 21, 2017. www.nytimes.com/2017 /03/21/arts/design/painting-of-emmett-till-at-whitney-biennial-draws-protests .html.

Kimmelman, Michael. "At the Whitney, Sound, Fury and Little Else." *The New York Times*, April 25, 1993. www.nytimes.com/1993/04/25/arts/art-view-at-the-whitney -sound-fury-and-little-else.html.

Miranda, Carolina A. "How one art museum has reckoned with race and its past." *Los Angeles Times*, Oct. 22, 2020. www.latimes.com/entertainment-arts/story/2020 -10-22/how-one-art-museum-has-reckoned-with-race-and-its-past.

Musée d'Orsay. *Le modèle noir de Géricault à Matisse*. Paris: Flammarion, 2019.

Nayeri, Farah. "Facing the Camera." *The New York Times*, Feb. 17, 2014. www .nytimes.com/2014/02/18/arts/international/facing-the-camera.html.

Nayeri, Farah. "France Vowed to Return Looted Treasures. But Few Are Heading Back." *The New York Times*, Nov. 22, 2019. www.nytimes.com/2019/11/22/arts /design/restitution-france-africa.html.

Nayeri, Farah. "To Protest Colonialism, He Takes Artifacts From Museums." *The New York Times*, Sept. 21, 2020. www.nytimes.com/2020/09/21/arts/design /france-museum-quai-branly.html.

Neuendorf, Henri. "It's Official, 80% of the Artists in NYC's Top Galleries Are White." Artnet, June 2, 2017. news.artnet.com/art-world/new-york-galleries -study-979049.

Pogrebin, Robin. "A New Zwirner Gallery with an All-Black Staff." *The New York Times,* Sept. 27, 2020. www.nytimes.com/2020/09/27/arts/design/zwirner-haynes -black-gallery.html.

Regan, Sheila. "After Protests from Native American Community, Walker Art Center Will Remove Public Sculpture." *Hyperallergic*, May 29, 2017. hyperallergic .com/382141/after-protests-from-native-american-community-walker-art-center -will-remove-public-sculpture/.

Saltz, Jerry, and Rachel Corbett. "How Identity Politics Conquered the Art World: An Oral History." *New York Magazine*, April 21, 2016. www.vulture.com/2016/04 /identity-politics-that-forever-changed-art.html.

Sheets, Hilarie. "Emmett Till's Coffin, a Hangman's Scaffold and a Debate Over Cultural Appropriation." *The New York Times*, May 31, 2017. www.nytimes.com /2017/05/31/arts/design/emmett-tills-coffin-a-hangmans-scaffold-and-a-debate-over -cultural-appropriation.html.

Shnayerson, Michael. *Boom: Mad Money, Mega Dealers, and the Rise of Contemporary Art*. New York: Public Affairs, 2019.

Smith, Roberta. "At The Whitney, A Biennial With A Social Conscience." *The New York Times*, March 5, 1993. www.nytimes.com/1993/03/05/arts/at-the-whitney-a -biennial-with-a-social-conscience.html.

Smith, Zadie. "Getting In and Out." *Harper's*, July 2017. harpers.org/archive/2017 /07/getting-in-and-out/.

Tomkins, Calvin. "Why Dana Schutz Painted Emmett Till." *The New Yorker,* April 3, 2017.

Tyson, Timothy B. *The Blood of Emmett Till*. New York: Simon & Schuster, 2017.

Whitney Museum of American Art. *Whitney Biennial: 1993 Biennial Exhibition*. New York: Whitney Museum of American Art in association with Harry N. Abrams, 1993.

CHAPTER 5

Abrams, Floyd. *Speaking Freely: Trials of the First Amendment*. New York: Viking, 2005.

Barry, Dan, and Carol Vogel. "Giuliani Vows To Cut Subsidy Over 'Sick' Art." *The New York Times*, Sept. 23, 1999. www.nytimes.com/1999/09/23/nyregion/giuliani -vows-to-cut-subsidy-over-sick-art.html.

Barstow, David. "Giuliani Is Ordered to Halt Attacks Against Museum." *The New York Times*, Nov. 2, 1999. archive.nytimes.com/www.nytimes.com/library/arts /110299brooklyn-museum.html.

Brenson, Michael. "Andres Serrano: Provocation and Spirituality." *The New York Times*, Dec. 8, 1989. https://www.nytimes.com/1989/12/08/arts/review-art-andres -serrano-provocation-and-spirituality.html.

Brenson, Michael. *Visionaries and Outcasts.*

Cotter, Holland. "As Ants Crawl Over Crucifix, Dead Artist Is Assailed Again." *The New York Times*, Dec. 10, 2010. www.nytimes.com/2010/12/11/arts/design/11ants .html.

Cotter, Holland. "He Spoke Out During the AIDS Crisis. See Why His Art Still Matters." *The New York Times*, July 12, 2018. www.nytimes.com/2018/07/12/arts /design/david-wojnarowicz-review-whitney-museum.html.

David Wojnarowicz Knowledge Base. A project of the *Artist Archives Initiative* at New York University. Information resource on the work of the artist. https://artistarchives .hosting.nyu.edu/DavidWojnarowicz/KnowledgeBase/index.php/Main_Page .html.

Foggatt, Tyler. "Giuliani vs. the Virgin." *The New Yorker*, May 21, 2018. www .newyorker.com/magazine/2018/05/28/giuliani-vs-the-virgin.

Holpuch, Amanda. "Andres Serrano's controversial Piss Christ goes on view in New York." *The Guardian*, Sept. 28, 2012. www.theguardian.com/artanddesign /2012/sep/28/andres-serrano-piss-christ-new-york.

Itzkoff, Dave. "Video Deemed Offensive Pulled by Portrait Gallery." *The New York Times*, Dec. 1, 2010. www.nytimes.com/2010/12/02/arts/design/02portrait.html.

Jonathan Jones, "Paradise Reclaimed." *The Guardian*, June 15, 2002. www .theguardian.com/artanddesign/2002/jun/15/artsfeatures.

Kimmelman, Michael. "David Wojnarowicz, 37, Artist in Many Media." *The New York Times*, July 24, 1992. www.nytimes.com/1992/07/24/arts/david-wojnarowicz -37-artist-in-many-media.html.

Mitter, Siddhartha. "Andres Serrano Lets Objects Do the Talking." *The New York Times*, April 10, 2019. www.nytimes.com/2019/04/10/arts/andres-serrano-lets -objects-do-the-talking.html.

Museum of Modern Art Website. "Chris Ofili, *The Holy Virgin Mary*, 1996." www .moma.org/collection/works/283373.

Ofili, Chris, and Judith Nesbitt. *Chris Ofili*. London: Tate Publications, 2010.

Okafor, Udoka. "Exclusive Interview With Andres Serrano, Photographer of 'Piss Christ.'" *Huffpost*, June 4, 2014. https://www.huffpost.com/entry/exclusive -interview-with-_18_b_5442141.

Pew Research Center Website. "In U.S., Decline of Christianity Continues at Rapid Pace." Oct. 17, 2019. www.pewforum.org/2019/10/17/in-u-s-decline-of-christianity -continues-at-rapid-pace/.

Reyburn, Scott. "Chris Ofili's 'The Holy Virgin Mary' to Be Sold." *The New York Times*, May 28, 2015. www.nytimes.com/2015/05/29/arts/design/chris-ofilis-the -holy-virgin-mary-to-be-sold.html.

Reynolds, David. *America, Empire of Liberty: A New History*. London: Penguin, 2009.

Rich, Frank. "Gay Bashing at the Smithsonian." *The New York Times*, Dec. 11, 2010. www.nytimes.com/2010/12/12/opinion/12rich.html.

Starr, Penny. "Smithsonian Christmas-Season Exhibit Features Ant-Covered Jesus, Naked Brothers Kissing, Genitalia, and Ellen DeGeneres Grabbing Her Breasts." *CNSNews*, Nov. 29, 2010. cnsnews.com/news/article/smithsonian-christmas -season-exhibit-features-ant-covered-jesus-naked-brothers-kissing.

Thompson, Derek. "Three Decades Ago, America Lost Its Religion. Why?" *The Atlantic*, Sept. 26, 2019. www.theatlantic.com/ideas/archive/2019/09/atheism -fastest-growing-religion-us/598843/.

Vogel, Carol. "An Artist Who's Grateful For Elephants." *The New York Times*, Feb. 21, 2002. www.nytimes.com/2002/02/21/arts/an-artist-who-s-grateful-for -elephants.html.

Zeigler, Joseph Wesley. *Op. cit.*

CHAPTER 6

Bailey, Martin. "How ethical can museums afford to be? We ask five major UK art institutions about funding challenges." *The Art Newspaper*, Sept. 3, 2019. www .theartnewspaper.com/news/how-ethical-can-uk-museums-afford-to-be.

BP Website. "In numbers, half a century of supporting the arts." https://www.bp .com/content/dam/bp/business-sites/en/global/corporate/pdfs/who-we-are/bp -arts-infographic.pdf.

Carrion-Murayari, Gary, and Massimiliano Gioni. *Hans Haacke: All Connected*. Catalogue of Hans Haacke exhibition at New Museum, New York, 2019–20. Phaidon Press Ltd., 2019.

Cascone, Sarah. "After Purdue Pharma Reached a $225 Million Settlement With US Authorities, the Met Says the Name of Its Sackler Wing Is 'Under Review.'" Artnet, Oct. 23, 2020. news.artnet.com/art-world/sacklers-name-museum-met -1917814.

Cheng, Scarlet. "SFMoMA releases a plan for diversity reforms." *The Art Newspaper*, July 17, 2020. www.theartnewspaper.com/news/sfmoma-releases-a-plan-for-reform.

Decolonize This Place website. https://decolonizethisplace.org/.

Gayle, Damien. "Climate activists bring Trojan horse to British Museum in BP protest." *The Guardian,* Feb. 7, 2020. www.theguardian.com/culture/2020/feb/07 /climate-activists-bring-trojan-horse-to-british-museum.

Giridharadas, Anand. "When Your Money Is So Tainted Museums Don't Want It." *The New York Times,* May 16, 2019. www.nytimes.com/2019/05/16/opinion /sunday/met-sackler.html.

Giridharadas, Anand. *Winners Take All.* London: Penguin Books, 2019.

Green, Matthew. "A crude performance: Semi-naked climate activists protest BP art sponsorship." *Thomson Reuters,* Oct. 20, 2019. www.reuters.com/article/instant -article/idAFL5N2750RR.

Marshall, Alex. "Louvre Removes Sackler Family Name From Its Walls." *The New York Times,* July 17, 2019. www.nytimes.com/2019/07/17/arts/design/sackler -family-louvre.html.

Marshall, Alex. "Museums Cut Ties With Sacklers as Outrage Over Opioid Crisis Grows." *The New York Times,* March 25, 2019. www.nytimes.com/2019/03/25 /arts/design/sackler-museums-donations-oxycontin.html.

Marshall, Alex. "Should Oil Money Fund the Arts? Leading British Artists Say No." *The New York Times,* July 5, 2019. www.nytimes.com/2019/07/05/arts/bp -sponsorship-national-portrait-gallery.html.

Marshall, Alex. "Tate Galleries Will Refuse Sackler Money Because of Opioid Links." *The New York Times,* March 21, 2019. www.nytimes.com/2019/03/21 /arts/design/tate-modern-sackler-britain-opioid-art.html.

Moynihan, Colin. "Guggenheim Targeted by Protesters for Accepting Money From Family With OxyContin Ties." *The New York Times,* Feb. 9, 2019. www .nytimes.com/2019/02/09/arts/protesters-guggenheim-sackler.html.

Pickford, James. "RSC brings curtain down on BP sponsorship." *The Financial Times,* Oct. 2, 2019. www.ft.com/content/4a71276e-e506-11e9-b112-9624ec9edc59.

Pogash, Carol. "Its Top Curator Gone, SFMOMA Reviews Its Record on Race." *The New York Times,* July 22, 2020. www.nytimes.com/2020/07/22/arts/design /sfmoma-gary-garrels-resignation.html.

Pogrebin, Robin, and Elizabeth Harris. "Warren Kanders Quits Whitney Board After Tear Gas Protests." *The New York Times,* July 25, 2019. www.nytimes.com /2019/07/25/arts/whitney-warren-kanders-resigns.html.

Radden Keefe, Patrick. *Empire of Pain.* New York: Doubleday, 2021.

Radden Keefe, Patrick. "The Family That Built an Empire of Pain." *The New Yorker,* Oct. 30, 2017. www.newyorker.com/magazine/2017/10/30/the-family-that-built -an-empire-of-pain.

Radden Keefe, Patrick. "The Sackler Family's Plan to Keep Its Billions." *The New Yorker,* Oct. 4, 2020. www.newyorker.com/news/news-desk/the-sackler-familys -plan-to-keep-its-billions.

Soueif, Ahdaf. "On Resigning from the British Museum's Board of Trustees." *The London Review of Books Blog.* July 15, 2019. www.lrb.co.uk/blog/2019/july/on -resigning-from-the-british-museum-s-board-of-trustees.

Stapley-Brown, Victoria. "Philanthropy, but at what price? US museums wake up to public's ethical concerns." *The Art Newspaper,* Aug. 28, 2019. www .theartnewspaper.com/news/what-price-philanthropy-american-museums-wake-up -to-public-concern.

Steinhauer, Jillian. "The Unlikely Connection Between the Whitney Museum and Riot Gear." *Hyperallergic,* July 1, 2015. hyperallergic.com/219311/the-unlikely -connection-between-the-whitney-museum-and-riot-gear/.

Taylor, Kate. "Sackler Family Members Fight Removal of Name at Tufts, Calling It a 'Breach.'" *The New York Times,* Dec. 19, 2019. www.nytimes.com/2019/12/19/us /sackler-opioids-tufts.html.

Qin, Amy. "Chinese Taxi Driver Turned Billionaire Bought Modigliani Painting." *The New York Times,* Nov. 10, 2015. https://www.nytimes.com/2015/11/11/arts /international/liu-yiqian-modigliani-nu-couche.html.

Voytko, Lisette. "Tufts Joins Long List In 2019 To Drop The Sackler Name." *Forbes,* Dec. 6, 2019. www.forbes.com/sites/lisettevoytko/2019/12/06/smithsonian-tufts -join-long-list-in-2019-to-drop-the-sackler-name/?sh=7b7804a618f0.

Weber, Jasmine. "A Whitney Museum Vice Chairman Owns a Manufacturer Sup- plying Tear Gas at the Border." *Hyperallergic,* Nov. 27, 2018. hyperallergic.com /472964/a-whitney-museum-vice-chairman-owns-a-manufacturer-supplying-tear -gas-at-the-border/.

CHAPTER 7

Bakare, Lanre. "Allyship or stunt? Marc Quinn's BLM statue divides art world." *The Guardian,* July 15, 2020. www.theguardian.com/world/2020/jul/15/allyship -or-stunt-marc-quinns-blm-statue-divides-art-world.

Berger, Joseph. "'Tilted Arc' To Be Moved From Plaza At Foley Sq." *The New York Times,* June 1, 1985. www.nytimes.com/1985/06/01/nyregion/tilted-arc-to-be -moved-from-plaza-at-foley-sq.html.

Bhambra, Gurminder K. "A Statue Was Toppled. Can We Finally Talk About the British Empire?" *The New York Times,* June 12, 2020. www.nytimes.com/2020 /06/12/opinion/edward-colston-statue-racism.html.

Brenson, Michael. "The Messy Saga of 'Tilted Arc' Is Far From Over." *The New York Times,* April 2, 1989. www.nytimes.com/1989/04/02/arts/art-view-the-messy -saga-of-tilted-arc-is-far-from-over.html.

Donadio, Rachel. "Jeff Koons Is Giving Sculpture to Paris to Remember Terror Vic- tims." *The New York Times,* Nov. 21, 2016. www.nytimes.com/2016/11/21/arts /design/jeff-koons-gift-to-paris-bouquet-of-tulips-terror-attacks.html.

Donadio, Rachel. "Jeff Koons Sent Paris Flowers. Can It Find the Right Vase?" *The New York Times*, June 20, 2017. www.nytimes.com/2017/06/20/arts/design/jeff -koons-bouquet-of-tulips-paris.html.

Hensley, Laura J. *Art for All: Public Art*. London: Raintree, 2011.

Kammen, Michael. *Visual Shock: A History of Art Controversies in American Culture*. New York: Alfred A. Knopf, 2006.

Landler, Mark. "'Get Rid of Them': A Statue Falls as Britain Confronts Its Racist History." *The New York Times*, June 8, 2020. www.nytimes.com/2020/06/08 /world/europe/edward-colston-statue-britain-racism.html.

Landler, Mark. "In an English City, an Early Benefactor Is Now 'a Toxic Brand.'" *The New York Times*, June 14, 2020. www.nytimes.com/2020/06/14/world /europe/Bristol-Colston-statue-slavery.html.

McGill, Douglas C. "Judge Rules Against 'Tilted Arc' Sculptor in Suit." *The New York Times*, July 16, 1987. www.nytimes.com/1987/07/16/arts/judge-rules-against -tilted-arc-sculptor-in-suit.html.

Mundy, Jennifer. "Lost Art: Richard Serra." Tate Website. www.tate.org.uk/art /artists/richard-serra-1923/lost-art-richard-serra.

"Non au 'cadeau' de Jeff Koons." *Libération*, Jan. 21, 2018. www.liberation.fr/debats /2018/01/21/non-au-cadeau-de-jeff-koons_1624159/.

Peltier, Elian. "Jeff Koons Inaugurates His Tulip Sculpture in Paris. Finally." *The New York Times*, Oct. 4, 2019. www.nytimes.com/2019/10/04/arts/jeff-koons -tulips-paris.html.

Serra v. US General Services Admin., 667 F. Supp. 1042 (S.D.N.Y. 1987). law.justia .com/cases/federal/district-courts/FSupp/667/1042/2158507/.

Tomkins, Calvin. "The Art World: 'Tilted Arc.'" *The New Yorker*, May 20, 1985.

Tomkins, Calvin. "Man of Steel." *The New Yorker*, Aug. 5, 2002.

Weyergraf-Serra, Clara, and Martha Buskirk. *The Destruction of Tilted Arc: Documents*. Cambridge, MA: MIT Press, 1991.

CHAPTER 8

"A Versailles le sculpteur Anish Kapoor découvre son oeuvre vandalisée." Video. *Le Monde*, Sept. 9, 2015. www.lemonde.fr/arts/video/2015/09/09/a -versailles-le-sculpteur-anish-kapoor-decouvre-son-uvre-vandalisee_4750070 _1655012.html.

Abdessemed, Adel. *Don't Trust Me*.www.adelabdessemed.com/oeuvres/dont-trust-me/.

"Anish Kapoor invite le chaos à Versailles." *Le Journal du Dimanche*, June 20, 2017. www.lejdd.fr/Culture/Anish-Kapoor-invite-le-chaos-a-Versailles-735120.

"Anish Kapoor: Versailles." Kamel Mennour. Video, Vimeo, 2015. https://vimeo .com/132831006.

Azimi, Roxana. "Les tags sur l'oeuvre d'Anish Kapoor révèlent les failles et les frilosités de Versailles." *Le Monde*, Oct. 6, 2015. www.lemonde.fr/culture/article/2015 /10/07/dans-les-failles-de-versailles_4784101_3246.html.

Bailey, Martin. "Revealed: secrets of the Tate Bricks." *The Art Newspaper*, April 30, 2011. https://www.theartnewspaper.com/archive/revealed-secrets-of -the-tate-bricks.

Barbieri, Claudia. "Anish Kapoor Avoids Niceties at Versailles." *The New York Times*, June 5, 2015. www.nytimes.com/2015/06/05/arts/international/anish -kapoor-avoids-niceties-at-versailles.html.

Bellet, Harry. "Adel Abdessemed, l'enfant terrible de l'art." *Le Monde*, Feb. 29, 2008. www.lemonde.fr/culture/article/2008/02/29/adel-abdessemed-l-enfant-terrible -de-l-art_1017311_3246.html.

Bellet, Harry. "Cruel mais pas forcément bête." *Le Monde*, March 17, 2009. www .lemonde.fr/culture/article/2009/03/17/art-contemporain-cruel-mais-pas -forcement-bete_1168944_3246.html.

"Bricks!" Documentary on Carl Andre controversy. BBC Four. www.bbc.co.uk /programmes/b07w6hdm.

Brown, James. "The Burlington Magazine and the 'Tate Bricks' Controversy." *Burlington Magazine Index Blog*, May 13, 2014. burlingtonindex.wordpress.com /2014/05/13/carl_andre/.

Cary Levine, *Pay for Your Pleasures: Mike Kelley, Paul McCarthy, Raymond Pettibon*. Chicago: University of Chicago Press, 2013.

DeBare, Ilana. "Art Institute halts exhibition showing killing of animals." *San Francisco Chronicle*, Feb. 9, 2012. www.sfgate.com/bayarea/article/Art-Institute-halts -exhibition-showing-killing-of-3221238.php.

Duponchelle. Valérie. "Anish Kapoor: 'Comme une fille violée qu'on condamne.'" *Le Figaro*, Sept. 21, 2015. www.lefigaro.fr/arts-expositions/2015/09/20/03015 -20150920ARTFIG00199-anish-kapoor-comme-une-fille-violee-qu-on -condamne.php.

Forbes, Alexander. "Vandalized Paul McCarthy Butt Plug Pulled from Paris Square." Artnet, Oct. 20, 2014. news.artnet.com/market/vandalized-paul-mccarthy -butt-plug-pulled-from-paris-square-137808.

Jacobs, Julia. "After Backlash, Philip Guston Retrospective to Open in 2022." *The New York Times*, Oct. 28, 2020. www.nytimes.com/2020/10/28/arts/design /philip-guston-retrospective-date.html.

Jacobs, Julia. "Philip Guston Blockbuster Show Postponed by Four Museums." *The New York Times*, Sept. 24, 2020. www.nytimes.com/2020/09/24/arts/design/philip -guston-postponed-museums-klan.html.

Jardonnet, Emmanuelle. "Chiara Parisi: 'Paul McCarthy n'est pas dans la provocation, mais dans la critique.'"*Le Monde,* Oct. 19, 2014. www.lemonde.fr/arts/article/2014/10/20/chiara-parisi-paul-mccarthy-n-est-pas-dans-la-provocation-mais-dans-la-critique_4509294_1655012.html.

Jardonnet, Emmanuelle. "McCarthy agressé pour l'érection d'un arbre de Noël ambigu, place Vendôme." *Le Monde,* Oct. 17, 2014. www.lemonde.fr/arts/article/2014/10/17/mccarthy-agresse-pour-l-erection-d-un-arbre-de-noel-ambigu-place-vendome_4507834_1655012.html.

Loret, Eric. "De Molière au 'Tree' de McCarthy: 350 ans de plug anal artistique." *Libération,* April 19, 2021. www.liberation.fr/culture/2014/10/19/de-moliere-au-tree-de-mccarthy-350-ans-de-plug-anal-artistique_1125226/.

Mayer, Musa. *Philip Guston.* London: Laurence King Publishing, 2020.

Mellor, Philip. "What a Load of Rubbish: How the Tate Dropped 120 Bricks." *The Daily Mirror,* Feb. 16, 1976.

Nayeri, Farah. "Adel Abdessemed: Tackling Themes of Everyday Cruelty and Extremism." *The New York Times,* Oct. 20, 2015. www.nytimes.com/2015/10/21/arts/international/adel-abdessemed-tackling-themes-of-everyday-cruelty-and-extremism.html.

Paglieri, Marina. "Non aprite quelle mostra." *La Repubblica.* Feb. 11, 2009.

"Paul McCarthy: 'All for the Gut.'" Heni Talks. Heni Publishing. Video, Facebook. fb.watch/4egxBzmfnG/.

Povoledo, Elisabetta. "Exhibition With Disturbing Videos of Animals Leads to Protests in Italy." *The New York Times,* Feb. 27, 2009. www.nytimes.com/2009/02/28/arts/design/28anim.html.

Rea, Naomi. "Respected Curator Mark Godfrey Will Leave Tate Modern Following His Blow-Up With the Museum Over Its Postponed Philip Guston Show." Artnet, March 11, 2021. news.artnet.com/art-world/mark-godfrey-leaving-tate-1950948.

Simpson, Colin. "The Tate Drops a Costly Brick." *Sunday Times,* London, Feb. 15, 1976.

Tate Website. "*The Bricks* controversy and 'Save the Stubbs.'" Archive Journeys: Tate History. 2003. www.tate.org.uk/archivejourneys/historyhtml/people_public.htm.

Tate Website. "Carl Andre, *Equivalent VIII,* 1966." www.tate.org.uk/art/artworks/andre-equivalent-viii-t01534.

Tomkins, Calvin. "The Materialist." *The New Yorker,* Dec. 5, 2011. https://www.newyorker.com/magazine/2011/12/05/the-materialist.

"Torino: Da domani la mostra di Adel abdessemed sospesa per proteste ambientalisti." *Adnkronos,* March 4, 2009.

"Vandals bring down sex toy shaped sculpture in Paris." *Reuters,* Oct. 18, 2014. fr.reuters.com/article/us-france-art-vandals-idUSKCN0I70F620141018.

Acknowledgments

I t gives me tremendous joy to see this, my first book, come to life. Writing is my favorite creative endeavor, the discipline that I have dedicated my life to. And *Takedown* has been a crucial turning point: the long-awaited opportunity to put my views on the page, and to probe the complicated politics of art and culture.

The writing of *Takedown* coincided with a deeply painful period of my life—the loss of my father, Dr. Abbas Nayeri. He was my guiding light in so many ways: a man of superior intellect and boundless humanity, and a first-class writer. Happily, I was able to share with him the news of my publishing deal. Under different circumstances, my first book would have been very much about him: a transgenerational memoir of Iran and of my diplomatic family. I have every intention of writing that book in the years to come, and of telling the story of my remarkable parents.

I owe the realization of this project to my family, first and foremost. My mother, Dori Nayeri, was a tower of love and strength; she taught me self-reliance from a young age, and let me be exactly who I wanted to be. My sister Nazanine, the book's very first reader, provided vital guidance in the run-up to this and every other career milestone. My sister Goly, wise beyond her years, was a precious and constant life coach. And our beloved nanny, Mohtaram, gave us a lifetime of devotion.

A huge debt of gratitude goes to two extraordinary mentors. Sylvie Albert, the great pianist and master whom I celebrated in a Paris concert, taught me everything I know about music and expression. Michael Brenson, the art historian, curator and author, has been a lifelong source of education and emulation.

ACKNOWLEDGMENTS

Takedown was born of a November 2019 *New York Times* article titled "Is It Time Gauguin Got Canceled?" It was all about a Gauguin exhibition at the National Gallery that examined the man and the artist. The article was spotted by Ross Harris of the Stuart Krichevsky Literary Agency, who reached out to me and suggested that I write a book on a similar theme. Ross has been the perfect agent: intelligent, responsive, and understanding. And Alessandra Bastagli, the editorial director of Astra House, has been the perfect editor. She has made this book infinitely better than it otherwise would have been, coaching me every step of the way, and persuading me to put more of myself in it. My sincere appreciation also goes to Astra House Publisher Ben Schrank, for his leadership, and to other key members of the Astra dream team: Rachael Small, Alisa Trager, Olivia Dontsov and Rola Harb.

Many of the articles that formed the backbone to this book appeared in the *New York Times*. I have my editors to thank, starting with Matt Anderson, for publishing that fateful Gauguin piece, and for his stewardship of the culture coverage in Europe; Barbara Graustark, for her judicious oversight of the *Times* visual-arts coverage; Michael Cooper, the deputy culture editor, for giving my stories generous play; and Jane Bornemeier, Gina Lamb, and Arlene Schneider, for their deft editing of *Times* special sections.

Numerous friends stood by me on the long and winding road to becoming an author: Andrew Franklin (who introduced me to everyone in the London book world), Andrew Whitworth (who provided expert legal advice), Catherine Frammery (a great writer who I hope will produce books of her own), Catherine Stavrakis, Linda Sandler, Annamaria Lodato, Alina Trabattoni, Leyla Boulton, and Irina Shumovich. Mitchell Spielberg was my New York twin and confidant; Rastine Merat and Frederic Martinez were my besties in life and in music; Ali Bagherzadeh was a genuine brother to me; Ali Azima believed in me and my literary ambitions; and David Matthews had my back.

Friends who were authors led by example, starting with Mark Beech, my longtime Bloomberg editor and boss, who tragically passed as I embarked on the writing of this book; Stephanie Theobald, my brilliant 'desert diva' friend; Anselmo Paolone; Michela Wrong; Ruth Scurr; and Agnès Poirier.

This book came together at a time of loss and lockdown. For their generosity, I am grateful to my cousin Shahrzad Khajenouri, in whose home *Takedown* originated; Marie-Catherine Arnal; and Fabio Benedetti-Valentini. Taraneh Farboud, my sister in all but name, was by my side. So were Nazenin Ansari, whose father and mine were as close as she and I are, and Nazanin Vishkai.

Takedown is the beginning of an exhilarating literary adventure.

I've only just begun.

ABOUT THE AUTHOR

FARAH NAYERI is an arts and culture writer for the *New York Times* and host of the *CultureBlast* podcast. Originally from Iran, she lives and works in London. Nayeri began her journalism career in Paris as a reporter for *Time* magazine and a contributor to *The Wall Street Journal*. She later became a correspondent of Bloomberg in Paris, Rome, and London, covering politics and economics, then culture. Nayeri is a public speaker and panel moderator, regularly chairing conferences for the *New York Times* and for institutions in Europe. She is a classically trained pianist and a devotee of flamenco dance.